T0324743

Enacting Research Methods in Information Systems:
Volume 1

Enacting Research Methods in Information Systems: Volume 1

Edited by

Leslie P. Willcocks
London School of Economics and Political Science, UK

Chris Sauer
Oxford University, UK

and

Mary C. Lacity
University of Missouri-St Louis, USA

Editors
Leslie P. Willcocks
London School of Economics and
Political Science, London, UK

Chris Sauer
Oxford University
Oxford, UK

Mary C. Lacity
University of Missouri-St Louis
St Louis, Missouri, USA

ISBN: 978-3-319-29265-6 (hardback)   ISBN: 978-3-319-29266-3 (eBook)
DOI: 10.1007/978-3-319-29266-3

Printed on acid-free paper

This Palgrave Macmillan imprint is published by Springer Nature
The registered company is Springer International Publishing AG Switzerland

Contents

v

List of Figures and Tables

Figures

Tables

Introduction

Leslie P. Willcocks, Chris Sauer and Mary C. Lacity

Overview

This series of three volumes on research methodologies follows on from an earlier collection of two volumes we edited entitled *Formulating Research Methods in Information Systems*. The original plan was to put together from 20 years of contributions to the *Journal of Information Technology (JIT)* a single volume on research methods and practices. However, as we read our way through the JIT issues starting with the most recent, we were quite startled to discover a very rich vein indeed on this theme going back as far as 1990. It became quite impossible to entertain the idea of omitting so many great papers with so much to say. Instead we decided to produce a more comprehensive text that would be of service to information systems (IS) scholars, PhD researchers and students, both as a reference and also as a re-presentation of valuable work and knowledge that was highly relevant, but, unsystematized and un-themed, would likely be overlooked.

Once we made this decision, the task then became to make a judicious selection that fulfilled these aims. Leaving many papers out was never going to be an easy process, but once we focused on the task, we were pleased to discover that we were more or less unanimous on which papers we needed, and how they should be classified.

Enacting research methods

The three volumes cover critical research, grounded theory, historical, interpretive, action research and design science approaches, as well as gender studies, semiotics and complexity theory applications. Looking through the content of 25 years of publication on research methods,

1

we are struck by the pluralism on this inherent in the IS field. To some extent, of course, this is not a wholly representative view of the actual methods used in practice, nor of empirical research papers getting into most IS journals. These tend to be positivist and quantitative, rather than qualitative or containing mixed methods approaches. Orlikowski and Baroudi (1991) pointed this out some 25 years ago, and urged greater recognition of what they termed then 'interpretive' (see our volume 2) and 'critical' (see below) research philosophies. While today positivist research philosophy remains dominant, at least in the more highly ranked IS journals, in more recent years one can observe a rising diversity, aided by the increasing number of papers – and books – published that also demonstrate how to conduct rigorous research in non-positivist, non-quantitative styles, for example Gallers and Currie (2011), Hirschheim et al. (2012), Klein and Myers (1999, 2011), Mingers (2001, 2011), Mingers and Willcocks (2004, 2014).

Without a comprehensive, codified pronouncement to this effect, the *JIT* has, over the years, taken a pluralist perspective on research methods, choosing to focus on the quality, relevance and interest likely to be generated, rather than insisting on, or tacitly preferring, specific methods and approaches. This is reflected in both the two volumes on *Formulating Research Methods in IS*, and also the present three volumes on *Enacting Research Methods in IS*. Happily Mingers (2011) has thoroughly thought through the issue of pluralist perspectives on IS research and he best hits on, and summarizes, what has turned out to be the *JIT*'s overall approach, though the papers the journal has published do not endorse critical realism so forcefully as he does. Given our objective of giving an overview of the approach to selecting papers for the present three volumes, and given the pluralist perspective those papers collectively embody, it is useful here to spend a little time on how the selection and the pluralism can be supported.

Mingers suggests that, in IS research, the main philosophical questions that can arise can be classified in terms of:

- Ontology – what kind of objects or entities may be taken to exist, and what are their types of properties, and forms of being?
- Epistemology – what is our relationship, as human beings, to the objects of our knowledge (including ourselves) and what distinguishes valid knowledge from belief or opinion?
- Methodology – given the first two, what methods should we use to acquire valid knowledge?

- Axiology – what are the purposes or values of science? What are the ethical or moral limits of science (if any)?

A particular set of assumptions about these four elements has been called a paradigm (Burrell and Morgan, 1979). For much of the twentieth century the prevailing natural and social scientific paradigm was empiricism, and more specifically positivism. Moreover, under naturalist assumptions, there is assumed only one general scientific approach, and that applies to all domains that can be considered under scientific scrutiny. This view of science has been extensively criticized, especially in the social sciences, and has led to a greater recognition of the social and psychological character of scientific activity. A more accepted view today is that the social world, constituted as it is through language and meaning, is intrinsically different from the natural world, and thus requires entirely different social constructivist, hermeneutic, or phenomenological perspectives and approaches. This view, and the plurality of views and approaches it suggests, is very prevalent in the present three volume set, and the previous set of two volumes. A third, more radical position is also represented, namely the denial of the possibility of objective or scientific knowledge altogether. Michel Foucault, for example, as represented in the first three chapters of the present volume, presents a strong sociology of knowledge that aims to undermine the fundamental categories of modernist rationality.

Mingers (2011) argues for a plurality not just of methods, but in all the four philosophical dimensions of ontology, epistemology, methodology and axiology. He suggests that this stance flows from both a systems perspective, seeing the world in a holistic way, and a critical realist perspective that accepts a plurality of objects of knowledge. There are, of course, other ways than through a critical realist perspective of arriving at the conclusion of plurality of objects of knowledge – and many of these routes are represented through our complete set of five volumes.

Habermas (1984) also provides a route into plurality – this time of forms of knowledge distinguished by different forms of truth. In constructing a methodology for operationalizing semiotics in IS, Mingers and Willcocks (2014) utilize Habermas's notion of three worlds the material, social and personal. We have, as human beings, different epistemological access to each of these ontological domains. We observe the material world consisting of all actual or possible state of affairs. We participate in our social world consisting of accepted and legitimate forms of behavior. We experience a personal world consisting of individual emotions, feelings and ideas. As Mingers (2011) points out, this generates the need for distinctive methodologies, which then need to be combined together to synthesize our understanding of the whole. For Habermas (1993) we also have distinct axiological relations to these worlds – pragmatic in relation to the material world, moral for the social world and ethical for the personal world. It follows from this that there are various types of knowledge, and that these are distinguished by different forms of truth, and, indeed, ways of validating that truth.

There are different, competing theories of truth, the main ones being correspondence, pragmatic, consensus and redundancy theories. This is not the place to elaborate on these theories. More important is to suggest two things: firstly that the notion of truth links inextricably with that of knowledge, usually defined as true, justified belief; and secondly that truth and knowledge are founding components of IS research and scholarship. Here Mingers (2011) is useful in suggesting four types of knowledge. Performative knowledge is knowing how to do something. Its truth claim lies in successful or unsuccessful performance. Experiential knowledge is knowing through personal experience a person, place, event etc. Its truth claim lies in personal sincerity about the experience, and supporting evidence of the claim. Propositional knowledge is knowing that a state of affairs is the case. Its truth claim lies in evidence that confirms a relation between the proposition itself, and the intransitive world it refers. Epistemological knowledge is knowing scientifically how and why something is the case. Its truth claim goes beyond propositional knowledge in going further than immediate appearances, and developing an underlying explanation of why, whether in the material, personal and/or social worlds, things appear as they do. Here scholars, including IS researchers, invest much time in attempting to ensure that the knowledge generated is reliable, whilst accepting there can be no certainty.

IS studies is interesting, and also peculiar, in being interdisciplinary and embracing variously, depending on the phenomena under study, the forms of knowledge and truth claims and validity tests inherent in all of what Kagan (2009) calls the 'three cultures' of natural sciences, social sciences and the humanities. Attempts to clone natural science approaches to truth, knowledge, validity claims and evidence and apply these to all IS phenomena being researched have not worked. Worse still, often the approaches have been informed by a naïve, A. J. Ayer – type logical positivism, that was refuted by Karl Popper the year after A. J. Ayer published his seminal book in English, and anyway has been discounted subsequently by most natural scientists working in their own fields. There have been many attempts to make the social sciences perform like natural sciences, but the phenomena under study frequently make this a very stretched task, as many IS researchers, as represented in these three volumes, have realized. Lee (2014) suggests that there are four kinds of science and usefully points out that unlike pure and applied natural sciences, IS is a science that studies artifacts, but also the world of people and their institutions, describing and explaining what exists or has existed or what could be created. This requires different assumptions and styles of research, with the methods being developed as fit for purpose, rather than adopted uncritically as techniques from hegemonic theory or as 'the scientific method'.

What lies tacit in all this is the role and influence of the humanities – the third culture – in the assumptions, theorizing and practices of both the natural and social sciences. In actual practice, the natural and social sciences have been shaped and are shot through with influences from humanities such as history, arts, philosophy, metaphysics, aesthetics, ethics, theology, and classics (Willcocks, 2014). The fact that this is not made explicit, or remains unrecognized, is both a mark of the attempt to distinguish 'science' as something different, and somehow 'unpolluted' by the humanities, but also a reflection of the lack of understanding of cultural and historical change and of the development of ideas that pervades much of the natural and social sciences. Worse still is the failure to recognize the metaphysical propositions and assumptions that pervade all processes of enquiry. This may well be a logical positivist inheritance, which, ironically, dismissed metaphysics as unscientific, while failing to recognize the metaphysical assumptions on which logical positivism itself was based. But as Charles Sanders Peirce once observed: 'you cannot avoid having a metaphysics, you can only fail to make it explicit'. The British historian R. G. Collingwood, along with Ludwig Wittgenstein, also pointed to the meta-assumptions that have to be unchallenged and stay in place as a foundation for the rest of an enquiry to take place. In short, the humanities have had, so far in IS studies, a largely hidden role to play. Hopefully, focusing on the approaches we do in these three volumes provide some sort of corrective to that reclusiveness.

From the foregoing discussion we come to the conclusion that actual human knowledge can never be known to be correct, can never be certain. We need to think in terms of types of knowledge, and in terms of confidence and warrantability or justification rather than 'truth' in any pure form. We need to think in terms of research approaches selected as appropriate for researching the phenomena under study, of making explicit the types of knowledge under investigation and of making clear the types of validity claims that can be made about the evidence chosen and analytical processes adopted. We hope that the reader will see such issues emerging much more clearly in what follows in these three volumes, and will be sensitized to debate each chapter's assumptions, line of approach, types of knowledge elicited, the validity of the method adopted and truth claims articulated, and the credibility of the evidence and its interpretation. In the light of this, the reader will be not surprised, but in fact energized by the diversity of research approaches enacted in these three volumes.

The present volume

Volume 1 of the Enacting Research Methods in Information Systems series collects compelling articles from the *JIT* pertaining to *critical, grounded theory and historical approaches*.

Critical approaches in IS focus on social issues – such as power, values, social control, freedom – when researching the development, use and impact of advanced information technologies. For IS researchers, critical research can challenge prevailing assumptions; the critical perspective reminds us of the constantly changing potential of humans who need not be confined by their immediate circumstances. Critical research remains under-represented in the IS literature. Orlikowski and Baroudi (1991) classify research as critical where a critical stance is taken toward taken-for-granted assumptions about organizations and IS, and where the aim is to critique the status quo through exposing deep-seated, structural contradictions within social systems. For Orlikowski and Baroudi the central concerns and recognitions of critical research relate to peoples' ability to change their material and social circumstances; the constraints on that capacity from prevailing political, cultural and economic systems; the contradictions in social forms that lead to conflicts and inequality and, which may also generate new social forms; and that knowledge is grounded in historical and social practices. The role of critical research is to expose, analyze and assist in transforming these power-asymmetric and alienating social conditions.

Critical research studies tend to have strong, certainly explicit theoretical and philosophical foundations. Within IS studies Klein and Myers (2011) found the three most used and influential critical theorists to be Jurgen Habermas (see Klein and Huynh, 2004), Michel Foucault (see Willcocks, 2004) and Pierre Bourdieu (see Levina, 2005). The work of these three theorists are significantly different, though all three, together with Theodor Adorno (used rarely in IS, but see Probert 2004) have been variously influenced by Marxian social theory and philosophy. Note that it is a major scholarly commitment to learn and find out how to apply their concepts and theorizations. However, detailed accounts of their work, as applied to IS studies, appear in Mingers and Willcocks (2004). That said, Klein and Myers (2011) identify three common elements across critical research: insight, critique and transformation. They also usefully develop a set of principles for conducting critical research. Klein and Myers state these as – use core concepts from critical social theorists, take a value position, reveal and challenge prevailing beliefs and social practices, aim for individual emancipation, work for improvements in society and look to improve social theories.

Grounded Theory approaches utilize a methodology for building theories 'grounded' in systematically gathered and analyzed data. This methodology was initially presented in *The Discovery of Grounded Theory* (Glaser and Strauss, 1967). As explained there, the purpose is to develop theoretically comprehensive explanations about a particular phenomenon. Strauss and Corbin (1990) locate their approach as inductively derived from studying the phenomenon represented. That is, it is discovered, developed and provisionally verified through systematic data collection: 'One does not begin with a theory, and then prove it. Rather, one begins with an area of study and what is relevant to that area is allowed to emerge' (Strauss and Corbin, 1990, p. 23). According to Baker et al. (1992), the purpose when using grounded theory method (GTM) is to provide an explanation of the social situation under investigation by establishing the core and subsidiary processes that operate within it. In terms of the core process, this guides and directs what is occurring and configures the analysis because it connects up most of the other processes within the explanatory network.

Strauss and Glaser developed the method over the years, but independently of each other, so there came about a split in approach. The subsequent debate characterizes a conceptualization (Glaserian) versus description (Straussian) approach to Grounded Theory. One can accept the validity of both approaches, but there are substantial differences between them. This is very marked in two specific areas: firstly the use of Strauss and Corbin's 'axial coding', and secondly the nature and form of what has been termed the theoretical outcome (Straussian 'full-description' versus Glaserian 'abstract-conceptualisation').

Matavire and Brown (2007) show widespread utilization of grounded theory in IS research, and reveal four main approaches. The authors classify these as the 'Glaserian' grounded theory approach, the 'Straussian' grounded theory approach, 'grounded theory' as component in a mixed methodology and the straightforward application of grounded theory techniques, most often for data analysis purposes. The most common usage of 'grounded theory' in IS has been just for data analysis purposes. Most studies tend to opt for the 'Straussian' approach, while the 'Glaserian' approach has been the least operationalized.

Whichever approach informs a particular study, there seem to be important principles to be observed by any study claiming to be using grounded theory. Reflecting on these principles, Urquhart (2001) highlights two key beliefs of grounded theory. Firstly, the researcher has to put aside theoretical ideas – avoiding preconceptions, if at all possible, is key to doing grounded theory. Secondly, regardless of the particular approach selected grounded theory cannot be developed without the concept of *constant comparison* being applied. This facilitates the development of complex theories. These theories will involve process, sequence and change in organizations, positions and social interaction. And the theories generated will be based closely on the data because constant comparison pushes the analyst to take into account diversity in the data. This diversity is surfaced by comparing between incidents and properties of a category, and trying to note all the underlying uniformities, patterns and diversities one can. Urquhart suggests that constant comparative method is flexible enough to be used in practice to produce either rich descriptive accounts or conceptualizations.

- **Historical approaches** have received all too little attention in IS research, and the adoption of historiographical theory and method is sparse indeed. This has little to do with lack of relevance, and much more to do with the training and dispositions of IS scholars, and how the IS community has chosen to attempt to construct itself as a scientific discipline. This situation has improved more recently with the *Journal of AIS* publishing a 2012 special issue on 'The History of the IS Field', though this did not really address bringing to the forefront historical methods (see Hirschheim et al., 2012). However, subsequently the *JIT* offered a 2013 special issue on historical methods. There Bryant et al. (2013) as editors make a strong case for the role of historical methods and historical perspectives in IS studies.

Bryant et al. (2013) point out that while there have been several attempts at the 'history of the IS field', there are few well-informed attempts in the top IS journals at 'history in the field', that is the use of history in researching the sort of phenomena of interest to IS researchers, e.g. the technical artifact, the systems development process, the use of information. If history is to inform IS research then an essential first step is to understand historical methods and techniques. A major obstacle has been that historians themselves have often been not particularly forthcoming about the techniques they deploy, or the assumptions they make. Another obstacle is that becoming competent at historical methods and embracing and working through the controversies on methods, evidence and 'truth' prevalent in the discipline of History requires a great intellectual investment on the part of any IS scholar. Porra et al. (2014) have addressed this directly more recently with their paper on the historical research method and IS research. They usefully provide a four tiered hierarchical research framework consisting of paradigms, approaches, methods and techniques, with distinctive historical research methods, steps and techniques increasingly proliferating in the bottom two layers of the hierarchy. In the section on historical approaches in this volume, three chapters also address the question of historical methods and their use.

Introduction to Section I – Critical Research

Section I consists of five chapters that offer critical perspectives for use in IS studies.

Chapter 1 is Bill Doolin's 1998 article for JIT 'Information Technology as Disciplinary Technology: Being Critical in Interpretive Research on Information Systems', *JIT*, Vol. 13, pp. 301–311. Bill Doolin addresses interpretive researchers and suggests that they need to become more critical and reflective about the role played by the information technologies they describe. In particular he points to the neglect in many studies of the role ICTs play in shaping social order and power relations in organizations. The chapter highlights potential deficiencies in interpretive research on IS and also offers a specific approach to studying information technology and organization that can overcome these weaknesses.

Doolin's perspective draws from Michel Foucault's discursive and disciplinary work but also on sociologists of technology. He argues that the thick description of interpretive research can be complemented within the larger perspective of critical social theory.

In **Chapter 2** 'What Does It Mean to Be "Critical" in IS Research?' *JIT*, 2002, Vol. 17, pp. 49–57, Carole Brooke provides a wide ranging review of critical thinking in the IS and organizational analysis fields of study. She addresses first the important question 'what is critical research?' She shows how, over time, definitions have changed and, and indeed, broadened. She then highlights two major themes. One concerns how we understand and study emancipation. The second involves the nature of power relations and the inequalities they shape in the workplace. Brooke then identifies an emerging tendency to use Habermas in critical IS inquiry. She assesses the reasons for this trend but warns against becoming locked into a particular discourse. She concludes by deliberating on how our frameworks of reference can be broadened, and, illustrates this, like Bill Doolin in Chapter 1 by reference to the work of Michel Foucault.

Carole Brooke complements these messages in **Chapter 3** – 'Critical Perspectives on Information Systems: An Impression of the Research Landscape', *JIT*, 2002, Vol. 17, pp. 271–283. This chapter follows on from Chapter 2 and opens up key questions about the potential valuable contribution critical research can make to IS studies. Brooke begins by pointing to the wide range of researchers for whom critical research has indeed become an important activity. She agrees with the calls from others for more empirical research, and then points to examples of specific empirical applications of a critical approach. She then considers how critical research impacts upon actual IS praxis. She looks in, in particular, at the IS professional's role, the conduct of systems development and how IS praxis can change organizational life itself. The chapter does not seek to provide a comprehensive review of the literature. Rather it aims to show the many developments in critical studies on organization and IS and the implications for future direction. To do this the author draws upon a sample of material covering a range of perspectives.

We would support the suggestion that, critical research must develop a strong emphasis on empirical work. Too often, as Brooke argues, there has been in the field of management an over-conceptual emphasis, and IS researches should not make the same mistake. We should note, however, that in both fields, in the time since Carole Brooke wrote her article, we have seen a lot more critically informed empirical work appear. For Brooke a critical project of this nature is applicable in the IS arena, and can link effectively with a growing IS tradition of qualitative inquiry. Despite having a relativist ontology, actor–network theory also places a large emphasis on the importance of empirical inquiry. In **Chapter 4** 'To Reveal Is to Critique: Actor–Network Theory and Critical Information Systems Research', *JIT*, 2002, Vol. 17, 69–78, Bill Doolin and Alan Lowe posit that actor–network theory endorses careful tracing and recording of heterogeneous networks. In this respect actor–network theory is well suited to generating contextual, detailed empirical knowledge about IS and their role in networks. In this chapter

Bill Dolin and Alan Lowe tease out how IS research informed by actor–network theory can pursue a broader critical research project not prevalent in earlier work.

Chapter 5 is 'The Rationality Framework for a Critical Study of Information Systems', *JIT*, 2002, Vol. 17, pp. 215–227. Here the three authors, Dubravka Cecez-Kecmanovic, Marius Janson and Ann Brown place the social study of IS within a broader context, namely of what they call 'progressive rationalization in modern organizations'. The heart of the chapter is their focus on the roles IS play in the rationalizing organizational processes and shaping and impacting on social interaction. The authors put forward a rationality framework. This synthesizes several approaches to reason and rationality. It provides a conceptual model for critical analysis of social and organizational consequences of organizational rationalization supported, even augmented by IS. The authors draw on a field study of three IS cases and interpret these to show the rationality framework at work. In the chapter they use the framework to explain different IS–organization relationships following increasing levels of rationality. The authors highlight that these rationalization processes entail not only substantial benefits but also considerable risks.

Introduction to Section II – Grounded Theory Approaches

Section II consists of two chapters that discuss grounded theory approaches for use in IS studies.

As qualitative research in IS has increased in recent years, we have also seen a concomitant increase in the use of GTM as a research method. But while the method offers a systematic way to generate theory from data, its full potential is infrequently tapped in IS. Why is this? Probably because a number of myths and misunderstandings about GTM are inhibiting researchers from making a bigger step. This problem is addressed, and knowledge of GTM advanced, in **Chapter 6** by Cathy Urquhart and Walter Fernandez, 'Using Grounded Theory Method in Information Systems: The Researcher as Blank Slate and Other Myths', *JIT*, 2013, Vol. 28, pp. 224–236. In this chapter the authors seek to make very clear critical aspects of the method because they have found that these are much misunderstood by casual observers and novice users. The chapter provides guidance that addresses common problems, and also uses examples drawn from the IS literature by way of illustrating the concepts. With this work, the chapter contributes usefully to the cause of raising the profile of GTM, and improving the quality of GTM-informed research.

Chapter 7 is by Stefan Seidel and Cathy Urquhart and is entitled 'On Emergence and Forcing in Information Systems Grounded Theory Studies: The Case of Strauss and Corbin', *JIT*, 2013, Vol. 28, pp. 237–260. Though GTM has been increasingly used in the IS field, it still remains a contested method. Indeed Bryant and Charmaz (2007) in the respected *Handbook of Grounded Theory* see it not as a method but as a family of methods. Part of the contestation also relates to the fact that its two founders Barney Glaser and Anselm Strauss fell out eventually over certain methodological issues. At heart the argument has been over the metaphor of 'emergence' and the most fundamental prescription of GTM – 'that researchers should not force preconceived conceptualizations on data' (Seidel and Urquhart). Glaser was particularly critical of Strauss for introducing an axial coding stage, and using one single coding paradigm. For Glaser, the Straussian paradigm is too rigid, it forces data, it hinders emergence and ultimately leads only to conceptual description instead of grounded theory. Surprisingly, however, there are few studies that provide empirical evidence that demonstrate that the Strauss (and Corbin) version of grounded theory results in forcing. In this chapter, Seidel and Urquhart analyze IS studies in top ranked journals, where Straussian grounded theory procedures are most frequently utilized. The chapter provides detailed insights into the use and impacts of axial coding and the coding paradigm. They find IS researchers' use of Straussian coding procedures both conscious and deliberative, and that axial coding as employed shows GTM an evolving method open to what they call 'idiosyncratic interpretations and flexible deployment'. Seidel and Urquhart see their findings consistent with recent developments in constructivist grounded theory. Here the proposition is that grounded theories are not discovered, but are constructed, and are based on conscious decisions and interpretive acts. Seidel and Urquhart also propose three propositions, and several guidelines that will help IS researchers to construct Straussian informed grounded theory that uses coding procedures, while still sticking to the principle of avoiding preconceptions as much as possible.

Introduction to Section III – Historical Approaches

Section III consists of three chapters that point to the value and neglect of historical approaches in IS studies.

Chapter 8, by Frank Land, entitled 'The Use of History in IS Research: An Opportunity Missed?' *JIT*, 2010, Vol. 25, pp. 385–394, is shaped by two regularly repeated clichés. Frank Land points to the first which is that 'History is bunk'. For Land, this well-known saying by Henry Ford has two implications: (1) that what is presented as 'history' is more often than not inaccurate if not a downright lie, and (2) that there is nothing to learn from history as 'modern innovations make the past irrelevant' (Land). Frank Land points to the second cliché the author points to, 'We will heed the lessons we have learned from past disasters'. Land points out how often that claim is made with respect to IS failures. Again, Land argues that there are two implications from this cliché. One is that history repeats itself. Thus if we learn how mistakes were made we can stop the same mistakes from recurring. The second implication is that we can analyze the past with enough accuracy as to identify all the problems and issues that led to the mistakes being made. In this chapter, Frank Land argues that Henry Ford's viewpoint is far too prevalent, and damaging to IS research. In practice, despite its neglect, the historiography of IS is important to understand IS and its evolution through time. Furthermore, even the most transformative, revolutionary innovations benefit from a close study of the historical context. Land's arguments and conclusions are supported by a number of telling examples.

In **Chapter 9** Natalie Mitev and Francois-Xavier de Vaujany offer 'Seizing the Opportunity: Towards a Historiography of Information Systems', *JIT*, 2012, Vol. 27, pp. 110–124. The authors argue that historical perspectives are 'timidly' entering the world of IS research when compared to advances in the use of historical research approaches in management and organization studies. Major IS journals have published history-oriented papers, but the number and range of historical papers – while increasing – remains low. (As at 2016 we, as editors, would add that it still remains low). The research reported in this chapter consisted of a thematic analysis of all papers on History and IS published between 1972 and 2009 as indexed on ABI and in Google Scholar. A typology developed by theorists Usdiken and Kieser was used. This classifies historical research into supplementarist, integrationist and reorientationist approaches. Mitev and de Vaujany discuss how these approaches link with positivism, interpretivism and critical research – epistemological stances well known in IS research and detailed in the present three volumes. The authors then describe the differences between these approaches and their historiographical characteristics. Mitev and de Vaujany found that most IS history papers are supplementarist, descriptive case studies with very limited uses of history and historical methods. They then argue that IS research would benefit from adopting integrationist and reorientationist historical perspectives. The chapter offers examples to illustrate how the adoption of integrationist and reorientationist theories would contribute to enriching, extending and challenging existing theories, research methods and consequently the research outcomes.

The call for historical research in IS is an explicit recognition of the predominance of what William Bonner calls 'presentism' in business research. How does this manifest itself? This is where the past is used purely to justify and validate current beliefs, or modern beliefs are inserted onto the past. One alternative would be to use the past to, for example, understand and reveal current assumptions and biases. There would seem to be a freedom in dismissing past, and even present time in order to center ourselves and our information and communications technology artifacts primarily in the future, looking to improve the future unburdened by the past. But what if that action and assumption are wrong. What if the present is fluid and unstable precisely because the past is embedded in the present which as a result remains tension filled and unresolved? This then raises fundamental challenges to the work that IS researchers do, raises questions about the value of that work to others and should cause reflection on our impact as educators. William Bonner addresses these issues in **Chapter 10**, 'History and IS – Broadening Our View and Understanding: Actor–Network Theory as a Methodology', *JIT*, 2013, Vol. 28, pp. 111–123.

In particular, Bonner uses a Canadian case study to argue, as an earlier chapter did, the merits of using actor–network theory, in this case as a methodology for historical IS research. The study is a revealing one, prompted by the apparent resolution of a privacy controversy, involving personal motor vehicle registration information in the province of Alberta. In the case controversy was resolved by an appeal to something called 'historical purposes and practices'. However, those, purposes and practices failed to be identified. This raised an important question, namely 'what was the substance of this argument and how come it was successful?' Bonner Traces actual 'purposes and practices', from the early 1900s to the present, and reveals tellingly how historical, and contextual understanding provides not only insights into, but can alter our very understanding of, the present.

References

Baker, C., Wuest, J., and Stern, P. (1992). Method Slurring: The Grounded Theory – Phenomology Example, *Journal of Advanced Nursing*, 17(11), 1355–1366.
Bryant, A. and Charmaz, K. (eds.) (2007). *The Sage Handbook of Grounded Theory*. Sage, London.

Bryant, A., Black, A., Land, F., and Porra, J. (2013). What is History? What is IS History? What is IS history? ... and Why Even Bother with History? *Journal of Information Technology*, 28(1), 1–17.

Burrell, G. and Morgan, G. (1979). *Sociological Paradigms and Organizational Analysis.* Heinemann, London.

Gallers, R. and Currie, W. (eds.) (2011). *The Handbook of Management Information Systems – Critical Perspectives and New Directions.* Oxford University Press, Oxford.

Glaser, B. and Strauss, A. (1967). *The Discovery of Grounded Theory,* Aldine Press, Chicago.

Habermas, J. (1984). *The Theory of Communicative Action1. Reason and The Rationalization of Society.* Heinemann, London.

Habermas, J. (ed.) (1993). *Justification and Application,* Polity, Cambridge, pp 1–17.

Hirschheim, R., Saunders, C., and Detmar Straub, D. (2012). Historical Interpretations of the IS Discipline: An Introduction to the Special Issue, *Journal of the Association for Information Systems,* 13(4), 1–7.

Kagan, J. (2009). The Three Cultures: Natural Sciences, Social sciences and the Humanities in the 21st Century. Cambridge University Press, Cambridge.

Klein, H. and Huynh, M. (2004). The Critical Social Theory of Jurgen Habermas and Its Implications for IS Research. In Mingers, J. and Willcocks, L. (eds.) (2004) *Social Theory and Philosophy For Information Systems.* Wiley, Chichester.

Klein, M. and Myers, M. (1999). A Set of Principles for Conducting and Evaluating Interpretive Field Studies in Information Systems. *MIS Quarterly,* 23(1), 67–93.

Klein, M. and Myers, M. (2011). A Set of Principles for Conducting Critical Research in Information Systems. *MIS Quarterly,* 35(1), 17–36.

Lee, A. (2014). Theory is King? But First, What Is Theory? *Journal of Information Technology,* 29, 350–352.

Levina, N. (2005). Collaborating on Multiparty Information Systems Development Projects: A Collective Reflection-in-Action View. *Information Systems Research,* 16(2), 109–130.

Matavire R. and Brown I. (2008). Investigating the use of 'Grounded Theory' in information systems research. *Proceedings of the 2008 SAICSIT conference on IT Research In Developing Countries,* pp. 139–147.

Mingers, J. (2001). Combining IS Research Methods: Towards a Pluralist Methodology. *Information Systems Research,* 12(3), 240–259.

Mingers, J. (2011). The Truth, The Whole Truth, and Nothing But The Truth – High Quality Research In Information Systems. In Gallers, R. and Currie, W. (eds.) (2011). *The Handbook of Management Information Systems – Critical Perspectives and New Directions.* Oxford University Press, Oxford.

Mingers, J. and Willcocks, L. (eds) (2004). *Social Theory and Philosophy For Information Systems.* Wiley, Chichester.

Mingers, J. and Willcocks, L. (2014). An Integrative Semiotic Framework for Information Systems: The Material, Social and Personal Worlds. *Information and Organization,* 24, 48–70.

Orlikowski, W. and Baroudi, J. (1991). Studying Information Technology in Organizations: Research Approaches and Assumptions. *Information Systems Research,* 2(1), 1–28.

Porra, J., Hirschheim, R., and Parks, M. (2014). The Historical Research Method and Information Systems Research. *Journal of Association for Information Systems*, **15**(9), 536–576.

Probert, S. (2004). Adorno: A Critical Theory for IS. In Mingers, J. and Willcocks, L. (eds) (2004). *Social Theory and Philosophy For Information Systems*. Wiley, Chichester.

Strauss, A. and Corbin, J. (1990) *Basics of Qualitative Research: Grounded Theory Procedures and Techniques*, Sage Publications, Newbury Park, CA.

Urquhart, C. (2001) An Encounter with Grounded Theory: Tackling the Practical and Philosophical Issues. In Trauth, E. (ed.). *Qualitative Research in Information Systems: Issues and Trends*. Idea Group Publishing, London.

Willcocks, L. (2004). Foucault, Power/Knowledge and Information Systems: Reconstructing The Present. In Mingers, J. and Willcocks, L. (eds) (2004). *Social Theory and Philosophy For Information Systems*. Wiley, Chichester.

Willcocks, L. (2014). Comments on Allan Lee's 2014 Paper 'Is Theory King? But First What Is Theory?' Panel on Is Theory King? At the *International Conference on Information Systems*, 14–17 December, Auckland, New Zealand.

Section I
Critical Research

1
Information Technology as Disciplinary Technology: Being Critical in Interpretive Research on Information Systems

Bill Doolin
Centre for Interdisciplinary Management Studies, University of Waikato, Hamilton, New Zealand

Introduction

The collection, analysis and interpretation of data are always conducted within some broader understanding of what constitutes legitimate inquiry and valid knowledge (Henwood and Pidgeon, 1993). It is the methodology adopted by a researcher that is the dominant influence on the research process and findings, rather than the methods employed, which remain data collection techniques (Putnam, 1983, Llewellyn, 1993). By discussing methodology, we reveal our choices of method and define the way these choices fit the research problem (Dobbert, 1990). However, choices in research methodology can not be unproblematically explained away simply by recourse to a researcher's beliefs and philosophical assumptions (cf. Burrell and Morgan, 1979; Chua, 1986; Guba, 1990; Orlikowski and Baroudi, 1991).

Research methodologies are the products of (and are constitutive of) the social context in which they are invoked. Particular contexts legitimate, justify and authorize some research choices and not others (Tinker and Yuthas, 1994). For example, the assumptions which underlie New Right political thought can be argued to derive from positivistic conceptions of science (Dixon and Kouzmin, 1994): 'The claim to moral neutrality and scientific objectivity suits an age in which economy has

Reprinted from 'Information technology as disciplinary technology: being critical in interpretive research on information systems', by B. Doolin in *Journal of Information Technology*, 13, 1998, pp. 301–311. With kind permission from the Association for Information Technology Trust. All rights reserved.

come to be regarded as more important than society and in which a brand of economics has claimed scientific qualities' (Rees, 1995, p. 17). The increasing dependence of research on powerful external agencies encourages the uncritical adoption of images of society held by those funding the research (Joerges and Czarniawska, 1998). It could be suggested that the tendency for large scale (positivistic) surveys to be used in policy evaluation reflects a demand for rapid results and instrumental explanations of societal reality (Agar, 1980). Quantification and enumeration play an important role in the construction of a 'rational' modern society (Bloomfield, 1991).

The inevitable presence of value choices in the research process suggests that 'the choice of a particular value system tends to empower and enfranchise certain persons while disempowering and disenfranchising others. Inquiry thereby becomes a political act' (Guba, 1990, p. 24, emphasis removed). Putnam (1983) points out that much organizational research utilizes a managerial perspective and, thus, perpetuates the status quo. Positivist research, which has an orientation towards technical control, is particularly prone towards managerial-based definitions of organizational reality. However, this tendency is not an inherent feature of positivist research, and equally, unreflective and uncritical interpretive organizational research is capable of perpetuating the status quo.

The central concern of this paper is to highlight the dangers of an unreflective treatment of technology in the developing interpretive research tradition in information systems research (Kaplan and Duchon, 1988; Orlikowski and Baroudi, 1991; Walsham, 1995; Doolin, 1996; Lee *et al.*, 1997; Nandhakumar and Jones, 1997). Technology is both a condition and a consequence of power relations in organizations and society (Knights, 1995), and in order for interpretive information systems research to be critical, the practices which surround and involve information technology need to be analysed in the context of a wider set of social and political relations. The suggestion made in the paper is that the potential lack of criticality in interpretive information systems research stems from a relatively unsophisticated consideration of technology which underplays the significance of technology proper. Without a critical consideration of technology, such research not only maintains taken for granted assumptions about technology, it also deflects criticism away from technology and encourages its reification (Joerges and Czarniawska, 1998).

The remainder of the paper is structured as follows. The paper first briefly reviews the basis for interpretive research in information systems and highlights the potential criticisms of such research which stem from its treatment of technology. The succeeding section discusses attempts to confront 'the question of technology' (Joerges and Czarniawska, 1998) in interpretive information systems research. A particular approach to studying information technology and organization which utilizes a perspective on technology and power drawn from the work of Michel Foucault is then presented. This approach is offered as a way of overcoming the weaknesses inherent in earlier treatments of technology in interpretive information systems research. The approach is then applied to a particular type of information system in the health care context to illustrate how information technology may act as a disciplinary technology.

Being critical about interpreting information technology

Arguments advocating interpretivism as a legitimate basis for understanding human activity are well rehearsed in the organizational studies literature (for example, Burrell and Morgan, 1979; Putman, 1983; Chua, 1988; Dyer and Wilkins, 1991; Orlikowski and Baroudi, 1991; Walsham, 1993; Jönsson and Macintosh, 1997). Interpretivism asserts that the positivist methodology of the natural sciences is inadequate for the understanding of human action. The primary rationale for this assertion is that human beings enact their own reality. Human products such as society or organizations are objectifications of the human mind. A different method of inquiry to that of the natural sciences is needed, one which recognizes 'the actions, events and artefacts from *within* human life not as the observation of some external reality' (Hughes, 1990, p. 90; Lee, 1991; Harper, 1992; Henwood and Pidgeon, 1993).

Interpretive information systems research might be charactized by an intention to understand the implication of information technology in organizational activity through 'an understanding of the *context* of the information systems, and the *process* whereby the information system influences and is influenced by its context' (Walsham, 1993, pp. 4–5). It is based on the belief that: 'the same physical artefact, the same institution, or the same human action, can have different meanings for different human subjects, as well as for the observing social scientist' (Lee, 1991, p. 347). Although information systems have a physical component which permits their technical operation, they are designed and used by people operating in a complex social context. Thus, an information system is understood (constructed) differently by different individuals, and is given meaning by the shared understanding of such phenomena which arises out of social interaction:

> Events, persons, objects are indeed tangible entities. The meanings and wholeness derived from or ascribed to these tangible phenomena in order to make sense of them, organize them, or reorganize a belief system, however, are *constructed realities*. (Lincoln and Guba, 1985, p. 84)

From this perspective, an information system is a human artefact which is drawn on and used to create or reinforce meaning by the interacting human participants involved with the technological aspects of the system. The concept of dynamic process is important since the information system itself is not static, either in terms of its physical components and data or in the changing human perceptions of the information system and its output (Walsham, 1993). Viewed thus, information technology forms part of an environment, within which managers, developers and users interact in order to develop shared meanings and interpretations of an ambiguous social reality. These shared meanings form a basis from which action is constructed (Boland, 1979).

However, interpretive information systems research has been criticized for its failure to explain the unintended consequences of action, which cannot be explained by reference to the participants and which are often a significant force in shaping social reality. It has also been criticized for its frequent neglect of historical change, and a failure to recognize the inherent conflict and contradiction in social relations (Jönsson, 1991; Orlikowski and Baroudi, 1991). In particular, Tinker (1998) criticizes recent ethnographic research on information systems for what he perceives as its uncritical appreciation of the social and historical context of technological developments. He suggests that this unreflective accommodation with technology reflects an equivocation which inadvertently helps to legitimate (and accelerate) technological changes which degrade the quality and quantity of work. (Of course, Tinker's argument is itself influenced by the values implicit in his particular approach to understanding technology and society. Hence his recourse to the literature on the deskilling aspects of technology (Braverman, 1974).) By disregarding the historical and social contexts in which information technology in organizations is designed and used, representations of information systems phenomena are grounded in the status quo (Orlikowski and Baroudi, 1991).

Many information systems researchers who would describe their research as interpretive would disagree with criticism of this nature. They would suggest that indeed it is hard to avoid being critical when conducting interpretive research (Walsham, 1993). Nevertheless, there is a danger that interpretive researchers may become preoccupied with exhaustive and comprehensive description in attempts to provide authoritative and definitive accounts of empirical reality (Knights, 1995). We need to consider the implications of unreflective accounts of technology in perpetuating the status quo in organizations. We can avoid this danger by connecting the interpretation to broader considerations of social power and control (Thomas, 1993). Interpretive information systems research can be critical by adopting a more politically informed position regarding the agency of information technology in social and technological change (Tinker, 1998).

By critical I mean questioning and deconstructing the taken for granted assumptions inherent in the status quo (Hull, 1997), and interpreting organizational activity and how information technology is implicated in it by recourse to a wider societal, historical, economic and ideological context. While interpretive information systems research is grounded in a desire to describe and understand organizational reality, it need not do so without questioning the power structures which maintain the status quo. Interpretive information systems research must extend beyond the historical development of information technology into the larger economic and societal framework within which such developments occur. The wider context of particular technological outcomes involves preconceptions of power that impact on present and future events – events which must be interpreted in light of these power relationships (Putnam, 1983).

It is worth noting that the critical interpretivism I am advocating is not necessarily reliant on the critical theory of Jurgen Habermas and the Frankfurt School. Although critical theory represents a valid approach for the critical interpretation of information technology in organizations, the position maintained in this paper is that interpretive researchers can be critically reflective while utilizing another theoretical apparatus. As Thomas (1993) notes, critical researchers range on a continuum of possible critical approaches. The use of critical theory and critical hermeneutics to inform a style of critical ethnography has been well developed in the information systems literature by Harvey and Myers (1995), Myers (1997) and Myers and Young (1997), and is not discussed further here.

Information technology, duality and determinism

An unreflective accommodation with technology in interpretive information systems research (Tinker, 1998) has its origins in received conceptions of technology and its relationship with the social. The information systems field, with its roots in engineering and social science disciplines based on a nature/society dichotomy, has difficulty in confronting technology (Joerges and Czarniawska, 1998). Early attempts to balance the technical with the social, such as the notion of socio-technical systems (Mumford and Weir, 1979) reflected this dichotomizing assumption. Even more sophisticated attempts to open up technology to social constructivist arguments tend to retain this implicit duality. The assumption of a dichotomy between the technical and the social leads to the adoption of various deterministic positions in relation to technology and technological development:

If we reduce technology to machines, as something other than ourselves as social beings, it is easy to fall into the trap of asking how such machines were socially determined, or alternatively, how such machines determine how we are socially. (Bloomfield et al., 1994b, p. 139)

Determinism is reflected in information systems research which treats information technology as having impacts. Either information technology is portrayed as the determining factor and users as passive, or users and organizations are viewed as acting in rational consort to achieve particular outcomes through the use of information technology (Kaplan and Duchon, 1988).

In the former portrayal, technology is assigned an internal dynamic, through which it becomes an autonomous and deterministic force in society (Winner, 1980; MacKenzie and Wajcman, 1985; Orlikowski, 1992). This technological determinism can be observed in the labour process literature, where specific aspects of technology are perceived to lead to the inevitable deskilling and degradation of work (Braverman, 1974). In the information systems field, the technological imperative is reflected in a technicist view of information technology, in which the computer is seen uncritically as an instrument of progress (Mowshowitz, 1981). The implication is that an objective and neutral information technology impacts on the functioning and structure of its organizational environment, causing changes in the structure of organizations towards flatter or networked forms, changes in the nature of managerial work, and either the upskilling or deskilling of workers (Markus and Robey, 1988). Much has been promised of the ability of information technology to change organizational forms and processes (Miles and Snow, 1986; Drucker, 1988; Rockart and Short, 1991; Applegate, 1994) based on its ability to not only automate, but 'informate' (Zuboff, 1988) and even 'transformate' (Scott Morton, 1991).

In the second portrayal of information technology mentioned above, subjective social values shape the design and use of the emerging technology towards some intentional outcome. This corresponds to a position that Orlikowski (1992) terms 'strategic choice', which focuses on the way that organizational context and the strategies of technology decision makers influence technology. This perspective argues that technology is not autonomous, and that instead technology is shaped by social or political interests, and is the instrument of particular groups in society (Bijker and Law, 1992; Scarborough and Corbett, 1992; Bloomfield *et al.*, 1994a, 1994b). For example, Kling (1980) suggests that little causal power can be attributed to information technology itself. The 'social impacts' or 'consequences' of computers are the consequences of the underlying social processes by which they are developed, adopted and used. However, the social shaping or construction of technology is also a form of determinism.

The work of Zuboff (1988) is a widely cited illustration of the interpretive approach to information systems research. In a comprehensive and influential study, she considered the implications and outcomes of computerization in eight US organizations. From her research, Zuboff suggested that information technology could have either an automating effect or an 'informating' effect. By informating, she meant the capacity of information technology to generate ongoing information about underlying productive and administrative processes. Zuboff argued that traditional management control perverts the potential of information technology. Instead, information technology can and should be designed with the intention to informate work, and thus enhance worker flexibility and autonomy. Used in this way, information technology would enable the decentralization of organizational power in new forms of networked, learning organizations peopled by knowledge workers empowered through technology (Bloomfield and McLean, 1996).

However, Zuboff's work has been criticized as naive and optimistic in the way it assigns an inherently progressive and liberating role to information technology in the transformation of organizational structures and processes (Knights and Murray, 1994).[1] Her emphasis on the autonomous informating power of information technology seems to make recourse to technological determinism. Orlikowski (1991) challenges this deterministic view, noting that 'there is nothing inherent in technology's informating potential that ensures a transformation in the workplace' (p. 34). At the same time, Zuboff suggests that it is the strategic choices of managers which influence the design and use of the emerging technology towards some intentional outcome. Information technology is viewed either as potentially empowering, liberating and upskilling or as disempowering and deskilling, *depending on how it is applied*. This simultaneous appeal to technological and social determinism appears unresolved:

> The task now is to determine the likelihood of such organizational innovations. It means exploring the relationship between managerial authority and the autonomous informating power of the technology. Can the technology transform authority? Or will authority impose restrictions on the informating process? (Zuboff, 1988, p. 218).

If we wish to go beyond such dichotomies, we need to replace the dualism usually assumed between the technical and the social with a view of reality as materially heterogeneous. In such a view, the social and the technical mutually define one another (Law, 1991, 1992, 1994; Knights and Murray, 1994; Latour, 1994; Law and Mol, 1995). For instance, Bloomfield (1991) suggests that information systems represent the organization, in that the collective understanding of the organization is mediated and redefined through the fabrication of the system. He argues that the fabrication of an information system presupposes certain organizational changes, rather than leading to change through the impact of the system upon the organization. Thus, information technology does not cause organizational changes so much as reflect them. However, the visibilities mobilized by the use of an information system may lead to other changes. The characteristics of a particular information system may open up new choices and constrain others, while a dominant organizational culture may promote certain ways of working at the expense of others (Kimble and McLoughlin, 1994).

Viewed in this way, information technology is neither the outcome of the logic of some technological reality, nor the reflection of social and organizational variables, but part of a process in which both technology and organization become redefined (Bloomfield *et al.*, 1994a). Technology and organization cannot be separated out. The study of modern organizations cannot exclude a consideration of technology, while technology is always developed in and for organizational contexts. Each presupposes the other. Social relations are instantiated and mediated through technology, and organizations are made relatively cohesive and stable by the way they are intimately bound up with the technical. Technology is society made durable (Latour, 1991; Callon and Latour, 1992; Bloomfield et al., 1994a; Bloomfield, 1995).

Technology does not *impact* on organizations or society; a change in social relations, task, skills and knowledge is already prefigured in the way that the technology is conceived of and constructed. Machines do not *control* social relations: they presuppose, mediate and reinforce them. (Bloomfield, 1995, p. 497).

In some ways, the apparent opposition between technological determinism and technology as the instrument of human agency can be read as a debate over whether the 'power' of information technology is ultimately enslaving or emancipating. Such views take for granted a simplistic equating of information with power, and thus information technology with power. This is a zero-sum notion of power which implies that shifts in organizational power are the result of corresponding changes in the organizational distribution of resources (such as information) which confer power on their possessors (see, for example, Pettigrew, 1972; Markus, 1981; Pfeffer, 1994). The weakness of such a mechanical and possessive conception of power is that it fails to consider that power must also be a property of relations (Clegg, 1989; Bloomfield and Coombs, 1992).

If reality is materially heterogeneous and relational, then we need to utilize a conception of power which is relational in its exercise. We need to be sensitive to the exercise of power in studying technology without reducing technological developments to either technological or managerial imperatives (Bloomfield and McLean, 1996). Although the development of information technology may be deliberate, with the intention of changing the nature of management and organizational practice, unintended consequences may arise from the contesting of information and representations of organizational reality between different groups (Bloomfield et al., 1994a). Foucault (1977, 1980) offers such a relational notion of power.

Information technology and disciplinary power

According to Foucault, power is exercised from within the social body. His concept of disciplinary power operates by enhancing the calculability of individuals. It is constantly exercised by surveillance, observation and comparative measures that reference the norm (Foucault, 1977, 1980).[2] Power is manifested in the ubiquitous heterogeneous instruments, techniques and procedures brought to bear on the actions of others, some concentrated and hierarchically organized and others socially dispersed (Hindess, 1996). Various technologies of evaluation and calculation make visible the activities of individuals and calculate the extent to which they depart from a norm of performance (Johnson, 1993; Miller, 1994). Contemporary examples include the comparative application of performance information, or other forms of surveillance (such as supervision, routinization, rationalization, formalization, mechanization) which seek to increase control of organizational members' behaviour (Clegg, 1989).

Linked to a centre of calculation, the individual is made calculable and made to calculate. Individuals learn to survey themselves and discipline themselves through forms of self-regulation and self-control (Clegg, 1989; Coombs *et al.*, 1992). Their actions are influenced through a mechanism of self-monitoring, rather than direct control and supervision. That is, individuals are constitued as subjects capable of operating a regulated autonomy (Miller and Rose, 1990; Rose and Miller, 1992; Humphrey *et al.*, 1993; Miller, 1994). What emerges is a regulated subjectivity (Miller, 1987), in which individuals are transformed into subjects who secure their sense of meaning, identity and reality through their participation in a range of disciplinary and discursive practices. These discourses and practices which they reproduce constitute the truth of what is normal in social and organizational relations. As Knights and Willmott (1989) note: 'the very exercise of power relies upon the constitution of subjects who are tied by the sense of their identity to the reproduction of power relations' (p. 537).

Increasingly, information technology mediates this process. Disciplinary power operates through the internalization of social and institutional norms and the construction of particular understandings of organizational reality among organizational participants. Information systems play an important role in mobilizing these values and norms through which individuals derive meaning and identity. Calculative practices such as those facilitated by information systems render social phenomena visible in a particular way. Some activities are given an existence and attention, while others are unrecognized. In the fabrication of information systems, the constitutive concepts of the dominant discourses and knowledges instituted in organizational practices have to be defined and organizational phenomena reconciled with them.

Information systems thus mediate and reinforce certain views and meanings, mobilizing particular representations of organizational reality. In doing so, they underpin the framework of meaning within which organizational participants regulate their own behaviour in accordance with the norms and values associated with these knowledges and discourses (Orlikowski, 1991; Bloomfield and Coombs, 1992; Bloomfield *et al.*, 1994a, Knights and Murray, 1994).

The majority of attempts to apply a Foucauldian perspective to information technology have been concerned with the capacity of information systems (the informational dimension of information technology) to make visible aspects of organizational activity. Surveillance and control is facilitated by giving complex, ambiguous phenomena 'hard' numerical values (Morgan and Willmott, 1993). Information technology facilitates enumeration, which can underpin categorization and, thus, what is made visible. Such technologies privilege formal, quantitative information, aiding in the construction of calculative realities (Webster and Robins, 1989; Bloomfield, 1991; Bloomfield and Coombs, 1992). However, the development of information systems to monitor and scrutinize particular organizational activities facilitates control by making individuals within an organization both calculable *and calculating* with respect to their own actions. This invokes the notion of an electronic panopticon, in which organizational participants are enlisted in their own control through their belief that they are subject to constant surveillance (Orlikowski, 1991; Sewell and Wilkinson, 1992, Webster and Robins, 1993; Bloomfield *et al.*, 1994a).

For example, Orlikowski's (1991) study of how the deployment of a particular information technology affected production workers in a single multinational software consulting firm provides a critical consideration of the way that information technology can reinforce established forms of organizing and intensify existing mechanisms of control. Orlikowski suggests that the mediation of work processes by information technology creates an information environment which enables a disciplinary matrix of power, knowledge and control. The way in which information technology 'renders events, objects, and processes so that they become visible, knowable, and shareable in a new way' (Zuboff, 1988, p. 9), lies at the heart of disciplinary power. The implication is that technology's informating capacity can be used to facilitate a more embedded and repressive means of control in organizations. Information technology is more likely to reinforce hierarchical power than undermine it (Orlikowski, 1991; Knights and Murray, 1994; Willmott, 1996).

Casemix information systems as a disciplinary technology

In another study, Doolin (1998) uses a Foucauldian perspective to examine the power effects involved in the deployment of a 'casemix' information system in a hospital context. A casemix system is an information system which links detailed information on individual patient clinical activity with the associated costs, for use by managers and service providers as a basis for contracting and for revealing the relative efficiency of clinical resource usage (Packwood *et al.*, 1991). The information provided by casemix information systems mobilizes new categories for construing medical activity (Bloomfield, 1991). Scrutinizing clinical procedures and explicitly linking patient treatment decisions to standard costs, makes clinical activity visible and susceptible to intervention by management, who can influence decisions on admissions, treatment, length of stay and discharge. Casemix systems provide a view on clinical practice which highlights variances between the performance of individual clinicians or clinical specialities. The intention is to place clinical activity under scrutiny and to persuade clinicians to confirm to 'normal' work practices (Feinglass and Salmon, 1990; Bloomfield and Coombs, 1992; Chua and Degeling, 1993; Covaleski *et al.*, 1993).

The detailed information provided by the casemix information system studied by Doolin (1998) offered hospital management the possibility to increase control over health professionals, either directly or indirectly. Direct control was attempted by monitoring and making visible the financial implications of clinical decisions. Using this information, managers could make stronger truth claims (Boland and Schultze, 1996) in their attempts to contain clinical resource usage. While the inscriptions generated by the casemix information system facilitated the attempted direct control over the financial aspects of clinical practice, surveillance through this system also had the potential to engender a degree of self-control in clinicians' behaviour. Through the provision of appropriate casemix information, it was hoped that a sense of resource efficiency would be induced in the clinicians as the consequences of their patient treatment decisions were made visible. Management's view was that the provision of objective information on resource usage would lead to rational decision making by clinicians and to more efficient and responsible medical practice as less expensive treatment protocols were pursued.

However, while managerial intentions behind the introduction of the casemix system may have related to increased control over medical professionals, resistance by the clinicians was possible. Foucault (1981) argues that the articulation of power relations requires that those over whom power is exercised are recognized and maintained as people who act. That power is exercised only over subjects who are free to act implies the necessary existence of resistance in power relations. Power effects have to be reproduced and are subject to the ambiguity of human agency. They are the contingently produced outcomes of the actions of people who could 'do otherwise' (Knights and Willmott, 1989; Knights and Morgan 1991). The result is a disciplinary, rather than a disciplined, society (O'Neill, 1987; Hindess, 1996). Disciplinary technologies such as comparative surveillance information systems are not exclusively constraining. Instead they open up a new and legitimate discursive space for action (Bloomfield and Coombs, 1992; Bloomfield *et al.*, 1994a). Organizational participants may appropriate and manipulate the information and rhetoric of such systems, diverting disciplinary practices to their own ends (Covaleski *et al.*, 1993; Whittington *et al.*, 1994).

Various strategies were utilized by clinicians in the hospital studied by Doolin (1998) to resist the monitoring and scrutiny afforded to management through the casemix information system. Clinicians were effective in resisting the application of a comparative surveillance system by challenging the validity of the construction of the casemix information or by pointing to other factors that potentially explained clinical outliers or variances between individual clinicians' practices. The 'double-edged' nature of the power exercised through the casemix information system meant that some clinicians were able to divert the casemix information towards their own ends, principally in arguing for more resources. Indeed, some of the senior clinicians had begun to explore the possibilities offered by the casemix system in assuming new roles as clinician managers (cf. Bloomfield and Coombs, 1992).

Casemix information systems increase the transparency of professional knowledge, expertise and work processes. The deployment of this comparative information provides management with both the technology and a rational justification for increased intervention in medical practice (Chua and Degeling, 1993; Davies and Kirkpatrick, 1995). Further, casemix management is becoming the prevalent framework within which discussions on resource allocation in health care are structured. Even to contest claims that are made on the basis of casemix information, one must use the medium of the disciplinary practices associated with casemix management (Covaleski *et al.*, 1993). Casemix information becomes the 'currency of debate, the principal media through which claims to legitimacy and control are processed'

(Morgan and Willmott, 1993, p. 12). In reproducing the practices associated with the casemix information system, clinicians internalize the norms and values inherent in the particular discourse in which case mix management is grounded, opening up the possibility of their self-control as self-disciplined subjects. This would represent a more subtle exercise of power than deliberate strategies to modify clinical behaviour through strengthening general management in hospitals or imposing a computerized surveillance on clinical activity.

Conclusion

The intention of the paper was to discuss how interpretive information systems research can involve a critical appreciation of the way in which information technologies are implicated in organizational activity. From an interpretive perspective, the requirements for researching information technology in organizations include focusing on action and interaction in organizational settings, analysing specific situations in which individuals experience phenomena, and recognizing the symbolic uses of technology while transcending the actors' purely subjective interpretation (Boland and Pondy, 1983). Accompanying these requisites should be a willingness to challenge commonsense assumptions and to question the status quo. In other words, to open up the 'black box' of information technology and scrutinize the power relations inscribed within it which may repress or constrain (Thomas, 1993; Knights and Murray, 1994).

In order for interpretive information systems research to be critical, information technology needs to be analysed as a condition and a consequence of a broader set of social and political relations. As Knights and Murray (1994) note, organizational realities are constructed, reproduced and changed within historically and spatially specific conditions of possibility. A critical approach to interpretive information systems research confronts issues of power in organizational and technological change. It challenges taken for granted notions regarding the inherently progressive nature of technology and avoids reducing technological developments to either technical or managerial imperatives (Bloomfield and McLean, 1996).

Interpretive research on information technology should go further than demonstrating the problematic and socially constructed nature of organizations by, for instance, attempting to show how particular technological outcomes define and stabilize (albeit temporarily) particular representations of organizational reality. That is, how the ensemble of practices, language, techniques *and* artefacts that make up information technology are implicated in the governance of the conduct and subjectivity of organizational participants (Knights, 1995; Hull, 1997). Using the relational notion of power developed by Foucault (1977, 1980), the concept of information technology as a disciplinary technology was outlined. The potential for this concept to provide a critical dimension in interpretive information systems research was discussed in relation to attempts to apply a Foucauldian perspective to studies of information technology and organization.

A hospital casemix information system provides an interesting illustration of information technology as a calculative and disciplinary technology. The increased monitoring and surveillance of clinical activity through a casemix information system is consistent with the concept of disciplinary power and 'the uninterrupted play of calculated gazes' (Foucault, 1977, p. 177). In this conception of power, disciplinary technologies of surveillance enhance the calculability of individuals through the comparative application of measures that reference the norm. Calculative practices such as those facilitated by casemix information systems render social phenomena visible in a particular way. In the health care context, the development of these sophisticated comparative information systems stems from the recognition that the control of health expenditure lies at the point of intervention by indi-vidual clinicians. Under the banner of improved financial efficiency and effectiveness, hospital management have attempted to intervene more directly in clinical practice and to demand greater cost consciousness from clinicians (Chua and Degeling, 1993).

However, casemix systems cannot be understood simply as management control pursued by electronic means, constituting clinicians as passive victims of surveillance. Power is always subject to resistance. Those over whom power is exercised are recognized and maintained as people who act and could do otherwise (Foucault, 1982; Knights and Morgan, 1991). There is a general tendency among those subject to power and control, to resist by means of challenging or diverting the systems and rules imposed on them (Clegg, 1989; Covaleski *et al.*, 1993). At the hospital discussed in the paper, surveillance through the casemix system was open to the circumvention of clinicians. Clinicians both challenged and diverted the casemix system in order to 'escape the implications of the gaze of normalizing judgement' (Chua and Degeling, 1993, p. 309).

To the extent that Foucauldian studies of technology and organization are able to assimilate the social and the technical in their treatment of technology, they offer a useful approach to studying technology in organizations from a critical perspective. However, Joerges and Czarniawska (1998) suggest that Foucauldian studies have often gone too far in their use of technical metaphors for organizational discipline, power and control to overwrite the social with the technical. Technology proper becomes once again largely taken for granted, its significance residing in its involvement as the material component of human practices (Hull, 1997; cf. Joerges and Czarniawska, 1998). To avoid an unreflective accommodation with technology, we need to retain a view of reality in which the social and the technical mutually define one another.

Notes

1. For a critique of the technological optimism in recent stories of empowerment through information technology see, among others, Lyon (1988), Knights and Murray (1994), Bloomfield and McLean (1996) and Willmott (1996).
2. Foucault (1977) uses Jeremy Bentham's central elevated watch-tower, the Panopticon, as a metaphor for the exercise of disciplinary power (Burrell, 1988). The impossibility of avoiding the supervisory gaze of the all-seeing (but unseen) observer in the tower, engenders a realization in the occupants of the surrounding cells that they are always subject to surveillance. The occupant becomes his or her own guardian. Even in the absence of the supervisor, the apparatus of power still operates, continuous, disciplinary and anonymous. This constitutes a new, internalized, discipline of norms and behaviour (Dreyfus and Rabinow, 1982; Clegg, 1989).

References

Agar, M.H. (1980) *The Professional Stranger: An Informal Introduction to Ethnography* (Academic Press, New York).

Applegate, L.M. (1994) Managing in an information age: transforming the organization for the 1990s, in Baskerville, R., Smithson, S., Ngwenyama, O. and DeGross, J.I. (eds) *Transforming Organizations With Information Technology* (North-Holland, Amsterdam) pp. 15–94.

Bijker, W.E. and Law, J. (ed.) (1992) *Shaping Technology/Building Society: Studies in Sociotechnical Change* (MIT Press, Cambridge, Massachusetts).

Bloomfield, B.P. (1991) The role of information systems in the UK National Health Service: action at a distance and the fetish of calculation. *Social Studies of Science*, 21(4), 701–34.

Bloomfield, B.P. (1995) Power, machines and social relations: delegating to information technology in the National Health Service. *Organization*, 2(3/4), pp. 489–518.

Bloomfield, B.P. and Coombs, R. (1992) Information technology, control and power: the centralization and decentralization debate revisited. *Journal of Management Studies*, 29(4), 459–84.

Bloomfield, B.P. and McLean, C. (1996) Madness and organization: informed management and empowerment, in Orlikowski, W.J., Walsham, G., Jones, M.R. and Degross, J.I. (eds) *Information Technology and Changes in Organizational Work* (Chapman and Hall, London) pp. 371–93.

Bloomfield, B.P., Coombs, R. and Owen, J. (1994a) The social construction of information systems: the implications for management control, in Mansell, R. (ed.) *The Management of Information and Communication Technologies: Emerging Patterns of Control* (Aslib, London) pp. 143–57.

Bloomfield, B.P., Coombs, R. and Owen, J. (1994b) A social science perspective on information systems in the NHS, in Keen, J. (ed.) *Information Management in Health Services* (Open University Press, Buckingham) pp. 135–46.

Boland, R.J., Jr (1979) Control, causality and information system requirements. *Accounting Organizations and Society* 4(4), 259–72.

Boland, R.J., Jr and Pondy, L.R. (1983) Accounting in organizations: a union of natural and rational perspectives. *Accounting, Organizations and Society,* 8(2/3), 223–34.

Boland, R.J., Jr and Schultze, U. (1996). From work to activity: technology and the narrative of progress, in Orlikowski, W.J., Walsham, G., Jones, M.R. and DeGross, J.I. (eds) *Information Technology and Changes in Organizational Work* (Chapman and Hall, London) pp. 308–24.

Braverman, H. (1974) *Labor and Monopoly Capital: The Degradation of Work in the Twentieth Century* (Monthly Review Press, London).

Burrell, G. (1988) Modernism, post modernism and organizational analysis 2: the contribution of Michel Foucault. *Organizational Studies,* 9(2), 221–35.

Burrell, G. and Morgan, G. (1979) *Sociological Paradigms and Organisational Analysis: Elements of the Sociology of Corporate Life* (Heinemann, London).

Callon, M. and Latour, B. (1992) Don't throw the baby out with the Bath school! A reply to Collins and Yearley, in Pickering, A. (ed.) *Science as Practice and Culture* (University of Chicago Press, Chicago) pp. 343–68.

Chua, W.F. (1986) Radical developments in accounting thought. *The Accounting Review* 61(4), 601–32.

Chua, W.F. (1988) Interpretive sociology and management accounting – a critical review. *Accounting, Auditing and Accountability,* 1(2), 59–79.

Chua, W.F. and Degeling, P. (1993) Interrogating an accounting-based intervention on three axes: instrumental, moral and aesthetic. *Accounting, Organizations and Society,* 18(4), 291–318.

Clegg, S.R. (1989) *Frameworks of Power* (Sage, London).

Coombs, R., Knights, D. and Willmott, H.C. (1992) Culture, control and competition; towards a conceptual framework for the study of information technology in organizations. *Organization Studies,* 13(1), 51–72.

Covaleski, M.A., Dirsmith, M.W. and Michelman, J.E. (1993) An institutional theory perspective on the DRG framework, case-mix accounting systems and health-care organizations. *Accounting, Organizations and Society,* 18(1), 65–80.

Davies, A. and Kirkpatrick, I. (1995) Performance indicators, bureaucratic control and the decline of professional autonomy: the case of academic librarians, in Kirkpatrick, I. and Lucio, M.M. (eds) *The Politics of Quality in the Public Sector: The Management of Change* (Routledge, London) pp. 84–107.

Dixon, J. and Kouzmin, A. (1994) The commercialisation of the Australian public sector: competence, elitism or default in management education? *International Journal of Public Sector Management,* 7(6), 52–73.

Dobbert, M.L. (1990). Discussion on methodology, in Guba, E.G. (ed.) *The Paradigm Dialog* (Sage Publications, Newbury Park, California) pp. 286–89.

Doolin, B. (1996) Alternative views of case research in Information Systems. *Australian Journal of Information Systems*, 3(2), 21–9.

Doolin, B. (1998) Discourse, technology and organisation in a New Zealand Crown Health Enterprise. Unpublished PhD thesis, University of Waikato, New Zealand.

Dreyfus, H.L. and Rabinow, P. (1982) *Michel Foucault: Beyond Structuralism and Hermeneutics* (Harvester Wheatsheaf, New York).

Drucker, P.F. (1988) The coming of the new organization. *Harvard Business Review*, 66, 45–53.

Dyer, W.G., Jr and Wilkins, A.L. (1991) Better stories, not better constructs, to generate better theory: a rejoinder to Eisenhardt. *Academy of Management Review*, 16(3), 613–19.

Feinglass, J. and Salmon, J.W. (1990) Corporatization of medicine: the use of medical management information systems to increase the clinical productivity of physicians. *International Journal of Health Services*, 20(2), 233–52.

Foucault, M. (1977) *Discipline and Punish: The Birth of the Prison* (Penguin, London).

Foucault, M. (1980) *Power/Knowledge: Selected Interviews and Other Writings 1972–1977* (Pantheon, New York).

Foucault, M. (1981) *The History of Sexuality: An Introduction* (Penguin, London).

Foucault, M. (1982) The subject and power, in Dreyfus, H.L. and Rabinow, P. (eds) *Michel Foucault: Beyond Structuralism and Hermeneutics* (Harvester Wheatsheaf, New York) pp. 208–26.

Guba, E.G. (1990) The alternative paradigm dialog, in Guba, E.G. (ed.) *The Paradigm Dialog* (Sage Publications, Newbury Park, California) pp. 17–27.

Harper, D. (1992) Small N's and community case studies, in Ragin, C.C. and Becker, H.S. (eds) *What is a Case? Exploring the Foundations of Social Inquiry* (Cambridge University Press, Cambridge) pp. 139–59.

Harvey, L.J. and Myers, M.D. (1995). Scholarship and practice: the contribution of ethnographic research methods to bridging the gap. *Information Technology and People*, 8(3), 13–27.

Henwood, K.L. and Pidgeon, N.F. (1993) Qualitative research and psychological theorizing, in Hammersley, M. (ed.) *Social Research: Philosophy, Politics and Practice* (Sage, London) pp. 14–32.

Hindess, B. (1996) *Discourses of Power: From Hobbes to Foucault* (Blackwell, Oxford).

Hughes, J. A. (1990) *The Philosophy of Social Research*, (2nd edn) (Longman, London and New York).

Hull, R. (1997) Governing the conduct of computing: computer science, the social sciences and frameworks of computing. *Accounting, Management and Information Technologies*, 7(4), 213–40.

Humphrey, C., Miller, P. and Scapens, R.W. (1993) Accountability and accountable management in the UK public sector. *Accounting, Auditing and Accountability Journal*, 6(3), 7–29.

Joerges, B. and Czarniawska, B. (1998) The question of technology, or how organizations inscribe the world. *Organization Studies*, 19(3), 363–85.

Johnson, T. (1993). Expertise and the state, in Gane, M. and Johnson, T. (eds) *Foucault's New Domains* (Routledge, London) pp. 139–52.

Jönsson, S. (1991). Action research, in Nissen, H.-E., Klein, H.K. and Hirschheim, R. (eds) *Information Systems Research: Contemporary Approaches and Emergent Traditions* (North-Holland, Amsterdam).

Jönsson, S. and Macintosh, N.B. (1997) CATS, RATS and EARS: making the case for ethnographic accounting research. *Accounting, Organizations and Society,* 22(3/4), 367–86.

Kaplan, B. and Duchon, D. (1988) Combining qualitative and quantitative methods in information systems re-search: a case study. *MIS Quarterly,* 12(4), 571–86.

Kimble, C. and McLoughlin, K. (1994) Changes to the organisation and the work of managers following the introduction of an integrated information system, in Mansell, R. (ed.) *The Management of Information and Communication Technologies: Emerging Patterns of Control.* (Aslib, London) pp 157–77.

Kling, R. (1980) Social analyses of computing: theoretical perspectives in recent empirical research. *Computing Surveys,* 12(1), 61–110.

Knights, D. (1995) Refocusing the case study: the politics of research and researching politics in IT management. *Technology Studies,* 2(2), 230–54.

Knights, D. and Morgan, G. (1991) Corporate strategy, organizations and subjectivity: a critique. *Organization Studies,* 12(2), 251–73.

Knights, D. and Murray, F. (1994) *Managers Divided: Organization Politics and Information Technology Management* (Wiley, Chichester).

Knights, D. and Willmott, H. (1989) Power and subjectivity at work: from degradation to subjugation in social relations. *Sociology,* 23(4), 535–58.

Latour, B. (1991) Technology is society made durable, in Law, J. (ed.) *A Sociology of Monsters: Essays on Power, Technology and Domination* (Routledge, London) pp. 103–31.

Latour, B. (1994) On technical mediation – philosophy, sociology, genealogy. *Common Knowledge,* 3(2), 29–64.

Law, J. (1991) Introduction: monsters, machines and sociotechnical relations, in Law, J. (ed.) *A Sociology of Monsters: Essays on Power, Technology and Domination* (Routledge, London) pp. 1–23.

Law, J. (1992) Notes on the theory of the actor-network: ordering, strategy, and heterogeneity. *Systems Practice,* 5(4), 379–93.

Law, J. (1994) *Organizing Modernity* (Blackwell, Oxford).

Law, J. and Mol, A. (1995) Notes on materiality and sociality. *Sociological Review,* 43(2), 274–94.

Lee, A.S. (1991) Integrating positivist and interpretive approaches to organizational research. *Organization Science,* 2(4), 342–65.

Lee, A.S., Liebenau, J. and DeGross, J.I. (ed.) (1997) *Information Systems and Qualitative Research* (Chapman and Hall, London).

Lincoln, Y.S. and Guba, E.G. (1985) *Naturalistic Inquiry* (Sage, Beverly Hills).

Llewellyn, S. (1993) Working in hermeneutic circles in management accounting research: some implications and applications. *Management Accounting Research,* 4, 231–49.

Lyon, D. (1988) *The Information Society* (Basil Blackwell, Oxford).

MacKenzie, D.C. and Wajcman, J. (1985) *The Social Shaping of Technology* (Open University Press, Milton Keynes).

Markus, M.L. (1981) Implementation politics: top management support and user involvement. *Systems, Objectives, Solutions,* 1, 203–15.

Markus, M.L. and Robey, D. (1988) Information technology and organizational change: causal structure in theory and research. *Management Science*, **34**(5), 583–98.

Miles, R.E. and Snow, C.C. (1986) Networked organizations: new concepts for new forms. *California Management Review*, **28**(3), 62–73.

Miller, P. (1987) *Domination and Power* (Routledge and Kegan Paul, London).

Miller, P. (1994) Accounting and objectivity: the invention of calculating selves and calculable spaces, in Megill, A. (ed.) *Rethinking Objectivity* (Duke University Press, Durham) pp. 239–64.

Miller, P. and Rose, N. (1990) Governing economic life. *Economy and Society*, **19**(1), 1–31.

Morgan, G. and Willmott, H. (1993) The 'new' accounting research: on making accounting more visible. *Accounting, Auditing and Accountability Journal*, **6**(4), 3–36.

Mowshowitz, A. (1981) On approaches to the study of social issues in computing. *Communications of the ACM*, **24**(3), 146–55.

Mumford, E. and Weir, M. (1979) *Computer Systems in Work Design – the ETHICS Method: Effective Technical and Human Implementation of Computer Systems*, (Associated Business Press, London).

Myers, M.D. (1997) Critical ethnography in information systems, in Lee, A.S., Liebenau, J. and DeGross, J.I. (eds) *Information Systems and Qualitative Research* (Chapman and Hall, London) pp. 276–300.

Myers, M.D. and Young, L.W. (1997) Hidden agendas, power and managerial assumptions in information systems development: an ethnographic study. *Information Technology and People*, **10**(3), 224–40.

Nandhakumar, J. and Jones, M. (1997) Too close for comfort? Distance and engagement in interpretive information systems research. *Information Systems Journal*, **7**(2), 109–31.

O'Neill, J. (1987) The disciplinary society: from Weber to Foucault. *British Journal of Sociology*, **37**(1), 42–60.

Orlikowski, W.J. (1991) Integrated information environment or matrix of control? The contradictory implications of information technology. *Accounting, Management and Information Technologies*, **1**(1), 9–42.

Orlikowski, W.J. (1992) The duality of technology: rethinking the concept of technology in organizations. *Organization Science*, **3**(3), 398–427.

Orlikowski, W.J. and Baroudi, J.J. (1991) Studying information technology in organizations: research approaches and assumptions. *Information Systems Research*, **2**(1), 1–29.

Packwood, T., Keen, J. and Buxton, M. (1991) *Hospitals in Transition: The Resource Management Experiment* (Open University Press, Milton Keynes).

Pettigrew, A.M. (1972) Information control as a power resource. *Sociology*, **6**(2), 187–204.

Pfeffer, J. (1994) *Managing with Power* (Harvard Business School Press, Boston, Massachusetts).

Putman, L.L. (1983) The interpretive perspective: an alternative to functionalism, in Putnam, L.L. and Pacanowsky, M.E. (eds) *Communication and Organizations: An Interpretive Approach* (Sage, Beverly Hills) pp. 31–54.

Rees, S. (1995) The fraud and the fiction, in Rees, S. and Rodley, G. (eds) *The Human Costs of Managerialism: Advocating the Recovery of Humanity* (Pluto Press, Liechhardt, NSW) pp. 15–27.

Rockart, J.F. and Short, J.E. (1991) The networked organization and the management of interdependence, in Scott Morton, M. (ed.) *The Corporation of the 1990s* (Oxford University Press, Oxford).

Rose, N. and Miller, P. (1992) Political power beyond the State: problematics of government. *British Journal of Sociology,* **43**(2), 173–205.

Scarbrough, H. and Corbett, J.M. (1992) *Technology and Organization: Power, Meaning and Design* (Routledge, London).

Scott Morton, M. (ed.) (1991) *The Corporation of the 1990s* (Oxford University Press, Oxford).

Sewell, G. and Wilkinson, B. (1992) 'Someone to watch over me': surveillance, discipline and the just-in-time labour process. *Sociology,* **26**(2), 271–89.

Thomas, J. (1993) *Doing Critical Ethnography* (Sage, Newbury Park, California).

Tinker, T. (1998). Hamlet without the prince: the ethnographic turn in information systems research. *Accounting, Auditing and Accountability Journal,* **11**(1), 13–33.

Tinker, T. and Yuthas, K. (1994) Social change and theoretical structures in MIS. Fourth Interdisciplinary Perspectives on Accounting Conference, University of Manchester, 11–13 July.

Walsham, G. (1993) *Interpreting Information Systems in Organizations* (Wiley, Chichester).

Walsham, G. (1995) The emergence of interpretivism in IS research. *Information Systems Research,* **6**(4), 376–94.

Webster, F. and Robins, K. (1989) Plan and control: towards a cultural history of the Information society. *Theory and Society,* **18**(3), 323–51.

Webster, F. and Robins, K. (1993) 'I'll be watching you': comment on Sewell and Wilkinson. *Sociology,* **27**(2), 243–52.

Whittington, R., McNulty, T. and Whipp, R. (1994) Market-driven change in professional services: problems and processes. *Journal of Management Studies,* **31**(6), 829–45.

Willmott, H. (1996) 'Smart Machine derailed' – engineers accuse passengers. *Electronic Journal of Radical Organisational Theory.* 2(2) at http://www.mngt. waikato.ac.nz/depts/sm&l/journal/vol_3/willmott.htm.

Winner, L. (1980) Do artifacts have politics? *Daedalus,* **109**(1), 121–36.

Zuboff, S. (1988) *In the Age of the Smart Machine: The Future of Work and Power* (Basic Books, New York).

2
What Does It Mean to be 'Critical' in IS Research?

Carole Brooke
Faculty of Business and Management, University of Lincoln, Brayford Pool, UK

Introduction

The main aim of this paper is to explore what it means to conduct 'critical' research in IS. In order to begin this, it is necessary to look beyond the scope of IS inquiry itself to other disciplines, especially organizational analysis. A preliminary review is made of the state of critical thinking in the fields of information systems and organization. In addressing the question 'what is critical research?' the paper shows how definitions have changed and broadened over time.

In critical research more generally it has been suggested that there are several major weaknesses in theory and application. Two key themes in particular need further attention. They are emancipation and power relations. The paper outlines some of the reasons why these two issues have been highlighted and discusses their relevance within the context of critical IS research.

A recent emerging trend is identified towards the use of Habermas in the specific area of critical IS inquiry. Some of the reasons for this apparent trend are considered and the main features of thinking as applied in this regard are summarized and commented on. Finally, the paper argues that unless we wish to become locked into a Habermasian discourse, IS research must continue to push beyond this thinking in order to enrich our work. The work of Foucault is used to illustrate how the weaknesses identified in critical theory at the beginning of this paper

Reprinted from 'What does it mean to be "critical" in IS research?' by C. Brooke in *Journal of Information Technology*, 17, 2002, pp. 49–57. With kind permission from the Association for Information Technology Trust. All rights reserved.

might be addressed. It concludes by contrasting the contributions made by Habermas and Foucault to critical research in IS.

What is critical information systems research?

Traditionally, critical theory has been described as a form of historical materialism and is much influenced by issues of class, ethnicity, and gender. Critical theory tends to view situations through a lens of local domination by powers-that-be, with the potential for localized resistance. Hegemony is a characteristic, with conflict and contradictory tensions featuring in the analysis. It is generally agreed that critical theory has substantial (though not exclusive) roots in the Frankfurt School of the late 1920s. This intellectual movement was a reaction to the perceived domination of thinking at the time by positivism and can be understood against a backdrop of a post-Enlightenment, Modernist social context. Key thinkers include Theodor Adorno, Erich Fromm, Max Horkheimer, Jürgen Habermas and Herbert Marcuse.

The Frankfurt School identified taken-for-granted assumptions about aspects of their contemporary society and argued that their form and nature were shaped by existing social and historical contexts. They also highlighted that the very ways in which such shaping was recorded and represented were themselves the product of their time, and could (and should) be called into question. This has given rise to critical theory's claim to be able to mount a self-critique of its own knowledge claims as well as to be able to mount a critique of social conditions. Underlying the focus of the Frankfurt School was the desire not only to expose inadequacies in society but also to encourage reflection upon and *emancipation* from such inadequacies as were identified. Emancipation is a key distinguishing feature of critical theory.

Writing from two very different theoretical strands of 'criticality', both Walsham (1993) and Boje (2001) remind us that critical theory should be carefully distinguished from interpretivity approaches. One of the reasons for this is that both positivism and interpretivity tend to focus on description and understanding rather than on emancipation and the importance of values and assumptions at the individual level. This cautionary note is particularly relevant today, given the discussion below of the increased impact of interpretivist approaches upon the realm of critical IS research.

More recently critical research has focused on the extent to which the modern organization can be regarded as *the* primary institutional carrier for the diffusion of technical or instrumental rationality in Western industrialized society. Rational bureaucracy tends to be presented as *the* strategic social mechanism embodying technical or instrumental reason as a legitimizing principle and as an operational norm (Reed, 1993). This has become a site for critical inquiry. The political theme is a common thread that runs through much of the discussion in critical research.

In addition to the more traditional critical theory approach, other perspectives that are being brought to bear on the critical agenda notably include interpretivism, post-structuralism, and postmodernism. A very brief note on these approaches follows.

From an interpretivist perspective (also called social constructionism) reality is individual and socially constructed but becomes reified as objective knowledge. Making sense through research involves exploring differences between different social constructions.

Post-structuralism views organizational life as a 'textual turn'. Everything is formed from inter-textualities and there is no 'outside' to these texts. We learn by deconstructing the narratives. These narratives are ideological and have political consequences. Postmodernism can be viewed in two parts. One part is a focus on the historical aspects of late capitalism (hence 'epochal postmodernism') recruiting scepticism and ironic analyses. The other part adopts a focus on different epistemologies, viewing knowledge and power as fragmented. Understanding is achieved through the 'reading' and 'writing' of a plethora of juxtaposed narratives.

To summarize, then, critical research in practice has developed over time into a broad church that extends beyond traditional forms of critical theory. Consequently, we need a broader definition of what it means to be 'critical' (Alvesson and Deetz, 2000). If all this should sound daunting, even inconsistent, Alvesson and Willmott (1992, p. 3) draw attention to the fact that critical theory has always encouraged the creative borrowing of ideas from different schools of theory and practice. The common thread is usually the emancipatory interest rather than the detailed following of any one particular theorist.

Given that this is the case, it is all the more important to explore the alleged weaknesses outlined at the beginning of this paper relating to emancipation and power relations.

Emancipation, power and resistance

It has been said that critical research has grown in popularity as a response to disillusionment with traditional forms of inquiry (see Alvesson and

Willmott, 1992, p. 3). It is now 10 years since Kalle Lyytinen pointed out the paucity, fragmentation and limited accomplishments of critical theory research in IS (Lyytinen, 1992, p. 171). By 1996 the situation had not altered much:

> The application of CT [critical theory] in IS is comparatively recent and is still at an early stage. It has yet to progress much beyond a critique of existing approaches to systems development. (Alvesson and Willmott, 1996, p. 149)

Before we draw any specific conclusions from this state of affairs, we must take into account the fact that a number of writers have highlighted weaknesses in both the epistemology and the methodology of critical research generally. Two of the most commonly cited ones are the lack of a social theory, specifically on the nature of emancipation, and an inadequate conceptualization of power. These weaknesses are closely linked.

The language of critical theory emphasizes 'emancipatory intent' because it acknowledges that an emancipatory outcome cannot be guaranteed. Hence, the focus is on process rather than outcomes. Any approach that claims an emancipatory intent should be able to promote participation and take account of unequal power relations. Lyytinen and Klein (1985) are quick to point out that the emancipatory interest requires full participation because the rationality of the goals of IS development call for a dialogue to take place between *equals*.

In their evaluation of seven different IS methodologies, Klein and Hirschheim (1991) concluded that although there was some identification of barriers to communication and possible solutions, current IS development methodologies did not address the issue of emancipatory rationality in a systematic way. A value gap was evident between users and systems developers that reflected resistance and a lack of consensus. Resistance, they said, always points to a lack of consensus. They saw the key challenge for IS development as striking a balance between communicative and formal rationality.

In general terms labour process theory has made an important contribution to the debate about power in the workplace. More recently research has taken on a heightened critical theme. Instead of viewing labour relations in terms of the oppressor and the oppressed, this view itself has become the locus of critical analysis and has led to new insights into workers' abilities to resist and self-organize (e.g. Ackroyd and Thompson, 1999). More specifically, labour process theory has played a key role in the development of critical IS research, including the deployment of technology (see Doolin and Lowe, this issue). However, in terms of the relationship between technology and people, it has been argued that the focus has tended to be partial, focused on the 'embodiment of new technology' and sometimes ignoring aspects that make up an information system, such as software and hardware (Beirne *et al.*, 1998). It has also been argued that issues of domination concerning gender and race need to be more fully incorporated into any theory of the labour process (Willmott, 1993, p. 701).

In Scarbrough and Corbett's interesting book on technology and organization, they attempted to evaluate technology through the three different lenses of power, meaning and design (Scarbrough and Corbett, 1992). They see power as relating to the impact of technology upon organizational structure and the way in which this affects balances of power. Yet in denying individuals the possibility of constructing their own meanings through use, they, too, seem to fall into the trap of negating employee power and resistance. Their over-emphasis on objectified organizational process limits their ability to push beyond traditional analyses.

In their respective chapters, John Mingers and Kalle Lyytinen both argue that critical theory is unable to theorize the causes and preconditions of power constraints and self-interest (Mingers, 1992; Lyytinen, 1992). Indeed, as Lyytinen points out, even Habermas' own work lacks a discussion of power and his view of emancipation is purely attitudinal; that is, he sees radical change coming about from a transformation of attitudes (*ibid.*). Despite this, the use of Habermas is gradually becoming more prevalent in contemporary critical IS literature. The next section explores this in more detail before going on to consider how the theoretical weaknesses already outlined might be addressed.

The Habermasian project

The work of Habermas is generally accepted as one of the key contributions to thinking from the Frankfurt School. His work is set against a backdrop of disillusionment with modernist notions of 'progress', especially in response to social conditions of alienation and anomie. Although anti-positivist in his stance, Habermas does not recommend the total abandonment of the Modernist project. Rather, as McCarthy puts it, he urges for an 'enlightened suspicion of the enlightenment' (Habermas, 1984). This attitude is important to our understanding of why his work is attractive to researchers in critical IS. Although Habermas did not discuss his ideas with reference to technology per se, his apparently sceptical stance together with his normative approach (more on this later) lends itself well to the evaluation of technological contexts where notions of 'progress' or post-industrial work intensification are implicit. The use of the word 'enlightened' is significant because when we begin to consider his three knowledge-constitutive interests, we see that within the interest of emancipation, the main purpose is enlightenment not emancipation per se. As with the language of critical theory in general, we see here that Habermas' focus is on process rather than outcome.

Lyytinen and Klein (1985) promote the application of Habermas' typology of action to IS research. There is not room to rehearse all the details here but the typology includes purposive-rational action, that is action geared towards achieving a particular objective (divided into either strategic or instrumental), and communicative action, that is directed through language towards achieving mutual understanding. In discussing the relationship between Habermas' social action typology and information systems research, they argue that Habermas can be used in at least two ways: as a means to classify IS research itself and as a way of encouraging a broader approach to inquiry (Lyytinen and Klein, 1985, p. 211).

Habermas reflects the Frankfurt School by concerning himself with dismantling the dominance of positivism. He asserts that whilst positivism's focus is on obtaining understanding, critical theory's focus is upon emancipation. Emancipation requires what he calls 'communicative action'. One of the key themes in his writings is the need for mutual understanding through undistorted communication/language. This is not to suggest that Habermas thought that such an ideal would necessarily be achievable but that social scientists should strive to identify and bring to our attention the obstructions to such a discourse. His beliefs are based on the (some would say Modernist) notion of rationality. A major goal for Habermas is the eliciting of a discursive rationality, that is, an understanding of the rationale that underlies the way in which individuals express themselves. So, Habermas goes on to develop a theory of communicative action (TCA).

He takes a Kantian turn in that he argues that a rationality can be constructed so long as it is able to be subjected to critique (falsifiability). Here we begin to get a self-reflective flavour of critical theory. Habermas proposes that knowledge claims of validity with respect to TCA can be exercised discursively. In other words, a truth claim can be redeemed by the evidence. This is key to the notion of emancipation because, if it can be redeemed, it can be emancipated.

Since the idea of discursively redeemable validity claims is so central to his work, Habermas develops these ideas in some detail, giving rise to a set of argumentation types. Habermas makes the controversial claim that in any communicative act the specific forms of his argumentation types are unavoidable. To this extent he seems to be putting his concepts beyond critique.

The concept of 'lifeworld' is central to TCA. Habermas describes lifeworld as a transcendental site where speaker and hearer meet. His description is reminiscent of a Euclidean space in that communicative actors are always moving within the boundary of the lifeworld, they cannot step outside of it. In the lifeworld speaker and hearer both make claims that their expressions fit the world and they negotiate and settle their differences and reach a consensus (not necessarily an agreement). TCA singles out two aspects in particular: the teleological aspect of realizing one's own claims or actions, and the communicative aspect of interpreting a situation and arriving at some form of agreement. In communicative action participants pursue their goals cooperatively on the basis of a shared definition of the situation. If a shared definition has first to be negotiated or if agreement is not possible then consensus rather than agreement may become the aim, consensus being a necessary pre-condition to pursuing goals. The criteria for success in dealing with a situation is two-fold: the success achieved by teleological action and the consensus brought about by acts of reaching understanding. Participants cannot attain their goals (through communicative action) if they cannot meet the need for mutual understanding called for by the possibilities of acting in the situation. The lifeworld is the last resort to resolving semantic difficulties.

Waving not drowning?

Having conducted a brief excursion into Habermas' lifeworld, we can now pose the question, why is his approach currently becoming popular with researchers in critical IS? One possibility is that he provides a more easily 'modelled' set of frameworks for application than some other writers. It is not so surprising that such an objectifiable (contentiously, a more 'realist') methodological approach should have an appeal for the IS discipline, even though his work was not developed with IS research in mind. Several dangers have been brought to our attention here. Mingers has commented that Habermas' work is too abstract and removed from organizational experience to be of any direct help on its own (Mingers, 1992, p. 101). Also, Lyytinen, though endorsing the value of a Habermasian approach, warned against its mechanistic use, particularly of the three knowledge-constitutive interests (Lyytinen, 1992). Now, 10 years on, another apparent danger is emerging; that of over-use.

Key to understanding this recent development is Critical Systems Thinking (CST). As Valero-Silva has pointed out, it is important to note that most of the CST literature through the mid-1980s to mid-1990s almost exclusively drew upon the work of Habermas for its critical inquiry (Valero-Silva, 1996). Indeed, although there have been calls for increased pluralism recently (see a future special issue of the *Journal of Information Technology*) on the whole the impact of Habermasian thinking within CST still remains.

In brief, the argument proposed here is that critical IS research is becoming increasingly influenced by developments in CST and, therefore, by Habermas. Like a Mexican wave, Habermasian theory has (re) arrived at the doorstep of critical IS. If we want to avoid becoming locked into a Habermasian discourse then we need to continue to broaden our frameworks of inquiry. It is evident that writers such as Adorno, Latour, Bourdieau and Heidegger have received attention by critical researchers in IS (e.g. Doolin and Lowe, and O'Donnell and Henriksen, this issue) but their influence is currently limited in relative terms when compared to the recent rise of Habermas.

Introducing Foucault

In the following sections the work of Foucault will be introduced to show how the ideas of another thinker can be used to move beyond a Habermasian framework. It may seem ironic to advocate the increased use of a theorist such as Foucault within critical IS – a theorist that for other researchers (especially in the field of organizational analysis) equates with Habermas in terms of application saturation! Of course, the choice of Foucault at this point is far from random. The works of Habermas and Foucault have been compared on a number of occasions by writers in other fields of inquiry. It seems appropriate, therefore, to draw upon Foucault in order to address the specific weaknesses of critical theory outlined earlier in this paper.

In a paper of this length it is not possible to do justice to the richness of the Habermas versus Foucault debate and in a sense this is not critical to our current concern. The intention is not to propose one major theorist in order to replace the other but rather to open up a space for reflection. Of more importance is to give a flavour of the contrasts between the two thinkers and indicate, thereby, how understanding these contrasts might enrich critical IS inquiry. Furthermore, these contrasts are not necessarily mutually exclusive, but before going on to consider Foucault's ideas in more detail, it is useful to sketch a brief backdrop to the nature of the Foucault–Habermas debate.

Foucault himself admits that he was not aware of the work of the Frankfurt School when he conducted his earlier work and, therefore, was unfamiliar with Habermas' ideas. Some writers argue that there are more differences between them than similarities. Others argue the opposite (for a good overview see Ashenden and Owen, 1999). Nevertheless, it would be false to assume that Habermas and Foucault share no points of agreement or that they have no respect for each other's thinking. As Foucault said:

> I am interested in what Habermas is doing. I know he does not agree with what I say – I am a little more in agreement with him – but there is always something which causes me a problem. (Taken from an interview with Foucault, in Conway, 1999).

Foucault's work has been variously labelled as post-structuralist (Boje, 2001) and postmodern (Walsham, 1993). One explanation for this could be the way in which his ideas tend to be applied within philosophical contexts at variance with Foucault's original roots. This may especially apply to translation of his ideas into contexts involving material technology. Although Foucault discusses 'technology' it is in relation to concepts such as power, self and knowledge and not information systems per se.

Both Habermas and Foucault recognize the decentred subject; that is, the tendency for fragmentation to occur between an individual and their claims to 'truth'. But Foucault, in typical critical self-reflection, goes further and calls into question the nature of the decentring of subjects and highlights it contingent nature. This enables him to open up the topics of emancipation and power relations to critical inquiry in a way that Habermas cannot.

More about emancipation and power

It may seem strange to suggest that Foucault has more to offer researchers than Habermas with respect to notions of emancipation. It has been said that Foucault offered very little in the way of a rigorous analysis of 'democracy' whereas Habermas put the question 'is democracy possible?' at the centre of his work. But this serves to misconstrue the differences between the two. The contrast is not so much one of interest or attentiveness to the topic but of analytical style, as we will demonstrate.

Habermas' theory of communicative action (TCA) was developed precisely to indicate *what is required in the way of process* to enable democracy to take place. His approach is to set out the conditions necessary for democratic activity and propose a way of implementing these. In contrast, Foucault concentrates his attention on the historical conditions under which democracy can emerge and on *how we can assert ourselves within systems that regard themselves as democratic.* Habermas takes more of an etic stance by focusing on what democracy looks like from the outside, whereas Foucault adopts a more emic stance and considers what democracy is like from the inside.

Foucault challenged an idea central to critical theory: that relations of power are not something bad in themselves and something from which one must be emancipated. Rather he argues that there are often aspects of power that are beneficial for the stakeholders involved. Indeed, he does not believe that there can be a society without relations of power, by which he means power in the sense of trying to conduct or influence the behaviour of others. He also argued that any production of knowledge contains within itself the potential for contradictory outcomes. For instance, generating insights into a set of power relationships with the intention of opening up the relationships can actually result in them becoming more entrenched and inscribed. Thus, emancipatory intentions do not always lead to desired outcomes.

Despite this discussion some writers (e.g. Clegg, 2001; Ackroyd and Thompson, 1999) see Foucault as not only neglecting issues of worker resistance but failing to provide space within which such a debate can take place. As Clegg puts it, after Foucault (and others such as Laclau and Mouffe) it becomes extremely difficult to maintain a radical view of power, repression and hegemony. The essential problem is that within Foucault's frame of thinking, the notion that there is something beneath the surface, a substructure that stands in tension with the dominant structure, is removed. In its post-structuralist wake, the dissolving of this apparatus removes the capacity for 'radical theory' to be radical.

Clegg presents an ironic picture. The effect of dissolving the apparatus is to remove the possibility for identifying the 'repressed other'. Consequently, he says the democracy of popular opinion is inimical to the intellectual power expressed in radical theory:

> At the end of Marxism, radical theory reveals its fundamental elitism, representing in its practice, paradoxically, precisely what it sought to critique in the world (Clegg, 2001).

A point related to this is made by O'Donnell and Henriksen (this issue) when they say that Habermas, shorn of his Marxian determinism, provides a more modest conceptualization of the relationship between theory and practice.

But these objections fail to take into account several features of Foucault's conceptualization of power. In particular, his treatment of the way in which power is exercised (the microphysics of power) and his argument that Marxism (and liberal and Freudian critiques, too) actually contributes to the reification of authority itself. As Foucault says, to define power in terms only of repression is to adopt a purely juridical view of power. This is dangerous because power then becomes synonymous with law, law is presented as above reproach (and beyond critique) and carries with it the weight of obedience. Foucault is not presenting authority as a benign institution here. Far from it, rather he is attempting to reveal a more complex conceptualization of power.

Habermas' conceptions of 'lifeworld' and 'system' are bereft of any analysis of the bases of their construction or of the practices that give rise to them, even though these practices might eventually become part of the 'normalized' construction which Habermas seeks to produce. The norms are not objects but language; hence the normalization of language enables mutual understanding (and an ideal speech situation). He provides no account of the way in which these 'norms' are generated. His lifeworld struggles to reproduce itself through communicative action while the state and economy (power and money) attempt to colonize it (see O'Donnell and Henriksen, this issue). This problem is intensified because Habermas wants his universal norms to be the basis of legitimate lawmaking. He wants to introduce the principle of normalization into the systems of rule and law.

Habermas cannot account for the normalizing powers that are needed for the construction of his project. He does not provide an analysis of the values, assumptions and practices that constitute the discursive practices he wishes to encourage.

At the end of the nineteenth century, especially in Germany, the moral, juridical and political sciences redefined themselves as 'normative sciences'. Coming from this heritage it is not surprising that for Habermas uncovering the nature of procedures and structures is necessary in order to clarify the 'norms' that can create a democratic environment. In contrast, for Foucault it is the analysis of modern forms of 'authority' that constitutes the task of an on-going critical inquiry. Foucault's historical analyses lead us to critically reflect upon the conditions of contemporary existence, both in the sense of the organizational practices we seek to explore and of our own research practices in doing so. It is partly for this reason that many researchers have emphasized the usefulness of Foucault's approach in conducting critical inquiry.

Foucault tackles the issue of power head on and views power relations in terms of situated action. He identifies two dimensions to power: juridical and microphysical. Juridical power refers more to the 'what' of power, to the mechanisms and rules of law governing behaviour and is seen as repressive. Microphysical power is more concerned with the 'how' of power, to methods of domination and how power is exercised. Foucault sees discursive practice as part of the microphysics of power, and as fragmented and dispersed (we could say a patchwork, a bricolage) where a network of sites is involved. It is not located simply with a thinking knowing subject/individual (Foucault, 1972). Power is seen as relational and based in action; in other words, it is situated. He does not focus on an abstract definition of power but rather sees it as constituted in relationships within and between localized networks of actions. He emphasizes the way in which power and knowledge are inextricably intertwined; co-created, in fact. Technology is often seen as an instrument of power that can reproduce and reify certain dominant discursive practices. As Foucault says:

> There is no knowledge without a particular discursive practice; and any discursive practice may be defined by the knowledge that it forms. (Foucault, 1972, p. 183)

This propels us into another currently popular arena for debate, beyond the scope of this discussion: knowledge management. Researchers who view technology in the workplace as discursive practice will need to pay attention to the close relationship between the key issues of power, knowledge and technology.

There are links here between Foucault and Habermas to the extent that discursive practice is a key site for critical analysis. However, Foucault's approach to communication is very different. Referring to Habermas' theory of communicative action, Foucault says:

> The thought that there could be a state of communication which would be such that the games of truth could circulate freely, without obstacles, without constraint and without coercive effects, seems to me to be Utopia. (Taken from an interview with Foucault, in Conway, 1999).

For his part, Habermas commends Foucault's thinking for its self-critical capacity but at the same time points out that his method of analysis (historical genealogy):

> . . . enters on the scene in an irritating double role. On the one hand, it plays the empirical role of an analysis of technologies of power that are meant to explain the functional social context of the science of man. . . . On the other hand, the same genealogy plays the transcendental role of an analysis of technologies of power that are meant to explain how scientific discourse about man is possible at all. (Habermas quoted in Conway, 1999, p. 62)

Habermas is attempting to expose a double standard here. He is saying that when Foucault unpicks the historical conditions that give rise to power and its expressions in a particular context, he fails to apply the same principles to his own analytical project. After all, Foucault insists that we are all implicated in the regimes of power that we oppose precisely in the very act of opposing them. Thus, in failing to hold up the mirror to his own genealogy, Habermas proposes that Foucault disguises the origins of his own conceptualizations of power. Not only that but he also accuses Foucault of relying on an unacknowledged preconception of a theory of power. This conceptualization presents individuals as inevitable 'dupes' in a network of anonymous regimes and yet nowhere does his genealogical analysis provide any justification for resistance to authority as opposed to adaptation.

This can be seen, however, as a misrepresentation of Foucault's conceptions. Although he situates the individual agent within a set of economic relations of production and linguistic networks of signification that involve power relations, in another sense Foucault provides more of a space within which human agents can develop power than does Habermas.

By viewing power in terms of situated action, Foucault sees that each situation arises out of a different set of historical circumstances and transformations. It follows, then, that there can be no generalizable set of norms for this analysis. Instead, he prefers to treat each instance as unique and his analysis of it as requiring an on-going process of critical self-reflection. Foucault refers to this as a process of 'constant checking'. Foucault argues that to produce an explanatory theory of power is tantamount to the normalization of power, and the normalization of power simply reinforces its own ability to be used as a legitimating force (for good or bad). It certainly does not facilitate critical inquiry.

Thus, not only does Foucault refute the claim that his treatment of power should be more overtly theorized but he also presents a case for deliberately avoiding doing so.

In summary, then, it could be argued that Foucault's approach to emancipation seems less naïve, in that he recognizes the role of unequal power relations and the potential for contradictory outcomes. Habermas evaluates power in abstraction from its underlying processes whereas Foucault more directly analyses power relations themselves and the forces of domination that result from inequalities in power.

Complementarism versus confusion

Not even those who declare themselves to be sceptics of Foucault would necessarily accept all the criticisms placed at his door. As Fleming (2001) points out, sometimes the criticism can be viewed rather as misinterpretation. Many more would argue that Foucault's ideas have a lot to offer, especially when one considers the alleged weaknesses of critical theory regarding emancipation and power relations. It has been said, for example, that anyone with a concern for freedom and autonomy will prefer Foucault's approach to that of Habermas (Tully, 1999, p. 129).

Tully asserts that Habermas is the humanist and Foucault the anti-humanist, and not vice versa as has often been argued (*ibid.*). Whilst this may be an unhelpful way to distinguish between the two thinkers, it is relevant to note that Foucault views humanism as tending to be presented as a universal set of ethics against which society can be modelled. From this angle, it is apparent that any IS methodology based within a humanist tradition could be in danger of putting itself beyond critique. This is antithetic to a critical approach and, hence, Foucault harbours reservations. It is this sort of attention to self-critique that characterizes much of Foucault's thinking, and lends an impression of his work being more obviously self-critical at times than that of Habermas. Another way of looking at it would be to say that Habermas tends towards prescription whereas Foucault tends towards a deconstructive analysis.

Habermas and Foucault each recommend their respective methodologies as providing a superior understanding of the practical choices available to individuals. Nevertheless, it may be more useful to direct our energies away from which of these two approaches is better, towards a more collaborative attitude, where complementarity replaces competition. The key question is whether or not the two approaches are incommensurable and, therefore, whether or not they can be usefully combined.

At this point we must note the potential dangers of methodological complementarism. Foucault does not provide a normative guide for action. In contrast, Habermas does. The scientific and positivistic heritage of IS research will tend to favour adoption of approaches that are more easily 'modelled'. It is reasonable to suggest that any line of research that seeks to use a normatively articulated framework will tend to favour a Habermasian approach rather than a Foucauldian one. As suggested earlier, the impact of CST upon the field of critical IS inquiry today is noticeable and one of their current concerns is the search for new methodologies and the practical means with which to apply critical theory (Valero-Silva, 1996). It has also been argued that CST is mainly inspired by managerial interests and practices rather than by a critique of theory and practice (Valero-Silva, 2001). As we have already seen, from a Foucauldian perspective it is not acceptable simply to apply particular methodological frameworks, we have also to subject them to on-going critique. This leads us to ask how 'critical' is CST and, by association, any research that makes use of it?

CST has recently been looking at a number of other approaches in the search for pluralism and, thereby, a set of increased 'critical' credentials (see a future special issue of the *Journal of Information Technology*). Postmodernism is one example of this attempt at paradigmatic bridge building (e.g. Jackson, 2000). Such instrumental use of multiple perspectives overlooks the fact that their axiological bases remain largely unchallenged. This undermines the notion of critical inquiry at the same time as Foucault's critical attitude of 'constant checking' would seem to undermine the very usefulness of the bridge building project itself. Certainly, unless CST is prepared to undertake a form of self-critique then it cannot be considered fully 'critical' (Valero-Silva, 1996) and just the same assertion applies to critical IS inquiry. Thus, we return to the theme with which we opened this paper: what does it mean to be 'critical' in IS research? The emancipatory interest rather than the detailed following of any one particular theorist may be a suitable binding force that holds these diverse approaches together. Nevertheless, as the espoused practice of critical inquiry broadens, so the values and assumptions that underpin its theoretical execution needs to be more explicitly articulated, and reflexively critiqued within each research context.

This brings us to recent debates within critical inquiry in general concerning pluralism and incommensurability. This is a rich area of debate but goes beyond the scope of this particular paper. However, in the second of these special issues these debates will be taken up and explored in more depth for their relevance to critical IS research.

The dance goes on

Taking all these points together, it would seem that the trajectory of critical IS inquiry soon could be at odds with a Foucauldian perspective, providing even more opportunity for colonization by Habermasian (and other normalizing types of) theory. Does our response to this need to be antagonistic?

Several writers have argued that Foucault deliberately initiated some of the philosophical jousts in which the two thinkers have taken part, so that Habermas', sometimes angry, attacks need not draw respective supporters into a battle stance. Rather, the dialogue between them (albeit conducted mainly in an indirect and impersonal fashion) can be viewed as a positive sign. As Conway puts it, if the greatest tribute to Nietzsche's thinking is to make it groan and protest, then why complain when Habermas does this for Foucault (Conway, 1999, p. 86)?

From this perspective Foucault and Habermas are not so much locked in mortal combat as co-creating a dialectical dance. Their dance is a form of communication and as we watch it unfold we see them 'collaboratively spin the web of genealogical communication'; evidence of their 'philosophical twinship'. This dance serves to define the agenda of contemporary political philosophy. Any attempt to stop or control the dance (as in declaring a 'winner') would effectively disrupt what some see as a productive and much neglected counter-discourse of modernity (Conway, 1999, p. 61).

Although a political theme is common throughout much of the discussion within critical IS, not everyone will see themselves as engaged primarily in political philosophy. There is a helpful message here, nonetheless. Instead of focusing our energies on slugging it out for a 'biggest and best' approach to inquiry, we could focus on helping each other to generate better self-critique. This is not navel-gazing. Our ability to generate self-critique informs our practice. Through 'constant checking' we can create our own dialectical dance that enriches our present and propels the trajectory of critical IS research into the future.

References

Ackroyd, S. and Thompson, P. (1999) *Organizational Misbehaviour* (Sage, London).
Alvesson, M. and Deetz, S. (2000) *Doing Critical Management Research* (Sage, London).

Alvesson, M. and Willmott, H. (eds.) (1992) *Critical Management Studies* (Sage, London).

Alvesson, M. and Willmott, H. (1996) *Making Sense of Management: a critical introduction* (Sage, London).

Ashenden, S. and Owen, D. (eds.) (1999) *Foucault contra Habermas* (Sage, London).

Beirne, M., Ramsay, H. and Panteli, A. (1998) Developments in Computing Work: control and contradiction in the software labour process. In Thompson, P. and Warhurst, C. (eds.) *Workplaces of the Future*. (Macmillan Business, Basingstoke), 142–62.

Boje, D. (2001) *What is Critical Postmodern Theory?* Available online at http://cbae.nmsu.edu/~dboje/

Clegg, S.R. (2001) *Changing Concepts of Power, Changing Concepts of Politics.* Available online at: aom.pace.edu/cms/Washington/clegg.htm

Conway, D.W. (1999) Pas de Deux: Habermas and Foucault in Genealogical Communication. In Ashenden, S. and Owen, D. (eds.) *Foucault contra Habermas*, (Sage, London), 60–89.

Dean, M. (1999) Normalising Democracy: Foucault and Habermas on democracy, liberalism and law. In Ashenden, S. and Owen, D. (eds.) *Foucault contra Habermas*, (Sage, London), 166–94.

Fleming, P. (2001) Beyond the Panopticon? Book Review of *Organizational Misbehaviour* by Ackroyd and Thompson (1999). *Ephemera*, 1, 2, 190–4.

Foucault, M. (1972) *The Archaeology of Knowledge* (Routledge, London).

Habermas, J. (1984) *The Theory of Communicative Action: Volume 1: Reason and the Rationalization of Society; Volume 2: Lifeworld and System: A Critique of Functionalist Reason.* Translated by Thomas McCarthy. (Heinemann, London).

Heidegger, M. (1962) *Being and Time* (Blackwell, Oxford).

Jackson, M.C. (2000) *Systems Approaches to Management* (Kluwer, New York).

Klein, H.K. and Hirschheim, R. (1991) Rationality Concepts in Information System Development Methodologies. *Accounting, Management and Information Technologies*, 1, 2, 157–87.

Lyytinen, K. (1992) Information Systems and Critical Theory. In Alvesson, M., and Willmott, H. (eds.) *Critical Management Studies*. (Sage, London), 159–80.

Lyytinen, K. and Klein, H.K. (1985) The Critical Theory of Jürgen Habermas as a Basis for a Theory of Information Systems, in Mumford, E., *et al*. (eds.) (Elsevier Science, North-Holland), 207–25.

Mingers, J. (1992) Technical, Practical and Critical OR: past, present and future? In M. Alvesson and H. Willmott (eds.) *Critical Management Studies*. (Sage, London), 90–112.

Reed, M. (1993) Organizations and Modernity: continuity and discontinuity in organization theory. In Hassard, J. and Parker, M. (eds.) *Postmodernism and Organisations*. (Sage, London), 163–82.

Scarbrough, H. and Corbett, J. M. (1992) *Technology and Organization: power, meaning and design.* (Routledge, London).

Tully, J. (1999) To Think and Act Differently. In Ashenden, S. and Owen, D. (eds.) *Foucault contra Habermas*. (Sage, London), 90–142.

Valero-Silva, N. (1996) A Foucauldian Reflection on Critical Systems Thinking. In Flood, R. and Romm, N. (eds.) *Critical Systems Thinking: current research and practice*. (Plenum Press, New York), 63–79.

Valero-Silva, N. (2001) Demystifying the Theory and Practice of Critical Systems Thinking. In Wilby, J. and Allen, J.K. (eds.) *Proceedings of the 45th Annual Conference of the International Society for the Systems Sciences.* Asilomar, California, July 8–13.

Walsham, G. (1993) *Interpreting Information Systems in Organizations.* (John Wiley & Sons, Chichester).

Willmott, H. (1993) Breaking the Paradigm Mentality. *Information and Organization,* **14**, 5, 681–719.

3

Critical Perspectives on Information Systems: An Impression of the Research Landscape

Carole Brooke
Faculty of Business and Management, University of Lincoln, Brayford Pool, UK

Who does critical research speak to?

Klein and Hirschheim (1991) predicted that the future of information systems (IS) research would

> . . . belong to methodologies that are able to combine a high level of formal rationality with a sufficient level of communicative rationality under emancipatory conditions (p. 15).

Despite this prediction, not so long ago it could be argued that the dominant rationality in IS research was still rational and positivist and that to break away from this in order to adopt a different paradigm could lead to marginalization (Harrington, 1995; Brooke and Maguire, 1998). But has the pendulum now swung too far in the opposite direction? More importantly, is critical IS research of any real value outside of a limited field of application?

As was discussed in an earlier special issue of this volume of the *Journal of Information Technology* (Brooke, 2002b) definitions of 'critical' research have considerably broadened over time. One of the consequences of this is that many more research paradigms now include themselves within the label of 'critical inquiry'. This is often achieved through a call to pluralism. The paper opens by examining the rise of pluralism and issues of paradigm incommensurability. It then goes on to sketch the theoretical territory of critical research by considering three distinctive manifestations: critical systems thinking (CST), critical realism and critical post-modernism. This brief theoretical introduction is followed by detailed examples of empirical IS research conducted from each of the three perspectives and then reflects upon the impact of critical research on IS praxis. The paper closes by identifying common themes for critical IS research.

The rise of pluralism

The call to pluralism in critical research is perhaps today nowhere more apparent than within CST. Systems thinking claims to have moved a long way since its inception, from the general systems theory of Von Bertalanffy through the soft systems of Peter Checkland to the CST discussed by Jackson (2000) and others today. According to Jackson (2000), CST came into being in the 1980s and during the 10 years between 1990 and 2000 had 'come of age' (p. viii). It is against this backdrop that there seems to be a rising dominance of CST in critical IS research. One influence of this, as was argued in the special issue mentioned above (Brooke, 2002b), is an emerging tendency towards an increased use of Habermas in the specific area of critical IS and, indeed, it has been said that CST itself is partly grounded on the critical social theory of Habermas (Gregory, 1996).

Jackson (2000, p. 363) stated that the appropriate relationship between CST and emancipation became clearer once Habermas' three knowledge-constitutive interest had been embraced (Habermas, 1984a, b). Thus, the emancipatory intent became a universal search for improvement rather than self-emancipation. Lyytinen and Klein (1985) put it like this:

> We suggest that information associated with the use and development of information systems can be regarded as knowledge for social action (p. 209).

Jackson's (2000) measure of the extent to which CST has matured was its success in severing automatic connections with emancipatory approaches. Not only that but he suggested that this severing was a necessary step towards adopting pluralism and multimethodology use. Not all critical researchers would agree with this statement by any means (Saravanamuthu, 2002). Jackson (2000, p. 424) pointed out that CST, having come of age, no longer seeks complete understanding. Rather, it now recognizes the limitations and partiality of understanding. He rebutted the criticisms of post-modernists (and others) that CST can be used unknowingly for managerial ends and instead framed it in terms of a highly reflective process. Gregory (1996) helped to clarify this potentially messy area of pluralism by building on some of Flood's (1990) earlier work and identifying various forms of pluralism. She discussed four approaches to management research: isolationism, imperialism, pragmatism and complementarism. Understanding the difference is particularly crucial to the conduct of critical IS research since the implications relate closely to issues of power and emancipation.

Isolationism adopts multiple perspectives, but sees each one as 'going their own way' and with no cross-fertilization between them. Imperialism tends to favour one paradigm above others and, although it can integrate different perspectives, will do so only if the central tenets of the dominant framework remain intact. Pragmatism (using Jackson's definition rather than Churchman's) uses whatever tool seems workable at the time. It is eclectic and has been accused of lacking rigour and grounding. White and Taket (1997) and Taket and White's (2000) form of pragmatic pluralism, which is called PANDA (participatory appraisal of needs and the development of action), throws up common concerns relating to pragmatic pluralism in general (Jackson, 2000). The method emphasizes doing 'what feels good' for the participants and the facilitators and could be exploited by some as a means for abrogating responsibility. More seriously, this has implications for ethical practice. Much is dependent on the ability of the facilitators and, as Taket and White (2000) themselves admitted, it is difficult to reflect critically upon issues of equitable participation and challenge existing power relations. These are serious areas of weakness for a method that claims to be critical in its approach.

The fourth area Gregory (1996) addressed was complementarism. She argued that complementarism has replaced the term pluralism in much of the systems literature. This is problematic since its obscures the possibility of other pluralist approaches. Central to complementarism are the aims of openness and conciliation (a reflection of Habermasian thinking) and attempts to integrate different strands of thinking. Jackson's main contribution to this, which was begun in 1983/1984, is his 'system of system methodologies' (SOSM). Through her discussion of SOSM, Gregory (1996) illustrated that Jackson's approach to pluralism was primarily complementarist. She identified a tendency for one perspective to suck in others that it investigates and for the SOSM to map situations and then freeze-frame them. Implied here is that pluralism has to be able to respond dynamically to interactions in the research process. Thus, she proposed an alternative, discordant pluralism, the features of which are to view different theoretical positions as supplementing one another rather than competing and to promote learning through radical differences. This supplementary approach focuses on differences as much as similarities and is able to accommodate the tension so important to maintaining a critical stance. Jackson (2000) argued in favour of pluralism on the basis that it contributes to diversity – a strength rather than a weakness. Gregory (1996) recommended pluralism, but with careful attention to its particular type.

So where does this leave us? The concept of critical research can no longer be confidently assigned to a particular paradigm 'box' to the extent that the call for critical research is becoming partially obscured by the call to pluralism. This is a key issue since not all critical researchers believe that pluralism is possible at all. A major objection is the claim that different paradigms cannot be combined. This view was perhaps most clearly presented by Burrell and Morgan (1979) in their mapping of sociological paradigms. Since then the tension between the call to pluralism and paradigm incommensurability has become quite a feature of critical research (Jackson and Carter, 1991).

For some to deny paradigm incommensurability is to deny the potential for resistance. It can be seen as a 'soft option'. What choice do we make in the face of multiple perspectives? Jackson (2000) accepted that making choices remains a human responsibility and there is no escape from that, but he tended to suggest that more apparent choice equates with more assured choice. As Willmott (1993, p. 704) reminded us, this is not necessarily so because choice depends upon the ability to examine the underlying values of these choices critically and to reject all of them if they are found wanting. Anything else is a form of intellectual power play that runs counter to the central values of critical research, even mirroring the forms of power play reported in IS development. The potential for resistance is important to critical IS at all levels – theoretical, methodological and practical. From this perspective paradigm incommensurability remains an important plank in the radical theory project.

In an attempt to build bridges Willmott (1993) argued for a third way. In the tradition of Kuhn he acknowledged aspects of incommensurability, but pointed to the connectivity and continuity that characterizes theory development and suggested that efforts should be directed towards resolving anomalies within existing theories. Reed

(1993) also observed that organizational theory development was moving away from a focus on paradigm incommensurability towards what he called 'a more realistic and sober assessment' (p. 179) of mediation between competing perspectives. He concluded that making a useful contribution to future theory development would be dependent upon the ability to

> ... tell a new story that critically engages with older narratives which will be in need of radical overhaul, but continue to speak to present problems and projected futures (Reed, 1993, p. 182).

The next section attempts to show the variety and breadth of theoretical territory now claimed under the critical banner and indicates how researchers are harnessing different paradigms in the cause of critical IS research.

A brief sketch of the theoretical territory

The discussion here is brief since more detail is given through the empirical examples that follow on. The examples chosen are intended to be indicative only. They represent three distinctive and contrasting approaches of critical IS research. CST and post-modern systems thinking occupy a middle ground between objectivity and subjectivity. Critical realism represents a more objective and rationalist route to critical research whereas critical post-modernism offers a more relativist approach.

Critical post-modern systems

CST has already been introduced and so here we focus on a specific development within it: post-modern systems. Whoever thought we would see the day when the words 'post-modern' and 'systems thinking' would appear side by side? Jackson (2000) noted that the rise of post-modernism in organizational research has forced systems theorists to think again. He traced common roots for post-modernism and the emancipatory systems approach:

> Postmodernism diverged from the Enlightenment tradition when it followed Nietzsche and Heidegger in pursuit of self-emancipation rather than Hegel, Marx and the Frankfurt School (Jackson, 2000, p. 334).

Jackson (2000, p. 348) produced a set of constitutive rules for the application of critical systems practice that sits within his pluralist frame of thinking and attempts to embrace post-modernism. Unsurprisingly, this involves adopting multiple perspectives and multimethodologies. Jackson (1997, p. 371) re-emphasized the importance of maintaining attention to the 'emancipatory option', but that it is not the job of pluralism or of CST to privilege a radical paradigm. Rather, meta-paradigmatic pluralism, he said, has the advantage of being committed to emancipatory potential without being tied to emancipatory practice, as this would be predetermining the outcomes. It is here that he found post-modernism an attractive option because it seeks to avoid meta-narratives and is focused on promoting diversity and difference. He added that

> Postmodern thinking has weakened faith in our ability to actually know anything for certain about how to design organisations and society (and quite right, too, given the disastrous experiments carried out in the name of certainty) . . . The emancipatory option must remain on the agenda (Jackson, 1997, p. 375).

However, if you do not adopt a realist stance to some degree then how do you know if you have been emancipated (Adam, 2002; Thompson and McHugh, 2002). Thompson and McHugh (2002) presented a cogent argument. If a researcher treats each and every tool or approach to inquiry as of equal value then this can lead to the very things which critical inquiry seeks to avoid: uncritical consumption and the absence of rigorous analysis and debate. Furthermore, Clegg (2001) and Thompson and McHugh (2002) drew our attention to the issue of democracy within the context of pluralism. Clegg (2001) reminded us that pluralism requires 'co-presence', that is the presence of the full range of stakeholders. Any absence from dialogue can be viewed as the result of repression. Thompson and McHugh (2002) concluded that the distinction between representation and reality must be made, otherwise the outcomes will be both unhealthy and undemocratic.

Critical realism

Thompson and McHugh (2002) pointed to at least two issues that critical researchers must address: the tendency for critical research to demolish without rebuilding and the partiality of competing theories. They urged for rethinking and resituating within a more democratic context. They concluded that

> While a reflexive attitude is a feature of any critical approach, hyper-reflexivity in which everything is deconstructed or problematised, while solving nothing, is ultimately arid and self-defeating. There are still practices and a world to remake (Thompson and McHugh, 2002, p. 395).

Whilst they welcomed theoretical pluralism, they argued that complementarity is more of a realistic goal than synthesis. They identified the problem not as paradigm incommensurability, but as reality incommensurability. They saw grounds for dialogue and for the progression of knowledge, but in identifying an aspect of relativity that needs to be overcome they proposed critical realism as the middle ground between positivism and relativism.

Bhaskar's critical realism has been embraced for some time by critical researchers in the field of accounting, for example Power and Laughlin (1992). Some interesting debates have taken place recently in other disciplines. In operational research, for instance, Ormerod and Mingers (2002) debated and disagreed on what critical realism has to offer. One author (Ormerod) referred to a dictionary of philosophy in order to reassure himself that the concept of 'critical realism' is a tried and tested approach, but he found it wanting, while the other author (Mingers) warned us that devices such as dictionaries tend to be teleological and represent only what has already become concretized as history.

One reading of this exchange is that Ormerod found critical realism 'a bridge too far'. His response was ironically reminiscent of the time when soft systems methodology emerged and systems thinking moved (was dragged?) towards the more subjective end of Burrell and Morgan's (1979) framework. So whilst some people view critical realism as too relativistic others, like Thompson and McHugh (2002), see it as a way of bridging a relativistic divide.

Critical post-modernism

To an extreme relativist the existence of anything 'real' independent of sense experience and the concept of closure in interpretation are insupportable. The critical version of post-modernism does not go this far, but it is certainly more relativist than critical realism. Nevertheless, Boje (2001) proposed critical postmodernism as being able to overcome the sort of problems of relativity that were highlighted by Thompson and McHugh (2002).

Boje (2001) theorized critical post-modernism as a mid-range theory exploring the middle ground between epochal post-modernism (or post-modernism à la Hassard and Parker (1993)), epistemological post-modernism and critical modernism. Boje (2001) drew our attention to the 'dark side' of post-modernism that is missed by non-critical approaches. Post-modernism is inherently ambiguous and plural. He pointed out that interpretivism (or social construction theory) is often confused with post-modernism and he warned that this is dangerous since it leaves out any consideration of the material conditions of political economy, even to the extent that some post-modern approaches effectively result in 'carnivalesque resistance'. In other words, by totally rejecting any form of grand narrative and negating the possibility for any 'real' material condition, there is a danger that, instead of engaging with the issues and seeking to transform conditions, one simply attempts to find what Boje (2001) called 'a more festive path' through the quagmire. Boje's (2001) warning and his search for a middle way is certainly reminiscent of Thompson and McHugh's (2002) reservations. They observed that

> A multi-paradigm perspective is primarily influenced by postmodernists trying to draw back from extreme relativism and seek greater dialogue (Thompson and McHugh, 2002, p. 389).

Thus, critical post-modernism is proposed as a way of bridging the relativistic gap between postmodernism and critical theory (Boje, 2001).

The contribution of empirical research

All three theoretical perspectives so far have claimed to be able to address the substantive issues of critical research, particularly emancipation and power relations. This section looks in more depth at examples of empirical work that have been conducted from each of the perspectives presented here and sees these claims in action. It indicates a response to the call from Alvesson and Deetz (2000) for more empirical work and provides an opportunity for greater dialogue (Thompson and McHugh, 2002).

Critical systems thinking: pluralism, post-modernism and platforms

Between 1997 and 2000 Carrizosa (2000, 2002) conducted research that adopted a pluralist and multimethodology approach including aspects of postmodernism within a gas turbine manufacturing company in the UK (KGT). His work is a good example of what Jackson (2000, p. 417) described as critical systems practice, where different techniques are applied in the service of methodologies that reflect different paradigms and are employed as appropriate to individual circumstances.

Throughout the duration of the research KGT were experiencing high levels of churn due to changes in market share and, in turn, changes in ownership and directorship. Carrizosa (2000, 2002) argued that a pluralist approach helped him to be flexible and responsive to the levels of change experienced by the participants and their impact on the direction of the research as it unfolded. An action research design was adopted and all participants in the study were referred to as 'co-researchers'. The emphasis was on participation and the open sharing of views. Carrizosa's (2000, 2002) main role was that of facilitator. Much of his success in enabling individuals to overcome reservations about politics and power play were down to his gaining their trust and confidence over an extended period of time. This point cannot be over-emphasized given that he recognized the potential for political, cultural or practical constraints in limiting the range of methodologies used and thereby the integrity of the pluralism (Carrizosa, 2002, p. 4). The research constituted engagement in what he termed 'informed pluralism' by virtue of the facilitation towards the co-researcher status of all the participants (Carrizosa, 2000, p. 11).

There is only space here to present a brief vignette of the total research, but fortunately it can be broken down into five subprojects. We will focus on the final three of these subprojects: the thinking space, the book and the walls workshops since these demonstrate the pluralist and post-modern nature of the research more obviously. Carrizosa (2000) coined the term 'platforms' for describing the intellectual and reflective organizational space that these three devices opened up for the participants.

The thinking space was both an activity and a way of doing things. It provided a space within which the co-researchers could have structured conversation and engage in equal participation. A range of techniques was used including rich pictures, root definitions, conceptual models, viable systems methodology, systems metaphors and system dynamics.

The book emerged from this engagement and proved to be a useful way of addressing power relations. The book was created in an interactive way and consisted of writings by the participants of their experiences in implementing new organizational structures. In writing the book the co-researchers were objectifying an organizational theory about the company itself and this newly co-created theory of the firm propelled the company into further action grounded in the diverse and subjective experiences of the individuals. In this sense it was a new way of standing out in contrast to senior management views of the *status quo*. The walls workshops were described as follows:

> On walls, accessible to all actors, systems diagrams and various visual representations were set up as outputs of continuous interaction among participants . . . Once an issue was raised natural conversation took over which led to a WW [walls workshop] if participants thought it appropriate. All this was intended to be founded on the spirit of collaboration, commitment and within the framework of a serious and organised effort, whose progress was visualised on the wall at all stages. Using this device the process was available for scrutiny, validation, revision and feedback (Carrizosa, 2000, p. 8).

Carrizosa (2002) subscribed to Gregory's (1996) discordant pluralism and was careful to guard against an imperialist subsumption of perspectives during his application of methodologies. Indeed, Carrizosa (2002) claimed that

> . . . the TS [thinking space], the Book and the WW [walls workshop] became buffers where reflection on the use of methodologies and paradigms resulted from interaction among co-equal actors. The rule of co-equal actors encouraged participants regardless of their formal position, their predominantly engineering background and somewhat technocratic culture, to temporarily reflect about and try what other tools, methods and methodologies pertaining to different paradigms could offer in terms of approaching a particular problem situation (p. 9).

The post-modern and critical values underpinning this work are manifested in several ways. The highly contingent, open and emergent nature of the platforms as devices for communication reflects a post-modern view of emancipation and improvement. Jackson (2000, p. 420) noted that the creation of the thinking space was based on a generic interpretive methodology, although it gave equal prominence to eman-cipatory concerns. It should be noted though that, whilst the learning achieved by the co-researchers constituted an emancipatory outcome, the project design focused on emancipatory intent, i.e. the research recognized that emancipatory outcomes could not be predetermined. In addition, the platforms encouraged creativity and diversity and 'ethical alterness'. Before the research took place the organizational members were not aware of the 'human activity system' as a matter for research or for daily reflection. Subsequent to the creation of the platforms the organization did become a research matter to be reflected upon. It also enabled them to challenge power relations and to encourage diversity as well as to have 'fun' (Carrizosa, 2002, p. 16). Carrizosa (2002) noted that the 'joy' of embarking on platforms as a device lay not in implementa-tion *per se*, but in opening up possibilities for sensing and creating new ones to follow. He seemed to suggest that the research was an ongoing journey of new learning.

An important aim of this research was to generate learning amongst the participants, even those who were not directly involved in the pro-jects themselves. The multiple perspectives adopted were said to have enriched communications overall. Carrizosa (2002, p. 10) went on to claim that a pluralist, multimethodology approach where paradigm incommensurability is managed could result in double loop learning and that interventions such as the platforms described here were an effective way of doing this. It is important to note that the co-research-ers considered the platforms to be a local improvement in their own right (Carrizosa, 2002, p. 14). Ultimately, in critical tradition, Carrizosa (2002) reflected that any notion of improvement must depend upon the actors. So it is significant to note that KGT are still using platforms today.

Critical realism: emotional labour and the new workplace

Taylor's (1998) work on emotional labour in the service sector makes an interesting if somewhat disturbing read. He conducted ethnographic research within a telephone sales operation of a British airline and applied labour process theory in order to make sense of his findings. One of his major conclusions was that emotional labour is a key fea-ture of the new service sector workplace. Following Hochschild (1983) emotional labour is defined here as feeling management where it is performed as part of paid work, where it serves the interests of the employer in capital accumulation, is undertaken during social interaction with clients and where there is some managerial supervision or measurement of performance.

Technology was central to the performance of work at the airline – all staff worked with a headset, a telephone system and a computer system. The aim of the job was to convert as many calls as possible into airline bookings. The role of emotional labour is probably best illustrated here in the term 'customer intimacy' which was used by the head of telephone sales worldwide for describing the 'most important goal' (Taylor, 1998, p. 88). Customer intimacy meant being proactive – getting to know the customer so well that their needs could be anticipated and exceeded rather than just responded to in a reactive way. Management monitored work performance through a 50:50 split between hard targets (e.g. statistical analyses of call conversion) and soft targets (e.g. good teamwork). The latter was difficult for them to define and the former was seen as a benevolent system that encouraged staff to deliver business through their own personal skills development. The measurement of these targets determined the performance-related pay of individual staff.

The research identified a contradiction between management and staff perceptions of the nature of the work as well as inherent contradictions between the airline's espoused theory and actual operator practices. Management described the nature of the work as encouraging individual 'autonomy' and 'discretion' whereas staff reported an ethos of strict monitoring (mainly tapping) of calls taken and an official policy of standardization of technique and style. An electronic managerial control system was used for individual supervision and evaluation in order to ensure that any divergence from prescribed policy was of a 'positive' nature. Yet when interviewed the supervisors emphasized that staff were encouraged to be themselves and, indeed, that to do anything else would appear false and discourage customers. However, management's account does not sit well with the accounts of the operators. As one of them put it

> They either want us to be natural when interacting with customers or they don't, they can't have it both ways (Taylor, 1998, p. 95).

There was also a suggestion from the staff that the customers did not like the style that the operators were told to adopt.

Hochschild (1983) identified two forms of emotional labour: surface acting and deep acting. Surface acting refers to the act of displaying emotions to others that one does not feel, whereas deep acting suggests that it deceives oneself as much as others. Deep acting is shaped by managerial control and can even impact on the personality of the individual employee. In Taylor's (1998) research call operators employed both types of acting in the course of their emotional labour. One interviewee expressed deep acting when they reported that

> . . . a lot of people keep telling me I've actually mellowed since I came here so it's done something for me (Taylor, 1998, p. 94).

Staff were trained to treat customers in a certain way, most notably to 'always feel sorry for the ignorant customer . . . put sympathy on to him and not yourself'. And as another put it

> You've got to be on your guard all the time . . . I suppose in some ways you can't just be yourself (Taylor, 1998, p. 93).

However, the research also revealed that in many instances the call operators did not comply with this policy. They had devised a way of assessing whether or not their call was being tapped and, if not, slipped back into their own natural ways. A member of staff admitted that

> . . . when I am positive she is not listening, I have been really short with bad customers, it's a great feeling (Taylor, 1998, p. 95).

This suggested that even the surface acting was only displayed when managerial monitoring took place. It also suggested that Hochschild's (1983) theory was too simplistic. Examples were found of sophisticated surface acting and of deep acting for pragmatic purposes (i.e. deep acting which was not fully self-deceptive).

Taylor (1998) argued that labour process theory could inform studies of emotional work in the electronic workplace in at least four ways. It reveals the extraction of surplus value, it shows the capitalist 'logic of accumulation', it reveals the control imperative of management and exposes the underlying antagonistic nature of capital–labour workplace relations. None of this will surprise anyone familiar with labour process theory. However, some other interesting aspects were also revealed.

The control of people's thoughts and feelings was shown to be of a normative type (the electronic monitoring systems), but it was also shown that this control was partial, incoherent and contradictory. Even where behaviour would seem to suggest to management that staff were complying with official policy, in practice this was not always the case.

Furthermore, this study also illustrated that emotional labour was a gendered phenomenon. Indeed, Hochschild's (1983) work in the USA showed that women carried out a high proportion of jobs (between one-third and one-half) that were characterized by emotional labour.

Finally, Taylor (1998) set the findings of his own research against the backdrop of a number of other similar studies and concluded that contemporary electronic workplaces serve to shift the focus away from the technicalities of the work to the actual way in which the work is performed. At a superficial level it could be argued that this has long been established, but then this interpretation would miss at least two other points. The first is obvious and has a long tradition: that techno-logical intensification can just as easily lead to deskilling. The second is less obvious. In a workplace where employees have been 'empowered' or 'informated' through technology, then managerial expectations are both raised and shifted to focus on areas that are less tangible to evalu-ate. The performance of a less tangible labour effort (as in emotional labour) requires more subtle forms of management and more diverse forms of resistance on the part of the workers (Ackroyd and Thompson, 1999). Hard-edged analysis will not suffice in such contexts. Research approaches that can somehow 'take account of' the nuances of diffuse workplace interactions are not enough. We also need approaches that are purposefully driven to expose issues of power, autonomy, emancipa-tion and gender. Critical approaches contribute to meeting that need.

Critical post-modernism: consultancy as storytelling

The contribution that post-modernism can make to IS practice has been recognized by a variety of writers. The example that follows focuses on the practice of consultancy and views it through the lens of organiza-tional storytelling. Organizational storytelling can be viewed from a less radical (critical) perspective or a more radical (critical post-modern) per-spective. From the less radical viewpoint stories are elaborations upon actual events, wish fulfilments and expressions of deeper organizational and personal realities. From the more radical perspective, everything is discourse and narrative and there is no distinction between fact and fantasy or between text and context. It is this latter perspective which will be considered here. As Boje (1995) put it

> the storyteller and story listener are co-constructors of each story event as a multiplicity of stories get enacted simultaneously in a mul-tiplicity of sites, of brief encounter, in and around organisations (p. 5).

Organizational storytelling can be seen in practice at three different levels: as a way of organizational sense making, as defining management and as business itself. The research by Clark and Salaman (1996) on consultancy falls into the latter category. They argued that management consultants successfully satisfy and retain clients by telling 'strong stories'. The unregulated nature of management consultancy means that the customer's ability to assess the value of a consultancy's service prior to purchase is crucial. They proposed that the management consultancy industry is characterized by the following.

1. Intangibility (of the product).
2. Social interaction (between consultant and client).
3. Heterogeneity (of consultancy types).
4. Perishability (products are time and context specific).

The short-term and sporadic nature of the client–supplier relationship means that clients are often first-time buyers and, therefore, clients do not know what they are getting until they get it. Furthermore, consultancy knowledge is a social product and impression management is very important. This inherently ambiguous nature of the consultancy process lends itself to a focus on the manipulation of images and symbols. Clark and Salaman (1996) pointed to the production of organizational myths and in particular the creation of managers themselves into 'mythical manager heroes' (e.g. leader, strategist and saviour).

They discovered two types of consultancy story building: the solving of mysteries and the deconstruction of apparent certainties.

> Consultants' knowledge offers representations of organisation structures, processes and purposes to managers. Within these representations is an identity for managers themselves – a positive description stressing the importance of the manager's role (Clark and Salaman, 1996, p. 179).

Consultants demonstrate mastery and credibility through their ability to reduce uncertainty and through their competence in managing meanings, particularly in an economic (concise and resolute) way. This reflects organizational experience of what they call 'information anxiety' and the dominance of the resource metaphor in business. Consultants may appear to reflect the real world as experienced by the client manager, but equally it could be argued that the consultant is regulating what management do because management are working within the textual framework described by the consultant. The work of management consultants therefore not only constitutes organizational reality, but also constitutes managers themselves. Consequently, the process of management itself becomes redefined through the storytelling activities of the consultant.

Technology (particularly computers) features prominently in organizational stories. A number of research projects have shown this. Technology appears in organizational stories as physical objects, as living beings (through anthropomorphism) and as a resource or tool (a particularly powerful metaphor). Our everyday language suggests that we view computers as if it had agency (human qualities of action). In contrast, organizational stories often stress the importance of remaining in control of computers, of avoiding becoming their servants and of retaining skills and experience. Power and control are important themes here.

> If power is one of the hidden agendas of computer stories at the workplace, especially of stories recounted by experts and managers, then discomfort and apprehension are the underlying message of many. It is interesting to note that in no stories did the computer feature as the friend of the user ('my old and trusty PC') nor as party to heroic deeds. At the heart of these apprehensions may lie the sense that computers are already too clever and too powerful to be controlled by humans, while at the same time we have become too dependent on them to be able to function without them (Gabriel, 2000, p. 167).

In contemporary organizations stories have to compete with other forms of narrative, particularly against 'information' and 'data', but also against 'facts', jargon, numbers, images, arguments, opinions and so on. Stories and the accompanying engagement and meaning negotiation begin to shrivel away or are silenced (Brooke, 1994, 2001). People become deskilled in narrative ability and become information handlers not storytellers. All this highlights the potentially fragile nature of experience. It also highlights the interesting potential for critical postmodernism in IS research. We will return to some of these issues when we consider IS praxis and the work of Lash (2002).

How does critical research impact upon actual information systems praxis?

We now go on to consider three key issues that critical inquiry has illuminated in relation to IS praxis: the role of the IS professional, the nature of systems development and the changing nature of organizational life itself. Once again, each example broadly reflects the three approaches of CST, critical realism and critical post-modernism.

Information systems professionals claim too much

It has been suggested that practitioners regard systems thinking as too abstract for practical use so it is worth considering here a contribution from the CST camp that would seem to refute this. According to Ulrich (2002) critical systems heuristics was first developed in Berkeley in the late 1970s. Heuristic is taken from the Greek *heurisk-ein* meaning to find or discover and, thus, heuristics refers to the practice of discovery. Ulrich's work on critical systems heuristics was the first major text in the 1980s to present an emancipatory systems approach and it more or less plugged a gap in existing systems thinking, providing possibilities for action within coercive power situations where soft systems thinking had not (Jackson, 2000). Ulrich (2002) claimed that his work represented an independent strand of CST in which 'critical' implies both an emancipatory and a reflective effort. He attempted to work out the generic critical significance of the systems idea for reflective practitioner practice and presented a thesis that is highly relevant for critical IS development and critical practice in general (Ulrich, 2001a,b).

The essence of Ulrich's (2000, p. 25) argument is that what we observe and how we evaluate it depends on how we bound the system of concern. He therefore constructed a set of boundary categories. He argued that 'improvement' is an eminently systemic concept since, unless the system of reference is known, suboptimization will occur. Using Kantian logic he argued that no statement about boundaries could be made without certain assumptions concerning what does and what does not count in a situation. Therefore (unlike Kant) he derived his categories from the views and intentions of the social actors themselves that constitute the system of focus rather than from Aristotelian formal logic. Ulrich (2000) constructed 'an eternal triangle' to show the dialectical relationships involved. He mapped out three elements: boundary judgements (the system under concern), values (evaluations) and facts (observations). The decision about which stakeholders should be involved in any decision situation is itself a boundary judgement that needs to be subjected to scrutiny and this highlights the self-reflective nature of the approach. In his paper he worked through a practical example in order to show how the concept of boundary judgements can be applied in practice:

> The emancipatory employment of boundary judgements aims to make visible the operation of power, deception, dogmatism or other

non-argumentative means behind rationality claims. It accomplishes this purpose by creating a situation in which a party's unreflecting or even consciously covert use of boundary judgements becomes apparent (Ulrich, 2000, p. 259).

Ulrich (2000) argued that professionals (and others) tend to 'claim too much' and do so as an unreflective consequence of assuming their expertise is not limited by their particular knowledge of a situation. In other words, professionals tend to appropriate discursive space by exaggerating (consciously or unconsciously) their expertise. This observation is not limited to CST (Brooke and Maguire, 1998). Nevertheless, Ulrich went on to say that CST has shown that there is a deep symmetry of all claims to knowledge and rationality, irrespective of whether or not they are professionally derived. This enabled Ulrich to move beyond the professional–lay divide.

He was not arguing against professionalism *per se,* but against contemporary notions of professional competence that, he argued, tend to put members of society in a situation of incompetence even as they are meant to serve them. Thus, he suggested that the ultimate source of legitimacy should lie with the social actors. He proposed that in any situation both 'professionals' and 'citizens' could contribute a set of core competences to reflective practice. In this way he proposed a methodological route to professional practice. This is clearly pertinent to the field of IS. Nonetheless, Ulrich's work focused on exposing the exercising of power rather than on theorizing the nature and construction of power itself. This may be why Jackson (2000) classified critical systems heuristics as 'simple coercive' within the SOSM framework, i.e. as only able to deal with situations where there are obvious imbalances of power rather than where power relations are less clear. It is important to note though that Ulrich (2002) himself rejected this method of classification. Indeed, he proposed that the core methodological principle of boundary critique is a generic principle that is indispensable not only for 'coercive' problem situations, but for all problem-structuring and problem-solving processes. Technological systems design is a classic site in IS research for exploring problem situations. It is to this activity that we now turn.

Information systems development is still an unholy alliance

Systems development activities are often overtly interest-based in nature and, therefore, provide fertile ground for academic inquiry into one of the central concerns of critical theory: power relations. An example is the 'unholy alliance' that can be struck between the interested parties during systems development (Brooke and Maguire, 1998). The unholy alliance is a form of technical subterfuge whereby technical experts, in an attempt to compensate for their own lack of change management expertise, project a false image of their knowledge and its representativeness of the wider context. This phenomenon is referred to as 'virtual know-how'. In essence, virtual know-how is produced when the experts (systems developers) promote the efficacy of their own territory at the expense of exploring less familiar territory, even though the latter could be more conducive to reaching a 'successful' conclusion to the project.

Technical professionals have been criticized occasionally for producing solutions that are looking for problems (embodied in the notion of technological determinism), but they also occasionally produce problems as well. The interest-based nature of systems development means that there may be competing agendas amongst groups with each group wanting to ensure that the system is successful in their own terms. This can lead to the perceived advantages of the system being promoted while potential disadvantages are underemphasized. This dishonest or unholy alliance between different stakeholder groups (for instance internal users, systems developers, consultants/ suppliers, external clients and academic researchers) can result in major problems, with systems remaining largely hidden until they have been implemented. A rationality is adopted by the different groups as a common ideology, not so much because it is perceived as a natural reflection of the way things are, but because it serves to hide the use of power and legitimates and obscures the actual choices that are taking place (Pfeffer, 1981). Smith (1989) summarized it well when he said

> There are many prescriptions as to how work ought to be organised and how managers ought to manage the introduction of new technology. Yet the thoroughly rational management strategy for technical change has proved to be an elusive chimera (p. 377).

The unholy alliance is not struck between groups of equal power, quite the reverse. If Pfeffer's (1991) warning concerning rationality as a mask for the actual use of power and choice is accepted then it is essential that critical IS research strives to promote self-awareness and enable the assumptions that underpin management goals to be made more explicit. If this is not attempted then consultants and technical experts could become evangelists and spin doctors for a technocratic management. This warning no less applies to researchers. Willmott (1993) urged critical researchers to be vigilant against a potential lapse into uncriticality when he said that

> By becoming more practically reflexive about the conditions of theorising, we move away from an external and seemingly authoritative form of analysis and towards an immanent, self-consciously situated form of critique that places at issue the categories in terms of which it initiates critical play (p. 708).

Reflexivity is an essential element of conducting critical research, but it requires intellectual and organizational space. The inter-relationship between this need and the nature of the contemporary workplace is well explored in the next example.

Technological forms of life

Critical studies can shed light on changes in the very nature of daily existence itself.

The example discussed here concerns a broadly critical post-modern view of technology and the workplace. In his new book *Critique of Information* Lash (2002) discussed a phenomenon not too dissimilar to Parker and Cooper's (1998) cybernetically inspired concept of cyborganization. Lash (2002) differed from Parker and Cooper (1998) mainly in that he saw humans not so much as cyborgs but as an organic–technological interface. In declaring ourselves 'unable to function' without our personal computer, mobile telephone, etc. we are reinforcing this view of ourselves. We operate as

> a man–machine interface – that is, as a technological form of natural life – because I must necessarily navigate through technological forms of social life (Lash, 2002, p. 15).

We have to navigate through technological culture and, since this is constituted in 'at a distance' forms of life, then we also become life at a distance. We cannot achieve sociality in the absence of technological systems, except by interfacing with communication and transportation machines. Taking this further Lash (2002) drew in developments in human genetics in order to show how even details of our internal nature and bodily workings are externalized and stored in information databases. Through this process of being opened up we become part of a wide-open system of nature and technology, open to flows of information and communication.

The biggest implication of this proposition is that, whereas positivist researchers would argue for epistemological–ontological dualism, from Lash's (2002) perspective everything becomes flattened out into a radical monism of technology. The proposition of technological forms of life negates positivism's subject–object divide in favour of a form of empiricism where the observer is not fundamentally different from the observed. This echoes the philosophical position expressed by some critical theorists and postmodernists. Indeed, in a previous work Lash (1988) described post-modern social theory as a process of de-differentiation. In his latest thesis, the shift is away from the transcendental and philosophical phenomenology of Husserl and Heidegger towards the empiricist phenomenology of Garfinkel. The human actor is not substantially different to the actions they observe (cf. the parity within actor network theory of human and non-human 'actors'). Deep meaning disappears to be replaced by empirical meaning and this empirical meaning becomes everyday and contingent. In other words, meaningful knowledge is not separate from action but is intrinsic to it. We gain knowledge in a reflexive manner, but the reflexivity is of a particular type – it is a fusion of theory and practice. Theory is incarnate actually within the very act of practice itself. Sense making is no longer a private, personal act. Sense making is now for others and becomes a process of 'account giving', of 'glossing' and of communication. Implicit in this is an accountability and responsibility within each context or community. You give an account and you are then accountable for the consequences.

A major implication is that there is no longer any 'outside' (see Cooper, 1990), no external place for reflection and critique or representational space (Brooke, 2001). The suggestion is that we can no longer 'critique' as we used to – we can only 'articulate' processes and objects and attempt to modify boundaries (cf. Ulrich, 2000). Critique must be interior to the information not external to it and (given the fusion of thought, act and meaning) as was noted 'there is no time out' (Lash, 2002, p. 201). Lash (2002) concluded that power no longer works through discourse and ideology, but instead is manifested in the immediacy of information and communications. Power no longer works through reflective intellect or the unconscious but through tacit knowledge. The organism itself has become a self-regulating IS. In technological life those who work in scientific and technological centres (such as laboratories) will play a very significant role. The overall message is that technological life forms are not so much based on the notion of exploitation but exclusion. Social standing will accrue to those who have rights of access and intellectual property. This is a theme reflected in the now well-established term 'digital divide' (e.g. Remenyi, 2002; Sauer and Willcocks, 2002).

Lash (2002), in citing the human genome project as an example, showed how the incorporation of technology into our daily lives not only results in limited access to resources for some people and their accompanying disenfranchisement but also to our own commodification in the process. The accumulation of capital and the extraction of emotional labour illustrated in the earlier case examples are taken a step further in Lash's (2002) account of the accumulation of life forms. We might benefit here from a sharp reminder that the word 'emancipation' comes from the Latin for 'to release' as in to free a person from some form of constraint. Unfortunately, Lash's (2002) description suggests that we have nowhere left to go. This state of affairs suggests the need for increased vigilance and an increased role for critical research, not its redundancy.

Conclusions

Whilst not purporting to be a comprehensive literature review, this paper has attempted to demonstrate the range of contributions which critical approaches to IS research and praxis can make. It has been noted that many research paradigms now identify with the call to critical inquiry and that this is often achieved through a pluralist approach. Glancing across the critical research landscape has reconfirmed the impressions given in the special issue mentioned earlier in the paper (Brooke, 2002a) that the central themes of concern remain power relations and emancipation. However, the rise of pluralism has brought to light concerns about a loss of intellectual tension where one paradigm comes to dominate another and where loss of resistance results in insufficient attention to power relations such that voices are ignored or silenced.

Several other common themes have emerged in this review, notably the appropriation of feelings and humanity itself and the growing need for representational space. Against the backdrop of such workplace technology analyses such as those of Taylor (1998) and Lash (2002), we might view the current popularity amongst managers of Goleman's emotional intelligence and Zohar's spiritual intelligence with much scepticism. The recent surge of interest in knowledge management could conceivably lead decision makers to believe that organizations must apply technology in such a way that it can extract, objectify and commodify what makes us human in order to achieve business 'success'. Such a possibility (whether or not exaggerated) gives some insight into why critical IS research is necessary and critical knowledge management research is already demonstrating its potential (see Swan and Scarbrough (2001) for a good overview).

All this serves to reinforce the importance of opening up intellectual and representational spaces within organizations (Brooke, 1994, 2001; Clark and Salaman, 1996; Carrizosa, 2000, 2002, Lash, 2002). This paper suggests that critical approaches to IS will be more sensitive to identifying the need for such spaces as well as better equipped to help create them. If all this sounds like a rather pessimistic justification for critical research perhaps we can take some words of comfort from the phenomenologist Merleau-Ponty (1964) who wrote extensively about the primacy of perception. Building upon Weber's ideas he said that in the 'cultural sciences' there can be no system and no end. Unless some 'sclerosis' of life disaffects us, there will always be changes, new questions and disparate points of view, on what constitutes reality (Merleau-Ponty, 1964, p. 206). The overriding message of this paper is that critical approaches to IS have a valuable role to play in keeping up this momentum – even if occasionally accused of being the irritant rather than the pearl.

References

Ackroyd, S. and Thompson, P. (1999) *Organizational Misbehaviour* (Sage, London).

Adam, A. (2002) Exploring the gender question in critical information systems. *Journal of Information Technology*, **17**(2), 59–67.

Alvesson, M. and Deetz, S. (2000) *Doing Critical Management Research* (Sage, London).

Boje, D. (1995) Stories of the storytelling organization. *Academy of Management,* **38**(4), 997–1035.

Boje, D. (2001) *Narrative Methods for Organizational and Communication Research* (Sage, London).

Brooke, C. (1994) Information technology and the quality gap. *Employee Relations,* **16**(4), 22–34.

Brooke, C. (2001) Information systems in use: a representational perspective. *TAMARA,* **1**(3), 39–52.

Brooke, C. (2002a) Editorial: critical research in information systems: issue 1. *Journal of Information Technology*, **17**(2) 45–47.

Brooke, C. (2002b) What does it mean to be critical in IS research? *Journal of Information Technology*, **17**(2), 49–57.

Brooke, C. and Maguire, S. (1998) Systems development: a restrictive practice? *International Journal of Information Management*, **18**(3), 165–80.

Burrell, G. and Morgan, G. (1979) *Sociological Paradigms and Organisational Analysis* (Gower, Aldershot).

Carrizosa, A. (2000) Enacting thinking spaces towards purposeful actions: an action research project. Paper presented to the *World Congress of the Systems Science and the 44th Annual Meeting of the International Society for the Systems Sciences,* Toronto, Canada. CD-ROM.

Carrizosa, A. (2002) 'Platforms' for critical systems practice: an organisation-based action research project. In *46th Conference of the International Society for the System Sciences,* Janet K. Allen and Jennifer Wilby (eds.) International Society for the System Science/ISSS, 2–6 August 2002, Shanghai, China. CD-ROM.

Clark, T. and Salaman, G. (1996) Telling tales: management consultancy as the art of storytelling. In *Metaphors and Organisations,* Grant, D. and Oswick, C. (eds) (Sage, London), pp. 166–84.

Clegg, S.R. (2001) Changing Concepts of Power, Changing Concepts of Politics. *Administrative Theory and Prascis,* **23**(2), 126–50.

Cooper, R. (1990) Organization/Disorganization. In *The Theory and Philosophy of Organizations,* Hassard, J. and Pym, D. (eds) (Routledge, London), pp. 167–97.

Flood, R.L. (1990) *Liberating Systems Theory* (Plenum, New York).

Gabriel, Y. (2000) *Storytelling in Organisations: Facts, Fictions and Fantasies* (Oxford University Press, Oxford).

Gregory, W. (1996) Discordant pluralism: a new strategy for critical systems thinking. *Systems Practice,* **9**(6), 605–25.

Habermas, J. (1984a) *The Theory of Communicative Action: Volume 1: Reason and the Rationalization of Society* (Heinemann, London) (translated by T. McCarthy).

Habermas, J. (1984b) *The Theory of Communicative Action: Volume 2: Lifeworld and System: A Critique of Functionalist Reason* (Heinemann, London) (translated by T. McCarthy).

Harrington, J. (1995) *Paradigms Lost and Gained: Are We the Victims of a Paradigmatic Hegemony?* (Newcastle Business School Working Paper Series, University of Northumbria).

Hassard, J. and Parker, M. (1993) *Postmodernism and Organisations* (Sage, London).

Hochschild, A.R. (1983) *The Managed Heart: The Commercialisation of Human Feeling* (University of California Press, Berkeley, CA).

Jackson, M.C. (1997) Pluralism in systems thinking and practice. In *Multimethodology: The Theory and Practice of Combining Management Science Methodologies,* Mingers, J. and Gill, A. (eds) (John Wiley, Chichester), pp. 347–77.

Jackson, M.C. (2000) *Systems Approaches to Management* (Kluwer, New York).

Jackson, N. and Carter, P. (1991) In defence of paradigm incommensurability. *Organization Studies,* **12**(1), 109–27.

Klein, H.K. and Hirschheim, R. (1991) Rationality concepts in information systems development methodologies. *Accounting, Management and Information Technologies,* **1**(2), 157–87.

Lash, S. (1988) Discourse or figure? Postmodernism as a regime of signification. *Theory, Culture and Society,* **5**(2), 311–36.

Lash, S. (2002) *Critique of Information* (Sage, London).

Lyytinen, K. and Klein, H.K. (1985) The critical theory of Jurgen Habermas as a basis for a theory of information systems. In Mumford, E., Hirscheim, R., Fitzgerald, G. and Wood-Harper, T. (eds) *Research Methods in Information Systems.* (Elsevier Science, North-Holland), pp. 219–36.

Merleau-Ponty, M. (1964) *The Primacy of Perception* (Northwestern University Press) (collection edited by J.M. Edie).

Ormerod, R. and Mingers, J. (2002) Viewpoint. *Journal of the Operational Research Society,* **53,** 347–59.

Parker, M. and Cooper, R. (1998) Cyborganization: cinema as nervous system. In *Organization Representation,* Hassard, J. and Holliday, R. (eds) (Sage, London), pp. 201–28.

Pfeffer, J. (1981) *Power in Organisations* (Pitman, Marshfield).

Power, M. and Laughlin, R. (1992) Critical Theory in Accounting. In *Critical Management Studies,* Alvesson, M. and Willmott, H. (eds) (Sage, London), pp. 113–35.

Reed, M. (1993) Organizations and modernity: continuity and discontinuity in organization theory. In *Postmodernism and Organisations,* Hassard, J. and Parker, M. (eds) (Sage, London), pp. 163–82.

Remenyi, D. (2002) As the first 50 years of computing draw to an end . . .: what kind of society do we want? *Journal of Information Technology,* **17**(1), 3–7.

Saravanamuthu, K. (2002) Information technology and ideology. *Journal of Information Technology,* **17**(2), 79–87.

Sauer, C. and Willcocks, L. (2002) Editorial: winners and losers in the digital divide. *Journal of Information Technology,* **17**(1), 1–2.

Scarbrough, H. and Corbett, M. (1992) *Technology and Organization: Power, Meaning and Design* (Routledge, London).

Smith, S. (1989) Information technology in banks: Taylorization or human-centred systems? In *Computers in the Human Context: Information Technology, Productivity and People,* Forester, T. (ed.) (Basil Blackwell, Oxford), pp. 377–90.

Swan, J. and Scarbrough, H. (2001) Editorial: knowledge management: concepts and controversies. *Journal of Management Studies,* **38**(7), 913–21.

Taket, L. and White, A. (2000) *Partnership and Participation: Decision-making in the Multiagency Setting* (John Wiley & Sons, Chichester).

Taylor, S. (1998) Emotional labour and the new workplace. In *Workplaces of the Future,* Thompson, P. and Warhurst, C. (eds) (Macmillan Business, Basingstoke), pp. 84–103.

Thompson, P. and McHugh, D. (2002) *Work Organisations: A Critical Introduction,* 3rd edn (Palgrave, Basingstoke).

Ulrich, W. (2000) Reflective practice in the civil society: the contribution of critically systemic thinking. *Reflective Practice,* **1**(2), 247–68.

Ulrich, W. (2001a) A philosophical staircase for information systems definition, design and development: a discursive approach to reflective practice in ISD (part 1). *Journal of Information Technology Theory and Application,* **3**(3), 55–84.

Ulrich, W. (2001b) Critically systemic discourse: a discusive approach to reflective practice in ISD (Part 2). *Journal of Information Technology Theory and Application,* **3**(3), 85–106.

Ulrich, W. (2002) Personal communication.

White, A. and Taket, L. (1997) Continuing multimethodology as metamethodology: working towards pragmatic pluralism. In *Multimethodology: The Theory and Practice of Combining Management Science Methodologies,* Mingers, J. and Gill, A. (eds) (John Wiley, Chichester), pp. 379–405.

Willmott, H. (1993) Breaking the paradigm mentality. *Information and Organization,* **14**(5), 681–719.

4

To Reveal Is to Critique: Actor–Network Theory and Critical Information Systems Research

Bill Doolin and Alan Lowe
University of Waikato Management School, Hamilton, New Zealand

Introduction

This paper examines some of the issues for critical researchers of information systems (IS) arising from the post-modern turn (Lyotard, 1984; Seidman, 1994). The emphasis of the paper is to explore the increased interest and significance of research styles that have been developed within this genre and their application to IS research. The paper will approach this issue by giving particular attention to an examination of the relevance of research informed from an actor–network theory perspective. We see actor–network theory as an important addition to a broader critical research project (Alvesson and Deetz, 2000).

Alvesson and Deetz (2000) suggested that the challenge for critical management research is developing research that is not too easily dismissed as unfair and irrelevant. They argued that this requires a strong emphasis on empirical work as opposed to the conceptual work that has characterized critical scholars in management so far. It is believed that a critical project of the nature proposed by Alvesson and Deetz (2000) would be applicable in the IS literature, where a growing tradition of qualitative empirical inquiry may be particularly suited to such an expanded conception of the critical research agenda. In particular, it is argued that adopting an actor–network theory perspective to researching within organizations is well suited to the generation of such detailed empirical knowledge that is local and contextual.

In this sense, actor–network theory can be placed broadly within a post-modern mode of thinking that emphasizes the local and situated nature of all knowledge (Lee and Hassard, 1999). Modern forms of knowledge, whether in positivist, hermeneutic or Marxist guise, claim legitimacy by relying on universal standards and categories, what Lyotard (1984) called an 'incredulity toward grand narratives'. In contrast, postmodern knowledge undermines these traditional conceptions of knowledge and legitimacy in favour of heterogeneity and a decline of ideological hegemony in society. Post-modern knowledge emphasizes 'local, historically contextualised, and pragmatic types of social inquiry' (Seidman, 1994, p. 5).

The paper is structured as follows. The next section presents a discussion of the development of a critical research literature in IS. That section concludes that the definition of 'critical' used thus far in IS research is too limiting. Consequently, a broader definition of critical is pursued in the subsequent section, based on the work of Knights (1995), Alvesson (1999) and other organizational theorists. The paper then briefly reviews the concepts underlying actor–network theory before considering the ontological characteristics of actor–network theory that lend itself to such a broader critical research project. Finally, the paper discusses how IS researchers can use actor–network theory's performative view of social relations in being critical.

The critical turn in information systems research

The presence of a critical stream in IS research is nascent at best. In their seminal review of the mainstream IS research literature, Orlikowski and Baroudi (1991) found no articles they could classify as critical. The criteria they used in their review for defining a study as critical were as follows.

> Evidence of a critical stance towards taken-for-granted assumptions about organizations and information systems, and a dialectical analysis which attempted to reveal the historical, ideological, and contradictory nature of existing social practices (p. 6).

A similar definition of critical research was used by Myers (1997) in his discussion of qualitative research in IS.

> The main task of critical research is seen as being one of social critique, whereby the restrictive and alienating conditions of the

status quo are brought to light. Critical research focuses on the oppositions, conflicts and contradictions in contemporary society, and seeks to be emancipatory i.e. it should help to eliminate the causes of alienation and domination.

The emphasis placed in these definitions of critical on challenging the *status quo* and on uncovering fundamental and alienating structural contradictions in society can be traced to the influence of the work of Jurgen Habermas and the Frankfurt School. Much of the critical research in the IS literature has drawn upon the critical social theory of Habermas (e.g. Ngwenyama, 1991; Lyttinen, 1992; Hirschheim and Klein, 1994; Ngwenyama and Lee, 1997). Indeed, as Ngwenyama and Lee (1997) acknowledged 'his work has had greater impact on the IS discipline than any other CST [critical social theory] school of thought' (p. 151).

Motivating IS researchers working in this tradition is an emancipatory interest in seeking less constraining alternatives to existing social conditions (Ngwenyama, 1991). This is a deliberate attempt to move beyond an interpretation and representation of IS phenomena that implicitly accepts and helps preserve the *status quo* to 'the emancipation of organizational actors from false or unwarranted beliefs, assumptions, and constraints' (Ngwenyama and Lee, 1997, p. 151). For example, Ngwenyama and Lee (1997) emphasized the importance of communication richness in electronic mail in the emancipation of organizational actors from distorted communicative acts. Similarly, Hirschheim and Klein (1994) discussed the potential emancipatory role of participation in IS development methodologies.

Although the critical social theory of Habermas represents a valid approach for the critical interpretation of information technology (IT) in organizations, the relative dominance of this approach in critical IS research is unnecessarily limiting. There exists a continuum of possible critical approaches (Thomas, 1993) and IS researchers can be critical while using other theoretical perspectives. Although not necessarily well represented in the IS research literature, there are alternative critical approaches to IT that draw on other fields of organization studies.

For example, Doolin (1998) argued that researchers need consciously to adopt a critical and reflective stance in relation to the role that the ITs that they describe play in maintaining social orders and power relations in organizations. He suggested that using a perspective drawn from the work of Michel Foucault on power is one way of accomplishing this. IT is both a condition and a consequence of power relations in organizations and society (Knights, 1995) and, in order for IS research to be critical, the practices that surround and involve IT need to be analysed in the context of a wider set of social and political relations. Doing so requires opening up the 'black box' of IT and scrutinizing the power relations inscribed within it that may repress or constrain (Thomas, 1993; Knights and Murray, 1994).

Concern over the alienating potential of IT in the workplace, which has been voiced by some critical IS scholars working in a Habermasian tradition, is echoed by other academics using a Marxist perspective. For instance, Tinker (1998) criticized recent ethnographic research on IS for what he perceived as its uncritical appreciation of the social and historical context of technological developments. He suggested that this unreflective accommodation with IT reflects an equivocation that inadvertently helps legitimate (and accelerate) technological changes that degrade the quality and quantity of work.

The revitalized labour process theory that emerged following the publication of Braverman's (1974) monograph on the deskilling and alienating tendencies of technology has provided a significant critique of the managerial deployment of ITs in organizations (e.g. Knights and Willmott, 1988). Labour process theorists continue to provide a critique of how IT is implicated in the labour process in various IT-intensive contexts such as software development (e.g. Beirne *et al.*, 1998), business process re-engineering (e.g. Knights and McCabe, 1998) and call centres (e.g. Mulholland, 1999).

Another important source of critical research related to IS has grown out of a feminist critique of gendered assumptions about technology (e.g. Wajcman, 1991). Feminist scholars have been concerned with gender issues in the design of IS and IT (e.g. Green *et al.*, 1993) and with the gendered division of labour (Webster, 1996). In many cases their work connects with a political and emancipatory project for developing gender–technology relations that liberate (Gill and Grint, 1995).

The question this paper addresses is whether actor–network theory provides another suitable vehicle for critical theorizing in IS research. Before doing so, the paper will revisit the definition of critical research, constructing the meaning of critical in a different and more encompassing way to that of critical social theory.

Critical research as the intellectualization of method

Sayer (1992) argued that, in an orthodox conception, the 'basic aims of social science are taken for granted as the development of a "scientific" objective, propositional knowledge which provides a coherent description and explanation of the way the social world is' (p. 233). However, Sayer (1992) argued that, if we are to address the 'difficult' questions of social science research, the orthodox conception generates 'unreasonable and contradictory expectations' (p. 233). Instead, he argued for an alternative critical theory conception. However, the open nature of social systems compared to those that are the concern of the natural sciences makes such a project difficult. Putnam (1978) described the objects of interest to the social sciences as being a 'structured mess', but perhaps the most apparent difficulty lies in the 'internality of social science to its object which makes the latter susceptible to change by the former' (Sayer, 1992, p. 234).

In responding to such doubts in regard to case study research into organizationally embedded IS, Knights (1995) recommended that the researcher dispel the illusion of neutrality that many academics and particularly positivists seek to cultivate around their activities. He argued that a more reflexive approach to both the self and other is necessary. Knights (1995) suggested that the contribution of case research lies in adding depth to more conventional approaches, but also that in-depth analysis facilitates the disruption of existing assumptions and certainties. However, the disruption of one set of representations involves the elevation of another that, in its turn, remains to be disrupted. Thus, case research sets in motion continual possibilities of the production, transformation and reproduction of representation. Positivism draws its appeal in part from its determination to ignore 'the ontological discontinuity between natural and social phenomena [and] leave its representations unreflexive and unproblematical' (Knights, 1995, p. 248). Knights (1995) suggested that case research ought not to concern itself with generalizability, but instead should seek to emphasize its strengths. These include the telling of convincing stories and the ability to express the uncertainty and undecidability of organizational life.

Alvesson and Skoldberg (2000) argued that good qualitative research is not so much a technical project as an intellectual one. They attempted to raise the level of empirically based qualitative social science through an eclectic 'intellectualization of method'. They sought to demystify a variety of post-structuralist ideas by treating them pragmatically as sensitizing devices for the qualitative researcher. In doing so, they abstracted 'principles and ideals from hermeneutics, critical theory and postmodernism, with a view to endowing qualitative research with a more reflexive character' (Alvesson and Skoldberg, 2000, p. 8).

In particular, Alvesson and Deetz (2000) identified three very broadly cast elements that make up the intellectual role of the critical researcher and which may have different emphases on critical research: insight, critique and transformative redefinition. Insight is associated with hermeneutic understanding in the critical tradition, while critique is regarded as illustrated by the genealogy of Foucault or the deconstruction of the post-structuralists. Those authors suggested that interpretive work aiming for insight may be complemented by limited elements of critique and transformative redefinition. They acknowledged that critique may also take a central place, but suggested that use of the empirical case study is typically more limited in such research. Alvesson and Deetz (2000) still wished to provide space for transformative redefinition, although wanting to avoid 'hyper-critique' and argued that it should not dominate empirical research.

For Alvesson and Skoldberg (2000) research was premised on access to empirical material and involved a belief that qualitative enquiry must have a value as a source of subjective meaning and insight into participants' experiences of a complex social world. This is a stream of thinking that Alvesson (1999) advanced strongly, arguing that we must 'give some space in research for knowledgeable subjects to say something that is well-informed . . . about their experiences and social practices' (p. 19).

Alvesson and Deetz (2000) argued that critical studies should offer images that counter the dominant ideals and understandings spread by dominant groups and mainstream management thinking through 'drawing attention to hidden aspects and offering *alternative readings*' (p. 17, emphasis added). This is seen as a way of involving the same issues and qualities in critical research that are important for organizations themselves. However, Alvesson and Deetz (2000) cautioned that care needs to be taken in order to avoid simply replacing the ideas present in existing hierarchies and undemocratic social relations with equally naïve Utopian ideals.

This leads us to the contribution of actor–network theory to a broader critical project. This paper suggests that actor network theory offers a particularly effective 'alternative reading' of social interactions within organizations through its emphasis on empirical enquiry and its lack of constraining structure and ontology. In its early years actor–network theory was involved with sociological studies of science. Callon (1986a) and Latour (1987) wrote about scientists and scientific laboratories, 'strategic loci' that are representative of key institutions through which society and social values are moulded. This paper will argue for the extension of such conceptions to IS. These systems are implicated within organizations as sociotechnologies of calculation and control. As such, they might reasonably be depicted as strategic loci, as perhaps suggested by Callon *et al.* (1986):

> And may we expect further revolutions in the means of translation, possibly in relation to what is sometimes called the information society? . . . This approach implies that such control is not mono-lithic. Rather, there is a wide range of struggling actors and there are periodic changes in both the means of control and the strategic loci (p. 229).

What is this thing called actor–network theory?

There are dangers in naming and labelling – particularly in the construc-tion of 'actor–network theory' and its abbreviation ANT (Latour, 1999; Law, 1999). In using the term actor–network theory we are speaking of what the initial work on actor–networks and the sociology of transla-tion (Callon, 1986a,b; Latour, 1987; Law, 1987) has become and at the same time contributing to its 'black boxing'. This simplification has meant that actor–network theory has become easily transportable and translated into many different arenas of academic research. However, it has also tended to reduce some of its power in apprehending complex-ity (Law, 1999) and to lead to normative pronouncements of 'what is' actor–network theory and 'what is not'. As Law (1999) reminded us, that which has been labelled actor–network theory is not a fixed theo-retical position (performed in part through the act of its naming), but rather a 'heterogeneous work in progress' (p. 9).

Nevertheless, for those who are not familiar with actor–network theory, the paper attempts here a brief representation of some of the concepts associated with it. Actor–network theory perceives contem-porary society as constituted by heterogeneous collectivities of people, but always together with technology, machines and objects. It is the intricate inter-relations among the heterogeneous elements of tech-noscience that make up our society and organizations (Knorr-Cetina, 1997). These interrelationships are theorized as networks of human and non-human actors, each of which is itself the effect of a network of heterogeneous elements – hence 'actor–network' theory, for an actor is also a network (Callon, 1991).

A fundamental aspect of actor–network is their relationality. Actors, both individual and collective, are defined and interactively constituted in their relationships with other actors in the actor–network (Law, 2000). An actor, in the (semiotic) sense used here, is something that acts or to which activity is granted by others. Actor is accepted to be the source of an action, regardless of its status as a human or non-human. Differences in agency and size between actors are the result or outcome of some process of negotiation involving power relations (Callon and Latour, 1981). All are relational achievements, that is uncertain effects generated by an actor–network and its mode of interaction. Such actors are constituted as objects only to the extent that the actor–network stays in place (Law, 1992).

The relative durability of actor–networks is a consequence of their heterogeneity. Actor–networks come in a variety of material forms, such as people, texts, machines and architectures. Actor–networks are made relatively cohesive and stable by the way they are intimately bound up with the material and the technical (Latour, 1991; Joerges and Czarniawska, 1998). The ordering of the social is never purely social, but rather sociotechnical in that the social and the technical mutually define one another (Law, 1991; Knights and Murray, 1994). The corollary is that society and technology cannot be conceptualized as ontologically separate (though interrelated) entities (Latour, 1994).

Entities establish themselves as agents, building a network of alliances by defining, mobilizing and juxtaposing a set of materially heteroge-neous actors, obliging them to enact particular roles and fitting them together to form a working whole (Law, 1988). The agent becomes the spokesperson of the actors constituted in this translation (Callon, 1986b; Law 1992). This 'enrolment' of allies in a network involves per-suading other actors that they share a common interest or problem. The agent seeks to enrol other actors into a network by a process of 'problematization' (Latour, 1987), presenting a problem of the latter in terms of a solution belonging to the former. However, resistance is possible and translation is only achieved when actors accept the roles defined and attributed to them. If an actor resists enrolment and defines itself differently it becomes complex, possibly leading to the modifica-tion or disintegration of the actor–network system (Callon, 1986a,b).

Actor–network theory's theoretical constructs place great reliance on the tracing of intricate networks and associations among human and non-human actors (Whitley, 1999). While powerful, these networks and alliances place constraints and limits on technoscience and its systems. We are continually reminded by Latour (1987, 1993, 1999) of the dependence of technoscience upon its networks of relations, of the significance of centres of calculation, of enormous volumes of mundane inscriptions and of the importance of the enrolment of people and objects into the technoscience project. Without substantial resources and effort, ideas do not travel, prototypes do not become common-place and knowledge does not produce centres of calculation that become 'obligatory points of passage'. It is only after all these resources have been successfully assembled and brought to bear that controversies are settled and black boxes are produced (Preston *et al.*, 1992).

Ontological considerations

This paper will now focus on the ontological aspects of actor–network theory, which are at one and the same time the reason for a substantial critique and the source of its explanatory power. Drawing on Callon (1986b), Michael (1996) summarized these as (1) an agnosticism or impartiality towards the nature of the actors involved in a controversy, (2) a generalized symmetry in treating human and non-human actors with the same analytic framework and vocabulary and (3) a repudiation of a priori distinctions between the social and the natural or technical.

Lee and Hassard (1999) argued that what actor–network theory can offer to our understanding of sociotechnical relations is essentially consequent on an acceptance of a relativist view of the nature of soci-ety. Yet, actor–network theory gains much of its notoriety from the way in which human and non-human, the social and the technical, are brought together in the same analytic view (Hassard *et al.*, 1999). Walsham (1997) outlined a number of criticisms of actor–network theory that arise from the organizational theory literature, including an inadequate consideration of social structures, the symmetric treatment of humans and non-humans and moral relativism. Although Walsham (1997) did not explicitly mention them as such, these criticisms con-stitute a major obstacle to operating under the received view of critical theory as described in an earlier section of this paper.

The first criticism relates to actor–network theory's emphasis on the local and the contingent and how these contribute to the production of social order. Critics of actor–network theory argue that this emphasis neglects the reverse role that institutionalized social structures play in influencing the local process of social interaction (Walsham, 1997). Traditional critical theory tends to assume the inevitable presence of conflict brought about through predetermined and pre-existing social structures. Yet, in actor–network theory social structures are themselves the relational achievements. Whether entities are kings, countries or classes, they are as much an effect, the outcome of the interaction between networks of forces, as a cause of subsequent events (Callon and Latour, 1981; Law, 1992; Law and Mol, 1995). As Latour (1991) put it 'the macro-structure of society is made of the same stuff as the micro-structure' (p. 118).

This emphasis on 'relational materiality' (Law, 1999), i.e. that entities achieve their form and attributes as a consequence of their relations with other entities, reflects an unwillingness to accept a priori the pre-existence of social structures and differences as somehow inherently given in the order of things. This enables actor–network theory to explore how particular social relations are translated and performed in different localized contexts. For, as Law (1999) observed, entities are performed in, through and by the very relations that define them. This is not to say that differences do not occur (Callon and Latour, 1992) or that some network effects are not relatively stable and enduring (Gill and Grint, 1995). What actor–network theory is interested in is how it is that this durability is achieved: 'How is it that things get performed (and perform themselves) into relations that are relatively stable and stay in place' (Law, 1999, p. 4).

Actor–network theory avoids the tendency to reify social relations as given entities that are 'constructed as macro-actors and shut away into black boxes' (Ormrod, 1995, p. 44) focusing instead on how they are actively enrolled as resources in sustaining an actor–network system. The aim is to open up these black boxes, these simplifications that we take for granted all too often and expose the way that translations occur and associations are generated (Somerville, 1999) and, in doing so, explore how social relations are ordered so as to 'generate effects like organizations, inequality, and power' (Law, 1992, p. 381).

Similarly, actor–network theory does not assume the pre-existence of interests attributed to various actors. Rather than modes of domination obscuring or distorting the 'real interests' of organizational participants (subject to a 'false consciousness'), interests (and domination) are treated as relational effects, which are the 'temporarily stabilized outcomes of previous processes of enrolment' (Callon and Law, 1982, p. 622).

A consequence of relational materiality is the symmetric treatment of humans and non-humans. The implication is that what is an actor is an empirical matter. As Callon (1991) observed, 'in this ontology actors have both variable content and variable geometry' (p. 140). Both human and non-human actors should be treated with the same analytical framework and vocabulary (Callon, 1986b; Latour, 1987, 1993; Law, 1987), that is all should be considered as actors who may play a role in the patterning of sociotechnical networks. This refusal to privilege the human has caused some controversy in sociology, such as in the exchange between Callon and Latour (1992) and Collins and Yearley (1992). The focus in critical social theory tends to be on questions of human agency (Whitley, 1999). Technology is often ignored or relegated to a role as a tool of oppression, domination and control. However, it is important to realize that actor–network theory does not seek to diminish the importance of humans, but instead to highlight the role of what Latour (1992) called the 'missing masses' in stabilizing the heterogeneous actor–networks that make up organizations and society. As Walsham (1997) noted, in this age of (sociotechnical) hybrids challenging the rigid separation of human and non-human seems valuable, particularly where the boundaries between the social and the technical are continually negotiated and defined, such as in IS (Bloomfleld and Vurdubakis, 1994).

Finally, actor–network theory is frequently grouped with social constructivism, which attracts charges of apoliticism or moral relativism. The agnosticism inherent in actor–network theory (Ormrod, 1995) derives from the position that the various perspectives, interpretations and identities of actors implicated in the actor–network should not be presumed or fixed by an observer when they are subject to negotiation (Callon, 1986b). However, Latour (1991) argued that actor–network theory is not indifferent to the possibility of moral judgement, but rather rejects judgements that transcend the network, somehow originating from outside the empirical events and relationships that actor–network theory describes. In this sense, actor–network theory is similar to Foucault's rejection of the possibility of normative justification in that the imposition of moral consequences from beyond the actor–network is itself an operation of power (cf. Ormrod, 1995) in which one form of domination is exchanged for another.

To reveal is to critique

Walsham (1997) concluded that, for actor–network theory to examine ethical and moral implications related to IS, there is a need to include political, ethical and moral theories from outside the actor–network. He is not alone. For instance, Whitley (1999) attempted to combine Habermas with actor–network theory in proposing a critical theory for a new collective of humans and non-humans. Ciborra and Hanseth (1998) invoked Heidegger alongside actor–network theory in their work on information infrastructures. Knights *et al.* (1997) drew on Foucault in their study of computer networks in the financial services industry, as did Brigham and Corbett (1997) in their discussion of how electronic mail is implicated in organizational power relations and control at a distance. Even Latour (1996) seemed to hint that something else needs to be added to the network when asked to provide policy or pass judgement. Hull (1999) picked up the hint in his examination of knowledge management, where he attempted to show how a focus on 'conduct' (drawing on the work of Gillian Rose) 'provide[s] an example of a form of critical activity that can complement ANT, that can add a "something else" to network-tracing activity' (p. 415).

This is one possible route open to researchers working with actor–network theory and this paper does not wish to deny the value of insights gained through social theorizing of this nature. However, the paper is concerned with the idea that the introduction of such theories to actor–network theory studies of IS reflects an assumption that the network-tracing activity (Hull, 1999) of actor–network theory is unreflexive and acritical. This paper has already discussed the claims and critiques of actor–network theory in relation to agnosticism and it is important to remind ourselves that most of the research performed under the rubric of actor–network theory is concerned with the empirical description of the actor–network systems that have stabilized around various ITs, whether hospital IS (Bloomfield *et al.*, 1997), electronic data interchange standards (Hanseth and Monteiro, 1997) or software (Baxter, 2000).

The present authors do not accept that the agnosticism and ontological relativism of actor–network theory precludes critique. Instead, the paper will argue that the very act of tracing the network and the actions of its constituents, combined with a refusal to a priori make distinctions or grant status, enables a critical light to be shone on the assumed, the mundane and the status quo. While this paper supports the view that actor–network theory has offered new ways of understanding the sociotechnical nature of IS (cf. Walsham, 1997), the authors believe that IS researchers need to move beyond this understanding and explore how distinctions are produced, status is constructed and social relations are stabilized. Actor–network theory is a useful way of defamiliarizing the taken for granted (Calas and Smircich, 1999). As Ormrod (1995) suggested 'If we are to successfully challenge the relations . . . we think are worse, unfair, wrong, then we need to be able to discuss them in all their specificity and difference' (p. 45).

Returning to the paper's earlier discussion of a broader critical project advocated by Alvesson and Deetz (2000), it is the reflexive and empirical inquiry that actor–network theory offers which makes it effective as a critical research perspective. Actor–network theory is concerned with unravelling the heterogeneous materials and processes in which networks and actors are shaped and stabilized. It makes no a priori assumptions about the nature or character and the similarity or difference of the relations it describes (Law, 1999). These are not determined, permanent or universal (Wise, 1997). Instead, they are treated as matters of historical contingency (Michael, 1996), the outcome of processes of translation and negotiation.

This agnosticism means that it is able to 'record the discriminations that are performed and the boundaries that are constructed in the activities it studies' (Lee and Hassard, 1999, p. 392). There are differences between 'the powerful and the wretched', but these are 'differences in the methods and materials that they deploy to generate themselves' (Law, 1992, p. 390, emphasis removed). As Michael (1996) observed, it is through exposing this contingency that critique derives. In doing so, actor–network theory reveals how things could have been otherwise (Law, 1992; Michael, 1996).

For example, Walsham and Sahay (1999) provided some critical insights into an actor–network analysis of geographic IS in India. Their initial choice of exploring IT use in a developing country suggests some empathy with a critical agenda and in tracing the networks implicated in their case studies they questioned the desirability of global pressures and influences in these contexts. In particular, by providing an analysis situated in the social, political and cultural context of India, they were able to demonstrate how the inscription of Western values in the geographic IS technology reflected assumptions about rational decision making, spatial thinking and coordinated action, assumptions that to some extent conflicted with Indian values in the implementation of the geographic IS there.

Part of revealing how things could have been otherwise involves attempting to represent more than one point of view within an actor–network, addressing what Star (1991) called the 'distribution of the conventional' (p. 43). This is the heterogeneity of actor–networks: a sense of the multiplicity of humans and non-humans, an understanding of the work that keeps networks stable and an acknowledgement that networks are not necessarily stable for all. For instance, consider who an automatic door closer might discriminate against (Latour, 1988) or the plight of someone allergic to onions ordering a burger at McDonalds (Star, 1991).

A stabilized network is only stable for some, and that is for those who are members of the community of practice who form/use/maintain it. And part of the public stability of a standardized network often involves the private suffering of those who are not standard – who must use the standard network, but who are also non-members of the community of practice (Star, 1991, p. 43).

As Star (1991) observed, we are all members of more than one social world or actor–network and, in this sense, we are all marginal to some extent through the differing degrees of our various member-ships. Multiple memberships and multiple marginalities need to be incorporated into actor–network theory (Michael, 1996).

Conclusion

Actor–network theory, with its central concern being the understand-ing and theorization of the role of technology and technological objects within society, is an attractive candidate for researchers of IS and their implications within organizations. IS, but, even more directly, software packages, standards, rules, methods and conventions are particularly apt examples of technology or knowledge systems that together represent influential sociotechnologies of management. Research studies informed by actor–network theory might reasonably look to provide understandings and explanations of these phenomena in organizations. Walsham (1997) emphasized the potential contribution of actor–network theory in enabling us to think about the increasing hybridization of humans and IT. As Latour (1996) observed,

It is no longer clear if a computer system is a limited form [of] organization or if an organization is an expanded form of computer system. Not because, as in the engineering dreams and the sociolo-gists' nightmares, complete rationalization would have taken place, but because, on the opposite, the two monstrous hybrids are now coextensive (p. 302).

Lee and Hassard (1999) argued that actor–network theory is *'ontologi-cally relativist* in that it allows that the world may be organized in many different ways, but also *empirically realist* in that it finds no insurmount-able difficulty in producing descriptions of organizational processes' (p. 392, emphasis in original). Such a categorization provides a useful framework for those unfamiliar with the philosophical rhetoric that Latour (1993), in particular, has erected around his theoretic constructs. Lee and Hassard (1999) contended that actor–network theory has much to commend it in the investigation of key contemporary developments in organizational thinking, practice and form.

Using actor–network theory as a research strategy puts a strong emphasis on empirical inquiry, despite actor–network theory's relativist ontology. This empirical aspect is in part composed of the careful tracing and recording of heterogeneous relational networks. What actor–network theory offers is a clear way of seeing these relations for what they are. They are powerful because of the relatively sophisticated combinations of resources and people that they mobilize. By using approaches such as actor–network theory we can seek to demystify the facts and data that they produce. Actor–network theory enables us to analyse the interrelationships that comprise actor–networks and show just how ordinary and mundane they often are. In doing this, actor–network theory offers the hope of a more fundamental appreciation and critique of the underlying relationships that pervade contemporary society. It is precisely these sociotechnical relations that we need to explicate in order to come to terms with a world where ITs are 'part of our everyday mode of existence, and our interactions with machines incrementally define our life experiences' (Calas and Smircich, 1999, p. 664).

Acknowledgement

A previous version of this paper was presented at the (Re-)Defining Critical Research in Information Systems Workshop, University of Salford, UK, 9–10 July 2001.

References

Alvesson, M. (1999) *Beyond Neo-positivists, Romantics and Localists: A Reflexive Approach to Organizational Research*, working paper (Lund Institute of Economic Research).

Alvesson, M. and Deetz, S. (2000) *Doing Critical Management* Research (Sage, London).

Alvesson, M. and Skoldberg, K. (2000) *Reflexive Methodology: New Vistas for Qualitative Research* (Sage, London).

Baxter, L. (2000) Bugged: the software development process. In *Managing Knowledge*, Prichard, C., Hull, R., Chumer, M. and Wilmott, H. (eds) (Macmillan, Basingstoke), pp. 37–48.

Beirne, M., Ramsay, H. and Panteli, A. (1998) Developments in computing work: control and contradiction in the software labour process. In *Workplaces of the Future*, Thompson, P. and Warhurst, C. (eds) (Macmillan, Basingstoke), pp. 142–62.

Bloomfield, B.P. and Vurdubakis, T. (1994) Boundary disputes: negotiating the boundary between the technical and the social in the development of IT systems. *Information Technology and People*, 7(1), 9–24.

Bloomfield, B.P., Coombs, R., Owen, J. and Taylor, P. (1997) Doctors as managers: constructing systems and users in the National Health Service. In *Information Technology and Organizations: Strategies, Networks and Integration*, Bloomfield, B.P., Coombs, R., Knights, D. and Littler, D. (eds) (Oxford University Press, Oxford), pp. 112–34.

Braverman, H. (1974) *Labour and Monopoly Capital: The Degradation of Work in the Twentieth Century* (Monthly Review Press, New York).

Brigham, M. and Corbett, M. (1997) E-mail, power and the constitution of organisational reality. *New Technology, Work and Employment*, **12**(1), 25–35.

Calas, M.B. and Smircich, L. (1999) Past postmodernism? Reflections and tentative directions. *Academy of Management Review*, **24**(4), 649–71.

Callon, M. (1986a) The sociology of an actor–network: the case of the electric vehicle. In *Mapping the Dynamics of Science and Technology: Sociology of Science in the Real World*, Callon, M., Law, J. and Rip, A. (eds) (Macmillan, London), pp. 19–34.

Callon, M. (1986b) Some elements of a sociology of translation: domestication of the scallops and the fishermen of St Brieuc Bay. In *Power, Action and Belief: A New Sociology of Knowledge?*, Law, J. (ed.) (Routledge and Kegan Paul, London), pp. 196–233.

Callon, M. (1991) Techno-economic networks and irreversibility. In *A Sociology of Monsters: Essays on Power, Technology and Domination*, Law, J. (ed.) (Routledge, London), pp. 132–61.

Callon, M. and Latour, B. (1981) Unscrewing the big Leviathan: how actors macro-structure reality and how sociologists help them to do so. In *Advances in Social Theory and Methodology: Toward an Integration of Micro- and Macro-sociologies*, Knorr-Cetina, K. and Cicourel, A.V. (eds) (Routledge and Kegan Paul, Boston), pp. 277–303.

Callon, M. and Latour, B. (1992) Don't throw the baby out with the bath school! A reply to Collins and Yearley. In *Science as Practice and Culture*, Pickering, A. (ed.) (University of Chicago Press, Chicago), pp. 343–68.

Callon, M. and Law, J. (1982) On interests and their transformation: enrolment and counter-enrolment. *Social Studies of Science*, **12**, 615–25.

Callon, M., Law, J. and Rip, A. (1986) Putting texts in their place. In *Mapping the Dynamics of Science and Technology: Sociology of Science in the Real World*, Callon, M., Law, J. and Rip, A. (eds) (Macmillan, London), pp. 221–230.

Ciborra, C.U. and Hanseth, O. (1998) From tool to *Gestell*: agendas for managing the information infrastructure. *Information Technology and People*, **11**(4), 305–27.

Collins, H. and Yearley, S. (1992) Epistemological chicken. In *Science as Practice and Culture*, Pickering, A. (ed.) (University of Chicago Press, Chicago), pp. 301–26.

Doolin, B. (1998) Information technology as disciplinary technology: being critical in interpretive research on information systems. *Journal of Information Technology*, **13**(4), 301–11.

Gill, R. and Grint, K. (1995) Introduction. In *The Gender–Technology Relation: Contemporary Theory and Research*, Grint, K. and Gill, R. (eds) (Taylor & Francis, London), pp. 1–28.

Green, E., Owen, J. and Pain, D. (1993) *Gendered by Design? Information Technology and Office Systems* (Taylor & Francis, London).

Hanseth, O. and Monteiro, E. (1997) Inscribing behavior in information infra-structure standards. *Accounting, Management and Information Technologies*, 7(4), 183–211.

Hassard, J., Law, J. and Lee, N. (1999) Preface. *Organization*, 6(3), 387–90.

Hirschheim, R. and Klein, H.K. (1994) Realizing emancipatory principles in information systems development: the case for ETHICS. *MIS Quarterly*, 18(1), 83–109.

Hull, R. (1999) Actor network and conduct: the discipline and practices of knowledge management. *Organization*, 6(3), 405–28.

Joerges, B. and Czarniawska, B. (1998) The question of technology, or how organizations inscribe the world. *Organization Studies*, 19(3), 363–85.

Knights, D. (1995) Refocusing the case study: the politics of research and researching politics in IT management. *Technology Studies*, 2(2), 230–54.

Knights, D. and McCabe, D. (1998) 'What happens when the phone goes wild?' Staff, stress and spaces for escape in a BPR telephone banking work regime. *Journal of Management Studies*, 35(2), 163–94.

Knights, D. and Murray, F. (1994) *Managers Divided: Organisation Politics and Information Technology Management* (Wiley, Chichester).

Knights, D. and Willmott, H. (1988) *New Technology and the Labour Process* (Macmillan, Basingstoke).

Knights, D., Murray, F. and Willmott, H. (1997) Networking as knowledge work: a study of strategic inter-organizational development in the financial services industry. In *Information Technology and Organizations: Strategies, Networks and Integration*, Bloomfield, B.P., Coombs, R., Knights, D. and Littler, D. (eds) (Oxford University Press, Oxford), pp. 137–59.

Knorr-Cetina, K. (1997) Sociality with objects: social relations in postsocial knowledge societies. *Theory, Culture and Society*, 14(4), 1–30.

Latour, B. (1987) *Science in Action: How to Follow Scientists and Engineers Through Society* (Harvard University Press, Cambridge, MA).

Latour, B. (1988) Mixing humans and nonhumans together: the sociology of a door-closer. *Social Problems*, 35(3), 298–310.

Latour, B. (1991) Technology is society made durable. In *A Sociology of Monsters: Essays on Power, Technology and Domination*, Law, J. (ed.) (Routledge, London), pp. 103–31.

Latour, B. (1992) Where are the missing masses? The sociology of a few mundane artifacts. In *Shaping Technology/Building Society: Studies in Sociotechnical Change*, Bijker, W.E. and Law, J. (eds) (MIT Press, Cambridge, MA), pp. 225–58.

Latour, B. (1993) *We Have Never Been Modern* (Harvard University Press, Cambridge, MA).

Latour, B. (1994) On technical mediation – philosophy, sociology, genealogy. *Common Knowledge*, 3(2): 29–64.

Latour, B. (1996) Social theory and the study of computerized work sites. In *Information Technology and Changes in Organizational Work*, Orlikowski, W.J., Walsham, G., Jones, M.R. and DeGross, J.I. (eds) (Chapman & Hall, London), pp. 295–307.

Latour, B. (1999) On recalling ANT. In *Actor Network Theory and After*, Law, J. and Hassard, J. (eds) (Blackwell, Oxford), pp. 15–25.

Law, J. (1987) Technology and heterogeneous engineering: the case of Portuguese expansion. In *The Social Construction of Technological Systems: New Directions in* the *Sociology and History of Technology*, Bijker, W.E., Hughes, T.P. and Pinch, T.J. (eds) (MIT Press, Cambridge, MA), pp. 111–34.

Law, J. (1988) The anatomy of a socio-technical struggle: the design of the TSR2. In *Technology and Social Process*, Elliott, B. (ed.) (Edinburgh University Press, Edinburgh), pp. 44–69.

Law, J. (1991) Introduction: monsters, machines and sociotechnical relations. In *A Sociology of Monsters: Essays on Power, Technology and Domination*, Law, J. (ed.) (Routledge, London), pp. 1–23.

Law, J. (1992) Notes on the theory of the actor–network: ordering, strategy, and heterogeneity. *Systems Practice*, 5(4), 379–93.

Law, J. (1999) After ANT: complexity, naming and topology. In *Actor Network Theory and After*, Law, J. and Hassard, J. (eds) (Blackwell, Oxford), pp. 1–14.

Law, J. (2000) *Networks, Relations, Cyborgs: On the Social Study of Technology* (Centre for Science Studies and the Department of Sociology, Lancaster University, Lancaster. Available at http://www.comp.lancs.ac.uk/sociology/soc042jl.html).

Law, J. and Mol, A. (1995) Notes on materiality and sociality. *Sociological Review*, 43(2), 274–94.

Lee, N. and Hassard, J. (1999) Organization unbound: actor–network theory, research strategy and institutional flexibility. *Organization*, 6(3), 391–404.

Lyotard, J. (1984) *The Postmodern Condition: A Report on Knowledge* (University of Minnesota Press, Minneapolis).

Lyttinen, K. (1992) Information systems and critical theory. In *Critical Management Studies*, Alvesson, M. and Willmott, H. (eds) (Sage, London), pp. 159–80.

Michael, M. (1996) *Constructing Identities: The Social, the Nonhuman and Change* (Sage, London).

Mulholland, K. (1999) Back to the future: a call centre and new forms of direct control. In *17th Annual International Labour Process Conference*, Royal Holloway, University of London.

Myers, M.D. (1997) Qualitative research in information systems. Paper presented at the MISQ Discovery, June 1997, at http://www.misq.org/misqd961/isworld/index.html.

Ngwenyama, O.K. (1991) The critical social theory approach to information systems: problems and challenges. In *Information Systems Research: Contemporary Approaches & Emergent Traditions*, Nissen, H.-E., Klein, H.K. and Hirschheim, R. (eds) (North-Holland, Amsterdam), pp. 267–80.

Ngwenyama, O.K. and Lee, A.S. (1997) Communication richness in electronic mail: critical social theory and the contextuality of meaning. *MIS Quarterly*, 21(2), 145–67.

Orlikowski, W.J. and Baroudi, J.J. (1991) Studying information technology in organizations: research approaches and assumptions. *Information Systems Research*, 2(1), 1–28.

Ormrod, S. (1995) Feminist sociology and methodology: leaky black boxes in gender/technology relations. In *The Gender–Technology Relation: Contemporary Theory and Research*, Grint, K. and Gill, R. (eds) (Taylor & Francis, London), pp. 31–47.

Preston, A.M., Cooper, D.J. and Coombs, R.W. (1992) Fabricating budgets: a study of the production of management budgeting in the National Health Service. *Accounting, Organizations and Society*, 17(6), 561–93.

Putnam, H. (1978) *Meaning and the Moral Sciences* (Routledge and Kegan Paul, London).

Sayer, A. (1992) *Method in Social Science: A Realist Approach* (Routledge, London).

Seidman, S. (1994) *The Postmodern Turn: New Perspectives on Social Theory* (Cambridge University Press, Cambridge).

Somerville, I. (1999) Agency versus identity: actor–network theory meets public relations. *Corporate Communications*, 4(1), 6–13.

Star, S.L. (1991) Power, technology and the phenomenology of conventions: on being allergic to onions. In *A Sociology of Monsters: Essays on Power, Technology and Domination*, Law, J. (ed.) (Routledge, London), pp. 26–56.

Thomas, J. (1993) *Doing Critical Ethnography* (Sage, Newbury Park, CA).

Tinker, T. (1998) Hamlet without the prince: the ethnographic turn in information systems research. *Accounting, Auditing, and Accountability Journal*, 11(1), 13–33.

Wajcman, J. (1991) *Feminism Confronts Technology* (Allen & Unwin, North Sydney).

Walsham, G. (1997) Actor–Network theory and IS research: current status and future prospects. In *Information Systems and Qualitative Research*, Lee, A.S., Liebenau, J. and DeGross, J.I. (eds) (Chapman & Hall, London), pp. 466–80.

Walsham, G. and Sahay, S. (1999) GIS for district-level administration in India: problems and opportunities. *MIS Quarterly*, 23(1), 39–66.

Webster, J. (1996) *Shaping Women's Work: Gender, Employment and Information Technology* (Longman, London).

Whitley, E.A. (1999) *Habermas and the Non-humans: Towards a Critical Theory for the New Collective* (Centre for Social Theory and Technology, Keele University, Keele. Available at http://www.keele.ac.uk/depts/stt/cstt2/papers/whitley.htm).

Wise, J.M. (1997) *Exploring Technology and Social Space* (Sage, Thousand Oaks, CA).

5

The Rationality Framework for a Critical Study of Information Systems

Dubravka Cecez-Kecmanovic
School of Information Systems, Technology and Management, Faculty of Commerce and Economics, University of New South Wales, Sydney, Australia

Marius Janson
Department of Information Systems, University of Missouri-St. Louis, USA

Ann Brown
Faculty of Management, Cass Business School, City University, Frobisher Crescent, London, UK

Introduction

This paper focuses on the relationship between information systems (IS) and organizational processes from the perspective of the rationality of actors and their actions. The terms rational and rationality that are used in theoretical writings and in everyday life denote a multiplicity of meanings. The idea of reason has been connected with the disposition of actors to give rational grounds for or logical explanations of their beliefs and actions. Similarly, the actions by which actors achieve desired ends are regarded as rational. Furthermore, organizational processes that embody and are governed by rational actions are considered rational. More generally, an increase in the rationality that characterizes modern organizations and society is called rationalization. This paper explores the relationship between IS and organizations within the light of the progressive rationalization of organizational processes.

The relationship between IS and organizations has been a key theoretical issue since the early years of conceptual thinking about the

---

organizational use of information technology (IT). In particular, understanding the role and impacts of IS in organizational processes has been the central focus of a wide range of quantitative and, more recently, interpretative and critical empirical studies. As the role of IS evolved from process automation and optimization (e.g. inventory control systems) to supporting decision makers (by decision support systems) and integrated management (by enterprise resource planning and executive IS) and to enabling communication and cooperation across the organization, so too did the criteria for their assessment. The impact of IS on organizational processes was consequently first assessed in terms of the efficacy of control, cost minimization and profit maximization, then in terms of improvements in the efficiency and effectiveness of decision makers and organizations and, more recently, in terms of organizational transformation, which involved the flattening of structure, increasing flexibility, empowering employees, downsizing, etc. In order to make sense of empirical data about organizational use of IS and to improve understanding of the role and impacts of IS, researchers have adopted a variety of theories ranging from organization theory, organizational behaviour and management to sociology, social psychology, anthropology and philosophy (Bjorn-Andersen and Eason, 1980; Attewell and Rule, 1984; Boland, 1985; Orlikowski and Robey, 1991; Ang and Pavry, 1994; DeSanctis and Poole, 1994; Avison and Myers, 1995; Galliers and Baets, 1998; Robey and Bourdeau, 1999; Gopal and Prasad, 2000).

This paper deconstructs the relationship between IS and the rationalization of organizational processes from a critical theory perspective. It explores the rationality potential of IS in a range of organizational processes and the resulting social and organizational consequences. For this purpose the paper proposes a rationality framework founded on the broad-ranging concepts of rationality that were defined primarily by Weber (1978) and later redefined by critical theorists (Adorno and Horkheimer, 1944; Habermas, 1984, 1987). It also draws from contributions by a number of IS researchers who have applied critical social theory to explaining the social and political impacts of IS development in an organizational context (Lyytinen and Klein, 1985; Lyytinen and Hirschheim, 1988; Klein and Hirschheim, 1991; Ngwenyama, 1991; Lyytinen, 1992; Hirschheim et al., 1996; Myers and Young, 1997). Of particularly interest to this study was Klein and Hirschheim's (1991) consideration of IS development as a form of social action and the taxonomy of rationality types they proposed for assessing various IS development methodologies. They assessed a methodology based on the degree to which it adopted a particular rationality type. While this study draws from similar sources and considers a similar range of rationality concepts, its purpose is different: it aims to develop a taxonomy of rationality types that may help explain the role of IS in the rationalization of organizational processes and the ensuing social consequences.

More specifically, the paper proposes that the social implications of IS could be better assessed (and predicted) if there is an understanding of how the use of IS in organizational processes affects the rationalization of these processes, such as increased efficiency and effectiveness. The assessment of organizational benefits and values becomes relative and will change with the rationality criteria. Systems fully justified under one rationality type could be of dubious value seen from another point of view. Similarly the use to which systems are put could change from one rationality type to another. The failure to understand the actual impact of IS on rationality could lead to surprising social consequences and, ultimately, hurt an organization. Consequently, it is suggested that, if it is possible to determine a type of rationality supported or enabled by an IS, then the expected social and organizational implications of such a system may be better understood and assessed based on the predicted or observed increase of this type of rationality.

The aims of this paper are twofold: first, the paper develops a rationality framework that provides a categorical apparatus for understanding the essential types of rationality affected by the use of IS in organizational processes and, second, by applying this framework to several case examples of IS the paper aims to demonstrate how critical analysis of the role of IS in increasing rationality (of a particular type) provides new insights into their social and organizational consequences. This paper seeks to establish that, so long as more than one rationality exists, the choice between available options will be an important factor in understanding the role and social nature of the use of IS.

In the following section the paper presents a brief historical account of rationality and rationalization in organizations and society. By drawing on different conceptions of reason and rationality it then proposes the rationality framework for examination and critical analysis of IS in organizational processes. The study then interprets three IS cases from a field study and demonstrates how the rationality framework helps explain different IS–organization relationships in the light of increasing levels of rationality that entail both substantial benefits and risks. Finally, in the concluding section the paper briefly outlines lessons learned from its interpretation and puts forward arguments for a rationality theory of IS.

On the notion of rationality

In this brief account of rationality the paper will begin with Weber's (1978) analysis of rational action and rationality as an organizing principle in society and organizations. Weber's (1958) analysis of Western rationalism marked the break with 'optimistic faith [of the Enlightenment] in the theoretical and practical rationalisation of reality' (p. 85), that is pre-Weberian thinking of reason and the rationality of actions and society, often naïvely celebrating progress, that has long been regarded as empirically oversimplified and morally overoptimistic (Brubaker, 1987). In contrast, Weber's (1978) empirical and methodological investigations of rationality and the progressive rationalization of social institutions and practices as major determinants of modernity in Western societies were profoundly critical in a way that can be thought of as being relevant for the analysis of IS in contemporary organizations.

More specifically, Weber's (1978) distinction between formal rationality and substantive rationality, which was fundamental to his empirical analysis of modern bureaucratic organizations and society as well as for his moral response to it, can be drawn on. For Weber (1978) formal rationality was 'a matter of fact' and referred primarily to the calculability of means and procedures for achieving predefined given ends. Substantive rationality, on the other hand, was 'a matter of value' and referred to the relationship between an action and some substantive end, belief or value. Bureaucracies and administrative systems, as Weber's (1978) analysis demonstrated, are governed by purely formal rationality. This is a result of processes of rationalization that are characterized by increasing reliance on expert knowledge, in particular technical knowledge, by objectification or depersonalization of power structures and authority and by more efficient control over organizational processes (including material and human components as means of production). Above all, Weber (1978) was concerned with technically enabled rationalization through efficient calculation of means to achieve given ends, without considering the value or significance of these ends, through optimization of the functionality of organizations and industrial production that reduces individuals to material means of production. Formal rationality underpinned by technology thus resulted in organizations operating like 'technically rational machines' (Weber, 1978, p. 811).

Whether these formally rational actions, organizational processes and organizations are substantively rational depends on the ends, beliefs and values, that is substantive purposes, as standards of rationality. Weber (1964) claimed that, not only are modern bureaucratic organizations governed by formal rationality, but that they are increasingly 'substantially irrational' from the point of view of egalitarian, fraternal and caritative values. Here Weber (1964) not only described the rising tensions between the formal rationality and substantive irrationality of modern organizations and society but also expressed his own position, claiming that their 'institutional foundations are morally and politically problematic' (Brubaker, 1987, p. 38).

According to Weber (1978) rationality, as an organizing principle of social life, has its basic limits. Even if actors are subjectively rational and committed to some beliefs and values and, thus, inclined to substantive rationality, their mutual judgements of rational action differ and conflict to the degree to which their beliefs and values differ and conflict. Weber (1978) maintained that belief and value conflicts cannot be resolved in a rational way. Therefore, because irreconcilable value conflict is endemic in modern organizations, substantive rationality is inherently limited.

Following Weber's (1978) critical analysis of rationality and the processes of rationalization, Adorno and Horkheimer (1944), who were renowned critical thinkers of the first generation of the Frankfurt School, viewed organizational processes and advanced capitalist societies that were governed and shaped by 'instrumental rationality'. Instrumental rationality, which is derived from the concept of formal rationality, refers to the capacity for maximizing efficiency and optimizing control of organizational and societal processes through the application of technical knowledge. (Weber's (1978) concept of *Zweickrationalitat* is translated as instrumental rationality or purposive rationality.) Predominant institutionalization of instrumental rationality and progressive rationalization of processes and society is linked to increased formalization and bureaucratization and increased coherence, calculability and control, with socially disastrous consequences. For Adorno and Horkheimer (1944) it led to 'totally administered society' and 'closed, totalitarian systems'.

In contrast to Weber (1978) and critical theorists of the first generation, Habermas (1984) did not regard rationalization as a process that inevitably leads to instrumentalization, bureaucratization, control and domination, but as an inherently ambivalent process that also entails a potential for human cooperation, emancipation and freedom. The basic thrust of Habermas' (1984, 1987) theoretical approach was his conceptual distinction between instrumental and strategic rationality (as a derivative of Weber's (1978) formal rationality) on one hand and communicative rationality (as a new conception) on the other. This distinction reflects two fundamentally different orientations of actors: an orientation towards success in the former conception of rationality and an orientation towards understanding in the latter conception of rationality. Actors oriented primarily to success can be either instrumentally or strategically rational. Habermas (1984) considered a purposeful action to be instrumental when it is performed according to technical rules and when it is judged in terms of the effectiveness of its intervention in a physical world. Similarly, an action is strategic when actors achieve their ends by influencing others. Both instrumentally and strategically rational actors intervene in the objective world in order to change its state of affairs and disregard the interests, values and norms of other fellow human beings affected by the intervention. (This paper adopts Habermas' (1984) definition here of the objective world as 'the totality of states of affairs that either obtain or could arise or could be brought about by purposeful intervention' (p. 87).)

In contrast, actors oriented to understanding are communicatively rational. While also aiming to achieve specific ends, they do so by developing inter-subjective interpretation of a situation through social interaction, thereby leading to rationally motivated agreement and coordination of their actions. Habermas (1984) called such actions communicative actions. The very nature of communicative actions implies that, unlike instrumental and strategic actions, they are essentially linguistic in nature. That is to say the actors use language for effectively building mutual understanding and a common interpretation of a situation (White, 1988). Based on this common understanding the actors coordinate their actions, thereby achieving their ends (Koningsveld and Mertens, 1992). According to Habermas (1993)

> 'Rationality' refers in the first instance to the disposition of speaking and acting subjects to acquire and use fallible knowledge. As long as the basic concepts of the philosophy of consciousness lead us to understand knowledge exclusively as knowledge of something in the objective world, rationality is assessed by how the isolated subject orients himself to representational and propositional contents. Subject-centred reason finds its criteria in standards of truth and success that govern the relationships of knowing and purposively acting subjects to the world of possible objects or states of affairs. By contrast, as soon as we conceive of knowledge as communicatively mediated, rationality is assessed in terms of the capacity of responsible

participants in interaction to orient themselves in relation to validity claims geared to intersubjective recognition. Communicative reason finds its criteria in the argumentative procedures for directly or indirectly redeeming claims to propositional truth, normative rightness, subjective truthfulness, and aesthetic harmony (p. 314).

Of particular importance for the analysis of the roles of IS is how the potential of communicative rationality can be achieved in social interaction. The key assumption here is that participants in communication understand the internal relationship between the raising of inter-subjective validity claims and the commitment to give and be receptive to arguments. Communicative rationality in essence 'signifies a mode of *dealing with* (raising and accepting) validity claims' (emphasis in the original) (Wellmer, 1994, p. 52). Besides, no validity claim is exempt from critical examination. Communicative rationality could thus be said to express a reflexive conception of human speech, which means that all validity claims can only be redeemed in human discourse and can only be justified through argumentation. This further implies that participants should inhabit a pressure-free environment where the constitutive power of the better argument reigns. Habermas (1984) also explained that validity claims are not limited to the objective world of facts (as in instrumental and strategic rationality) but also refer to the social world of values and norms, as well as to the subjective world of individual experiences, desires and feelings. (Habermas (1984) defined the social world as a 'normative context that lays down which interactions belong to legitimate interpersonal relations' (p. 88). The social world embodies moral practical knowledge in the form of norms, rules and values. Complementary to the objective and social worlds, which are external to an actor, Habermas (1984) defined an internal or subjective world 'as the totality of subjective experiences to which the actor has privileged access' (p. 100).)

The rationalization of organizations: a theoretical framework

The paper begins here with two basic conceptualizations of organizations that are distinguished by different ontological assumptions. One is organization as a system, which conceives of organizations as concrete facticities, such as aggregations of actors, physical artefacts (machinery, buildings and technology), processes and structures that are integrated in order to achieve certain goals. Accordingly, management is then defined as the activity of actors with formal status and legitimate authority intervening into the system (Gephart *et al.*, 1996). Systems such as production systems, administrative systems, decision-making processes, financial systems and the like are defined in terms of the objects, processes, states and events about which it is claimed that they exist, have happened or are likely to happen. In other words organization is defined as part of the objective world.

Alternatively, organizations may be conceived as both the system and socio-cultural life world of its members. The socio-cultural life world is the symbolically created, taken-for-granted universe of daily social activities of organizational members, which involves language, social structures and cultural tradition as the background knowledge that members share. While material production refers to the system aspect of an organization, cultural reproduction, social integration and socialization refer to the life world of its members (Habermas, 1987). Whatever happens in an organization and whatever organizational members believe, thematize, contest and talk about refer to the three worlds within the horizon of their life world. The life world 'is constitutive for mutual understanding *as such,* whereas the formal world-concepts constitute a reference system for that *about which* mutual understanding is possible' (emphasis in the original) (Habermas, 1987, p. 126). For actors in social interaction the life world is always intuitively present as the context for inter-subjective understanding of a situation and coordination of their actions. In this process elements of the life world context become explicit and subject to contestation and revision. As a result, actors engaged in social interaction simultaneously draw from and recreate their life world.

Two conceptualizations of organizations that are based on two sets of ontological assumptions determine what is considered to be subject to rationalization: systems in the first conception and both systems and the life world in the second conception. The ontological assumptions (and two concepts of organization) are used as one classification dimension for formulating the basic types of rationality and rationalization of organizations. The second dimension is determined by different approaches to reason and rationality.

As has been seen, there are two fundamentally different and mutually opposing approaches to reason and rationality. One is subject-centred reason, which is concerned with self-assertive individual interests that determine the goodness of goals and means for achieving them. Subject-centred reason is behind the individual perspective of rationality. The other is reason situated in social interaction, which is exemplified by the inter-subjectivity of mutual understanding of the participants that denotes the collective perspective of rationality. The individual and collective perspectives of rationality coupled with two views of organization (as a system or as both a system and life world) form a framework that distinguishes four basic types of rationality (Table 5.1).

From an individual perspective, assuming the view of organizations as systems (that is cell 1 in Table 5.1), rational actors pursue their interests and make decisions so as to intervene in a system and achieve predefined ends. This type of rationality, following Weber (1978), will be called formal rationality. Using Habermas' (1984) categorization, it is further differentiated as instrumental rationality and strategic rationality. Instrumentally rational actors calculate means based on technical knowledge in order to achieve given ends and disregard other human beings involved. Strategically rational actors follow rules of rational choice and achieve given ends by influencing other actors, who are perceived as rational opponents. The more an actor's knowledge of the target system is accurate, the more effective his/her intervention in the system and, therefore, the more instrumentally rational the actor. Similarly, the better an actor's knowledge of other actors (opponents) and their likely counteractions, the more effective his/her influence on these actors and, therefore, the more strategically rational the actor.

When the ontological assumptions are changed and all three worlds are included, while still looking from an individual perspective, the nature of rationality changes as actors are oriented to achieving ends that are not only related to systems (e.g. increased performance and efficiency of material production, which are defined within the objective world) but also those referring to their life world: norms and values,

Table 5.1 The rationality framework

	Ontological assumptions	
	Organizations as systems (part of the objective world)	Organizations as both the systems and life world of their members (involving the objective, social and subjective worlds)
Individual perspective (subject-centred reason)	Cell 1: formal rationality Instrumental rationality Strategic rationality	Cell 2: substantive rationality
Collective perspective (reason situated in inter-subjectivity)	Cell 4: quasi-communicative rationality or distorted communicative rationality	Cell 3: communicative rationality

justice and fairness, political or ideological affiliations, etc. (which are related to their shared social world and their inner subjective worlds). Following Weber (1978) this cell is called substantive rationality (cell 2 in Table 5.1). The issue here is that different actors pursuing their (different) interests and driven by their (different) substantive ends and values will usually disagree in their judgement of rational action. Klein and Hirschheim (1991) outlined the key assumptions behind effective application of substantive rationality, i.e. that individual actors can and do share a common set of values. Each is 'held accountable for the degree to which his actions are consistent with an ultimate value ideal' (Klein and Hirschheim, 1991, p. 160). Clearly the potential for conflict arises when actors hold differing values about either or both of their shared objective and social worlds. Conflict of this nature is particularly difficult to handle in situations where the lack of agreement over values is hidden and there is no mechanism for identifying it.

An alternative, collective perspective of rationality that becomes of great significance when viewing the organization as both a system and life world is communicative rationality, which is the third type in the framework (cell 3 in Table 5.1). As has been seen, instead of rationality defined from the position of a success-oriented, self-interested individual, Habermas (1984, 1987) defined communicative rationality from the perspective of social actors oriented to mutual understanding. Communicatively rational actors use language for developing inter-subjective understanding of a situation as a basis for a rationally motivated agreement and coordination of their action plans (aimed at achieving their, in principle, different ends). It is via communicative rationality that the hidden disagreements of substantive rationality can be identified and possibly resolved.

It has to be noted here that this study adopted what is believed to be an original idea of Habermas (1984) of communicative rationality. This paper does not see justification for distinguishing between communicative rationality and emancipatory rationality as proposed in the earlier mentioned paper by Klein and Hirschheim (1991). When communication works to create an effective shared understanding of all significant elements of a situation, it may emerge that differences of opinion among the actors are extreme enough to prevent 'consensually orientated action'. Emancipatory rationality is proposed as a way of dealing with such conflict so as to improve conditions for rational discourse. This is a departure from Habermas' (1971) original idea that emancipatory interest and emancipatory potential are implied by communicative rationality. Namely, the essence of communicative rationality is unconstrained communication, free from any force that inherently involves emancipatory potential. While 'recognizing the barriers to rational communication' and 'finding remedies on how to overcome distorting tendencies in communication' (Klein and Hirschheim, 1991, p. 171) is a relevant aspect of emancipation in social interaction, more than communicative rationality cannot be expected when dealing with it. It is communicative rationality that enables the achievement of emancipatory potential. As this study accepted Habermas' (1984) original comprehensive definition of communicative rationality that inherently involves an emancipatory potential, no need is seen for formulating a distinct emancipatory rationality.

In addition, a number of authors have criticized the concept of communicative rationality as idealistic and claimed that conditions for the realization of emacipatory potential could not be met in any practical organizational situation (Wilson, 1997). As a response to such criticism Habermas (1990) noted that a degree of communicative rationality is necessarily assumed in any practical discourse up to the point where communication breaks down. Similarly, for participants in social interaction it is meaningful to strive to realize the emancipatory potential to a satisfactory degree while understanding that the ideal of emancipation could never be fully achieved.

The conditions for communicative rationality in practice may be restricted in many ways. First, the processes of reaching understanding and communicatively achieved agreement might be limited by competing interests, underlying power asymmetry, different levels of communicative competence among actors and unequal access to knowledge and resources. For instance, actors in power positions or with privileged access to knowledge may unintentionally exert influence on others while believing to be oriented to understanding. In another scenario, they may pretend to be oriented to understanding while in fact being oriented to success, thus intentionally deceiving others. In both cases communicative rationality is distorted: unconsciously in the former and consciously in the latter. Distorted communicative rationality (paradoxically) assumes a collective perspective in order to preserve the appearance of communicative rationality and, thus, enable covert strategic acting. However, the practice of distorted communicative rationality does not genuinely take into account or refer to the life world of participants but rather remains concerned only with systems aspects (cell 4 in Table 5.1). The above distinction between the distorted and genuine communicative rationality types is conceptually very clear but may be somewhat blurry in practical situations (as will be discussed later in this paper).

Second, actors that do not belong to the same life world may engage in a cooperative activity (e.g. employees from different, geographically dislocated organizations coordinate their electronic commerce activities). They may honestly seek mutual understanding of a situation, but their ability to achieve it is limited due to the lack of their shared background knowledge. In such circumstances (cell 4 in Table 5.1) there are partial conditions for communicative rationality. Therefore, it is proposed to name it quasi-communicative rationality. While the criteria for distinguishing genuine from quasi-communicative rationality are unambiguous, in real life situations any collective (a group or organization) oriented to mutual understanding would find itself on a spectrum between the two pure types.

Table 5.1 presents a rationality taxonomy that defines three fundamental types of rationality: (1) formal rationality (instrumental and strategic), (2) substantive rationality and (3) communicative rationality. In addition, it defines a fourth type of rationality, quasi-communicative rationality and distorted communicative rationality, as derivatives of the third type of rationality.

The rationality framework presented here suggests several lines of IS inquiry. First, it indicates the rationality potential of IS–organization relationships in relation to the four (or more precisely three plus one) types of rationality. Second, it helps in understanding the meaning of rationalization (to be potentially) achieved by an IS for each type of rationality and the resulting consequences. It helps in understanding how the actual rationality (not necessarily the intended one) affected by the use of an IS determines the nature of social and organizational consequences. Third, it also provides a conceptual foundation for analysis and classification of different types of IS and the development of standards for their evaluation. The authors think that confusion as to rationality type is a significant factor in the continuing high level of dissatisfaction with IS and their failures. Next this paper briefly presents the field study and then gives examples of IS in order to illustrate these lines of inquiry.

Research methodology

This paper draws from a field study conducted in the Colruyt Company, which is a discount food chain and Belgium's third largest food retail company. The Colruyt Company evolved from a one-store enterprise in the 1960s to a highly profitable food retail chain, currently comprising some 120 stores located throughout Belgium. The company's success is attributed among other things to its innovative use of IT and its integration with the company's management philosophy regarding workers empowerment and their participation in decision making. Namely, as the late Jo Colruyt, the founder and former company board chairman, explained in a 1993 interview, from its very beginning the company used IT for exploring new innovative organization structures and enabling and supporting open and inclusive management practices that stimulated employees' initiative, responsibility and risk taking.

The field study started in 1992 and continues to this day. Initially it was an interpretive field study conducted by non-participant observers (two of the authors were among them) (Janson *et al.*, 1997a,b). Gradually, as the observers became concerned with the assumptions behind the application of IT and with the ways in which IS are used for achieving improvements in work processes and decision making, this added a critical dimension to the study. Namely, on one hand, the observers experienced the company's attempts to build genuine participative decision making and empower employees, in which the use of IS played an important role. On the other hand, the observers noted unions' accusations that company management had hidden agendas and had used IS for masking their pure commercial interests and objectives. As a result, the study adopted a critical orientation, with the aim of not only interpreting and explaining but also informing and changing practice (Cecez-Kecmanovic and Janson, 1999). Consequently, informed by critical social theory, the authors' interpretation and analysis turned the study into a critical field inquiry (Klein, 1999; Cecez-Kecmanovic, 2001).

Document analysis, in-depth interviews and non-participant observation research techniques that were developed for interpretive field studies were used in the empirical study (Walsham, 1993, 1995). However, by setting a particular research agenda (the rationalization of organizational processes) focusing on specific explanatory substantive problems (such as the assumed rationality of actors, the intended and achieved rationalization due to the use of IS and the manipulation and control of employees versus emancipation and participation) and adopting a historic perspective, the study became a critical inquiry (Cecez-Kecmanovic, 2001).

Over 30 company and union documents (both hard copies and electronic ones) were collected and analysed. Eighteen in-depth semi-structured interviews (five with the company's founder and high level managers, three with shop managers and clerks and three with union members) were conducted and analysed (e.g. interview transcripts by

M. Lengeler in 1992, 1993, 1994, 2000, 2001 and an interview with J. Colruyt in 1993) and several meetings were observed. The authors reconstructed stories from these sources about the company's IS, including the purpose and history of their development, assumptions about the context in which they were developed and implemented, the types of rationality addressed and the rationalization aimed and achieved, as well as other intended and experienced effects, risks and dangers. For the purpose of this paper, three cases of IS were selected for illustrating how the rationality framework assists understanding their roles and long-term social effects.

Interpretation of information systems from the field study within the rationality framework

Information systems for fresh food shipments

Fresh food products are shipped from the company's warehouse to individual stores in carts that have hollow outer walls. During transportation the fresh products are kept at a low temperature that is maintained by injecting a coolant into a cart's walls. Delays in unloading carts after they arrive at the store and before the fresh food products are placed in the stores' freezers are frequent. Government regulations require that fresh foods be kept below a certain maximum temperature at all times. Rejecting a fresh food shipment because its temperature exceeded the government-established temperature is expensive. In order to keep records of rejected fresh food shipments the company decided it needed to store each cart's inside temperature in a database.

Dockworkers behave in a rather robust manner when unloading delivery trucks and rough handling would result in frequent computer damage if one were located on the loading dock. Yet the loading dock is the location where the carts' temperatures need to be recorded and entered into the systems database. In short, the company needed a system that enabled measuring a cart's temperature and entering the measurement into the IS database without using a standard keyboard.

The company formed a functional group comprising a work simplification expert, an expert familiar with various instruments that measure temperature and an IS analyst. During the functional group's meeting it became clear that an exact recording of the carts' temperatures was not needed. The essential nature of any temperature measurement was binary, that is to say a cart's interior is either below or above the critical temperature. This realization led to the following solution: (1) a thermometer was used for reading a cart's inside temperature and (2) a two-colour plastic strip was glued to the loading dock's wall. One colour indicated a temperature below the critical point while the second colour meant a temperature that was above the critical point. All the dockworker had to do was to read the thermometer and point a laser gun at the appropriate colour which then resulted in entering the carts' temperature condition into the IS database. The laser gun was attached to a personal computer that was mounted out of harm's way high up the loading dock's wall. The IS was a resounding success.

When reflecting on the system's success it seems that the key issue was the correct assumption concerning the rationality of the actors involved in the process. The IS was based on the functional group's view that the reordering process was inherently instrumental. That is to say, the designers assumed that the system served an optimal distribution of fresh food products based on a temperature criterion. The real issue here is that the system designers modelled the process as involving inanimate elements of the 'objective world'. However, the computer being one of these inanimate objects that could be easily damaged by human action was the reason that the computer had to be placed out of harm's way. In short, the solution to the problem accorded with instrumental rationality and, hence, fell into the first cell of the framework used here (the organizational process of fresh food distribution as a system individual perspective). However, it could be argued that the IS used dockworkers for feeding data into the system and, thus, treated human beings as objects. The push to increase speed in the fresh food manipulation and temperature reading (that is to increase rationality) may have exerted high pressure on the dockworkers that remained hidden in the initial assessment of the IS impacts.

By viewing the IS within the rationality framework it is possible to judge the appropriateness of the rationality type chosen (in this case instrumental rationality, i.e. cell 1 in the rationality framework) and assess (1) the value of the IS based on increased instrumental rationality and (2) the potential risks involved in it (see the summary in Table 5.2).

Information systems assisting in the decrease of customer waiting times

After completing serving a customer the checkout clerk enters the number of waiting customers into the IS. This enables the calculation of customer waiting times. At the end of the shift the clerk receives the waiting times of those three customers who experienced the longest waiting time. Company documents revealed that the information is provided to nobody but the clerk. Summarized figures are made

Table 5.2 Impacts of the Colruyt Company IS on rationality

	Intended IS use and expected benefits	Observed IS use and its effects	Risks and challenges
IS for product distribution	Increase in instrumental rationality – optimization of the fresh food shipping process	IS succeeded due to focus on the instrumental rationality that governed the fresh food shipping process	Dockworkers measure temperature and feed data into the IS and are thus treated as objects; increased rationality of food shipping would imply pressure on dockworkers to speed up feeding the data
IS for decreasing customer waiting times	Increase in substantive rationality – achievement of congruent goals related to improved customer service	Increased efficiency and improved customer service Selection of checkout clerks for additional training Clerks' self-evaluation and improvement	There is a risk that managers and supervisors misuse the IS in order to obtain detailed customer waiting times and spy on individual clerks Introduction of clear policies preventing IS misuse and nurturing shared values and norms regarding employees' rights (through training) was considered key to achieving intended goals
ISID	Increase in communicative rationality – increase in mutual understanding of issues, thereby enabling cooperative interpretation of problems and assisting members in reaching agreement and consensus in decision making	Generally improved communication: open, public and efficient company-wide communication Raised awareness of company problems and increased workers' participation in problem solving	An actor can deceive others by pretending to act communicatively while in fact acting strategically The challenge is to train company members to be communicatively competent and capable of detecting the misuse of ISID and potential deception A further challenge is to ensure access to as wide a range of information as possible

available to the store and district managers and to members of upper management. An interview with a store manager confirmed that confidentiality of customer waiting time data was indeed a fact. The manager further indicated that, while it was technically possible for him to access individual clerk data, it would violate company policy.

Checkout clerks receive regular training that provides them with the necessary skills and motivation for this important task. It is the company's philosophy that employees should be supplied with information that makes self-evaluation possible. According to Colruyt (1984)

Enabling the employee to measure his own performance furthers self-appreciation [for a job well done] and being able to monitor his own performance makes the employee more independent in relation to his surroundings (p. 54).

The system has a threefold purpose: to support top managers in increasing efficiency and improving customer service, to assist selection of checkout clerks for additional training and to help clerks' self-evaluation and improvement. This is clearly an IS that assumes and impacts on all three worlds (staff are perceived not as objects, but as individuals with their experiences and desires). Moreover, rationalization is seen from the individual perspectives of clerks and managers. Consequently, the system falls into cell 2 of the framework used here (organization as a system and life world individual perspective). The Colruyt Company is a company with a carefully nurtured and articulated value system that all stakeholders share to a large degree. Central to the company's philosophy is the importance of employee work satisfaction, self-realization and social relationships. Staff members are expected to be committed to the company's goals and participate fully in the company's activities. In return the company commits to designing an environment for 'meaningful' work. In this case the clerks, the company management and the union subscribe to the same value position, namely that the clerks are independent self-directing individuals and not 'parts of the customer-serving system'. Because there is a congruency of goals between top management, store manager and clerks, founded on shared values and norms, the IS successfully serves substantive rationality.

Many retail organizations use point-of-sale systems for employee control purposes by collecting data on worker productivity, worker accurateness and worker honesty (Klein and Alvarez, 1987). Such systems can develop from an (erroneous) assumption that instrumental rationality applies (as for the previous system). Since we are clearly in the social world, a multitude of counterproductive patterns of behaviour on the part of the clerks can and has been observed to occur. Alternatively, systems like these could be considered to be based on substantive rationality but often with an implicit value system as that, for example, embodied in the 'Taylorist' work role design. Counterproductive behaviour will occur if staff do not share the value system.

So prevalent was this approach that the Colruyt Company's union members were critical of the stated system goals and declared a contribution to substantive rationality. The union suspected the use of IS for decreasing customer time in fact enabled management to exercise control and direct monitoring and constant surveillance of clerks in order to influence their behaviour (in a covert way) and, thus, achieve better performance. A union document stated that 'We do not dare think of the working conditions [of the checkout clerks] when customers are promised to be checked out within some pre-specified time period' (Adele *et al.*, 1984, p. 77). If this claim is interpreted within the rationality framework, it implies that the IS is not in fact used for increasing substantive rationality-based shared values (cell 2), but is instead used for supporting covert strategic action by management and increasing their strategic rationality (cell 1). In other words, the union pointed to the risk of misuse of the IS, which compromises its intended purpose and benefits. As a result, clear policies regarding the use of the system were introduced, thereby ensuring its contribution to substantive rationality. Understanding the impact of IS on a rationality type (in this case substantive rationality) and conditions of sustaining that impact, that is remaining committed to substantial rationality and not slipping into strategic rationality, is an important contributor to systems' success (Table 5.2).

Groupware: an interactive system for information dissemination

In keeping with the idea that information should be available to anyone, the Colruyt Company developed an interactive system for information dissemination (ISID). The system was designed for meeting the company's objectives for open, public and efficient company-wide communication. Company policy ensured that information about decisions, actions and events, as well as inter-office correspondence, outbound and inbound communication and minutes of meetings, were captured by the ISID. An important system feature was its wide accessibility (80% of information is accessible to all company members and union stewards and 20% is confidential with access limited to authorized individuals).

The key role of the ISID is to assist all employees in engaging in problem identification and problem resolution and becoming genuine actors in the decision-making process. Any employee can raise a problem via the ISID and initiate its resolution. Other employees may respond (via the ISID) with relevant information or, perhaps, a ready-made solution. If no immediate solution exists a team of self-nominated individuals is created in order to explore the problem further and to propose possible courses of action. The team chooses a moderator, based on self-nominations or nominations by others. Next, the team members establish a common understanding of the problem situation and develop one or more potential solutions to the problem at hand. This is then communicated via the ISID so that other company employees with an interest in the problem or its solution get promptly informed and participate in the problem solving. Once publicly announced on the ISID, the problem definition and its proposed solutions are open to questioning, criticism and counter-proposals. New inputs to the problem definition and its solution may trigger reassessment by team members and this process continues until, ideally, an agreement is reached. However, this is not always feasible due to time limitations (usually a period of 3 weeks) or deep-seated personal differences. In this case, the team moderator weighs all arguments, comments and counter-proposals and makes a final decision and communicates it to all employees via the ISID. The decision, for which the moderator carries ultimate responsibility, is then implemented. While the whole decision-making process is lengthy, the democratically assigned rights of the moderator ensure that the process stays within time limits that are tolerable for the retail industry.

The company has an extensive range of in-house courses available to all employees in order to assist in their personal development, i.e. improving their self-knowledge, assertiveness, job skills, inter-personal skills and communication skills, thereby encouraging free discourse regarding employees emancipation and company values, policies and practices. Employees attend these courses at their own discretion and during their regular working hours. Employees so trained share a common perspective and participate in company affairs significantly less constrained than would normally be the case. The ISID creates the technologically enabled environment that makes communicative action a reality, i.e. access to knowledge and an ability to raise and contest validity claims and provide arguments in an unconstrained discourse, thereby leading to co-created inter-subjective meanings and shared understanding of a situation. Such an understanding provides the basis for consensually motivated agreement. This IS falls into cell 3 (organization as a systems and life world collective perspective). The history of the ISID's company-wide use demonstrates how communicative rationality can be achieved in practice and how it affects all forms of life. The company has been remarkably successful in a very competitive retail industry. At the same time, it has experienced the lowest staff turnover as compared to other retail companies, the decision making has been devolved with broad-ranging employee participation and the company culture is characterized by highly valued work ethics, a cooperative spirit, self-realization and emancipation through work and collaboration.

However, the ISID carries with it the danger of being misused. Several instances of use of the ISID in which employees made an appearance of communicative rationality while in fact acting strategically have been discovered. On one occasion an employee searched and collected all submissions by another employee and used this evidence for mounting accusations against that employee. Moreover, some members of the company were worried that restricted access to confidential documents and information stored in the ISID may systematically distort communication and, thus, compromise the whole purpose of the ISID. Misuse of the ISID leads to distorted communicative rationality and the system in these instances would be classified in cell 4 rather then cell 3. In order to identify and prevent potential misuse of the ISID, the Colruyt Company introduced the practice of critical reflection and public debate about such incidents, which in some cases led to the introduction of new norms and rules.

The evidence from the Colruyt Company indicates that the application and use of a system such as an ISID for supporting communicative rationality in a social group involves the risks of dishonest use and deterioration of conditions for genuine communicative rationality. It is notable that, as for the previous IS, the use to which the ISID is put and the social conditions in which it operates are as important as the system design in establishing its communicative potential.

Conclusion

This paper proposes use of the rationality framework for critical examination of the use of IS in organizations. The types of rationality proposed are rooted in the social theories of Weber (1959, 1978),

Adorno and Horkheimer (1944) and Habermas (1984, 1987) and draw on the work of IS researchers such as Lyytinen (1992) and Klein and Hirschheim (1991). The taxonomy of rationality types is based on two dimensions: (1) organization ontology (organization as a system versus organization as both a system and life world) and (2) the orientation of actors and location of reason (an individual versus collective perspective). As a result three fundamental types of rationality are identified: (1) formal rationality (instrumental and strategic), (2) substantive rationality and (3) communicative rationality. In addition, the taxonomy identifies a fourth type, quasi-communicative rationality and distorted communicative rationality as derivatives of the third type of rationality.

This framework extends the dominant decision theoretic approach in two ways. It adds the socio-cultural life world perception of the organization to the traditional 'hard' facts and measures description that the system view of an organization takes. It differentiates between our perspectives as (self-interested) individuals and as members of a social group (a collective). Three of the rationality types (cells 1, 2 and 3) offer positive potential for an IS. An appropriate choice between the cells and effective application of the designated rationality (instrumental, strategic and substantive and communicative) will go a long way to supporting the development of IS that add business value to an organization. From the analysis here of the fourth cell, it is suggested that one factor that may be contributing to the poor value delivered by some IS supporting a social group (a team or an organization) may be perception of its needs predominantly in system terms, thereby ignoring the life world (social integration, cultural reproduction and socialization) of its members.

The IS case examples provide powerful support for the proposed framework. The first example of an IS in supporting fresh food shipments established the continuing value of the decision theoretic approach where physical factors dominate. It also shows inherent risks of increasing instrumental rationality. The second IS, which was for customer waiting times, was of particular interest. Because the case company, i.e. the Colruyt Company, had such an unusual culture and set of values this IS demonstrated how differing values produce differing results for similar IS. Substantive rationality allows this issue to be identified. The last case exemplifies the company-wide use of IS in increasing communicative rationality that achieves significant benefits for both the company and its employees. It demonstrated the way in which an IS can support and enhance the collective perspective. These examples demonstrate how, by focusing on the nature and meaning of the rationality achieved or supported by the use of an IS, the critical analysis led to improved understanding of the system's actual and potential roles in increasing the rationality of organizational processes and, thus, enabled new insights into its social and organizational consequences.

The major claim of this paper is that basic types of rationality, i.e. formal (instrumental and strategic), substantive and communicative rationality (with two derivatives, quasi- and distorted communicative rationality), with their well-established theoretical foundations (presented here only briefly) are useful constructs for examining both the potential benefits and risks of increased rationalization of organizations that are enabled and supported by IS.

Based on this study, it is suggested that the rationality framework provides a starting point for the development of a rationality theory of IS. Such a theory should further advance our understanding of the nature of the rationalization of organizations and society that is achieved by the use of IS and should help in identifying and exploring their less obvious social consequences. The rationality theory of IS would, for instance, be concerned with the contribution of IS to increasing formal rationality and the associated issues of bureaucratization and subordination, increased formalization and depersonalization of workplace relations and increased control and alienation. It would also assist researchers and practitioners in exposing (a disregard for) substantive ends and values in the design and implementation of IS and revealing attempts at using IS for concealing real objectives or illegitimate and dishonest purposes. The primary task of the rationality theory of IS would be to contribute to the critical analysis of social and organizational use of systems by drawing attention to and exposing the hidden social consequences of increased rationalization enabled and supported by IS. Conversely, the rationality theory of IS should indicate the ways in which IS can be used for meeting the communicative needs of a social group and assisting actors in increasing their communicative rationality. It is also noted here that such a theory is not intended to replace but rather to complement many other theories and perspectives that inform our understanding of IS phenomena in contemporary society and organizations.

References

Adele, B., Martens, A., Tordeur, G., Van der Smissen, B. and Muelenaer, G. (1984) *Dossier Colruyt* (EPO, Antwerp).

Adorno, T.W. and Horkheimer, M. (1944) *Dialectic of Enlightenment* (Herder and Herder, New York) (translated by J. Cumming).

Ang, J. and Pavry, F. (1994) A survey and critique of the impacts of information technology. *International Journal of Information Management*, **14**, 122–33.

Attewell, P. and Rule, J. (1984) Computing and organisations: what we know and what we don't know. *Communications of the ACM*, **27**, 1184–92.

Avison, D.E. and Myers, M.D. (1995) Information systems and anthropology: an anthropological perspective on IT and organisational culture. *Information Technology and People*, **8**, 43–56.

Bjorn-Andersen, N. and Eason, K. (1980) Myths and realities of information systems contributing to organisational rationality. In *Human Choice and Computers*, Mowshowitz, A. (ed.) (North Holland, Amsterdam), pp. 92–110.

Boland, R. (1985) Phenomenology: a preferred approach to research on information systems. In *Research Methods in Information Systems*, Mumford, E., Hirschheim, R., Fitzgerald, G. and Wood-Harper, A.T. (eds) (North Holland, Amsterdam), pp. 193–203.

Brubaker, R. (1987) *The Limits of Rationality – An Essay on the Social and Moral Thought of Max Weber* (Routledge, London).

Cecez-Kecmanovic, D. (2001) Doing critical IS research: the question of methodology. In *Qualitative Research in Information Systems: Issues and Trends*, Trauth, E. (ed.) (Idea Group Publishing, Hershey, PA), pp. 142–63.

Cecez-Kecmanovic, D. and Janson, M. (1999) Communicative action theory: an approach to understanding the application of information systems. In *Proceedings of the Tenth Australasian Conference on Information Systems ACIS'99*, Wellington, New Zealand, pp. 183–95.

Colruyt, J. (1984) What is different at Colruyt? In *There are no Gentlemen Here, Sir*, Penneman, T. (ed.) (Druco, Halle) (in Flemish), pp. 53–6.

DeSanctis, G. and Poole, M.S. (1994) Capturing the complexity of advance technology use: adaptive structuration theory. *Organization Science*, **5**(2), 121–47.

Galliers, R.D. and Baets, W.R.J. (1998) *Information Technology and Organisational Transformation* (John Wiley & Sons, Chichester).

Gephart Jr, R.P., Boje, D.M. and Thatchenkery, T.J. (1996) Postmodern management and the coming crises of organisational analysis. In *Postmodern Management and Organization Theory*, Boje, D.M., Gephart Jr, R.P. and Thatchenkery, T.J. (ed.) (Sage, London), pp. 1–18.

Gopal, A. and Prasad, P. (2000) Understanding GDSS in symbolic context: shifting the focus from technology to interaction. *MIS Quarterly*, **24**(3), 509–44.

Habermas, J. (1971) *Knowledge and Human Interests* (Beacon Press, Boston, MA).

Habermas, J. (1984) *The Theory of Communicative Action – Reason and the Rationalisation of Society*, Vol. I (Beacon Press, Boston, MA).

Habermas, J. (1987) *The Theory of Communicative Action – The Critique of Functionalist Reason*, Vol II (Beacon Press, Boston, MA).

Habermas, J. (1990) *Moral Consciousness and Communicative Action* (The MIT Press, Cambridge, MA).

Habermas, J. (1993) *The Philosophical Discourse of Modernity* (The MIT Press, Cambridge, MA).

Hirschheim, R., Klain, H. and Lyytinen, L. (1996) Exploring the intellectual structures of information systems development: a social action theoretic analysis. *Accounting, Management and Information Technology*, **6**(1/2), 1–64.

Janson, M., Brown, A. and Taillieu, T. (1997a) Colruyt: an organization committed to communication. *Information Systems Journal*, 7, 175–99.

Janson, M., Guimaraes, T., Brown, A. and Taillieu, T. (1997b) Exploring a chairman of the board's construction of organisational reality: the Colruyt case. In *Information Systems and Qualitative Research*, Lee, A., Liebenau, J. and Degross, J.I. (eds) (IFIP, Chapman & Hall, London), pp. 303–32.

Klein, H.K. (1999) Knowledge and methods in IS research: from beginnings to the future. In *New Information Technologies in Organization Processes – Field Studies and Theoretical Reflections on the Future of Work*, Ngwenyama, O., Introna, L., Myers, M.D. and DeGross, J.I. (eds) (IFIP, Kluwer Academic Publishers, Boston), pp. 13–25.

Klein, H. and Alvarez, R. (1987) The collective resource approach to systems design. In *Computers and Democracy: A Scandinavian Challenge*, Bjerknes, G., Ehn, P. and King, M. (eds) (Avery, Brookfield, VT), pp. 97–116.

Klein, H.K. and Hirschheim, R. (1991) Rationality concepts in information system development methodologies. *Accounting, Management and Information Technology*, 1(2), 157–87.

Koningsveld, H. and Mertens, J. (1992) *Communicatief and Strategisch Handelen* (Muiderberg, Coutinho, The Netherlands) (in Dutch).

Lyytinen, K. (1992) Information systems and critical theory. In *Critical Management Studies*, Alvesson, M. and Willmott, H. (eds) (Sage, London), pp. 159–80.

Lyytinen, K. and Hirschheim, R. (1988) Information systems as rational discourse: an application of Habermas's theory of communicative action. *Scandinavian Journal of Management*, 4(1/2), 19–30.

Lyytinen, K. and Klein, H.K. (1985) The critical theory of Jurgen Habermas as a basis for a theory of information systems. In *Research Methods in Information Systems*, Mumford, E., Hirschheim, R., Fitzgerald, G. and Wood-Harper, A.T. (eds) (North Holland, Amsterdam), pp. 219–36.

Myers, M.D. and Young, L.W. (1997) Hidden agendas, power and managerial assumptions in information systems development. *Information Technology & People*, 10(3), 224–40.

Ngwenyama, O.K. (1991) The critical social theory approach to information systems: problems and challenges. In *Information Systems Research: Contemporary Approaches and Emergent Traditions*, Nissen, H.E., Klein, H.K. and Hirschheim, R. (eds) (Elsevier Science Publishers, New York), pp. 267–80.

Orlikowski, W.J. and Robey, D. (1991) Information technology and the structuring of organizations. *Information Systems Research*, 2(2), 143–69.

Robey, D. and Bourdeau, M.-C. (1999) Accounting for contradictory organisational consequences of information technology: theoretical directions and methodology implications. *Information Systems Research*, 10(2), 167–85.

Walsham, G. (1993) *Interpreting Information Systems in Organisations* (Wiley, Chicester).

Walsham, G. (1995) The emergence of interpretivism in IS research. *Information Systems Research*, 6(4), 376–94.

Weber, M. (1958) *The Protestant ethic and the spirit of capitalism* (Scribner's, New York) (translated by T. Parsons).

Weber, M. (1964) *Wirtschaft und Gesellschaft, Studienausgabe*, 4th edn, Winckelmann, J. (ed.) (Kiepenheurer & Witsch, Koln) (in German).

Weber, M. (1978) *Economy and Society*, Roth, G. and Wittich, C. (eds) (University of California Press, Berkeley, CA).

Wellmer, A. (1994) Reason, Utopia, and the dialectic of enlightenment. In *Habermas and Modernity*, Bernstein, J.R. (ed.) (The MIT Press, Cambridge, MA), pp. 35–66.

White, S. (1988) *The Recent Work of Jürgen Habermas: Reason, Justice, and Modernity* (Cambridge University Press, New York, NY).

Wilson, F.A. (1997) The truth is out there: the search for emancipatory principles in information systems design. *Information, Technology and People*, 10(3), 187–204.

Section II
Grounded Theory Approaches

6
Using Grounded Theory Method in Information Systems: The Researcher as Blank Slate and Other Myths

Cathy Urquhart
Manchester Metropolitan University Business School,
Manchester Metropolitan University, Manchester, UK

Walter Fernández
Research School of Accounting & Business Information Systems,
Australian National University, Canberra, Australia

Introduction

Grounded theory method (GTM) was developed in the field of sociology during the 1960s (Glaser and Strauss, 1967) and has been adopted in many fields of research, including information systems (IS). The use of GTM in IS studies echoes the progress of interpretive research from insignificance in the 1980s (Orlikowski and Baroudi, 1991) to its current mainstream status in the IS community (Markus, 1997; Klein and Myers, 2001). Grounded theory research has been published in the major journals of IS and the methodology has gained enough support to have its own special interest group within the Association of Information Systems.

While the adoption of GTM is increasing, it is also true that as *lateadopters* of the method IS researchers confront a number of issues surrounding this methodology. A recurrent issue is the mislabelling of studies as GTM (e.g., Suddaby, 2006; Urquhart and Fernandez, 2006; Jones and Noble, 2007). Mislabelling, at best, suggests a level of ignorance; and at worst, a possible lack of integrity when the GTM label is

Reprinted from 'Using grounded theory method in information systems: the researcher as blank slate and other myths', by C. Urquhart and W. Fernández in *Journal of Information Technology*, 28, 2013, pp. 224–236. With kind permission from the Association for Information Technology Trust. All rights reserved.

used as a legitimising jargon, without a deep understanding of fundamental concepts (Glaser, 2009). For example, using the label 'GTM' as
a generic term to categorise qualitative studies where anything goes so
long the study is claimed to be grounded in empirical data (Jones and
Noble, 2007). In addition, Urquhart and Fernández (2006) described
concerns with myths regarding the nature of GTM and how these
negatively influence the adoption and the use of GTM in IS research
(see also Suddaby, 2006).

Therefore, there is significant value in addressing the case of mislabelling of GTM arising from the perspective of misinterpretations, rather
than misrepresentations. This is so because misinterpretations are often
the product of unreflective methodological knowledge, which can be
addressed by scholarly discussion. In this paper we extend our previous work (Urquhart and Fernandez, 2006) by addressing the issue of
misconceptions and myths from the perspective of the expert grounded
theorist. Hence, the objective of this paper is to advance the discussion
and treatment of unfounded, yet common, myths or beliefs that delay
the diffusion of GTM as it was intended – a rigorous methodology that
facilitates high-quality theory development. To that end, this paper lists
major misconceptions, provides ways of addressing potential shortcom-
ings and suggests practical approaches to address common problems.
The rest of this paper is structured as follows. First, we briefly describe
the nature of GTM. Second, we discuss how grounded theory has been
applied in IS to date. Third, we identify some prevalent misconceptions
about GTM in the IS community. Fourth, we then offer some flexible
guidelines to help maximise the quality of grounded theory studies,
and thus their potential for publication. Before concluding, we discuss
the status of GTM in IS as an *essentially contested concept* (Gallie, 1956).

The GTM

The GTM originated in the social sciences, with the aim of generating
empirically grounded theory (Glaser and Strauss, 1967) based on the
systematic exploration of a phenomenon. The method aims 'to discover
what is going on, rather than assuming what should go on' (Glaser,
1978: 159). In this context, the 'discovery' relates to the identification
of useful theoretical conceptualisations based on a rigorous, systematic
and comprehensive approach to data collection and analysis (Fernandez
and Lehmann, 2005).

The method, adopted in sociology and nursing during the 1970s,
took more than two decades to be used in IS. Scholars in the IFIP

Working Group 8.2 Conference Proceedings presented the first papers using GTM in IS research: Toraskar (1991) and Calloway and Ariav (1991). Two years later Orlikowski's seminal (1993) paper on CASE use in organisations significantly contributed to the legitimacy of grounded theory as a method in IS. Orlikowski (1993) justified her use of GTM on three counts: it was useful for areas where no previous theory existed, it incorporated the complexities of the organisational context into the understanding of the phenomena, and the method was uniquely fitted to studying process and change.

Thus, GTM provides an attractive research approach to IS researchers interested in issues of process and context: key concerns when studying new organisational phenomena (Van de Ven and Poole, 1989). By conducting research in its social and historical context, researchers are able to obtain a good appreciation of the work of people as active builders of their own physical and social reality (Orlikowski and Baroudi, 1991). Further, the close study of actors, their actions and their context facilitates the production of meticulous *substantive theory* (a theory developed for a particular empirical area of enquiry) that can then be integrated with existing theory (Orlikowski, 1993).

In GTM, concepts are developed through *constant comparison*. This is the process of constantly comparing instances of data in a particular category against other instances of data, to see if these categories fit and are workable. Constant comparison is the driving technique of GTM's data analysis, the facilitator of *theoretical sampling*, and thus the means to reach what Glaser and Strauss (1967) call *theoretical saturation;* the point at which data gathering stops and the substantive grounded theory begins to emerge. Theoretical sampling requires the collection of *slices of data* of varied nature, seeking both converging and diverging evidence. Theoretical sampling provides researchers with limitless options for data gathering, including different collection techniques and data types – for example, observations, interviews, historical records and surveys. The aim of theoretical sampling is to generate 'different views or vantage points from which to understand a category and to develop its properties' (Glaser and Strauss, 1967: 65). Theoretical sampling enables the researcher to sample along an emergent storyline, deciding on analytic grounds where to sample from next.

We should also emphasise that while following the GTM coding procedures are necessary, slavish adherence to those procedures is not on its own sufficient to produce good theoretical outcomes. It is possible to follow the mechanics of method and yet fail to contribute with valuable conceptualisations (Suddaby, 2006, Urquhart *et al.*, 2009, 2010).

As Klein and Myers (1999) warned with regard to their principles for interpretive field studies in IS, the analytical guidelines offered by GTM cannot be applied mechanistically; rather, the grounded theorist has to use considerable judgement to determine their applicability, pacing and relevance. Furthermore, by following the coding rules, without a deeper understanding of the method, it is possible to end up with raw data that has been mechanically elevated to a substantive theory without interpreting what is happening at each stage of coding (Suddaby, 2006).

The key purpose of grounded theory research is to propose theories that are primarily and strongly connected to data collected in a substantive field (Glaser and Strauss, 1967). However, the application of grounded theory in IS has ranged from its use purely as a qualitative data analysis method producing context-bounded descriptions, through to its use to generate full-blown theory (Urquhart *et al.*, 2010). Yet, the remodelling of GTM into a tool for qualitative descriptions (Glaser, 2001) is not unique to IS as other disciplines have noted that GTM is often used for purposes other than generating theory (Becker, 1993; Benoliel, 1996; Green, 1998; Elliott and Lazenbatt, 2005).

Although GTM guidelines can enable researchers to derive theory that is empirically valid (Glaser and Strauss, 1967; Martin and Turner, 1986; Eisenhardt, 1989), these guidelines are designed to allow for flexibility (Charmaz, 2006); this underlines the need to have a good comprehension of the overall method, its demands and its possibilities.

Like all sophisticated research approaches, GTM requires a degree of careful training to master. Researchers new to GTM can benefit from substantial training in conducting empirical fieldwork, and from expert guidance in all stages of analysis, including how to integrate the extant literature during the different phases of the study. If these aspects of GTM are not sufficiently mastered, it is likely to fail in the same way that simply running a bunch of numbers that one picks up from various sources through statistical analysis software can fail the under-trained quantitative analyst.

To better understand GTM misconceptions, in the next two sections we use examples from articles showing a high 'degree of conceptualisation and theory scope' (a criterion proposed by Urquhart *et al.*, 2010) found in the top two IS journals, *Information Systems Research* and *MIS Quarterly*. We selected these journals for practical reasons: they provide sufficient evidence to illustrate our discussion without turning the article into a literature review. However, we strongly advise to read the excellent body of GTM work published at outlets such as *Journal of Information Technology*, *European Journal of Information Systems*,

Information Technology & People, Journal of the Association of Information Systems, Information & Management, and *Information Systems Journal*.

In addition, it is important to note the proceedings of IFIP 8.2 Conferences, whose scholars played a pioneering role in the diffusion of GTM in IS as well as the strong tradition of grounded theory articles in the *European Journal of Information Systems*, dating from the early 1990s. For an early example of theory building using Strauss and Corbin, for instance, we recommend Galal (2001). For an early example of innovative adaptations of grounded theory in IS, see Lings and Lundell (2005).

Addressing key misconceptions

This section discusses the most common misconceptions about GTM that need to be addressed. There is a deceptive simplicity to a number of key misconceptions about GTM, which, in our view, act as a significant obstacle to leveraging the theory building potential of GTM in IS research.

Misconception 1 – The researcher as a blank slate

The premise that the grounded theory researcher is a 'blank slate', who launches into data collection without first looking at the literature, is a particularly pervasive misconception (McCallin, 2003; Andrew, 2006). This misconception about GTM is possibly most harmful, because understanding the role of the literature in GTM is essential to producing good grounded theories. Also, one reviewer noted: *[b]lank slater thinking seems to mean the grounded theorist is to forget what they know in order to learn what they need. This naïve articulation is one of the most pernicious symptoms of ignorance regarding the demands that grounded theory approaches place on the scholar.*

The origin of this misconception can be attributed to a misinterpretation of one of the basic tenets of grounded theory: *the researcher must set aside the extant theory.* Yet, this tenet does *not* imply GTM researchers must *ignore* the existing literature and become a *tabula rasa.*

The idea of the researcher as a blank slate has at its base a superficial reading of the literature. Glaser and Strauss (1967: 33) warned researchers against the extant literature *dictating prior to the research, 'relevancies' in concepts and hypothesis.* However, construing this warning as a dictum requiring a blank mind is either a misrepresentation or a misinterpretation. The very crux of GTM is the rigorous generation of theory using systematic procedures, analytical skills and theoretical sensitivity, which emanate from knowledge of the extant literature. We must also emphasise that *all* the key texts of GTM stress the need to engage the resultant theory with the literature; these texts also explain how this integration should be done (including Glaser and Strauss, 1967; Glaser, 1978; Strauss, 1987; Strauss and Corbin, 1990; Glaser, 1998).

In GTM, known theories are set aside for potential future comparison, which are done only *if* the analysis of the data indicates the relevance of these theories. This is the manner in which the GTM researcher enables the emergence of patterns from the empirical data, and also the way in which extant theory is integrated into the study. *Setting aside* implies that the theorist understands the role of both knowledge and detachment to a grounded study. Theoretical and practical knowledge can enhance the theoretical sensitivity of researchers while their ability to detach from the acquired knowledge is critical to set aside preconceptions and look the data anew (Charmaz, 2006). This skill allows researchers to access existing knowledge of theory without being trapped in the view that it represents the final truth (as also suggested by Walsham, 1995).

Thus, grounded theory offers a way to deal with pre-existing knowledge bias and a way of integrating this knowledge with empirical data. This is necessary because *[e]ach of us brings to the analysis our own biases, assumption, patterns of thinking, and knowledge gained from experience and reading* (Strauss and Corbin, 1990: 95). At times, this may require delaying readings on the substantive area of research that might *stifle or contaminate or otherwise impede the researcher's effort to generate categories* (Glaser, 1992: 31).

Related to bias and contamination is the researcher's level of maturity. Strauss (1987) explains that the recommendation to delay the scrutiny of related literature applies less to experienced researchers, as they are more practiced at subjecting theoretical statements to comparative analysis – that is, testing and contrasting empirical data against the researcher's biases, assumptions and knowledge. GTM considers the researcher's knowledge, experiential and theoretical, as critical to achieving the required level of theoretical sensitivity and thus to enabling theoretical memoing, constant comparison and theoretical integration (Glaser, 1992)

In the section 'Addressing the misconceptions: some guidelines' of this paper we will provide some guidelines for engaging with the literature in a GTM study, and for integration of the literature at write-up stage.

Misconception 2 – GTM is inflexible

Because of its complex nature and conflicting guidance about how to apply the method, GTM is sometimes seen as inflexible and difficult to apply. One reason for the conflicting guidance is the well-documented split between Glaser and Strauss in 1990, on the publication of *Basics of Qualitative Research* by Strauss and Corbin. Glaser objected to Strauss and Corbin's coding paradigm, which was at the centre of their book. The coding paradigm suggested that the researcher looks for context, conditions, action/interactional strategies, intervening conditions and consequences as a guide to grouping and establishing relationships between codes, and seemed to be mandatory. Glaser (1992) objected to the coding paradigm and to the line-by-line coding proposed by Strauss and Corbin (1990). Glaser argued that the way of doing research presented by Strauss and Corbin was no longer grounded theory due to the forcing effect of the coding paradigm. The often quoted statement *If you torture the data long enough, it will give up!* (p. 123) represents the most condensed version of Glaser's appreciation of the Straussian approach, as it was to be called, to differentiate it from the Glaserian approach (Stern, 1994). Glaser also asserted that *forcing by preconception constantly derails it [the research] from relevance* (Glaser, 1992: 123).

However, restrictive it may be perceived by some grounded theorists, the Strauss and Corbin approach to GTM was a publishing success. The book was effectively promoted and distributed by a major publishing company; since then it has been widely available and adopted.

In contrast, Glaser published his books using a small publishing company, Sociology Press, which he founded in 1970 to preserve the integrity of the method while contributing to its development.[1] The narrow focus of the publishing company and its more modest operation restricted the diffusion of what Glaser calls *classic* grounded theory. Classic grounded theory scholars mainly congregate around Sociology Press, the Grounded Theory Institute and the *Grounded Theory Review Journal*; all these entities were either created or facilitated by Glaser. Thus, the diffusion of classic GTM to a great extent depends on these scholars and their 'word-of-mouth' promotions.

Each strand has its adherents. This split among GTM researchers can be partially attributed to fuelling the debate about the very nature of grounded theory. The Glaserian approach suits researchers seeking flexibility. The Straussian approach suits those seeking a more prescriptive method. It should also be noted that the dispute has an interesting codicil: after 18 years, the coding paradigm is all but abandoned in Corbin and Strauss (2008), where it is no longer mandatory, and is simply represented as one of many possible analytical tools.

The conflicting advice on approaches also leads some people to think that GTM is difficult, and perhaps risky for Ph.D. students, as they may find themselves in the firing line of competing approaches, each with passionate supporters. An example of this kind of thinking can be seen in a recent blog (Myo, 2012). This contrasts markedly with our own positive experiences, and that of our students, in using GTM. In our view, it is simply a case that one needs to be aware of the intellectual history of GTM, as opposed to being worried by that history. We will return to this issue of positioning in our guidelines section.

Moreover, the notion that GTM is inflexible is not borne out when one considers its widespread use. Furthermore, while the Straussian approach can be perceived as less flexible, and with a higher risk of forcing preconceptions, evidence from IS literature depicts a more positive outlook (see Table 6.A1 in Appendix). On the basis of this evidence, we cannot conclude that GTM is inherently inflexible, *in any of its forms,* at least when it is used by expert researchers. In other words, the reasons for the debate between the espoused views on GTM are not corroborated in practice at the top level of IS publishing.

In IS, as Table 6.A1 shows, GTM has been used in accordance with different research needs and epistemological positions; it has been applied as the sole method and in combination with others; it has produced new theories; and it has been used to show the relevance of extant theories from other fields to IS research. While each article in Table 6.A1 presents important aspects of the method and how it can be used, one example, Ransbotham and Mitra (2009), is particularly interesting, as it shows how theory generation and testing can be (a) conducted sequentially to generate theory and then test the generated theory; and (b) also effectively reported in a single article. This exemplar is likely to inspire those inclined to pursue multi-paradigm research.

Misconception 3 – GTM produces low-level theories that don't do much

This issue has its foundation in the view that GTM's concern with a limited substantive field prevents the development of theories with greater appeal in terms of usability or generalisability. Some scholars indicate the need to break away from focusing on micro-phenomena as this prevents the grounded theorist from enriching the research by considering macro-structures (Layder, 1993, cited in Walsham, 1995). In fact, the method encourages the production of theories that have explanatory and predictive powers beyond the substantive fields from which the theory emerged, as detailed in the original book (Glaser and Strauss, 1967). Below, we discuss reasons for low-level theoretical outcomes, ways to avoid common traps that could derail the achievement of valuable theoretical results.

One of the potential causes for low-level theory can be seen as a consequence of the type of 'bottom up' coding, which GTM employs. As Charmaz (2006) points out, the logic of 'discovery' in the GTM coding process enables researchers to look at the data anew and to produce rich theory, closely linked to the data. Indeed, this is a major strength of GTM. Closeness to empirical data is necessary to produce substantive grounded theory. However, one must not stop reading at this point. Closeness to data is a necessary but not sufficient condition to achieve a valuable theoretical outcome. The GTM literature acknowledged from its beginning that substantive theory development can shade into formal theories (Glaser and Strauss, 1965, 1967; Glaser, 1978, 2007; Strauss, 1987; Strauss and Corbin, 1990). Yet, the early definitions of substantive and formal theory were unclear (Alvesson and Sköldberg, 2000) and this lack of precision caused confusion and misinterpretations (Glaser, 2007).

Indeed, GTM places an obligation on the researcher to keep working on theory development, until what in grounded theory parlance is known as 'formal theory' is achieved (Strauss, 1987; Glaser, 2007).[2] The Straussian strand of grounded theory further considers the problem of scaling up by virtue of the conditional matrix (Strauss and Corbin, 1990: 161), which allows the integration of more 'macro' issues into the resulting theory. The conditional matrix considers conditions and consequences in a set of concentric circles, which represent successive layers of context – groups, sub-organisational, institutional level, organisations and institutions, community, national, and international.

While substantive theories can provide suitable explanation of a phenomena in a particular setting, formal grounded theories can transcend the areas from which the initial substantive theory emerged, becoming more general in explaining the core variable that emerged from the substantive theory. This is more useful in predicting or anticipating outcomes. The level of 'formality' refers to how well the theory (a) focuses only on general categories and hypotheses, (b) presents conceptualisations that are highly generalisable for practical application across a number of contexts, and (c) has been developed to generalise a core category emergent from a substantive grounded theory (Glaser, 2007). An early example of a formal theory is *social value of people,* which was partially derived from the substantive theory of *social loss of dying patients.* In both of these cases, the social loss or social value are calculated on the basis of apparent and learned characteristics of the person; however, the formal theory requires comparative analysis across different substantive groups (Glaser and Strauss, 1967).

Both substantive and formal grounded theories are expected to produce good research outcomes when the research is well planned and executed. Yet, the low level of theoretical outcomes in some studies often indicates a partial understanding (or a partial application) of the methodology – for example, studies that follow GTM techniques only to the extent that they produce rich descriptions based on coding, categorisation and sorting of data without due regard to conceptualisation (Suddaby, 2006). When the coding activity produces description rather than abstract conceptualisations, studies run the risk of not being scalable to theory, and thus remaining tied to the details of the substantive field without being able to achieve the desired theoretical outcome (Glaser, 2001). Reflecting on this bias for description, Glaser (2001: 94) stated *I am always amazed, given the pressure to generalize, the ease of doing it with GT, and the fact that all substantive GTs have general implications, at how many GT researchers do not develop or even mention the generalization of their basic social process or core variable, or sub-core categories.*

The partial application of GTM often occurs when studies are concluded before theoretical coding (establishing relationships between concepts) has been done. In these cases, researchers are likely to produce theories that are low in value: neither well presented nor well integrated with the relevant literature. Grounded theorists have the necessary freedom to apply a theoretical lens *that fits the data*, whatever that theoretical lens is, *so long as the lens fits and is not forced on the data.* This is particularly so in the case in *classic* grounded theory, but since Corbin's departure from demanding a particular coding paradigm (Corbin and Strauss, 2008) it applies to both Straussian and Glaserian approaches. Glaser (1978) suggests several routes to extending and scaling up the theory, including considering how the substantive theory relates to formal models and processes. To this end, researchers could opt to use *theoretical codes*, to assist in the relating of categories. Theoretical codes are useful extant theories that offer the potential to make the substantive codes relevant and understandable, integrating the substantive codes and relating them in new patterns (Glaser, 1978).

As the number of theoretical codes is ever-growing, the ability to see and to apply theoretical codes depends only on the researcher's *theoretical sensitivity.* That is, their awareness of extant formal theories from a range of fields (Glaser, 2005). This sensitivity is gained over time via constant interaction between the scientist and the literature, studying a myriad of theories. The theoretical coding polymorphism of classic GTM is possible precisely because *GT does not have an epistemology with an attached theoretical perspective that provides one set of TCs [theoretical codes] to the exclusion of others* (Glaser, 2005: 17).

The IS literature offers several instances where formal theories were used successfully as theoretical lenses to present a coherent view of the emerging substantive theories. For example, Levina's (2005) study of collaborative practices on information systems development (ISD) projects used Schön's (1983) concept of reflection-in-action to propose that multi-party collaborative practice can be cognizedas constituting a 'collective reflection-in-action'. This concept transcends the specific substantive field to be applicable to other multi-party collaborative projects, beyond the scope of ISD practice from which the theory emerged.

Barrett and Walsham (1999) also provide a good example of how to seek and use theoretical codes in grounded theory studies. In this case, the researchers were well aware of the literature and the different, often contradictory, viewpoints regarding the role information and communication technology (ICT) plays in transforming work practices. Yet, they consciously remained flexible and open to emergence, and it was only after completing the first round of data analysis that the relevance (or fit) of a particular theoretical lens became apparent. The usefulness of Giddens's theory on social transformation (Giddens, 1990, 1991) was not conceived *a priori* but rather *developed as part of an emergent process during periods of reflection between different stages of this intensive longitudinal research* (Barrett and Walsham, 1999: 6). Further, the theoretical lens was found after analysing 36 interviews and intensively reviewing the literature for theories that would fit the data. As such it was a valuable tool to understand the role of ICT in transforming the work at the London Market (Barrett and Walsham, 1999). By using Giddens's social transformation theory as a theoretical code, the researchers extended the substantive grounded theory, increasing its generalisability to other cases in which work practices are substantially transformed by technology adoption. In addition, the study contributed to the extension of social transformation theory to consider the role of information technology in the transformation process.

While GTM can be and has been used to produce rich descriptions of high quality and value (i.e., Gopal and Prasad, 2000), using GTM for descriptive work stops short of achieving its full potential – that is, producing theoretical conceptualisations that are well integrated with the extant theory. Our view on this issue is consistent with GTM literature: the conceptualisation level can be improved by the extra step of engaging formal theories to further explain and integrate the emerging substantive theory. While not mandatory, this step is an important component of the method that should be seriously considered in order to achieve the full potential of GTM.

Misconception 4 – GTM is positivist/interpretivist/critical

Grounded Theory has long been plagued with debates about its underlying philosophical position, a good example in IS being the Bryant (2002) and Urquhart (2002) debate about the inherently positivistic nature of GTM. In health research, Annells (1996) points to statements by Glaser (1992) about grounded theory focusing on *concepts of reality* (p. 14) and searching for *true meaning* (p. 55) as evidence of a critical realist position. In management research, Fendt and Sachs (2008) reject both the idea that theory is something neutral to be discovered in the data, and the idea that what is discovered is objective. However, the assumption that GTM is inherently positivist or interpretivist is not supported by the Straussian or Glaserian literature or by the extant GTM research literature.

Grounded theory was conceived as a *general method with no explicit correct epistemology* in which *all is data* is a key and consistent dictum (Glaser and Strauss, 1967; Glaser, 1978, 1998). Thus, GTM as a research method is orthogonal not only to the type of data used; it can be appropriated by researchers with different assumptions about knowledge and how it can be obtained.

Hence, the assertion that GTM *is* positivist, interpretive, critical realist or constructivist is neither supported by the grounded theory literature, nor based on research practice. GTM is in many ways neutral and should be seen as a container into which any content can be poured (Charmaz, 2006: 9). This level of epistemological neutrality makes GTM a highly useable research method.

The general nature of GTM is corroborated by the IS literature, where researchers with dissimilar epistemological stances successfully used grounded theory to attain valuable research outcomes. Orlikowski (1993) stated that the three characteristics of grounded theory – inductive, contextual and processual – fitted with an interpretive research orientation. This can be usefully contrasted with Levina and Ross (2003), which related their emergent findings to a positivistic theory of core competences and organisational design. However, Kirsch (2004) adopted a 'scientific realism' or 'soft positivist' approach (Madill *et al.*, 2000).

More broadly, a qualitative method, depending on its underlying epistemology, can be positivist, interpretivist or critical (Orlikowski and Baroudi, 1991; Myers, 1997; Klein and Myers, 1999, 2001). Similarly, qualitative GTM 'in use' is influenced by the different underlying epistemologies guiding the grounded theory studies. Thus, a good advice for grounded theorists can be found in Madill *et al.* (2000: 17) *qualitative researchers have a responsibility to make their epistemological position clear, conduct their research in a manner consistent with that position, and present their findings in a way that allows them to be evaluated appropriately.*

Finally, GTM embodies some practices that are useful for all qualitative researchers, regardless of philosophical position. The idea of overlapping data collection and analysis (Langley, 1999), where the emerging theoretical storyline directs successive data sampling, ensures a grounded approach to theory building even if GTM processes are not otherwise used. Similarly, the interplay between theorising and data categorisation in GTM is not dissimilar to the principle of dialogical reasoning in Klein and Myers (1999).

Addressing the misconceptions: some guidelines

In this section, we advance three guidelines that help to navigate some of the misconceptions discussed above. These guidelines give practical advice to researchers when they feel that they are coming across barriers to GTM use, and are based in our long-standing experience of many different GTM projects. The intention is for these to be working guidelines that are flexible, as is GTM.

Guideline 1 – Use a phased literature review

Glaser and Strauss (Glaser and Strauss, 1967: 3) argue researchers should not approach reality as a tabula rasa, but must have *a theoretical perspective* that will help them to abstract significant categories from the data. To define this perspective, a grounded theory investigation typically starts with a *pre-study* literature review to define the problem domain and the appropriate methodology for the study. Thus, the appropriate use of the literature in GTM can be seen as a question of *phasing* as shown in Figure 6.1 (McCallin, 2003; Martin, 2006). The first phase is *non-committal* in which the researcher scans the literature to develop theoretical sensitivity and find the research problem and learns about the methodology. The second phase is *integrative* in which the researcher compares the emergent theory with extant theories to render the new theory in the context of existing knowledge and thus make the substantive theory more valuable.

During the *non-committal phase*, the GTM researcher conducts a preliminary literature review to (a) help develop theoretical sensitivity

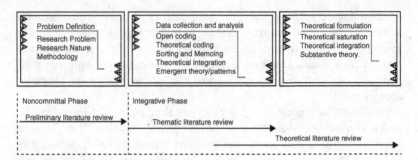

Figure 6.1   Key GTM activities and the continuous role of the literature review

before conducting fieldwork and (b) understand the nature and the form of the enquiry. The preliminary literature review informs about existing theories, how other investigators may have addressed aspects of our research problem or attacked similar situations in other areas. The objective is *not* to develop a research question, as in other types of studies, but rather to define the scope for exploring a wider research problem. During this phase, potentially relevant literature should be noted for future comparison. This is done keeping in mind the key objective of generating theory that will engage with the literature based on relevance and fitness. In short, this review is conducted *on the fundamental understanding that the generated grounded theory will determine the relevance of the literature, never the converse.*

For novel grounded theorists, the preliminary literature review must involve reading the central works explaining the method and the philosophy of research behind GTM (McCallin, 2003). This work enables would-be GTM researchers to understand the methodology, the method and the coding techniques to be used. Strauss and Corbin (1990: 4), define *methodology* as '*a way of thinking about and studying social reality*', *method* as '*a set of procedures and techniques for gathering and analyzing data*' and *coding* as '*the analytic processes through which data are fractured, conceptualized, and integrated to form theory*'. Failing to study the methodology in sufficient detail raises significantly the risk of doing a bad grounded theory study – that is, a study in which the emergence process is jeopardised, reaching saturation is difficult, and the result shows poor conceptual densification or inadequate integration with extant theories. It also raises the risk of mislabelling (Jones and Noble, 2007).

During the *integrative phase* we suggest that two types of literature reviews are conducted: thematic and theoretical. Once the empirical study is underway and the theoretical concepts start to emerge, the researcher returns to the extant literature to help develop the emerging concepts. This is called *thematic* literature review. The primary concern at this stage is to seek converging and diverging literature to compare against observed patterns and emerging theoretical conceptualisations. In this sense, the literature is treated as theoretical data that enrich the study.

It is likely that, while comparing emerging patterns or concepts against the literature, researchers will realise the need for further theoretical sampling, to progress toward saturation. Thus, the thematic review is a very important activity with a substantial role to play in the advancement of the study and also in the quality of the emerging conceptualisations, which become more robust and well-informed. This is also an intellectually stimulating process, as the researcher generates new ideas and theoretical memos, thanks to the exposure to the literature and its comparison against the substantive data. It should be noted that the role of theoretical memos is fundamental in theoretical emergence (Glaser and Strauss, 1967; Glaser, 1978, 1998).

Also during the integrative phase, the *theoretical* review becomes important. That is, once the core pattern has been defined, it is important to seek its integration with relevant theories before the theorist finally formulates a grounded theory. This integration relates the phenomenon observed in the substantive field to the wider literature in that same or a related field. By doing so, both the value of the proposed grounded study and its publication opportunities are enhanced.

An example from IS of this process of engaging with the literature can be found in Orlikowski's (1996) study of transformation of work practices and organisational structures. The study's central concern was to observe and learn from the actions of the participants via the analysis of rich empirical data from interviews, observations and documents. By letting the empirical evidence guide the study, Orlikowski was able to understand *what was going on* in the studied field.

Orlikowski (1996) shows how to use the data analysis process to guide conceptual emergence and to engage with the extant literature. Starting from a suitable question (an exploration of how actors were dealing with a particular problem), Orlikowski studied the substantive field to identify issues and topics, and to detect patterns. The data analysis provided Orlikowski with the fundamental knowledge to incorporate relevant thematic literature. In this study, the extant literature was used to increase theoretical sensitivity (being able to understand the observations in a wider theoretical context) and to enrich and integrate the emerging conceptualisations. By integrating emerging concepts and patterns with the literature, Orlikowski (1996) presented a valuable,

144 Cathy Urquhart and Walter Fernández

well-informed, substantive theory that advanced our knowledge on organisational transformation, changing long-held perspectives on planned change, technological imperative and punctuated equilibrium. This research outcome was achieved by following an effective interpretation of the canons of the method, which included a successful theoretical integration with the extant literature.

Guideline 2 – Use GTM flexibly but knowledgeably

Given that GTM in use can be flexible, how should IS researchers new to GTM maximise their chances of using GTM in a manner that suits their research objectives? We propose the following three action points:

1. Since GTM is more than a collection of techniques, it is critical to become acquainted first with Glaser and Strauss (1967) and then to read as much of the GTM as possible before proceeding to data collection (see Table 6.1). While reading the central books is essential during the preliminary phase of the study, researchers are certain to return to these texts seeking further understanding of the method (Ekstrom, 2006). This is simply good scholarship and can be described as understanding the intellectual tradition of GTM. It is also very practical advice – knowing the roadmap, as it was set by the originators of GTM, facilitates the research process, contributes to avoiding unnecessary confusion, enables conceptual emergence and improves research outcome.

2. The use of GTM in the IS literature shows that research value can be achieved in different ways. Thus, we advise IS researchers to be clear about the purpose for which they are using GTM – to leverage the strength of very well-defined coding procedures for the purposes of data analysis, or for the purposes of building theory.

3. Undeniably, the alignment of research objectives, philosophical position, skills, data and methods is as important in GTM as it is to any other form of research. Researchers should carefully appraise their skills against the multiple demands of the method. Chapter 15 of Glaser (1998) provides suitable ideas as to how to develop the necessary knowledge and skills, while Chapter 2 of Glaser (1978) provides a clear analysis of the demands imposed by the method.

Guideline 3 – When writing up the GTM article, consider exemplars in our field

The cycle of a GTM study is completed when the theorist can add to the current literature; once the theory has been generated from the data

Table 6.1 Central GTM books

Book	Description
Glaser, B.G., and Strauss, A.L. (1967) *The Discovery of Grounded Theory: Strategies for qualitative research*	Provides a good understanding of GTM historical background, its research philosophy and processes. Explains the key role of constant comparison. This book is a fundamental reading for any grounded theorist.
Glaser, B.G. (1978) *Theoretical Sensitivity*	Covers important aspects of theoretical sensitivity, pacing, sampling, coding, memos, sorting and writing, and provides a very important discussion on basic social processes. Introduces the idea of theoretical coding.
Strauss, A.L. (1987) *Qualitative Analysis for Social Scientists*	Provides advice for the first time user of GTM, especially around relating efforts to the technical literature, and the process of coding in a group.
Strauss, A.L. and Corbin, J.M. (1990). *Basics of Qualitative Research: Grounded theory procedures and techniques*	A widely read yet controversial book because of its rendering of GTM. Gives very clear procedures for GTM, but at the same time offers a narrower view of the method.
Glaser, B.G. (1992). *Emergence vs Forcing: Basics of grounded theory analysis*	This book is the response to Strauss and Corbin (1990). Helps to understand the divergent views held by Glaser and by Strauss and Corbin. It discusses in detail the significance of the issue of 'forcing' in GTM. Yet, reading this book without a good understanding of previous texts can obscure more than illuminate.
Glaser, B.G (1998) *Doing Grounded Theory: Issues and discussions*	This key book discusses practical aspects of the method, including: reading the literature, forcing, generating concepts, theoretical sampling, theoretical coding, memoing, sorting and writing.
Glaser, B.G (2005) *Grounded Theory Perspective III: Theoretical coding*	This book broke new ground in thinking about theoretical coding and the process of relating categories. It introduced 23 new 'coding families' to complement the original 18 coding families in the 1978 book.

through constant comparison and integration (Martin, 2006). Thus, considering how to present literature in a GTM article, and how a GTM article should be presented, are non-trivial issues for authors.

Clearly, there are tensions between the way grounded theorists work with the literature while doing the research and the way the literature is traditionally presented in journal articles. On the one hand, if the literature is discussed first, as is common with other methods, authors may feel that they are not truly representing the manner in which the literature was incorporated into the study. On the other hand, if the literature is presented later, the reader may not have the necessary information to appropriately follow and evaluate the argument. Suddaby (2006) provides a reasonable solution to this dilemma: *authors can note that, although they are presenting theoretical concepts in a traditional manner (i.e., up front in the study), the concepts did, in fact, emerge from the study.*

Several articles in the IS literature can serve as exemplars to those researchers aiming their papers at top-tier journals. This section is not intended to cover all these papers, but rather to present a few exemplars covering different types of application of grounded theory, as published in top IS journals. We first present a case of a full use of GTM (Barrett and Walsham, 1999); then a case of a full GTM study without adopting a single theoretical lens (Garud and Kumaraswamy, 2005); followed by a case in which a particular technique suitable for the method is explained (Hunter and Beck, 2000); and finally a case of partial use of GTM without incurring mislabelling (Montealegre and Keil, 2000).

The Barrett and Walsham (1999) article on electronic trading and work transformation in the London insurance market provides an excellent example of how to conduct and report GTM in a manner that is both comprehensive and easy to read and follow. The treatment of the literature during the study follows a grounded theory approach. Theoretical sensitivity was present and acknowledged (i.e., IT and transformation literature). Emerging data were sorted into themes, and these were analysed without a preconceived coding scheme, and then integrated with the extant literature. The grounded themes guided theoretical sampling during this intensive longitudinal exploration. Finally, the substantive theory was integrated with a Giddens (1991) theory on social transformation.

The core purpose of Barrett and Walsham (1999) was to present the conceptual scheme emerging from their study. The genius of the article is that while presenting the study to the reader in a traditional form, it also provides readers with a good appreciation of the sequence in which the theory was developed. The process is made explicit *The approach taken in research did not follow a top-down method where a conceptual scheme was developed and the fieldwork then conducted to confirm its value* (p. 6). The authors explained the research activities in sufficient detail, and readers of the article are informed about what they did, how they did it and why they did it during their research. Yet, the paper remained focused on the core objective of explaining the emerging conceptual scheme.

Another excellent example of research that followed the principles of GTM can be found in Garud and Kumaraswamy (2005). The paper reports a longitudinal study in which the authors engaged in a systematic exploration process of theoretical sampling, inductive data analysis and development of grounded theory, in order to generalise from case to theory (following the approach outlined in Lincoln and Guba, 1985). This paper shows how to integrate the literature and how to explain the research process the data analysed (interviews, ethnographic observations, reports, presentations, white papers and employee surveys). The paper also shows how a rich case description can be used to inform and situate the reader, before presenting the conceptualisation of the studied process.

The explanation of the use of GTM can be extensive or brief, depending on the nature of the article. Hunter and Beck's (2000) article on the use of repertory grids within a GTM study focused on describing how a particular technique, the role construct repertory test (RepGrid) developed by psychologist George Kelly. Thus, the paper spends little time on grounded theory itself, but a substantial effort was devoted to explaining how and why the proposed technique can be used to elicit information during qualitative interviews of experts in cross-cultural studies.

It should also be noted that GTM is not always the driving paradigm. Some studies only apply GTM techniques and principles to data analysis, without getting involved in theoretical sampling and often with the purpose of generating rich descriptions. In such cases, the study cannot claim to be GTM without incurring mislabelling. In these cases, Montealegre and Keil (2000) serve as an example of correct methodological labelling, as they do not claim that their study is GTM, but rather it is appropriately labelled as a case study that uses GTM data analysis techniques. These authors present their research procedures in detail in an appendix, allowing the reader to be informed about an important aspect of their approach, without getting distracted from the main argument.

Discussion

One motivation for writing this paper is that we were aware that GTM remains a contested concept in IS (Bryant and Charmaz, 2007). We have shown that there are important misunderstandings about GTM in IS (Suddaby, 2006; Urquhart and Fernandez, 2006) and that a more scholarly approach to GTM can serve to further the use of the methodology. In doing so we add to the plurality of IS research methods available to IS researchers (Lee, 2010; Taylor *et al.*, 2010).

When discussing the contested nature of GTM in general, Bryant and Charmaz (2007) argue that GTM has high recognition value, and claims for its use provide partial validation of a researcher's study. This methodological accreditation is one of the causes of 'mislabelled' grounded theory, where the label 'GTM' becomes a convenient description of any coding method, and confers respectability on that method because of the recognition value of GTM. Certainly there are many cases of mislabelling in IS, including instances of mislabelling where the role of GTM is downplayed for reasons of the review process – this also reveals the contested nature of GTM in IS.

An *internally complex character* is also a feature of a contested concept, and the fact that GTM has a long and complex intellectual history pays tribute to that character. The complexity of GTM, coupled with its surface simplicity, makes it subject to misconceptions. The complexity is manifested in the *delayed effect,* which characterises the method (Glaser, 1978, 1998). In IS, this internally complex character is no less obvious than in any discipline – we too have many different interpretations of GTM in evidence.

Contested concepts also have a variety of descriptions. This is well illustrated by how GTM has evolved into either Glaserian or Straussian versions, and other characterisations such as Charmaz (2006). In IS, this is evident in the different descriptions of the method (Orlikowski, 1993; Walsham, 1995) and also in debates on epistemological origins of GTM (Bryant, 2002; Urquhart, 2002).

The final aspect of a contested concept is that it must be able to admit unpredictable modifications in the light of circumstances. We see different applications and adaptation of GTM in IS research, including its use with: cases studies, both as the overarching method and as a subservient coding technique (Kaplan and Duchon, 1988; Webster, 1998; Barrett and Walsham, 1999; Levina and Ross, 2003); action research (Baskerville and Pries-Heje, 1999); phenomenology and hermeneutics (Trauth and Jessup, 2000); ethnography (Levina, 2005); surveys (Feller *et al.*, 2008; Ransbotham and Mitra, 2009); and, within a symbolic interaction methodological framework (Gopal and Prasad, 2000). As more IS researchers use GTM, we would call on those researchers to reflect on those adaptations, rather than perceiving their use as a deviation from 'pure' GTM.

Gallie's criteria also state that the continuous competition for acknowledgement should allow for *the original exemplar's achievement to be sustained and/or developed in optimum fashion*. For GTM in general, there can be no doubt that the exemplar is the *Discovery of Grounded Theory*. For IS specifically, it can be argued that Orlikowski (1993) represents an early exemplar, and that others have followed and developed the application of the method in IS. Our view is that, despite the notable exceptions that we have used as exemplars, GTM in IS research has not yet reached the optimum situation described by Gallie. An optimum situation would be where there are many examples of GTM being applied in high-level journals in IS.

Therefore, GTM in IS has the characteristics of an essentially contested concept. This is not surprising (Bryant and Charmaz, 2007). But, in this paper we have demonstrated how this contested nature of GTM as a concept is cause for misinterpretations and misrepresentations.

The core message of this paper is that GTM has a deceptive simplicity, which can induce the illusion that competence is possible without incurring in the necessary scholarly effort. In our view, the most damaging misconception is *the researcher as a blank slate* – nothing could be further from the truth in grounded theory. We believe that when the literature is addressed as intended by the method, including a deep study of the GTM literature during the non-committal phase of the study, the likelihood of incurring further misconceptions is greatly reduced, if not eliminated. Our suggested guidelines provide some flexible advice not only about the use of literature in the early stages, but also the much needed theoretical integration of the substantive theories produced by GTM, as seen in some of the existing exemplars in our discipline.

Conclusion

This paper is written to support and inform those people who wish to use GTM. As such it is useful for experienced academics, theorists new to GTM, and anyone curious about the potential of GTM as a rigorous and relevant method for IS research. Most of the misunderstandings we discussed tend to, intentionally or unintentionally, legitimise the view that GTM is an impractical research method, particularly for dissertation research. This has not been our experience, nor is it founded on evidence. The GTM has certain advantages, such as: relevance, as it has a built-in closeness to the data; rigour, in the form of clearly prescribed analysis procedures; and a clear pathway to generating substantive theories. It is also a flexible research method that is suitable for researching socio-technical processes and for building theory in unexplored areas – two strengths that could undoubtedly benefit IS research.

Future questions about the use of GTM include the consideration of whether, because of the unique nexus between people and technology in IS, this necessitates adaptations of GTM, and what type of adaptations they might be.

Finally, we turn to the question concerning the potential of GTM for theory-building in IS, given that theory- building has been identified as a key requirement for the further development of the IS field (Baskerville and Myers, 2002; Markus and Saunders, 2007). A more nuanced and reflective use of GTM should contribute to building rigorous IS theories, which are based in practice, and effectively engaged with the relevant literature. Such a use would enhance the potential of grounded theory to make a much bigger contribution to IS research.

Acknowledgement

The authors contributed equally to the paper.

Notes

1. See http://www.sociologypress.com/
2. The term 'formal' is used here in the sociological sense and should not be confused with other types of formality, such as those theories expressed in mathematical formal language.

References

Alvesson, M. and Sköldberg, K. (2000). *Reflexive Methodology: New vistas for qualitative research*, London, Thousand Oaks, CA: SAGE.

Andrew, T. (2006). The Literature Review in Grounded Theory: A response to McCallin (2003), *The Grounded Theory Review: An International Journal* 5(2/3): 29–41.

Annells, M.P. (1996). Grounded Theory Method: Philosophical perspectives, paradigm of inquiry, and postmodernism, *Qualitative Health Research* 6(3): 379–393.

Barrett, M. and Walsham, G. (1999). Electronic Trading and Work Transformation in the London Insurance Market, *Information Systems Research* 10(1): 1–22.

Baskerville, R. and Pries-Heje, J. (1999). Grounded Action Research: A method for understanding IT in practice, *Accounting, Management and Information Technologies* 9(1): 1–23.

Baskerville, R.L. and Myers, M.D. (2002). Information Systems as a Reference Discipline, *MIS Quarterly* 26(1): 1–14.

Becker, P.H. (1993). Common Pitfalls in Published Grounded Theory Research, *Qualitative Health Research* 3(2): 254–260.

Benoliel, J.Q. (1996). Grounded Theory and Nursing Knowledge, *Qualitative Health Research* **6**(3): 406–428.

Bryant, A. (2002). Re-grounding Grounded Theory, *Journal of Information Technology Theory and Application* **4**(1): 25–42.

Bryant, A. and Charmaz, K. (eds.) (2007). *The SAGE Handbook of Grounded Theory*, London, Thousand Oaks, CA: SAGE Publications.

Calloway, L.J. and Ariav, G. (1991). Developing and Using a Qualitative Methodology to Study Relationships among Designers and Tools, in H.E. Nissen, H. Klein and R. Hirschheim (eds.) *Proceedings of the IFIP WG 8.2 Working Conference*, 14–16 December 1991; (Copenhagen, DK) Amsterdam: North-Holland, 175–193.

Carlson, P.J. and Davis, G.B. (1998). An Investigation of Media Selection among Directors and Managers: From 'Self' to 'Other' orientation, *MIS Quarterly* **22**: 335–362.

Charmaz, K. (2006). *Constructing Grounded Theory: A Practical Guide through Qualitative Analysis*, Thousand Oaks, CA: SAGE Publications.

Corbin, J.M. and Strauss, A.L. (2008). *Basics of Qualitative Research: Techniques and procedures for developing grounded theory*, Los Angeles: SAGE Publications.

Eisenhardt, K.M. (1989). Building Theories from Case Study Research, *Academy of Management Review* **14**(4): 532–550.

Ekstrom, H. (2006). Aspects on McCallin's Paper, 'Grappling with the Literature in a Grounded Theory Study'? *The Grounded Theory Review: An International Journal* **5**(2/3): 45–47.

Elliott, N. and Lazenbatt, A. (2005). How To Recognise a 'Quality' Grounded Theory Research Study, *Australian Journal of Advanced Nursing* **22**(3): 48–52.

Feller, J., Finnegan, P., Fitzgerald, B. and Hayes, J. (2008). From Peer Production to Productization: A study of socially enabled business exchanges in open source service networks, *Information Systems Research* **19**(4): 475–493.

Fendt, J. and Sachs, W. (2008). Grounded Theory Method in management research: Users' perspectives, *Organizational Research Methods* **11**: 430–455.

Fernandez, W.D. and Lehmann, H.P. (2005). Achieving Rigour and Relevance in Information Systems Studies: Using grounded theory to investigate organizational cases, *The Grounded Theory Review: An international Journal* **5**(1): 79–107.

Galal, G. (2001). From Contexts to Constructs: The use of grounded theory in operationalising contingent process models, *European Journal of Information Systems* **10**(1): 2–14.

Gallie, W.B. (1956). Essentially Contested Concepts, in *Proceedings of the Aristotelian Society*, Vol. 56, Blackwell Publishing, pp. 167–198.

Garud, R. and Kumaraswamy, A. (2005). Vicious and Virtuos Circles in the Management of Knowledge: The case of Infosys Technologies, *MIS Quarterly* **29**(1): 9–33.

Giddens, A. (1990). *The Consequences of Modernity*, Stanford, CA: Stanford University Press.

Giddens, A. (1991). *Modernity and Self-identity: Self and society in the late modern age*, Stanford, CA: Stanford University Press.

Glaser, B.G. (1978). *Theoretical Sensitivity: Advances in the methodology of grounded theory*, Mill Valley, CA: Sociology Press.

Glaser, B.G. (1992). *Emergence vs. Forcing: Basics of grounded theory analysis*, Mill Valley, CA: Sociology Press.

Glaser, B.G. (1998). *Doing Grounded Theory: Issues and discussions*, Mill Valley, CA: Sociology Press.

Glaser, B.G. (2001). *The Grounded Theory Perspective: Conceptualization contrasted with description*, Mill Valley, CA: Sociology Press.

Glaser, B.G. (2005). *The Grounded Theory Perspective III: Theoretical coding*, Mill Valley, CA: Sociology Press.

Glaser, B.G. (2007). *Doing Formal Grounded Theory: A proposal*, Mill Valley, CA: Sociology Press.

Glaser, B.G. (2009). *Jargonizing: Using the grounded theory vocabulary*, Mill Valley, CA: Sociology Press.

Glaser, B.G. and Strauss, A.L. (1965). *Awareness of Dying*, New York: Aldine Publishing Company.

Glaser, B.G. and Strauss, A.L. (1967). *The Discovery of Grounded Theory: Strategies for qualitative research*, New York: Aldine Publishing Company.

Gopal, A. and Prasad, P. (2000). Understanding GDSS in Symbolic Context: Shifting the focus from technology to interaction, *MIS Quarterly* 24(3): 509–546.

Green, J. (1998). Grounded Theory and The Constant Comparative Method, *British Medical Journal* 316(7137): 1064–1065.

Hunter, M.G. and Beck, J.E. (2000). Using Repertory Grids to Conduct Cross-cultural Information Systems Research, *Information Systems Research* 11(1): 93–101.

Jones, R. and Noble, G. (2007). Grounded Theory and Management Research: A lack of integrity? *Qualitative Research in Organizations and Management: An International Journal* 2(2): 84–103.

Kaplan, B. and Duchon, D. (1988). Combining Qualitative and Quantitative Methods in Information Systems Research: A case study, *MIS Quarterly* 12(4): 571–586.

Kirsch, L.J. (2004). Deploying Common Systems Globally: The dynamics of control, *Information Systems Research* 15(4): 374–396.

Klein, H.K. and Myers, M.D. (1999). A Set of Principles for Conducting and Evaluating Interpretive Field Studies in Information Systems, *MIS Quarterly* 23(1): 67–93.

Klein, H.K. and Myers, M.D. (2001). A Classification Scheme for Interpretive Research in Information Systems, in E.M. Trauth (ed.) *Qualitative Research in IS: Issues and trends*, Hershey, PA: Idea Group Publishing.

Lamb, R. and Kling, R. (2003). Reconceptualizing Users as Social Actors in Information Systems Research, *MIS Quarterly* 27(2): 197–236.

Langley, A. (1999). Strategies for Theorizing from Process Data, *Academy of Management Review* 24(4): 691–710.

Layder, D. (1993). *New Strategies in Social Research: An introduction and guide*, Cambridge, UK: Polity Press.

Lee, A.S. (2010). Retrospect and Prospect: Information systems research in the last and next 25 years, *Journal of Information and Technology* 25(4): 336–348.

Levina, N. (2005). Collaborating on Multiparty Information Systems Development Projects: A collective reflection-in-action view, *Information Systems Research* 16(2): 109–133.

Levina, N. and Ross, J.W. (2003). From the Vendor Perspective: Exploring the value proposition in information technology outsourcing, *MIS Quarterly* 27(4): 331–364.

Levina, N. and Vaast, E. (2005). The Emergence of Boundary Spanning Competence in Practice: Implications for implementation and use of information systems, *MIS Quarterly* 29(2): 335–363.

Levina, N. and Vaast, E. (2008). Innovating or Doing as Told? Status Differences and Overlapping Boundaries in Offshore Collaboration, *MIS Quarterly* 32(2): 307–332.

Lincoln, Y.S. and Guba, E.G. (1985). *Naturalistic Inquiry*, Beverly Hills, CA: SAGE Publications.

Lings, B. and Lundell, B. (2005). On the Adaptation of Grounded Theory Procedures: Insights from the evolution of the 2G method, *Information Technology and People* 18(4): 196–211.

Madill, A., Jordan, A. and Shirley, C. (2000). Objectivity and Reliability in Qualitative Analysis: Realist, contextualist and radical constructionist epistemologies, *British Journal of Psychology* 91(1): 1–20.

Markus, M.L. (1997). The Qualitative Difference in Information System Research and Practice, in J.I. DeGross, J. Liebenau and A.S. Lee (eds.) *Information Systems and Qualitative Research*, London: Chapman & Hall.

Markus, M.L. and Saunders, C. (2007). Looking for a Few Good Concepts ... and Theories ... for the Information Systems Field, *MIS Quarterly* 31(1): iii–vi.

Martin, P.Y. and Turner, B.A. (1986). Grounded Theory and Organizational Research, *The Journal of Applied Behavioral Science* 22(2): 141–157.

Martin, V.B. (2006). The Postmoderm Turn: Shall classic grounded theory take that detour? A review essay, *The Grounded Theory Review: An International Journal* 5(2/3): 119–129.

McCallin, A.M. (2003). Grappling with the Literature in a Grounded Theory Study, *Contemporary Nurse* 15(1–2): 62–69.

Montealegre, R. and Keil, M. (2000). De-escalating Information Technology Projects: Lessons from the Denver International Airport, *MIS Quarterly* 24 (3): 417–447.

Myers, M.D. (1997). Qualitative Research in Information Systems, *MIS Quarterly* 21(2): 241–242.

Myo (2012). Grounded theory: 'Whenever possible, stay away from it' 'It is too complicated, and difficult to handle and manage', [WWW document] http://whatihavelearntrecently.blogspot.co.uk (accessed 26 April 2012).

Orlikowski, W.J. (1993). CASE Tools as Organizational Change: Investigating incremental and radical changes in systems development, *MIS Quarterly* 17(3): 309–340.

Orlikowski, W.J. (1996). Improvising Organizational Transformation Over Time: A situated change perspective, *Information Systems Research* 7(1): 63–103.

Orlikowski, W.J. and Baroudi, J.J. (1991). Studying Information Technology in Organizations: Research approaches and assumptions, *Information Systems Research* 2(1): 1–28.

Ransbotham, S. and Mitra, S. (2009). Choice and Chance: A conceptual model of paths to information security compromise, *Information Systems Research* 20(1): 121–139.

Schön, D.A. (1983). *The Reflective Practitioner: How professionals think in action*, New York: Basic Books.

Stern, P.N. (1994). Eroding Grounded Theory, in J. Morse (ed.) *Critical Issues in Qualitative Research Methods*, Thousand Oaks, CA: Sage Publications.

Strauss, A.L. (1987). *Qualitative Analysis for Social Scientists,* Cambridge: Cambridge University Press.

Strauss, A.L. and Corbin, J.M. (1990). *Basics of Qualitative Research: Grounded Theory Procedures and Techniques,* Newbury Park, CA: Sage Publications.

Suddaby, R. (2006). From the Editors: What grounded theory is not, *Academy of Management Journal* **49**(4): 633–642.

Taylor, H., Dillon, S. and Van Wingen, M. (2010). Focus and Diversity in IS Research: Meeting the dual demands of a healthy applied discipline, *MIS Quarterly* **34**(4): 647–667.

Toraskar, K. (1991). How Managerial Users Evaluate Their Decision Support: A grounded theory approach, in H.E. Nissen, H. Klein and R. Hirschheimeds (eds.) *Proceedings of the IFIP WG 8.2 Working Conference,* 14–16 December 1991; (Copenhagen, DK) Amsterdam: North-Holland, 195–225.

Trauth, E.M. and Jessup, L.M. (2000). Understanding Computer-mediated Discussions: Positivist and interpretive analyses of group support system use, *MIS Quarterly* **24**(1): 43–79.

Urquhart, C. (2002). Regrounding Grounded Theory – Or reinforcing old prejudices? A Brief Reply to Bryant, *Journal of Information Technology Theory and Application* **4**(3): 43–54.

Urquhart, C. and Fernandez, W.D. (2006). Grounded Theory Method: The researcher as blank slate and other myths, in *The International Conference on Information Systems,* 2006 (Milwaukee, WI, USA).

Urquhart, C., Lehmann, H. and Myers, M. (2010). Putting the Theory Back into Grounded Theory: Guidelines for grounded theory studies in information systems, *Information Systems Journal* **20**(4): 357–381.

Van de Ven, A.H. and Poole, M.S. (1989). Methods for Studying Innovation Processes, in A.H. Van de Ven, H.L. Angle and M.S. Poole (eds.) *Research on the Management of Innovation: The Minnesota studies,* New York: Harper & Row.

Vannoy, S.A. and Salam, A.F. (2010). Managerial Interpretations of the Role of Information Systems in Competitive Actions and Firm Performance: A grounded theory investigation, *Information Systems Research* **21**(3): 496–515.

Walsham, G. (1995). Interpretive Case Studies in IS Research: Nature and method, *European Journal of Information Systems* **4**(2): 74–81.

Webster, J. (1998). Desktop Videoconferencing: Experiences of complete users, wary users, and non-users, *MIS Quarterly* **22**(3): 257–286.

Appendix

Table 6.A1 Examples of GTM use in IS research

Study	Journal	How GTM was used
Kaplan and Duchon (1988)	MISQ	To study relationships between a computer system and the perceptions of its users. GTM used in a mixed method approach to case study research.
Orlikowski (1993)	MISQ	Classic GTM used to produce a theoretical model of strategic conduct in adopting and using CASE tools in organisations. Engaged with formal innovation theory.
Carlson and Davis (1998)	MISQ	To study the media selection behaviour of executives and managers. GTM (Glaser and Strauss, 1967; Strauss, 1987) was used to guide data analysis. Cluster analysis technique (SPSS) was used. Engaged with multiple theories of media selection.
Webster (1998)	MISQ	To study the use of desktop video conferencing. Classic GTM used to develop theory from a longitudinal case study (Eisenhardt, 1989). Engaged with communication media choice, systems analysis and design, and privacy.
Barrett and Walsham (1999)	ISR	To study the role of IT in organisational transformation. Pseudo-Straussian GTM used to study a single case. Engaged with and extended Giddens theory on social transformation.
Gopal and Prasad (2000)	MISQ	To study how group decision support systems were used in a university setting. Classic GTM techniques used within a symbolic interaction methodological framework. The article contributes rich descriptions from the field.
Hunter and Beck (2000)	ISR	To conduct cross-cultural research. Proposes the use of the RepGrid technique in GTM studies. Describes how the technique is used to address emic *vs* etic issues.
Trauth and Jessup (2000)	MISQ	To study computer-mediated discussions in group support systems. GTM (Glaser and Strauss, 1967; Strauss, 1987) used for the interpretive part of a study that combined and compared positivist and interpretive research. GTM was used in combination with ethnography and hermeneutics.
Lamb and Kling (2003)	MISQ	To study ICT use and to develop an alternative to the user concept found in the literature. Classic GTM used to develop a social actor model that can be used to conceptualise ICT research and design.

(continued)

Table 6.A1 Continued

Study	Journal	How GTM was used
Levina and Ross (2003)	MISQ	To study IT vendors value proposition in IT outsourcing. Classic GTM used with case study data. Primarily engaged with Milgrom and Roberts' complementarity in organisational design and with Hamel and Prahalad's core competency concept.
Kirsch (2004)	ISR	To study the dynamics of control during different phases of large IS projects. Used the Straussian approach with case study (two cases) adopting a soft-positivist stance (Madill *et al.*, 2000). Engaged with the control literature.
Garud and Kumaraswamy (2005)	MISQ	To study challenges faced by organisations in harnessing knowledge. Classic GTM used to analyse a data-rich longitudinal case study over a period of 3 years. Engaged with systems theory.
Levina (2005)	ISR	To study multi-party collaborative practices in IS development projects. Classic GTM used in an ethnographic study of IS development. Engaged with Schön's reflection-in-action theory.
Levina and Vaast (2005)	MISQ	To study the emergence of organisational competence in boundary spanning. GTM is used to analyse data from case studies. Presents an excellent integration with the extant literature and engages with Bourdieu's theory of practice.
Feller *et al.* (2008)	ISR	To study social mechanisms in open source service networks. Straussian GTM used to analyse data in a multi-method research guided by postpositivist epistemology.
Levina and Vaast (2008)	MISQ	To study offshore software development practices. Classic GTM used to build theory on offshoring following an interpretive cases study approach (Walsham, 1995). Engaged with Bourdieu's theory of practice.
Ransbotham and Mitra (2009)	ISR	To study information security. Classic GTM used to develop a conceptual model of paths to information security compromise using observations, interviews, document reviews and discussion groups. The model is empirically examined using alert data.
Vannoy and Salam (2010)	ISR	To study the utilisation of IS in top managers' competitive actions. GTM (Corbin and Strauss, 2008) used to produce a process model of IS, competitive action and firm performance. The relevant literature is engaged to discuss and present the model.

7

On Emergence and Forcing in Information Systems Grounded Theory Studies: The Case of Strauss and Corbin

Stefan Seidel[1] *and Cathy Urquhart*[2]
[1]*Institute of Information Systems, University of Liechtenstein, Vaduz, Liechtenstein;*
[2]*Manchester Metropolitan University Business School, Manchester Metropolitan University, Manchester, UK*

Introduction

Grounded theory method (GTM) (Glaser and Strauss, 1967; Strauss and Corbin, 1990; Charmaz, 2006) is characterized by the continuous interplay between the collection and analysis of data in order to generate theory that is firmly grounded in empirical phenomena (Glaser and Strauss, 1967; Strauss and Corbin, 1998). The method is now an accepted research approach in the information systems (IS) discipline (Urquhart *et al.*, 2010; Matavire and Brown, 2011). That said, there are many debates around the application of GTM, and the method is contested (Duchscher and Morgan, 2004; Bryant and Charmaz, 2007). Important debates relate to the underlying epistemology (Mills *et al.*, 2006), role of prior theory (Jones and Noble, 2007), and coding procedures (Kelle, 2007). As a result, there are now different strands of GTM, which differ in various aspects, including induction, deduction, and verification (Heath and Cowley, 2004; Matavire and Brown, 2011). Bryant and Charmaz (2007) argue strongly that GTM can be seen as a 'family of methods', and we would concur with that view. Mills *et al.* (2006) write that GTM 'can be seen as a methodological spiral that begins with Glaser and Strauss' original text and continues today' (p. 25). Specifically,

Reprinted from 'On emergence and forcing in information systems grounded theory studies: the case of Strauss and Corbin,' by S. Seidel and C. Urquhart in *Journal of Information Technology*, 28, 2013, pp. 237–260. With kind permission from the Association for Information Technology Trust. All rights reserved.

they use the terms 'traditional' and 'evolved' in order to distinguish the work of Glaser from that of Strauss, the two co-founders of the method. Similarly, in the IS discipline, Matavire and Brown (2011) identify four types of grounded theory use. In line with Mills *et al.* (2006), they characterize the Glaserian approach as 'classic' GTM (Type 1), and further developments as 'evolved' (Type 2), including work on interpretive and constructivist grounded theory (Charmaz, 2000, 2006; Bryant, 2002). They further highlight that GTM is often used as part of a mixed methodology (Type 3) and that researchers often make use of grounded theory techniques in order to analyse data (Type 4).

One important debate is about the all-important metaphor of *emergence*, which 'had a far-reaching impact on the methodological debate but, at the same time, was difficult to be translated into tangible methodological rules' (Kelle, 2007: 191), and which is particularly reflected in the discussion of coding procedures and recommended use of one singular coding paradigm by Strauss and Corbin (1990), arguably the most influential strand of GTM (Jones and Hughes, 2001; Duchscher and Morgan, 2004; Bryant and Charmaz, 2007; van Niekerk and Roode, 2009).

In the 1990 book *The Basics of Qualitative Research*, Strauss and Corbin (1990) proposed three (open, axial, and selective) coding stages. The stage of axial coding, in particular, 'is so foreign to Glaser's method that there is little basis for direct comparison' (Walker and Myrick, 2006: 554). Within axial coding, a coding paradigm (henceforth referred to as the S & C paradigm) is recommended to guide researchers in coding and defining relationships between concepts. Glaser (1992) felt that this resulted in 'forced conceptualization'. The 1990 book triggered a split between the two founders of grounded theory, and led Glaser (1992) to publish an angry rejoinder in the form of his book, *Basics of Grounded Theory Analysis: Emergence vs Forcing*. Other researchers have also criticized the Straussian strand for its rigidity (Keddy *et al.*, 1996) and lack of emergence (Robrecht, 1995). The S & C paradigm has also been alleged to hamper the creativity of the process of analysing data and building grounded theory (Heath and Cowley, 2004).

Indeed, the use of only one coding paradigm to help the process, as opposed to a range of coding 'families' suggested by Glaser (1978), raised serious questions about the nature of GTM itself. The dispute was no less than one about the heart and soul of GTM and has ramifications that persist to this day in many disciplines, including our own.

While the rigidity of procedures of Straussian GTM has long been debated by authors from different disciplines, including nursing, health studies, and the management sciences (e.g., Glaser, 1992; Robrecht, 1995; Keddy *et al.*, 1996; Locke, 1996; Melia, 1996; Heath and Cowley, 2004), this debate has largely been absent in the IS discipline, despite an increasing number of IS studies applying the method. Only relatively recently has the IS discipline started to pay increased attention to the issues related to the application of GTM (e.g., Urquhart *et al.*, 2010; Matavire and Brown, 2011).

Against this background, this article explores how axial coding and the S & C coding paradigm have influenced IS research, in the context of the controversy about forcing *vs* emergence (Kendall, 1999; Walker and Myrick, 2006; Matavire and Brown, 2011). Understanding this debate can teach us much about the important metaphor of emergence in grounded theory studies in the IS field. We also recognize that our examination of the effect of the Strauss and Corbin coding procedures in IS needs to be set in the context of a larger debate, as they are intimately linked to the different trajectories that different contributors have brought to the method (Bryant, 2002; Bryant and Charmaz, 2007).

Strauss and Corbin GTM is arguably the most influential strand of GTM, and is seen by scholars to have more reach and influence (Jones and Hughes, 2001; Boychuk Duchscher and Morgan, 2004; Bryant and Charmaz, 2007; van Niekerk and Roode, 2009). Over the last years, the Straussian strand of grounded theory (as one form of 'evolved' grounded theory) has been widely used in the IS discipline (Matavire and Brown, 2011). Matavire and Brown (2011) explicitly state that the 'extensive use of the paradigm model in Strauss and Corbin's (1990, 1998) evolved GTM is an important point of divergence from classic GTM' (p. 122). Charmaz (2006) says that the Straussian strand, in the form of the 1990 book 'serves as a powerful statement of the method and has instructed graduate students throughout the world' (p. 8). We contend that the use of Strauss and Corbin (S & C) as an important instance of evolved grounded theory in the IS discipline warrants further investigation.

In this article, we investigate how S & C GTM has been applied in the IS discipline from 1987–2010,[1] focusing on the use of axial coding and the coding paradigm. Our aim is not to compare different strands of GTM, as there are some excellent works that have already done so (e.g., Heath and Cowley, 2004; Walker and Myrick, 2006; Jones and Noble, 2007). Our objectives are to (a) understand the actual impact that the application of S & C GTM has had on the IS discipline, (b) interpret these findings in the context of larger debates and developments around grounded theory, and (c) develop some guidelines that can assist fellow researchers in their application of axial coding and the coding paradigm. It is not the intention of this article to favour one particular strand of GTM over another. Instead, we aim to respond to a call made by Matavire and Brown (2011) who say, with reference to the different approaches to grounded theory used in IS research: 'For each of these approaches further clarity is needed, in terms of criteria for judging the soundness and rigour of the research, and guidelines and principles to be followed' (p. 127).

Our overall research problem can be framed as follows:

What is the role of axial coding and the paradigm with regard to avoiding theoretical pre-conceptions and allowing for the emergence of categories?

We do this through the medium of two research questions. The first looks at the use of S & C Coding procedures in the IS discipline since the publication of Strauss and Corbin's controversial book in 1990. Our first question is:

Research Question 1: How, and as part of what research designs, are axial coding and the coding paradigm used in the IS discipline, from 1987–2010?[1]

We expect that answering this question may provide insights into how aware IS researchers have been of the forcing debate and the important issue of emergence in grounded theory studies, and how they have used axial coding and the coding paradigm. This first question also allows us to give a picture of how grounded theory has been taken up in the IS field generally, given that many IS researchers seem to be influenced by the dominance of the Strauss and Corbin strand of grounded theory.

Our second research question asks:

Research Question 2: How does the use of axial coding and the S & C coding paradigm impact on the results generated from IS studies that apply them?

This question relates to the results of research that are generated when the procedures of axial coding, and the S & C paradigm, are strictly followed. It is expected that the identification of the characteristics of these results can shed light on whether or not their application leads to forcing of data, and mere conceptual description, as claimed by Glaser (1992) and discussed by others (e.g., Robrecht, 1995; Keddy *et al.*, 1996; Heath and Cowley, 2004). We are also interested in how studies that strictly apply the S & C paradigm conceptualize the IT artefact, which is at the heart of the IS discipline (Orlikowski and Iacono, 2001). As the paradigm has been alleged to force data and lead to conceptual description, one may argue that using the paradigm may also tend to lead towards a limited number of conceptualizations of the IT artefact. This might lend weight to the argument that using the paradigm may hinder emergence and limit the potential for theorizing based on S & C GTM.

The remainder of this article is structured as follows. The next section provides an introduction into the forcing debate in GTM, and provides an overview of different coding procedures. We then present our analysis of IS studies that make use of S & C coding procedures. We follow this with a discussion of the implications of our study, and put forward some guidelines for those researchers interested in using the Straussian strand. The article concludes with a summary of limitations and contributions.

The forcing debate and coding procedures in grounded theory

The 'classic' strand of GTM, often referred to as 'Glaserian' grounded theory, is firmly rooted in the work by Barney Glaser (Glaser and Strauss, 1967; Glaser, 1978, 1992). This strand closely resembles the vision of GTM in the original 1967 book, which contains very little in the way of strictures and guidelines (Locke, 1996; Suddaby, 2006). Indeed, the original book (Glaser and Strauss, 1967) presents a method that is based on the concept of comparative analysis, that is, through the constant comparison of data with data and codes, categories, and relationships.

Strauss and Corbin (1990) introduced a new approach that provided much more detailed procedures to analyse data and build theory (Charmaz, 2006; Walker and Myrick, 2006), and initiated a very different formulation of GTM. One explanation for these different interpretations in the context of 'emergence' in GTM are the different backgrounds of Glaser and Strauss, as highlighted in Bryant (2002), Bryant and Charmaz (2007), Charmaz (2006), or Strauss and Corbin (1998). Glaser, who has his background in Columbia University positivism 'saw the need for making comparisons between data to identify, develop, and relate concepts' (Strauss and Corbin, 1998: 10). Strauss, on the contrary, was much influenced by American pragmatists such as Mead (1934) and Dewey (1922), and pragmatist works contributed to the method 'an awareness of the interrelationships among conditions (structure), action (process), and consequences' (Strauss and Corbin, 1998: 10), among others. The coding procedures, therefore, must be seen in the broader context of these different influences. While the new procedures introduced in Strauss and Corbin (1990) were also in Strauss (1987), it was only on publication of the 1990 book that the famous 'split' ensued. Their presentation of GTM received much criticism from Glaser who even requested the 1990 book to be withdrawn, arguing that Strauss' understanding of grounded theory 'misconceives our conceptions of grounded theory to an extreme degree, even destructive degree' (Glaser, 1992: 1).

A more recent development is that of constructivist grounded theory that is built upon the understanding that neither theories nor data are discovered; instead they are constructed by the researcher based on her interactions with the field (Charmaz, 2000, 2006; Bryant, 2002). Charmaz (2006) argues that 'we can use basic grounded theory guidelines with twenty-first century methodological assumptions and approaches' (p. 9) – a view that is shared by other influential authors, including Bryant (2002) and Clarke (2003, 2005). Here, it is important to note that constructivist grounded theory is in the tradition of pragmatism and symbolic interactionism – a background that is shared by Anselm Strauss.

Coding procedures

Coding procedures in GTM have evolved considerably during its history. Given that the forcing and emergence debate revolves around those procedures, this section subjects them to further scrutiny. Strauss (1987) and Strauss and Corbin (1990) break down the coding process into three stages of *open, axial,* and *selective* coding, Glaser (1978, 1992) nominates three stages of *open, selective,* and *theoretical coding,* and Charmaz (2006) discusses four types of *initial coding, focused coding, axial coding,* and *theoretical coding.*

The different coding procedures are summarized in Table 7.1.

Open coding, on which both Strauss and Glaser agree, is the process of going through the data, generally line by line but sometimes word by word, and attaching initial codes to those chunks of data. Charmaz (2006) uses the notion of *initial coding*; at this, initial coding is similar to what Glaser and Strauss refer to as open coding (Urquhart, 2013). Yet, in line with her constructivist view on grounded theory, Charmaz (2006) highlights: 'I agree with Glaser's approach of keeping initial coding open-ended yet acknowledge that researchers hold prior ideas and skills' (p. 48).

Axial coding forms the point of departure between the two strands and was first proposed by Strauss in 1987. Axial coding aims at discovering relationships between categories and subcategories (Strauss, 1987;

Table 7.1 Coding procedures in grounded theory

Book	Suggested coding procedure
Glaser and Strauss (1967)	Comparing incidents, integrating categories
Strauss (1987)	Open coding, axial coding, selective coding
Strauss and Corbin (1990)	Open coding, axial coding, selective coding
Glaser (1992)	Open coding, selective coding, theoretical coding
Strauss and Corbin (1998)	Open coding, axial coding, selective coding
Charmaz (2006)	Initial coding, focused coding, axial coding (optional), theoretical coding
Corbin and Strauss (2008)	Open coding, axial coding, and theoretical coding as distinct stages no longer appear, though open coding and axial coding appear as terms in one chapter. The emphasis is on a broader set of tools named context, process, and theoretical integration. Two coding paradigms are used as a foundation for context

Adapted from Urquhart, 2013, p. 23.

Strauss and Corbin, 1990, 1998). That is, the researcher codes around the 'axis' of a category, and links categories at the level of properties and dimensions (Strauss and Corbin, 1998). Strauss and Corbin (1990, 1998) mandate the use of a single coding paradigm in axial coding to assist with grouping and relating categories. Table 7.2 provides an overview of the paradigm elements as presented in Strauss and Corbin (1990).

Charmaz (2006), citing Strauss and Corbin (1998), describes axial coding as 'Strauss and Corbin's (1998) strategy for bringing data back together again in a coherent whole' (p. 60) (after initial or open coding). Still, in her version of grounded theory, axial coding is described as being an optional stage, which may or may not be helpful to the researcher (Charmaz, 2006).

Selective coding is a term that has different meanings depending on whether the Straussian or Glaserian strand is used. In the Straussian version, selective coding is coding around the core categories and is a final stage. In the Glaserian version, it is a middle stage of coding, where codes are grouped, based on emergent core categories before being related to each other later, in the *theoretical coding* stage, where a coherent theoretical scheme is developed. Charmaz (2006) uses the term *focused coding* in order to describe what is called selective coding in Glaserian grounded theory (Urquhart, 2013). She writes: 'Focused coding means

Table 7.2 Coding paradigm items

Item	Description
Causal conditions	'Events, incidents, happenings that lead to the occurrence or development of a phenomenon' (Strauss and Corbin, 1990: 96)
Intervening conditions	'The structural conditions bearing on action/ interactional strategies that pertain to a phenomenon. They facilitate or constrain the strategies taken within a specific context' (Strauss and Corbin, 1990: 96)
Context	'The specific set of properties that pertain to a phenomenon; that is, the locations of events or incidents pertaining to a phenomenon along a dimensional range. Context represents the particular set of conditions within which the action/interactional strategies are taken' (Strauss and Corbin, 1990: 96)
Action/interactional strategies	'Strategies devised to manage, handle, carry out, respond to a phenomenon under a specific set of perceived conditions' (Strauss and Corbin, 1990: 97)
Consequences	'Outcomes or results of action and interaction' (Strauss and Corbin, 1990: 97)

Strauss and Corbin (1990).

using the most significant and/or frequent earlier codes to sift through large amounts of data' (p. 57).

Finally, both Glaser (1978, 2005) and Charmaz (2006) recommend a stage of theoretical coding, where relationships (theoretical codes) are posited between categories and the theory begins to take shape. In the Straussian strand, categories are related in the axial phase and this stage is not applied.

Critiques of axial coding and the coding paradigm

The major criticism of the coding paradigm proposed by Strauss and Corbin (1990, 1998) is that it presents just one set of ideas for relating categories. Glaser (1992) points out that he had suggested 18 coding families in 1978, which cover ideas like dimensions and elements, mutual effects and reciprocity, social control, recruitment and isolation, and many other ideas for categories and relationships. Glaser (2005) has since expanded the number of coding families to 41 in total, introducing 23 new coding families. Glaser (1992) further argues that the paradigm forces data, hinders emergence, and leads to conceptual description rather than grounded theory. He writes:

> In grounded theory we do not link properties and categories in a set of relationships denoting causal conditions, phenomena, context, intervening condition '[sic],' action/interactional strategies and consequences. This would be preconception and forcing theoretical concepts on data to the max. (p. 63)

Charmaz (2006), in accordance with the basic assumptions of constructivist grounded theory that both data and the interpretation of data are constructed based on the researcher's interaction with the field, characterizes axial coding as 'a frame for researchers to apply' that 'may extend or limit your vision, depending on your subject matter and ability to tolerate ambiguity' (p. 61). It has also been suggested that the use of the paradigm means that researchers focus on the application of the paradigm, rather than the emergence of theory as the result of an interactive, highly creative process (Heath and Cowley, 2004). Suddaby (2006) points out that, in grounded theory, 'the act of research has a creative component that cannot be delegated to an algorithm' (p. 638). The potential threat of 'forcing' has also been highlighted by other authors (e.g., Locke, 1996; Melia, 1996; Kendall, 1999). In the IS discipline, Urquhart (2001) reports that in her research she encountered problems when applying the paradigm and uses the paradigm rather as a 'jumping off point to think about categories, as opposed to a coding guide' (p. 18). Similarly, Day et al. (2009) write that they used the coding scheme 'as a general guideline to make sense of our data while remaining alert of emerging themes' (p. 642).

Despite this criticism the coding paradigm has gained much popularity, and Kelle (2007) offers a potential explanation:

> However, the coding paradigm turned out much more instructive for many grounded theory users than the coding family conception. While Glaser had proposed a long and only loosely ordered list of more or less related groups of sociological and formal terms, Strauss and Corbin advise the researcher to use one general model of action rooted in pragmatist and interactionist social theory [...]. (p. 202)

Still, Kelle (2007) points out that the coding paradigm has its origins in one particular theoretical tradition, namely, that of sociological pragmatism of Peirce, Dewey, and Mead, and continues to say that 'Glaser's critique that the coding paradigm may lead to the forcing of categories on the data thus cannot be dismissed' (p. 203).

In summation, we observe that much of the criticism of Straussian grounded theory, and potential dangers, centres on the use of the coding procedures and the coding paradigm in particular.

The S & C coding paradigm over time

It is important to note that, over time, the role of the paradigm has been de-emphasized by Strauss and Corbin (1990, 1998) (Corbin and Strauss, 2008), possibly in response to the criticisms of Glaser and others. Table 7.3 shows how the paradigm has evolved.

In the 1990 book, the authors state that the use of the paradigm is all but mandatory: 'Unless you make use of this model, your grounded theory analyses will lack density and precision' (p. 99). In the 1998 book, however, Strauss and Corbin claim to have never intended a rigidly staged process (Heath and Cowley, 2004). In fact, they write: 'In actuality, the paradigm is nothing more than a perspective taken toward data, another analytic stance that helps to systematically gather and order data in such a way that structure and process are integrated' (Strauss

Table 7.3 The evolution of the Strauss and Corbin paradigm

Coding paradigm	Comment on evolving use of paradigm
Conditions, interactions, strategies and tactics, and consequences (Strauss, 1987)	In the 1987 book, it is clear that the coding paradigm is not an optional part of coding. Researchers are told to 'follow the coding paradigm' (p. 81)
Causal conditions, context, intervening conditions, actions/ interactions, and consequences (Strauss and Corbin, 1990)	In the 1990 book, the coding paradigm is a mandatory part of coding. Researchers are told that grounded theory analysis will lack density and precision without it
Conditions (causal, intervening, and contextual), actions/ interactions (strategic or routine tactics), consequences (immediate, cumulative, reversible, foreseen or unseen) (Strauss and Corbin, 1998)	In the 1998 book, conditions are clustered together, strategies are clustered under actions, and consequences are further elaborated on
Conditions, interactions and emotions, consequences (Corbin and Strauss, 2008)	In the 2008 book, the paradigm loses its prominence and is presented as an optional analytic tool for novice researchers

Adapted from Urquhart, 2013, p. 26.

and Corbin, 1998: 128). In the 2008 edition, the role of the paradigm is further weakened in favour of emphasizing a broader set of tools named context, process, and theoretical integration (Corbin and Strauss, 2008). The paradigm is hence only one of a number of so-called 'analytic strategies' or 'tools'. They write that: 'One tool for helping the researcher to identify contextual factors and then to link them with process is what we call the *paradigm*. The paradigm is a perspective, a set of questions that can be applied to data to help the analyst draw out the contextual factors and identify relationships between context and process' (Corbin and Strauss, 2008: 89). Throughout the book, the authors are careful to highlight that researchers must choose among a variety of analytical tools and 'make use of procedures in ways that best suit him or her' (p. x). One possible inference is that much of the criticism brought forward by Glaser in his 1992 book, and elaborated upon by different authors (e.g., Robrecht, 1995; Keddy *et al.*, 1996; Locke, 1996; Melia, 1996), may have some substance. However, the slow deemphasis of the paradigm over time does not obviate the need for a detailed examination of the application of S & C coding procedures in IS, especially when we look at it in the larger context of what it might mean for emergence in GTM coding practices in IS. There is also a very real need to unpack how precisely GTM has been applied in the IS field to date, precisely because the Straussian strand has been subject to change and at the same time extensively applied in our discipline.

Analysis of IS studies that use S & C grounded theory procedures

In this section, we present our analysis of IS studies that have used S & C grounded theory procedures. We first present our literature search strategy, and then we show how S & C grounded theory procedures have been used in IS research (Research Question 1) and how the use of the S & C paradigm has influenced the results of IS studies (Research Question 2).

Search strategy

In order to provide an empirical basis for our investigation, our search focused on the *Senior Scholars' Basket of Journals* shared by the *Association for Information Systems* (AIS, 2007), which includes the *European Journal of Information Systems* (EJIS), the *Information Systems Journal* (ISJ), *Information Systems Research* (ISR), the *Journal of the Association of Information Systems* (JAIS), the *Journal of Management Information Systems* (JMIS), and *Management Information Systems Quarterly* (MISQ). Our logic was that such studies, which would have gone through a rigorous reviewing process, would be a suitable object for an investigation into the use of axial coding and the coding paradigm. We applied a search strategy that would allow us to identify those studies where authors made use of Straussian coding procedures. All relevant details on our literature search process can be found in Appendix A.

The use of Strauss and Corbin coding procedures in IS research

In this section, we provide details of how axial coding and the coding paradigm have been used in IS research from 1987 to 2010, providing answers to Research Question 1. We first analyse the use of S & C coding procedures over time, because this tells us something about the growing uptake of the Straussian strand of grounded theory in IS research. Second, we analyse how (as part of what research designs) S & C procedures in general are used. Third, we analyse how specifically axial coding and the paradigm are applied.

The use of S & C coding procedures over time

The first empirical IS study drawing on Straussian grounded theory that we identified was published in 1993 (Orlikowski, 1993) and references the Strauss and Corbin (1990) coding procedures (three years later, the same author also published the second study in the top six journals). Figure 7.1 provides an overview of how the 96 empirical articles we identified that reference S & C grounded theory are distributed between 1993 and 2010. The graph needs to be seen in context – obviously, the overall number of articles published in top IS journals has increased over time, and new outlets have become available (e.g., *JAIS* started in 2000). While we considered approximately 140 articles published in 1993, we considered approximately 260 articles published in 2010.

From a slow start in 1993, there was a peak of articles using S & C procedures in 2010, showing that these procedures have become very well established in a period of 18 years.[2] Table 7.4 provides an overview of how the 96 empirical articles that reference S & C grounded theory in the context of the research method are distributed by journal.

EJIS and *ISJ*, with a total of 51 articles between them, account for over half of the grounded theory articles using S & C coding procedures in that period. This indicates that it may indeed be the case that 'European' journals, as opposed to 'North American' journals, have been historically more hospitable to qualitative research in general (Galliers *et al.*, 2007) and GTM in particular.

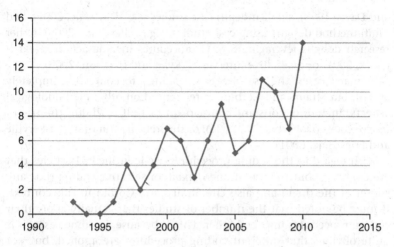

Figure 7.1 Absolute number of studies leveraging S & C coding procedures in IS top journals

Table 7.4 Number of studies referencing S & C grounded theory by journal

Journal	Number of studies referencing S & C grounded theory between 1993 and 2010
EJIS	31
ISJ	20
ISR	5
JAIS	9
JMIS	12
MISQ	19

The use of S & C coding procedures in different research designs

Our analysis suggests that IS researchers use S & C coding procedures to study a broad variety of different phenomena in a quite flexible manner and within a variety of research designs, most of which cannot be labelled 'pure' grounded theory. Specifically, many studies use these procedures to analyse the data (also compare Pauleen, 2003; Matavire and Brown, 2011).

Among the 96 empirical articles we analysed, case studies are by far and large the prevalent research strategy for studies that borrow from S & C grounded theory. Examples include multi case studies (e.g., Carlson and Davis, 1998), single indepth case studies (e.g., Day *et al.*, 2009), and multi-method designs using case studies (e.g., Feller *et al.*, 2008). Other research designs leveraging S & C procedures include action research (Kock, 2001) or qualitative interviews (Ryan and Harrison, 2000).

In many cases, the use of S & C coding procedures is completely absent, but Strauss and Corbin are referenced on other methodological aspects, including constant comparison (Schultze, 2000), the use of *in vivo* codes (Doherty *et al.*, 2006), or theoretical saturation (Baskerville and Pries-Heje, 2001).

With regard to the coding procedures, we identified 51 articles that are explicit about the use of open, axial, or selective coding (i.e., any subset of the three) and also cite Strauss and Corbin in this context. It must be noted that the number of studies that actually apply their coding procedures may be higher. This is because, in some cases, it is quite obvious that different coding procedures are applied, but not explicitly mentioned (e.g., the use of open coding in Ågerfalk and Fitzgerald, 2008). There are also some studies that make explicit use of open, axial, or selective coding, but do not reference the work of Strauss and Corbin in this context (e.g., Jones and Hughes, 2001; Lim *et al.*, 2005). Lim *et al.* (2005), for example, reference Orlikowski (1993) with regard to the selective coding process they applied in their study. It was somewhat surprising to see that, in many instances, it is said that grounded theory procedures are used in order to analyse the data, but no further insight into the process of data analysis is provided.

Only few studies that use S & C grounded theory explicitly state that they adhere to the entire framework and thus apply open, axial, and selective coding (e.g., Kirsch, 1997; Huang *et al.*, 2001).

On many occasions, IS researchers reference both Glaser and Strauss at the same time on the grounded theory approach they apply in their research (e.g., Hackney *et al.*, 2007). We consider the co-referencing of Straussian and Glaserian grounded theory to be relevant, as it has been argued that researchers should make explicit what school of grounded theory they apply, and should consistently adhere to that school's procedures in order to preserve the integrity of grounded theory and avoid inconsistencies and contradictions (Jones and Noble, 2007: 100). We interpret this as another indicator that the IS discipline has not yet fully engaged into the discussion on the differences between the different strands of grounded theory.

In summary, many IS researchers view S & C grounded theory – which is now well established as a research method in the top journals – as a toolbox that is combined with other qualitative techniques and methods (e.g., case study research, action research), rather than a research design that needs to be followed slavishly. First, researchers apply grounded theory as a coding technique, as opposed to building theory. Second, many researchers make selective use of coding techniques, as opposed to leveraging the entire framework. Third, researchers make selective use of S & C techniques in more general terms, including constant comparison, theoretical sampling, or the coding procedures. This flexible use of S & C procedures within various research designs may also provide an explanation for the finding that IS researchers typically do not explicitly state whether their work adheres to the Straussian strand of grounded theory or not.

The use of axial coding and the coding paradigm in IS research

Axial coding for us gave a marker of the use of S & C coding procedures (Walker and Myrick, 2006; Kelle, 2007). Altogether, we identified 38 studies that are explicit about the use of axial coding (see Appendix B). Notwithstanding the 'mandated' use of the paradigm in Strauss and Corbin (1990, 1998), axial coding is usually simply described as a process where categories are related to sub-categories and the relationships are explored, often without reference to the paradigm. Keil *et al.* (2007), for instance, who quote Strauss and Corbin (1998), write:

> The second stage of the qualitative analysis involved axial coding which is a process of systematically relating categories in terms of their properties and dimensions. (p. 75)

Similarly, Conboy (2010), who quotes Strauss and Corbin (1998), writes:

> whereas open coding fractures the data into categories, axial coding puts the data back together by making connections between the categories and sub-categories. (p. 278)

We could only identify very few articles where the authors actually mention the role of the coding paradigm within the stage of axial coding. Altogether, we identified *only seven* studies that are more or less explicit about the use of the paradigm. Table 7.5 provides an overview of these studies along with exemplary codes that illustrate to what extent the paradigm is applied. Given the subjective nature of this evaluation, we encourage our readers to take a look at the cited articles in order to follow our argument.

Table 7.5 Articles where authors are explicit about the use of the S & C coding paradigm

Article	Exemplary quote (mentioning of paradigm underlined)	Use of the paradigm
Scott (2000)	Graphical representation of the research process, including the paradigm items, in Figure 2 (p. 90)	Explicit
Galal (2001)	The concepts pertaining to individual levels of analysis (such as Domain, Organisation and Environment) *are systematically related to each other via the Paradigm Model as suggested by Strauss and Corbin (1990), later simply termed 'Paradigm' (Strauss and Corbin, 1998).* This model essentially provides a conceptual vehicle, through which a theory is developed, that articulates how concepts are causally or contextually related to each other (p. 7)	Explicit
Webb and Mallon (2007)	*The paradigm model is used to link categories and sub-categories in a set of relationships.* These relationships describe the phenomenon under study in terms of a set of conditions (causal, contextual, and intervening) and in terms of action/interaction strategies and their consequences. A simplified form of this model would look like this CAUSAL CONDITIONS [A]→PHENOMENON [B]→CONTEXT [C]→ACTION/ INTERACTION STRATEGIES [D]→CONSEQUENCES [E]; INTERVENING CONDITIONS [F] Thus, causal conditions (A) lead to a phenomenon (B), which leads to context (C), which leads to action/ interaction strategies (D), which then lead to consequences (E), under intervening conditions (F) (p. 371)	Explicit
Feller *et al.* (2008)	The next step (*axial coding*) was the process of determining hypotheses about the relationships between a category and its subcategories – *e.g., conditions, context, action/interaction strategies, and consequences* (p. 481)	Hints
Day *et al.* (2009)	*We analyzed our data using the Strauss and Corbin (1990) coding paradigm,* consisting of open, axial, and selective coding, as it provided a thorough and structured approach for examining the phenomenon of interest. It should be mentioned that we used the coding scheme as a general guideline to make sense of our data while remaining alert for emerging themes. We found the coding helpful for identifying impediments to information flows, their context, their possible origins, and their consequences (p. 642)	Explicit
O'Reilly and Finnegan (2010)	The next step (axial coding) is the process of determining hypotheses about the relationships between a category and its subcategories, *for example, conditions, context, action/ interaction strategies and consequences* (p. 467)	Hints
Strong and Volkoff (2010)	*We coded following Strauss and Corbin's paradigm,* but also included codes based on Glaser's six C's coding family and his dimension family as needed, always taking care to ensure the codes arose from the data, not from an external framework (p. 735)	Explicit

We identified one article that was published in 2007 (Webb and Mallon, 2007), one article that was published in 2009 (Day *et al.*, 2009), and two articles that were published in 2010 (Chakraborty *et al.*, 2010; Strong and Volkoff, 2010) that explicitly discuss the criticism that the coding paradigm has received, thus indicating that the IS discipline has started to engage with this arguably important discussion. This leads Chakraborty *et al.* (2010) to not use the paradigm at all, Strong and Volkoff (2010) to use it in combination with Glaser's (1978) coding families, and Day *et al.* (2009) to stress that they only use it as a guide, as opposed to a dogmatic principle. By contrast, Webb and Mallon (2007) applaud the more prescriptive nature of the paradigm and apply it quite rigidly.

Webb and Mallon's (2007) work is different from the other studies in that the authors use S & C grounded theory along with the paradigm specifically *because* of its more prescriptive nature, which suited their research aim of providing a method for narrative analysis. They write that they see the alleged weakness of S & C grounded theory (i.e., being more prescriptive) as a strength, and state that 'it is useful to the analysis of narrative (particularly by inexperienced researchers) because narrative analysis can quickly become complex in the absence of ready-to-hand procedures' (p. 370).

Overall, we found it somewhat surprising that relatively few studies refer to the forcing debate, even though it has been going on for more than two decades. Only recently, IS researchers have started to discuss the potential dangers that are associated with rigidly applying S & C grounded theory.

While in the seven articles presented in Table 7.5 it becomes apparent that the paradigm is applied, they are not necessarily explicit about the use of the same, but rather mention different paradigm items (e.g., O'Reilly and Finnegan, 2010). We did come across some other articles, where one may speculate about whether the paradigm may have been used, and these are detailed in Appendix C.

In summary, our analysis suggests that while axial coding in general is well established in IS top journals (and typically referred to as a stage where categories are related to their sub-categories and where relationships are explored), the paradigm model has gained relatively little popularity. It appears that criticism has been taken seriously, and researchers use axial coding flexibly, for instance, by using their own coding paradigm (e.g., Chakraborty *et al.*, 2010) as proposed by Kelle (2007), or combining it with using coding families as proposed by Glaser (e.g., Strong and Volkoff, 2010). Few researchers explicitly use the paradigm, and those who do typically do not claim that the paradigm is rigorously applied. The reasons for this disregard we will explore in the following section, where we discuss the results of research using the S & C paradigm and also further look into how the paradigm has been applied in research practice.

Characterizing the results of research using the S & C paradigm

In this section, we analyse how the application of axial coding and the coding paradigm may have impacted the results generated from IS studies, thereby providing answers to Research Question 2. We felt it was important to examine results of studies using axial coding and the coding paradigm in detail, given the debate about forcing of resultant theory. The seven studies we presented in Table 7.5 gave us that opportunity for that detailed examination.

In order to assess the outputs of these studies, we were faced with a challenge – how best to analyse and assess those outputs? Eventually, we decided to combine several approaches. First, we looked at the resultant theory or model itself. Second, we used two concepts about GTM suggested by Urquhart *et al.* (2010) – degree of conceptualization and theory scope – to help us understand how the theory had been built and its extent. Third, we analysed the result of the study in terms of Gregor's (2006) theory types. Finally, we used the classification of the IT artefact proposed by Orlikowski and Iacono (2001). Our use of the five analytical dimensions we chose is further elaborated on in Appendix D.

Overview of results

First, we provide an overview of our results for this section in Table 7.6. We then give a more detailed description of the findings, using each dimension.

Product of research

We were interested to see if there were any commonalities in the final products of research, and whether we would find traces of the paradigm model in those products, thus indicating the forcing of data. Let us first consider those studies that are explicit about the paradigm and also show how it was applied (Scott, 2000; Galal, 2001; Webb and Mallon, 2007; Day *et al.*, 2009; Strong and Volkoff, 2010).

Galal (2001: 8), in a study of software evaluation, explicitly acknowledges the role of the coding paradigm in the stage of axial coding and even writes that concepts were 'fitted' into the paradigm model. The

Table 7.6 Characteristics of studies that explicitly use the S & C coding paradigm

Study	Research design and focus	Final product	Degree of conceptualization	Theory scope	Theory type	Conceptualization of the IT artefact
Scott (2000) (JMIS)	Grounded theory study into inter organizational learning	Model of inter-organizational learning	Theory	Substantive	Explaining	Ensemble view/tool view
Galal (2001) (EJIS)	Use of grounded theory to create method of evaluation of software	Levels of theory and scenario for evaluation	Theory	Substantive	Analysing shading into explaining	Ensemble view
Webb and Mallon (2007) (JAIS)	Use of grounded theory to create method of narrative analysis, which is used to discuss communication breakdown in a software design example	Analysis of elements of interview, including causal elements Illustration of how grounded theory and narrative analysis can be combined Explicit goal of narrative analysis, not theorizing	Descriptive	Seed concepts	Analysing	Ensemble view
Feller et al. (2008) (ISR)	Grounded theory Case study where S & C procedures are used in order to analyse data about social exchange mechanisms in Open Source Service Networks	Theory on social mechanisms validated by survey	Theory	Substantive	Explaining and predicting	Ensemble view
Day et al. (2009) (JAIS)	Grounded theory case study of information flow in disaster relief supply chains	Model of information flows	Theory	Substantive	Explaining	Ensemble view/tool view
O'Reilly and Finnegan (2010) (EJIS)	Case study of electronic marketplace where S & C procedures used to analyse the data	Model of factors impacting on electronic marketplace performance	Theory	Substantive shading into formal concepts	Explaining and predicting	Proxy view
Strong and Volkoff (2010) (MISQ)	Longitudinal case study into ERP Misfits where grounded theory procedures were employed	Six categories of misfit	Descriptive	Substantive shading into formal	Analysing shading into explaining	Ensemble view/tool view

result of this research is theory at different levels (domain level, organizational level, and environment-level). The theories are then used in order to develop evaluative scenarios. The product of research (the need theories) is structured in accordance with the paradigm items and thus shows clear traces of the same.

Webb and Mallon (2007) also explicitly mention the use of the paradigm model. They propose a method for narrative analysis and apply axial coding in an illustrative case. They state that the purpose of the method is not to develop theory. These authors further say that the story takes its narrative shape through the application of the paradigm model. The authors say that the concepts 'are simply pulled into the paradigm model directly' (p. 376). When we look at the final product of research, the storyline resulting from selective coding, the structure of the paradigm model is still visible.

Scott (2000) investigates how and why information technology facilitates organizational learning. Her grounded theory study results in a model of organizational learning that is presented in a way that reflects the paradigm items: The main concepts are the phenomenon of virtual integration (phenomenon); environmental, organizational, and IT context in the disk drive industry (context); IT and trust (intervening conditions); and inter-organizational learning (action/interaction strategies). The structure of the paradigm is thus still visible in the final product of research. The results of the grounded theory analysis are then integrated with research literature in order to generate a conceptual model at a more abstract level. In this model, aspects of the coding paradigm are no longer visible.

Day *et al.* (2009), in their study of flow impediments in disaster relief supply chains, apply axial coding 'to match codes into the categories of the coding paradigm' (p. 642). While they write that they apply it 'as a guide instead of as a dogmatic principle by closely concentrating on emerging themes' (p. 642), the structure of the paradigm is still visible in the way the research is presented (e.g., information flow activities as the phenomenon, information flow impediments as intervening conditions, etc.). The authors state that they remained open for emergent themes, but they found 'that the coding paradigm and its categories fit the overall nature of our data very well' (p. 642).

Strong and Volkoff (2010) also acknowledge the dangers that are associated with using the paradigm and also use coding families as proposed by Glaser (1978) in their data analysis. They discuss how these different ways of looking at the data eventually led to emergent themes that do not show much resemblance with the paradigm items. So, in this case, the coding paradigm is explicitly used as only one way to look at the data and not applied in a strict and rigid fashion.

The other two articles presented in Table 7.5 are less explicit about the use of the paradigm. In both studies, it is stated that axial coding aims at discovering relationships between categories and sub-categories, considering 'e.g., conditions, context, action/interaction strategies and consequences' (Feller *et al.*, 2008: 481) and 'e.g., conditions, context, action/interaction strategies and consequences' (O'Reilly and Finnegan, 2010: 467). While the paradigm items are explicitly mentioned, the explaining and predicting theories produced provide unique conceptualizations of the phenomena being studied, that show no trace of the paradigm. Feller *et al.* (2008) and O'Reilly and Finnegan (2010) are the only two studies out of those that apply the paradigm that also present hypotheses.

Degree of conceptualization

By the degree of conceptualization, we mean the depth of analysis undertaken in coding terms, moving from description, interpretation through to the linking of categories to build theory, as suggested by Urquhart *et al.* (2010), and explained in Appendix D. By looking at this dimension, we hoped to be able to assess the level of conceptualization, given that one major criticism of the coding paradigm is that it results in low-level conceptualization. Altogether, in the seven studies, five get to, in our opinion, the level of theory. Only two remain at the level of description; these two studies, however, do not attempt to generate theory: Webb and Mallon (2007) state that their method of narrative analysis does not aim to develop a theory. Strong and Volkoff (2010) aim at identifying misfits and further theorizing about the conceptualization of the IT artefact in broader terms, and not at developing theory.

Those studies, however, that intend to develop theory, we believe, have been successful in their endeavours. Scott (2000), for example, in her study of inter-organizational learning, aims at explaining how and also why IT supports inter-organizational learning. The result of the study is a theory. In Galal (2001), a so-called need theory is presented. While the theory does not predict, it explains as it links causal conditions to strategies and consequences, and the statements are inferential. While substantive in nature, the result can still be framed as theory. Moreover, the three studies that do not explicitly claim that the paradigm is used, but mention the paradigm items, proceed to the level of theory.

Theory scope

We were interested in the scope of the theory produced by these studies, because Strauss and Corbin (1990) suggest the use of grounded theory for the generation of non-theory. Urquhart *et al.* (2010) identify three levels of theory in grounded theory studies – seed concepts, substantive theories, and formal theory. Most of the studies (six) produce theory at the substantive level, with some of those having a theory that shades into formal concepts. The theory proposed by Day *et al.* (2009), for example, comprises both concepts that are rather substantive in nature (e.g., inconsistent information and data formats) and that are rather formal (e.g., unwillingness). Some studies (Scott, 2000; Strong and Volkoff, 2010) engage with existent theory and thus succeed in proceeding to more formal concepts (Glaser and Strauss, 1967; Orlikowski, 1993).

Theory type

In our view, grounded theory affords great potential for theory building in our discipline. We were interested to see what types of theory might be generated by those studies that follow S & C coding procedures, including the use of the coding paradigm. Gregor (2006) distinguishes five types of theories, namely, theory for analysis (Type I), theory for explaining (Type II), theory for predicting (Type III), theory for explaining and predicting (Type IV), theory for design and action (Type V). As indicated by Gregor (2006), the different types of theories are closely related; that is, theory for explanation and prediction typically builds upon theory for analysing or description (i.e., taxonomies, frameworks). All our analysed studies at least provide analysis or description. Two studies (Webb and Mallon, 2007; Strong and Volkoff, 2010) remain at the level of description, while all other studies proceed to explaining (Type II) theories. This is in line with our finding with regard to the degree of conceptualization, where we have found that studies that apply the S & C paradigm tend to produce causal relationships; Type II theory explains how and why things happen and thus relies on causality (Gregor, 2006). The theoretical statements provided in some of these studies also shade into being predictive and thus become explaining and predictive (Type IV) theories. Prescriptive (Type V) theories are absent from the articles leveraging S & C coding procedures and the paradigm.

Conceptualization of the IT artefact

The IT artefact is at the core of IS research (Orlikowski and Iacono, 2001). Against this background, we were interested if, and in how far, the use of the S & C coding paradigm may impact on the conceptualization of the IT artefact. Orlikowski and Iacono (2001) identify 14 different conceptualizations of IT in the IS literature, which are further clustered into 5 broader views, namely, the tool view, the *ensemble* view, the *nominal* view, the *computational* view, and the *proxy* view. Definitions are given in Table 7.7.

Please note that the conceptualizations we identify below are tendencies, and often the studies are somewhere 'in between', as indicated in Table 7.6.

Scott (2000) investigates the role of technology in inter-organizational learning. While IT is seen as facilitating inter-organizational learning (which relates to the tool view of technology), the conceptualization views technology in relation to trust, collaboration, and learning, that is, the study also focuses on the dynamic interactions between people

Table 7.7 Conceptualizing the IT artefact according to Orlikowski and Iacono (2001)

Broad view	Detailed conceptualizations
Tool view of technology The tool view focuses on 'the engineered artifact, expected to do what its designers intend it to do' (Orlikowski and Iacono, 2001: 123). In this view, technology is typically the independent variable	As labour substitution tool As productivity tool As information processing tool As social relations tool
Proxy view of technology The *proxy* view focuses on conceptualizations that represent an 'essential aspect, property of value of the information technology' (Orlikowski and Iacono, 2001: 124)	As perception As diffusion As capital
Ensemble view of technology The *ensemble* view considers the dynamic interactions between people and technology in different contextual settings	As development project As production network As embedded system As structure
Computational view of technology The *computational* view focuses on the computational power of IT, thereby viewing technology as an algorithm or as a model	As algorithm As model
Nominal view of technology In studies that employ a *nominal* view, technology is referred to incidentally or in order to provide background information only	Technology as absent

and technology. Consider the following statement: 'An IOL [interorganizational learning] strategy, although potentially benefiting from IT, relies on face-to-face meetings to build trust and to encourage close collaboration' (p. 99). It thus becomes obvious that IT is seen as being only part of a larger, social context. Thus, this conceptualization is somewhere between a *tool* view and an *ensemble* view of technology.

Galal (2001) uses the S & C paradigm to systematically relate concepts to each other in order to formulate need theories in software development. These theories describe technology, and the use thereof, in its context. Concepts directly related to technology include 'Document management system that can be improved' (p. 9) (causal condition), 'Desired links to other existing IT systems' (p. 9) (context), or 'Current manual document management system' (p. 9) (intervening condition). Galal (2001) thus employs an *ensemble* view of technology and, more specifically, conceptualizes technology as an embedded system. That is, technology is 'neither an independent nor dependent variable but instead is seen to be enmeshed with the conditions of its use' (Orlikowski and Iacono, 2001: 126).

Webb and Mallon (2007) propose a method of narrative analysis that draws on grounded theory. They illustrate their example by means of a narrative of the history of an IS project. The result is a narrative of an IS development project, and like Galal (2001) can be framed as employing an *ensemble* view of technology, more specifically, technology as a development project. That is, it focuses on the social processes of the design, development, and implementation of an IS (Orlikowski and Iacono, 2001: 126).

Feller *et al.* (2008) investigate open source service networks, where an open source service network is a 'network of firms that collaborate in order to service customer software needs based on open source solutions' (p. 476). In their study, they 'explore how social mechanisms are used to overcome exchange problems, and thus facilitate the access to, and transfer of, strategic resources in OSSNs' (Feller *et al.*, 2008: 476–477). As the authors investigate social mechanisms in the context of the creation of software goods, we would contend that this study also employs an *ensemble* view of technology, specifically that of a production network. That is, the study looks at 'systems of alliances' that 'tie together inventors, research and development organizations, corporations, and governments who work together to develop new technologies and maintain their competitiveness' (Orlikowski and Iacono, 2001: 126). It must, however, be mentioned that the study clearly highlights that those mechanisms rely on the availability of appropriate IT infrastructures, thus indicating a view of technology as embedded system.

Day *et al.* (2009) investigate information flow impediments in disaster relief supply chains. The study uses concepts such as data collection, information processing, and information sharing. These constructs refer to the role of information technology in altering and enhancing 'the ways that humans and organizations process information' (Orlikowski and Iacono, 2001: 124), thus suggesting a tool view, more specifically technology as information processing tool. However, technology is not seen as in independent variable, but as being enmeshed with its social context: exemplary factors include *unwillingness* or *short supply chain life cycle* (Day *et al.*, 2009). We would thus contend that the study employs an ensemble view, at the same time as taking a tool view.

O'Reilly and Finnegan (2010) propose a theory of electronic marketplace performance, which is the central concept and dependent variable of this study; we contend that this is a proxy view of technology, as the authors investigate an element that represents an essential aspect, value of a specific information technology. Specifically, the authors investigate in how far electronic marketplace performance is impacted by strategic factors, contextual factors, structural factors, and fit.

Strong and Volkoff (2010) analyse organization–enterprise system fit and propose a new conceptualization of the Enterprise Systems artefact, thereby proposing implications for the IT artefact in general. These authors explicitly state that their conceptualization is 'somewhere between the tool and ensemble views of technology, as defined by Orlikowski and Iacono (2001)' (p. 752). While their conceptualization includes intended capabilities in the form of scripted structures (thus suggesting a tool view), they also highlight that 'the characteristics of the latent structures emerge from and depend on the other three structures [physical structures, deep structures, surface structures]' (p. 752), thereby suggesting an ensemble view.

Summary of key findings

Our findings suggest that for those studies that strictly apply the paradigm, it is obvious that this impacts on the process of data analysis and the results of research. That said, we would suggest that researchers have only proceeded with strict application of the paradigm where it has seen to be a good fit. Charmaz (2006) suggests that the paradigm helps to extend the analytic power of emerging ideas, and it is significant that the two studies that applied the paradigm closely (Scott, 2000; Galal, 2001) produced 'explaining' theory. Still, the question is whether the data are fitted into the paradigm or whether the paradigm fitted to the phenomenon. Many studies do not apply the paradigm in such strict fashion. Consequently, we cannot conclude that if the paradigm is used as 'nothing more than a perspective taken toward data, another analytic stance' (Strauss and Corbin, 1998: 128) this would lead to the forcing of data.

We also noted that applying the S & C coding paradigm leads to the identification of causal relationships. Therefore, one clear advantage of applying the S & C paradigm is that it does lead to theory development because it encourages the consideration of relationships between categories. We found that the application of the S & C paradigm only leads to non-theory, where researchers explicitly state that their aim is to generate non-theory. The accusation that the paradigm would result in low-level conceptualization is rebutted in our sample, at least. However, the conceptualization is restricted in that it is confined to relating categories according to the paradigm elements.

Our findings further suggest that those studies that apply the S & C paradigm tend to generate substantive concepts (i.e., concepts that are bound to a substantive area, and therefore, are said to be of high-practical relevance), sometimes shading into formal concepts (i.e., concepts that apply to a set of several substantive areas, and therefore, are more abstract in nature). We also noted that, in the studies we looked at, engaging with existent theory can help authors to proceed from the substantive concepts derived by allying S & C coding procedures to more formal concepts.

Our analysis also suggests that those studies that apply the S & C paradigm tend to move beyond mere description and provide explaining theory. Predictive and prescriptive statements are, by far and large, absent from those studies that apply the S & C paradigm.

Finally, from our analysis it becomes visible that the S & C paradigm is typically used in studies that employ an ensemble view to conceptualize the IT artefact, and there are at least two possible explanations: (a) the paradigm is intended to uncover the context in which certain phenomena occur and thus leads to according conceptualizations; (b) the paradigm is chosen in cases where the researcher is specifically interested in contextual factors and dynamic interactions. This seems likely, in that researchers will have proceeded with the coding paradigm if it provides a good fit with their research problem and can provide further insights into those contextual factors and dynamic interactions.

Discussion and implications

In this section, we discuss the findings from our analysis of data in the broader context of GTM with a particular focus on the basic principle of grounded theory – that the researcher should not force preconceived concepts on data. In this discussion, it is important to note that *both* Glaser's coding families and Strauss and Corbin's coding paradigm were intended to sensitize the researcher and make data analysis feasible (Kelle, 2007).

We first discuss the use of axial coding and the paradigm in IS research practice in the light of emergence and forcing of data, including the role of the paradigm in researchers' attempts to build theory instead of mere conceptual description. Second, we discuss how axial coding and the coding paradigm have been used in IS research practice, and conclude that this use is one that is conscious as opposed to accidental, where researchers deliberatively used these techniques in a way that is much in line with the pragmatist underpinnings of both Straussian and constructivist grounded theory. Third, we discuss advantages and disadvantages of axial coding and the paradigm, and attempt to provide an answer as to why Strauss and Corbin grounded theory has gained much popularity, despite all the – arguably justified – criticism it has been receiving over more than two decades, thereby relating our discussion to the nature of grounded theory as an evolving method. Fourth, we provide a discussion of the role that the experiences we and fellow researchers have had with Straussian grounded theory on the future of grounded theory, and provide a set of guidelines for using axial coding and the coding paradigm. Finally, we provide a brief outlook on the road ahead.

Axial coding, the paradigm, and emergence

With regard to the forcing debate as played out in IS research, we made two main observations: while, indeed, we found some evidence that the application of the S & C paradigm may lead to the forcing of data, we did not find any evidence that the application of the coding paradigm leads to conceptual description as opposed to theorizing *per se*.

Our findings suggest that where the S & C paradigm is used, this does indeed result in an emphasis on causal relationships between categories. One may, however, argue that the problem is that the paradigm leads to those relationships being defined in rather narrow terms. In some articles, we did see models that are very similar to the coding paradigm itself, so the accusation of 'forcing' is not entirely unwarranted. However, we must also contend that, from our analysis, we are not able to conclusively say whether the data are fitted into the paradigm or whether the paradigm fitted to the phenomenon. Still, some researchers state that the paradigm fits to the data (Day *et al.*, 2009). This is in line with what Charmaz (2006) says with regard to the use of axial coding in relation to the underlying research problem: 'The frame may extend or ' limit your vision, depending on your subject matter [...]' (p. 61).

It is worth noting that in some cases where the paradigm is applied rather rigidly, IS researchers do, in fact, put forward a theory. This observation becomes particularly relevant against the background that it has been argued that the IS discipline lacks foundational, or kernel, theories and thus requires more theory development (Watson, 2001). Specifically, we could observe a tendency of studies that apply the S & C paradigm to generate substantive concepts, sometimes shading into formal concepts. It has been argued by different researchers, and also by the originators of the method itself, that engaging with existent theory can lead to more general, or even formal, theory (Glaser and Strauss, 1967; Orlikowski, 1993). This process of 'scaling up' has also been discussed in depth in Urquhart *et al.* (2010), and we would like to reinforce this recommendation which, however, certainly applies to any type of grounded theory study. Besides, with regard to the type of theories generated, studies that apply the S & C paradigm tend to produce explaining theory, thus moving beyond description. One likely explanation is the focus of the paradigm on causality. Causality and explanation are closely interrelated (Gregor, 2006). We put forward the following proposition:

> **Proposition 1:** Using the paradigm, if done cautiously and with consideration of alternative coding families, may enhance one's theoretical sensitivity towards causal relationships and, in turn, proceed to explaining theory.

Whether the theory is entirely 'grounded' is a moot point, because, indeed, paradigm items may have been overlaid on the data. That said, Glaser (2005) points out that 'forcing' is a problem with all theoretical codes (he puts forward 41 such theoretical codes or paradigms), and that the theoretical code must have 'grab' and 'fit'. He also says better to have no theoretical code than a forced one (Glaser, 2005). Thus, it may be that these researchers have been successful in generating a theory precisely because the paradigm was appropriate for their research problem and focus – as indicated, a claim that is consistent with Charmaz (2006). Essentially, this is a discussion about theoretical sensitivity of the researcher, and their ability to develop categories without forcing preconceived ideas on the data (Kelle, 2007). Glaser and Strauss (1967) write: 'The sociologist should [...] be sufficiently *theoretically sensitive* so that he can conceptualize and formulate a theory as it emerges from the data' (p. 46). Against this background, we thus contend that the paradigm only constitutes one way of looking for relationships among categories, which brings us to the second important issue in our discussion, the conscious and flexible use of axial coding and the coding paradigm.

Conscious and flexible use of the coding paradigm

Our analysis provides clear evidence that, in the IS discipline, axial coding has been interpreted quite flexibly as a stage where categories are related to their subcategories, and where the paradigm is used in few cases. While the paradigm does not lead to conceptual description *per se*, it can be a useful device in order to become theoretically sensitive with regard to causal relationships between categories, in turn, leading to theory. It thus appears sensible for IS researchers to use the coding paradigm as one way to think about the data, as a jumping-off point (Urquhart, 2001), as opposed to a rigidly applicable schema. They could also access a far larger range of paradigms using Glaser (1978, 2005), as Strong and Volkoff (2010) do in their study, or draw on entirely different coding paradigms as done in Chakraborty *et al.* (2010) and proposed by Kelle (2007). This flexible use of axial coding is congruent with more recent developments of grounded theory, where the role of axial coding and the coding paradigm have been re-considered, specifically with regard to the sociological and philosophical underpinnings of the method, as we will outline in turn.

First, Charmaz (2006), in the context of constructivist grounded theory, describes axial coding as a stage that is optional and depends on the research problem at hand and the researcher's skills. She writes about her own use of axial coding:

> Although I have not used axial coding according to Strauss and Corbin's formal procedures, I have developed subcategories of a category and showed the links between them as I learned about the experiences the categories represent.
>
> (Charmaz, 2006: 61)

Interestingly, this is in line with the latest publication of Basics of Qualitative Research (Corbin and Strauss, 2008), where the authors write[3]:

> An important point to remember is that the paradigm is only a tool and not a set of directives. The analyst is not coding for conditions or consequences *per se*, but rather uses the tool to obtain an understanding of the circumstances that surround events and therefore enrich the analysis.
>
> (p. 90)

This understanding is further substantiated with the results from our analysis that show that while axial coding is consistently interpreted as the stage where categories are linked to their sub-categories, the S & C coding paradigm does not play the prominent role one may expect given that there have been three influential books (Strauss, 1987; Strauss and Corbin, 1990, 1998), where the coding paradigm is described as being all but mandatory. One likely explanation is that IS researchers, indeed, have taken the criticism seriously that has been put forward towards the use of the coding paradigm, and thus avoided to do so. And indeed, more recently, IS researchers have been increasingly aware of the debate around the potential dangers that are typically associated with applying the paradigm, most notably the threat of forcing the data.

Against this background, it appears that IS researchers have – quite naturally – used axial coding and the coding paradigm over the past 20 years in a much more flexible and adaptive way than intended by the referenced versions of the method by Strauss (1987) and Strauss and Corbin (1990, 1998). We find that the use of Straussian grounded theory procedures is one that is conscious; IS researchers deliberately choose strategies as they fit to the phenomena they study and adapt these coding procedures as they fit to the phenomena they study and the intent of their research. While we do see some evidence that the rigid application of the paradigm may lead to forcing, in most cases the researchers are well aware of the dangers associated with this. We put forward the following proposition:

> **Proposition 2:** The decision on whether or not and also how axial coding and/or the coding paradigm are used in order to construct theory should be a conscious decision, where researchers must consider the phenomena studied as well as the intent of their research.

This is in line with the basic idea of theoretical sensitivity, and with what Glaser and Strauss (1967) write on page 3 in *The Discovery of Grounded Theory*: 'Of course, the researcher does not approach reality as a *tabula rasa*. He must have a perspective that will help him see relevant data and abstract significant categories from his scrutiny of the data' (p. 3).

Moreover, this is much in line with constructivist grounded theory (Charmaz, 2006), where it is argued that neither theories nor data are discovered; instead they are constructed by the researcher based on her interactions with the field (Charmaz, 2000; Bryant, 2002; Charmaz, 2006). These interactions, we argue, include the deliberative choice of coding stages and coding paradigms to be used. As any grounded theory study needs to adhere to the basic principles of grounded theory – constant comparison and theoretical sensitivity – the challenge is how the construction can be done without forcing preconceived ideas on the data. Later in this chapter, we provide a set of guidelines grounded in our analysis that can assist researchers in using axial coding and the paradigm.

Axial coding, the paradigm, and grounded theory as an evolving method

The use of axial coding and the paradigm are an important marker and exemplar for the evolving nature of grounded theory. Not only is the method contested, but also characterized by a variety of options, techniques, and procedures that are now available to researchers across many disciplines. Bryant and Charmaz (2007) see GTM as 'a family of methods' and point out that the specific (idiosyncratic) ideas of researchers using GTM 'form a family of resemblances' (p. 11). Our study provides some insights into how this evolving nature has unfolded in the IS field. While 'evolved' grounded theory is now the predominant form of grounded theory (Matavire and Brown, 2011), few studies consistently and comprehensively use, for instance, Straussian grounded theory.

Against this background, we argue that it will be important that IS researchers clearly position their work and explain adaptations in order to contribute to the integrity of the method. We believe that such transparency will be beneficial to the current debates on the application of grounded theory. From the analysis of our study, we do not conclude that it will be necessary to label every study exclusively either 'Straussian' or 'Glaserian' or 'constructivist'. Instead, grounded theory studies need to adhere to the basic principles of the method – what Bryant and Charmaz (2007) call resemblances when they refer, for instance, to discussions about the 'primacy of grounded observation over preconceptions' (p. 11) – while grounded theory practices must be consciously used depending on the phenomenon being studied as well as the researchers' intent and skills. In order to accomplish such 'methodological fit', conscious decisions include the choice of coding procedures and paradigms. Charmaz (2006) writes: 'Antony Bryant (2002) and Adele Clarke (2003, 2005) join me in contending that we can use basic grounded theory guidelines with twenty-first century methodological assumptions and approaches' (p. 9). We put forward the following proposition:

> **Proposition 3:** Grounded theory is an evolving method, or even family of methods, and researchers need to adhere to the basic principles of the method, such as theoretical sensitivity and constant comparison, while choosing those techniques and guidelines that fit to the phenomenon being studied as well as their specific intent when constructing grounded theories.

Despite all the criticism that has been put forward against axial coding and the paradigm, it must be noted that there is some agreement in the literature about its advantages. Most notably, the paradigm seems to be more easy to handle than Glaser's coding families: 'one would need an advanced understanding of different thoughts of school [sic], their terminology, and their possible relations to make use of Glaser's list of coding families, to choose the coding families most adequate for the data and to combine different coding families in a meaningful way' (Kelle, 2007: 203).

Still, the question remains why Straussian coding procedures have gained so much popularity (remember that we identified 38 studies published in IS top journals that explicitly used axial coding), and here we present some possible explanations. Evolved grounded theory (most notably Straussian grounded theory) comes along with more detailed guidelines than classical grounded theory (Kelle, 2007), and this may lead to two consequences. First, novice researchers in particular may be attracted to what seem like well-signposted procedures (Urquhart, 2001). Second, following the proposed guidelines may allow researchers to more transparently report on the underlying research processes, thereby meeting the expectations of leading IS journals. Different scholars have indicated that qualitative research has not yet gained the acceptance as has quantitative research in the IS discipline, and researchers are asked to provide clear chains of evidence that lead empirical data to conceptualization (Walsham, 1995).

Using axial coding in practice – a set of guidelines

From our analysis of prior literature, and our findings about IS studies that use S & C coding procedures, we put forward below a set of guidelines. Combined with our key emerging propositions and prior discussion, we hope these guidelines may be of assistance to colleagues who have chosen to use S & C coding procedures. The guiding principle behind these guidelines is that any technique should enhance theoretical sensitivity, and not hinder emergence. Table 7.8 provides an overview of our suggested guidelines.

First, we call upon IS researchers to *flexibly* use axial coding as a stage where relationships between categories are identified (*Guideline 1*). The coding paradigm only constitutes one way to analyse data. If axial coding is interpreted as suggested in Strauss and Corbin (1990, 1998), IS researchers limit themselves to a specific way of coding, which, we would argue, may indeed hamper theoretical sensitivity and lead to the forcing of data. Our study has shown that the flexible use of axial coding has led to some good results, no forcing of data, and indeed some theorizing. We can then suggest that IS researchers are well advised to consider axial coding as a stage where categories are related to their sub-categories (i.e., where one codes around the axis of a category, so as to further develop that category), but do not follow the advice that axial coding must mandatorily and potentially exclusively apply the coding paradigm, as suggested in Strauss and Corbin (1990, 1998), for example. This is congruent with Kelle (2007), who even suggests that everybody should use their 'own coding paradigm'. This also is consistent with current advice from Corbin and Strauss (2008), where the paradigm is no longer mandatory as well as the interpretation of axial coding in constructivist grounded theory (Charmaz, 2006). It is also consistent with Glaser (2005), who clearly states that researchers both could and should seek to build their own theoretical codes, rather than applying a theoretical code that does not fit.

Second, we suggest that researchers should provide a clear rationale for adaptations that are made with regard to the use of S & C coding procedures (*Guideline 2*). This, we believe, will contribute to the integrity of the method. Adaptations are of interest and should be shared; grounded theory is an evolving method. Our study shows that grounded theory is frequently adapted, and that grounded theory techniques are used in a variety of research designs. This is congruent with findings from other studies (e.g., Matavire and Brown, 2011). Examples of grounded theory as an evolving method can be clearly seen in Charmaz (2006) and Clarke (2005).

190

Table 7.8 Guidelines for using S & C coding procedures

1. Flexible use of axial coding

This guideline suggests that IS researchers *flexibly* use axial coding as a stage, where relationships between categories are identified. The coding paradigm only constitutes one way to analyse data. If axial coding is interpreted as suggested in Strauss and Corbin (1990, 1998), IS researchers limit themselves to a specific way of coding, which, we would argue, may indeed hamper theoretical sensitivity and lead to the forcing of data

2. A rationale for adaptations

This guideline suggests that IS researchers provide a clear rationale for adaptions that are made with regard to using S & C coding procedures. This, we believe, will contribute to the integrity of the method. Adaptations are of interest and should be shared; grounded theory is an evolving method

3. Awareness of 'forcing' issues

This guideline suggests that IS researchers use the coding paradigm as a jumping-off point, rather than a rigid device, to avoid 'forcing'. Researchers need not to be aware of 'forcing' the data. If the coding paradigm is considered in conjunction with other coding families, as proposed by Glaser (1978, 2005), it can indeed enhance theoretical sensitivity. Many IS researchers using the S & C strand have opted not to use the paradigm; thus, they are already treating the paradigm as suggested by Corbin and Strauss (2008) – as an option

4. Theoretical sensitivity towards causality

This guideline suggests IS researchers to use the coding paradigm as a sensitizing device (Klein and Myers, 1999) that may help them to think about causal relationships in turn, leading to the discovery of 'theory to explain' (Gregor, 2006). Consequently, the paradigm appears to be suitable to study cause–effect relationships, for instance, in the context of IT appropriation, use, and effects. Again, one must be cautious as, of course, interpretive studies in particular are often not characterized by causality (Walsham, 1995). As indicated in Guideline 3, the paradigm should, however, be used in conjunction with other coding families

5. Contextualization

This guideline suggests IS researchers might consider the use of the S & C paradigm specifically in studies that seek to uncover the *context* in which certain phenomena occur, because context is a feature of the paradigm. For IS researchers, viewing technology as being enmeshed with the conditions of its development and use can be helpful

Third, researchers are encouraged to consider the coding paradigm as a jumping-off point, rather than a rigid device, to avoid 'forcing' (*Guideline 3*). If the coding paradigm is considered in conjunction with other coding families, as proposed by Glaser (1978, 2005), it can indeed enhance theoretical sensitivity. If the coding paradigm is applied rigidly, there is a possibility that it will show up in a strong resemblance in the final product of research. In many cases, however, the coding paradigm is used as a jumping-off point. Strong and Volkoff's (2010) approach of exploring other coding families (Glaser, 2005) is a good example.

Fourth, the coding paradigm may indeed enhance the theoretical sensitivity of researchers towards the identification of relationships that are causal in nature; in turn, leading to explaining theory (Gregor, 2006) (*Guideline 4*). Again, one must be cautious as, of course, interpretive studies in particular are often not characterized by causality (Walsham, 1995). As indicated in Guideline 3, the paradigm should, however, be used in conjunction with other coding families.

Fifth, researchers are encouraged to use the paradigm in studies that seek to uncover the context in which certain phenomena occur, thus viewing technology as being enmeshed with the conditions of its development and use (*Guideline 5*). Our study suggests a clear tendency towards the ensemble view of technology. Dey (1999) states that grounded theory focuses on the interaction of the individual with the phenomena under study – in our case, information technology.

The road ahead – using S & C coding procedures in the IS field

Through our analysis, we have shown that S & C coding procedures – despite much justified criticism – have been successfully used in the IS field. Consequently, we need to ask how we, as a discipline, can benefit from using S & C coding procedures. For instance, our study has shown that S & C coding procedures – including the paradigm – have been successfully used to develop explaining models, with a focus on cause–effect relationships. We would thus contend that, for instance, studies on IT appropriation, use, and effects (DeSanctis and Poole, 1994; Markus and Silver, 2008) can benefit from the use S & C coding procedures. In this context, more recently, the concept of functional affordances as relationships between technical objects and user groups has gained increased attention in IS research (Markus and Silver, 2008; Leonardi, 2011). Axial coding and the S & C paradigm could provide potential devices to understand the causal and intervening conditions (grounded in the material properties of IT), under which such affordances emerge. (Of course, other causal theoretical codes could be considered for causal relationships, for instance Glaser's (2005) theoretical code of conjectural causation, where causation is viewed more holistically.) Considering the potential of S & C coding procedures to uncover cause–effect relationships and capacity to investigate technology as it is enmeshed with the conditions of its development and use, we would like to encourage IS researchers to leverage S & C coding procedures in light of their potential to contribute to theory building. As it has been reinforced by our review of the literature, there is a tendency to think of grounded theory as an inductive coding technique, as opposed to a theory building method.

Limitations

This study has several limitations. First, our conclusions are based on the analysis of prior methodological literature and IS studies that have employed S & C coding procedures. By the very nature of our analysis, we were not able to study the unsuccessful attempts to use the S & C coding paradigm. Still, we would argue that the analysis of studies that actually employed S & C coding procedures adds important empirical evidence to a discussion that, until now, has been largely speculative and theoretical. Moreover, our critical analysis includes our discipline's six top journals as proposed by the AIS. While we believe that assessing those articles that have been rigorously peer reviewed will enable us to gain good insight into how S & C coding procedures have been used in the IS discipline, we cannot say with certainty that including other journals and also conferences may not produce a somewhat different picture and further insights.

Second, we focused on one specific aspect of the method, namely, that of axial coding and the coding paradigm – even though there are many more debates around GTM (Heath and Cowley, 2004). However, the prominent role of axial coding and the paradigm (Matavire and Brown, 2011), and their important role with regard to the basic principle of grounded theory to not force preconceived ideas on data warrant further investigation. We were then able to link the discussion to the larger debate about the evolving nature of GTM that has led some authors to even call it a 'family of methods' (Bryant and Charmaz, 2007).

Third, as the guidelines we propose pertain to S & C grounded theory in particular, they should be considered in conjunction with more general recommendations on the use of grounded theory; for instance, the basic principles of emergence, comparative analysis, and theoretical sampling (Glaser and Strauss, 1967; Strauss and Corbin, 1990), or the principles of scaling up and theoretical integration (e.g., Urquhart *et al.*, 2010).

Conclusions

With this study, we intend to contribute to the ongoing debate about the contested nature of GTM. Specifically, we discuss the most basic rule of grounded theory – that researchers should not force preconceived conceptualizations on data. Kelle (2007) writes about the important metaphor of emergence that was introduced in 1967 *The Discovery of Grounded Theory* that it 'had a far-reaching impact on the methodological debate but, at the same time, was difficult to be translated into tangible methodological rules' (p. 191). The stage of axial coding, and the S & C coding paradigm, were an attempt fill this void, and we can learn much if we understand how these procedures have impacted on research practice.

With our analysis of IS studies that have used Straussian grounded theory procedures, we add important empirical evidence to a discussion that, until now, has been largely theoretical and speculative as opposed to grounded in any evidence. In this article, we provide detailed insights into how axial coding and the coding paradigm have been used over approximately two decades of IS research published in top journals.

In conclusion, we learned through our analysis that axial coding and the coding paradigm have been used consciously by IS researchers against the background of the phenomena they studied, and the potential dangers of forcing of data and hindering emergence. We find that IS researchers deliberately choose and even adapt Straussian grounded theory procedures, as they fit to the phenomena they study and the intent of their research. We were further able to relate our findings to the broader developments of grounded theory, and argue that this is much in line with constructivist ideas of grounded theory: both data and interpretations are the result of constructions of researchers who engage with the field. We would suggest that it is important for IS researchers to look beyond the boundaries of their own discipline and consider their use of GTM within larger debates in other fields such as sociology. *The Sage Handbook of Grounded Theory* (Bryant and Charmaz, 2007) provides a good starting point in this regard – GTM can clearly be seen as an evolving method.

Finally, we were able to derive a set of guidelines that can assist researchers in constructing grounded theories using Straussian coding procedures, while adhering to the most basic rule of grounded theory – that preconception must be avoided in order to be true to the spirit of grounded theory.

Notes

1. The first publication of the coding paradigm was in fact in 1987 (Strauss, 1987); however, it was not a subject of controversy until the 1990 book of Strauss and Corbin. It turned out that the first article using S & C grounded theory published in the journals examined in this study was published in 1993.
2. For a comparison, see Matavire and Brown (2011) for GTM use in IS over the period 1985–2008.
3. Anselm Strauss died in 1996 and the changes in the 2008 book are solely the work of Juliet Corbin.

References

Ågerfalk, P.J. and Fitzgerald, B. (2008). Outsourcing to an Unknown Workforce: Exploring opensourcing as a global sourcing strategy, *MIS Quarterly* 32(2): 385–409.

AIS (2007). Senior scholar's basket of journals. [WWW document] http://home.aisnet.org/displaycommon.cfm?an=1&subarticlenbr=346 (accessed 5 August 2009).

Alvarez, R. (2008). Examining Technology, Structure and Identity During an Enterprise System Implementation, *Information Systems Journal* 18(2): 203–224.

American Psychological Association (2010). *Publication Manual of the American Psychological Association*, 6th edn, Washington DC: American Psychological Association.

Azad, B. and King, N. (2008). Enacting Computer Workaround Practices within a Medication Dispensing System, *European Journal of Information Systems* 17(3): 264–278.

Baskerville, R. and Pries-Heje, J. (1999). Grounded Action Research: A method for understanding IT in practice, *Accounting Management and Information Technologies* 9(1): 1–23.

Baskerville, R. and Pries-Heje, J. (2001). A Multiple-Theory Analysis of a Diffusion of Information Technology Case, *Information Systems Journal* 11(3): 181–212.

Baskerville, R. and Pries-Heje, J. (2004). Short Cycle Time Systems Development, *Information Systems Journal* 14(3): 237–264.

Bjørn, P. and Ngwenyama, O. (2009). Virtual Team Collaboration: Building shared meaning, resolving breakdowns and creating translucence, *Information Systems Journal* 19(3): 227–253.

Boychuk Duchscher, J.E. and Morgan, B. (2004). Grounded Theory: Reflections on the emergence vs forcing debate, *Journal of Advanced Nursing* 48(6): 605–612.

Bryant, A. (2002). Re-Grounding Grounded Theory, *Journal of Information Technology Theory and Application* 4(1): 25–42.

Bryant, A. and Charmaz, K. (eds.) (2007). Grounded Theory Research: Methods and practices, in *The Sage Handbook of Grounded Theory*, London: Sage, pp. 1–28.

Carlson, P.J. and Davis, G.B. (1998). An Investigation of Media Selection among Directors and Managers: From 'self' to 'other' orientation, *MIS Quarterly* 22(3): 335–362.

Chakraborty, S., Sarker, S. and Sarker, S. (2010). An Exploration into the Process of Requirements Elicitation: A grounded approach, *Journal of the Association for Information Systems* 11(4): 212–249.

Charmaz, K. (1983). The Grounded Theory Method: An explication and interpretation, in R.M. Emerson (ed.) *Contemporary Field Research: A collection of readings*, Boston, MA: Little, Brown & Co, pp. 109–126.

Charmaz, K. (2000). Grounded Theory: Objectivist and constructivist methods, in N.K. Denzin and Y.S. Lincoln (eds.) *Handbook of Qualitative Research*, 2nd edn, Thousand Oaks, CA: Sage, pp. 509–535.

Charmaz, K. (2006). *Constructing Grounded Theory: A practical guide through qualitative analysis*, Thousand Oaks, CA: Sage.

Clarke, A.E. (2003). Situational Analyses: Grounded theory mapping after the postmodern turn, *Symbolic Interaction* 26(4): 553–576.

Clarke, A.E. (2005). *Situational Analysis: Grounded theory after the postmodern turn*, Thousand Oaks, CA: Sage.

Conboy, K. (2010). Project Failure En Masse: A study of loose budgetary control in ISD projects, *European Journal of Information Systems* 19(3): 273–287.

Corbin, J. and Strauss, A.L. (1990). Grounded Theory Research: Procedures, canons, and evaluative criteria, *Qualitative Sociology* 13(1): 3–21.

Corbin, J. and Strauss, A.L. (2008). *Basics of Qualitative Research*, Thousand Oaks, CA: Sage.

Day, J.M., Junglas, I. and Silva, L. (2009). Information Flow Impediments in Disaster Relief Supply Chains, *Journal of the Association for Information Systems* 10(8): 637–660.

DeSanctis, G. and Poole, M.S. (1994). Capturing the Complexity in Advanced Technology Use: Adaptive structuration theory, *Organization Science* 5(2): 121–147.

Dewey, J. (1922). *Human Nature and Conduct*, New York: Holt.

Dey, I. (1999). *Grounding Grounded Theory: Guidelines for Qualitative Inquiry*, San Diego: Academic Press.

Doherty, N.F., Coombs, C.R. and Loan-Clarke, J. (2006). A Re-Conceptualization of the Interpretive Flexibility of Information Technologies: Redressing the balance between the social and the technical, *European Journal of Information Systems* 15(6): 569–582.

Espinosa, J.A., Slaughter, S.A., Kraut, R.E. and Herbsleb, J.D. (2007). Team Knowledge and Coordination in Geographically Distributed Software Development, *Journal of Management Information Systems* 24(1): 135–169.

Feller, J., Finnegan, P., Fitzgerald, B. and Hayes, J. (2008). From Peer Production to Productization: A study of socially enabled business exchanges in open source service networks, *Information Systems Research* 19(4): 475–493.

Galal, G.H. (2001). From Contexts to Constructs: The use of grounded theory in operationalising contingent process models, *European Journal of Information Systems* 10(1): 2–14.

Galliers, R.D., Whitley, E.A. and Paul, R.J. (2007). The European Information Systems Academy, *European Journal of Information Systems* 16(1): 3–4.

Glaser, B.G. (1978). *Theoretical Sensitivity: Advances in the methodology of grounded theory*, Mill Valley, CA: The Sociology Press.

Glaser, B.G. (1992). *Basics of Grounded Theory Analysis: Emergence vs. forcing*, Mill Valley, CA: Sociology Press.

Glaser, B.G. (2005). *The Grounded Theory Perspective III: Theoretical coding*, Mill Valley, CA: Sociology Press.

Glaser, B.G. and Strauss, A.L. (1967). *The Discovery of Grounded Theory: Strategies for qualitative research*, Chicago: Aldine Publishing Company.

Goo, J., Kishore, R., Rao, H.R. and Nam, K. (2009). The Role of Service Level Agreements in Relational Management of Information Technology Outsourcing: An empirical study, *MIS Quarterly* 33(1): 119–145.

Goode, S. and Gregor, S. (2009). Rethinking Organisational Size in IS Research: Meaning, measurement and redevelopment, *European Journal of Information Systems* 18(1): 4–25.

Goulielmos, M. (2004). Systems Development Approach: Transcending methodology, *Information Systems Journal* 14(4): 363–386.

Gregor, S. (2006). The Nature of Theory in Information Systems, *MIS Quarterly* 30(3): 611–642.

Hackney, R., Jones, S. and Lösch, A. (2007). Towards an E-Government Efficiency Agenda: The impact of information and communication behaviour on E-reverse auctions in public sector procurement, *European Journal of Information Systems* 16(2): 178–191.

Heath, H. and Cowley, S. (2004). Developing a Grounded Theory Approach: A comparison of glaser and strauss, *International Journal of Nursing Studies* 41(2): 141–150.

Holmström Olsson, H., Conchúir, E.Ó., Ågerfalk, P.J. and Fitzgerald, B. (2008). Two-Stage Offshoring: An investigation of the Irish Bridge, *MIS Quarterly* 32(2): 257–279.

Horton, K.S. and Wood-Harper, T.A. (2006). The Shaping of I.T. Trajectories: Evidence from the U.K. public sector, *European Journal of Information Systems* 15(2): 214–224.

Huang, J.C., Newell, S. and Pan, S.-L. (2001). The Process of Global Knowledge Integration: A case study of a multinational investment bank's Y2K Program, *European Journal of Information Systems* 10(3): 161–174.

Jones, R. and Noble, G. (2007). Grounded Theory and Management Research: A lack of integrity? *Qualitative Research in Organizations and Management: An international journal* 2(2): 84–103.

Jones, S. and Hughes, J. (2001). Understanding IS Evaluation as a Complex Social Process: A case study of a UK local authority, *European Journal of Information Systems* 10(4): 189–203.

Keddy, B., Sims, S.L. and Stern, P.N. (1996). Grounded Theory and Feminist Research Methodology, *Journal of Advanced Nursing* 23(3): 448–453.

Keil, M., Im, G.P. and Mähring, M. (2007). Reporting Bad News on Software Projects: The effects of culturally constituted views of face-saving, *Information Systems Journal* 17(1): 59–87.

Kelle, U. (2007). The Development of Categories: Different approaches in grounded theory, in A. Bryant and K. Charmaz (eds.) *The Sage Handbook of Grounded Theory*, London: Sage, pp. 191–213.

Kendall, J. (1999). Axial Coding and the Grounded Theory Controversy, *Western Journal of Nursing Research* 21(6): 743–757.

Khoo, H.M. and Robey, D. (2007). Deciding to Upgrade Packaged Software: A comparative case study of motives, contingencies and dependencies, *European Journal of Information Systems* 16(5): 555–567.

Kirsch, L.J. (1997). Portfolios of Control Modes and IS Project Management, *Information Systems Research* 8(3): 215–239.

Kirsch, L.J. (2004). Deploying Common Systems Globally: The dynamics of control, *Information Systems Research* 15(4): 374–395.

Klein, H.K. and Myers, M.D. (1999). A Set of Principles for Conducting and Evaluating Interpretive Field Studies in Information Systems, *MIS Quarterly* 23(1): 67–94.

Kock, N. (2001). Asynchronous and Distributed Process Improvement: The role of collaborative technologies, *Information Systems Journal* 11(2): 87–110.

Larsen, T.J., Niederman, F., Limayem, M. and Chan, J. (2007). The Role of Modelling in Achieving Information Systems Success: UML to the rescue? *Information Systems Journal* 19(1): 83–117.

Leonardi, P.M. (2011). When Flexible Routines Meet Flexible Technologies: Affordance, constraint, and the imbrication of human and material agencies, *MIS Quarterly* 35(1): 147–167.

Levina, N. and Ross, J.W. (2003). From the Vendor's Perspective: Exploring the value proposition in information technology outsourcing, *MIS Quarterly* 27(3): 331–364.

Lim, E.T.K., Pan, S.L. and Tan, C.W. (2005). Managing User Acceptance Towards Enterprise Resource Planning (ERP) Systems – Understanding the dissonance between user expectations and managerial policies, *European Journal of Information Systems* 14(2): 135–149.

Lindgren, R., Henfridsson, O. and Schultze, U. (2004). Design Principles for Competence Management Systems: A synthesis of an action research study, *MIS Quarterly* 28(3): 435–472.

Locke, K. (1996). Rewriting the Discovery of Grounded Theory After 25 Years? *Journal of Management Inquiry* 5(3): 239–245.

Maldonado, E. (2010). The Process of Introducing Floss in the Public Administration: The case of Venezuela, *Journal of the Association for Information Systems* 11(11): 756–783.

Markus, M.L. and Silver, M.S. (2008). A Foundation for the Study of IT Effects: A new look at desanctis and poole's concepts of structural features and spirit, *Journal of the Association for Information Systems* 9(10): 609–632.

Matavire, R. and Brown, I. (2011). Profiling Grounded Theory Approaches in Information Systems Research, *European Journal of Information Systems* 22(1): 119–129.

Mead, G.H. (1934). *Mind, Self and Society*, Chicago: University of Chicago Press.

Melia, K.M. (1996). Rediscovering Glaser, *Qualitative Health Research* 6(3): 368–373.

Miles, M.B. and Huberman, A.M. (1984). *Qualitative Data Analysis: A sourcebook of new methods*, Beverly Hills, CA: Sage Publications.

Mills, J., Bonner, A. and Francis, K. (2006). The Development of Constructivist Grounded Theory, *International Journal of Qualitative Methods* 5(1): 25–35.

Mourmant, G., Gallivan, M.J.M. and Kalika, M. (2009). Another Road to IT Turnover: The entrepreneurial path, *European Journal of Information Systems* 18(5): 498–521.

O'Reilly, P. and Finnegan, P. (2010). Intermediaries in Inter-Organisational Networks: Building a theory of electronic marketplace performance, *European Journal of Information Systems* 19(4): 462–480.

Orlikowski, W.J. (1993). Case Tools as Organizational Change: Investigating incremental and radical changes in systems development, *MIS Quarterly* 17(3): 309–340.

Orlikowski, W.J. and Iacono, C.S. (2001). Research Commentary: Desperately seeking the 'IT' in IT research – A call to theorizing the IT artifact, *Information Systems Research* 12(2): 121–134.

Pauleen, D.J. (2003). An Inductively Derived Model of Leader-Initiated Relationship Building with Virtual Team Members, *Journal of Management Information Systems* 20(3): 227–256.

Ramesh, B., Cao, L. and Baskerville, R. (2010). Agile Requirements Engineering Practices and Challenges: An empirical study, *Information Systems Journal* 20(5): 449–480.

Remus, U. and Wiener, M. (2010). A Multi-Method, Holistic Strategy for Researching Critical Success Factors in IT Projects, *Information Systems Journal* 20(1): 25–52.

Robrecht, L.C. (1995). Grounded Theory: Evolving methods, *Qualitative Health Research* 5(2): 169–177.

Ryan, G. and Valverde, M. (2006). Waiting in Line for Online Services: A qualitative study of the user's perspective, *Information Systems Journal* 16(2): 181–211.

Ryan, S.D. and Harrison, D.A. (2000). Considering Social Subsystem Costs and Benefits in Information Technology Investment Decisions: A view from the field on anticipated payoffs, *Journal of Management Information Systems* 16(4): 11–40.

Schultze, U. (2000). A Confessional Account of an Ethnography about Knowledge Work, *MIS Quarterly* 24(1): 3–41.

Scott, J.E. (2000). Facilitating Interorganizational Learning with Information Technology, *Journal of Management Information Systems* 17(2): 81–113.

Smolander, K., Rossi, M. and Purao, S. (2008). Software Architectures: Blueprint, literature, language or decision? *European Journal of Information Systems* 17(6): 575–588.

Spears, J.L. and Barki, H. (2010). User Participation in Information Systems Security Risk Management, *MIS Quarterly* 34(3): 503–522.

Strauss, A.L. (1987). *Qualitative Analysis for Social Scientists*, Cambridge, UK: University of Cambridge Press.

Strauss, A.L. and Corbin, J. (1990). *Basics of Qualitative Research*, 1st edn, Thousand Oaks, CA: Sage.

Strauss, A.L. and Corbin, J. (1994a). *Basics of Qualitative Research: Grounded theory procedures and techniques*, Newbury Park: Sage.

Strauss, A.L. and Corbin, J. (1994b). Grounded Theory Methodology: An overview, in N.K. Denzin and Y.S. Lincoln (eds.) *Handbook of Qualitative Research*, Thousand Oaks: Sage, pp. 273–285.

Strauss, A.L. and Corbin, J. (1998). *Basics of Qualitative Research: Techniques and procedures for developing grounded theory*, 2nd edn, London: Sage.

Strauss, A.L. and Corbin, J.M. (1997). *Grounded Theory in Practice*, Thousand Oaks, CA: Sage.

Strong, D.M. and Volkoff, O. (2010). Understanding Organization-Enterprise System Fit: A path to theorizing the information technology artifact, *MIS Quarterly* 34(4): 731–756.

Suddaby, R. (2006). What Grounded Theory Is Not, *Academy of Management Journal* 49(4): 633–642.

Urquhart, C. (2001). An Encounter with Grounded Theory: Tackling the practical and philosophical issues, in E.M. Trauth (ed.) *Qualitative Research in IS: Issues and trends*, Hershey, PA: IGI Publishing, pp. 104–140.

Urquhart, C. (2007). The Evolving Nature of Grounded Theory Method: The Case of the Information Systems Discipline, in A. Bryant and K. Charmaz (eds.) *The Sage Handbook of Grounded Theory*, London: Sage, pp. 339–359.

Urquhart, C. (2013). *Grounded Theory for Qualitative Research: A practical guide*, London: Sage.

Urquhart, C., Lehmann, H. and Myers, M.D. (2010). Putting the 'Theory' Back into Grounded Theory: Guidelines for grounded theory studies in information systems, *Information Systems Journal* 20(4): 357–381.

van Niekerk, J.C. and Roode, J.D. (2009). Glaserian and Straussian Grounded Theory: Similar or completely different? Paper presented at the Annual Research Conference of the South African Institute of Computer Scientists and Information Technologists, Vaal River, South Africa.

vom Brocke, J., Simons, A., Niehaves, B., Riemer, K., Plattfaut, R. and Cleven, A. (2009). Reconstructing the Giant: On the importance of rigour in documenting the literature search process. Paper presented at the Proceedings of the 17th European Conference on Information Systems (ECIS 2009), Verona, Italy.

Walker, D. and Myrick, F. (2006). Grounded Theory: An exploration of process and procedure, *Qualitative Health Research* 16(4): 547–559.

Walsham, G. (1995). Interpretive Case Studies in IS Research: Nature and method, *European Journal of Information Systems* 4(2): 74–81.

Watson, R. (2001). Research in Information Systems: What we haven't learned, *MIS Quarterly* 25(4): v–xv.

Webb, B. and Mallon, B. (2007). A Method to Bridge the Gap between Breadth and Depth in IS Narrative Analysis, *Journal of the Association for Information Systems* 8(7): 368–381.

Work, B. (2002). Patterns of Software Quality Management in Tickit Certified Firms, *European Journal of Information Systems* 11(1): 61–73.

Xu, P. and Ramesh, B. (2007). Software Process Tailoring: An empirical investigation, *Journal of Management Information Systems* 24(2): 293–328.

Yin, R.K. (2003). *Case Study Research. Design and Methods*, London: Sage Publications.

Appendix A

Details of literature search strategy

Table 7.A1 provides an overview of the searched IS journals, as well as the database coverage (for the relevance of transparently documenting the literature search process compare, for instance, vom Brocke *et al.*, 2009).

Table 7.A1   Journals reviewed in the literature review

Journal	Coverage
EJIS	1(1)(1991)–19(6)(2010)
ISJ [Volumes 1–5 as *Journal of Information Systems*]	5(4)(1995)–20(6)(2010)
ISR	1(1)(1990)–21(4)(2010)
JAIS	1(1)(2000)–11(12)(2010)
JMIS	1(1)(1984)–27(2)(2010)
MISQ	1(1)(1977)–34(4)(2010)

Our search strategy was as follows:

1. We started with a full text search using the search terms 'Strauss' and 'Corbin' in order to identify those articles citing the work of Anselm Strauss and Juliet Corbin. We justified this by arguing that any study that makes use of S & C coding procedures is most likely to reference their work. Table 7.A3 provides an overview of the (methodological) publications by Anselm Strauss and Juliet Corbin that IS researchers cite in the investigated articles. We soon realized that some articles refer to S & C coding procedures without referencing Strauss and Corbin. Lim *et al.* (2005), for example, cite Orlikowski (1993) when it comes to the stage of axial coding. We then also included 'axial coding' as a search term. Our initial search was a logical expression of the following form: <'Strauss' or 'Corbin' or 'axial'>. We then eliminated those articles where it was obvious that they do not relate to the use of S & C coding procedures, that is those articles

   • where other authors with the names Strauss or Corbin are cited, but not the aforementioned advocates of grounded theory, Barney Glaser and Anselm Strauss (e.g., a couple of articles cite Levi-Strauss), and that do not refer to axial coding (e.g., a couple of articles use notions such as 'coaxial' that are not related to the use of the paradigm); and
   • that only refer to work of Strauss in conjunction with Glaser (most notably Glaser and Strauss, 1967) and that do not refer to axial coding. This exercise produced a total of 115 articles (41 in *EJIS*, 23 in *ISJ*, 7 in *ISR*, 9 in *JAIS*, 12 in *JMIS*, and 21 in *MISQ*) that built the basis for our further analysis.

2. We then made a distinction between empirical and non-empirical studies, identifying 100 empirical studies and 15 non-empirical studies. While empirical studies were expected to help us answering the research questions by investigating the use of S & C coding procedures as well as the results of research, non-empirical studies were hoped to provide further insights into how S & C grounded theory is perceived and understood in the IS discipline. In some cases, we identified articles that are primarily conceptual, but use empirical data for illustration purposes. Of the 15 non-empirical articles, 9 are methodological, 3 are literature reviews, 1 a theoretical (conceptual) article, and 2 we classified as opinion pieces. For the classification scheme, we used the *Publication Manual of the American Psychological Association* (2010).

3. We then went through the 100 retrieved empirical articles in order to establish if the work of Anselm Strauss and/or Juliet Corbin is referenced in the

context of the applied research method or if, at least, axial coding is mentioned. We also excluded those articles where the work of Strauss and Corbin is not cited in the context of the underlying methodology, but with regard to their actual (empirical) research; this is the case in three articles (Horton and Wood-Harper, 2006; Azad and King 2008; Bjørn and Ngwenyama, 2009). We further identified one article where it is stated that grounded theory is not used (Khoo and Robey, 2007). This left us with 96 empirical articles that have been published in the top six journals of the IS discipline that reference Strauss and Corbin in the context of the applied research method.

4. In a last step, we performed a more detailed analysis of the 96 retrieved empirical studies in order to identify in what manner S & C coding procedures are used. We read the articles, with a focus on the applied data analyses, and searched for mentioning of open, axial, and selective coding as well as paradigm items such as conditions, actions/ interactions, strategies, and consequences, or the explicit notion of the coding paradigm.

Table 7.A2 provides an overview of our search strategy, which focused on the identification of those studies that applied axial coding and the paradigm. While we took great care in applying this procedure, we cannot exclude the possibility that a few articles may have been missed.

Table 7.A2 Overview of search strategy

Stage	Description	Number of articles deemed (potentially) relevant
Stage 1	• Full text search using the search terms 'Strauss', 'Corbin', and 'axial' • Elimination of those articles that are obviously irrelevant to the present study; for example, those articles that do not cite the work of Anselm Strauss and/or Juliet Corbin from 1987 onwards	115
Stage 2	• Identification of empirical studies	100
Stage 3	• Identification of empirical studies that reference the work of Anselm Strauss and/or Juliet Corbin in the context of the applied research method or at least mention the use of axial coding	96
Stage 4	• In-depth analysis, search for the mentioning of open, axial, and selective coding as paradigm items such as conditions, actions/ interactions, strategies, and consequences and the explicit the notion of the coding paradigm	96

Table 7.A3 Publications by Strauss and Corbin cited in the investigated studies in the context of the research method applied (references to Straussian grounded theory)

Publication	Title	Type
Strauss (1987)	*Qualitative Analysis for Social Scientists*	Book
Corbin and Strauss (1990)	*Grounded Theory Research: Procedures, Canons, and Evaluative Criteria*	Journal Article
Strauss and Corbin (1990)	*Basics of Qualitative Research: Grounded Theory Procedures and Techniques*	Book
Strauss and Corbin (1994a)	*Basics of Qualitative Research: Grounded Theory Procedures and Techniques*	Book
Strauss and Corbin (1994b)	*Grounded Theory Methodology: An Overview*	Book Section
Strauss and Corbin (1997)	*Grounded Theory in Practice*	Book
Strauss and Corbin (1998)	*Basics of Qualitative Research: Techniques and Procedures for Developing Grounded Theory*	Book
Corbin and Strauss (2008)	*Basics of Qualitative Research: Techniques and Procedures for Developing Grounded Theory*	Book

Appendix B

Table 7.B1 Articles that are explicit about the use of axial coding

Article	References on axial coding	Quote(s)
Orlikowski (1993)	Strauss and Corbin (1990)	'This is known as *axial coding* (Strauss and Corbin, 1990), and it relies on a synthetic technique of making connections between subcategories to construct a more comprehensive scheme' (p. 314)
Kirsch (1997)	Strauss and Corbin (1990)	'Next, axial coding (Strauss and Corbin, 1990) was applied, in which similar concepts are linked together into categories' (p. 225)
Scott (2000)	Strauss and Corbin (1990)	'This technique of open coding categorized concepts that were then used to develop relationships through axial coding and finally to develop a conceptual framework [...]' (p. 88)
Ryan and Harrison (2000)	Strauss and Corbin (1990)	'The resulting categories were reanalyzed using a synthetic technique called axial coding [...], which makes connections between categories to produce a more comprehensive scheme' (p. 18)

(*continued*)

Table 7.B1 Continued

Article	References on axial coding	Quote(s)
Galal (2001)	Strauss and Corbin (1990)	'The categories which emerge from open coding are systematically related, in a causal model, to describe the dynamic relationship between them using a coding paradigm referred to as the "Paradigm Model". The Paradigm Model makes use of the slots: Conditions, Contexts, Action/Interaction Strategies and Consequences; to relate concepts identified to each other' (p. 5)
Huang et al. (2001)	Strauss and Corbin (1990)	'Secondly, internal validity is achieved through three stages of coding: open, axial and selective coding (Strauss and Corbin, 1990)' (p. 163) 'Concepts and categories, such as subcultures, communication and program implementation, emerging from the open coding were used as a basis to proceed to the axial coding stage. Here the primary aim was to generate interconnections between these themes by building a paradigm model which was further refined to form the basis of the theoretical framework outlined in Figure 1' (p. 164)
Jones and Hughes (2001)	No direct reference	'As the number of categories increased they were related to each other and to sub-categories. This process is known as "axial" coding. The relationship between categories and sub-categories was explored' (p. 195)
Kock (2001)	(For all three: Glaser and Strauss, 1967; Glaser, 1978; Strauss and Corbin, 1990)	'Three main techniques developed in the context of grounded theory methodology (Glaser and Strauss, 1967; Glaser, 1978; Strauss and Corbin, 1990) were iteratively used in the summarization of the research evidence collected in both stages of this research: (1) open coding, whereby research variables have been identified; (2) axial coding, whereby causal effects linking research variables have been identified; and (3) selective coding, whereby sets of causal effects and related variables have been categorized according to main dependent research variables' (pp. 90–91)
Work (2002)	Strauss and Corbin (1990)	'The second technique is axial coding which develops the categories further. The specific features of each category, such as the conditions which cause the category to occur, are validated against the data' (p. 64)

(*continued*)

Table 7.B1 Continued

Article	References on axial coding	Quote(s)
Levina and Ross (2003)	Corbin and Strauss (1990)	'We then used causal diagrams and checklist matrices (Miles and Huberman, 1984) to help us discover relationships among concepts and to do axial coding (Corbin and Strauss, 1990)' (p. 338)
Pauleen (2003)	No direct reference	'During and after the second AL program, axial coding was used to put data together in new ways, by seeking to identify causal relationships between categories' (p. 235)
Baskerville and Pries-Heje (2004)	Strauss and Corbin (1990)	'The purpose of axial coding is to develop a better and deeper understanding of how the identified categories are related. Axial coding involves two tasks further developing the categories and properties. The first task connects categories in terms of a sequence of relationships. For example, a causal condition or a consequence can connect two categories, or connect a category and a sub-category. The second task turns back to the data for validation of the relationships' (pp. 241–242)
Goulielmos (2004)	Strauss and Corbin (1990)	'Axial coding helped to develop links among categories. With the identification of core categories, analysis shifted from a process of initial exploration to a process of elaborating key concepts and their properties' (p. 366)
Kirsch (2004)	Strauss and Corbin (1990)	'Open coding was followed by axial coding (Strauss and Corbin, 1990), which is a process of linking similar concepts into categories' (p. 381)
Lindgren et al. (2004)	Strauss and Corbin (1990)	'The transcribed material was analyzed by using the open and axial coding techniques (Strauss and Corbin, 1990)' (p. 445)
Lim et al. (2005)	Orlikowski (1993)	'Through the procedure of open and axial coding, we identified common patterns of interest across subjects from the unprocessed raw data. Still working independently, we categorized the patterns into a number of sub-themes, which are related to the research objective (Orlikowski, 1993)' (p. 140)
Ryan and Valverde (2006)	Strauss and Corbin (1990, 1998)	'These coding procedures (open coding, axial coding and selective coding) are explained in detail in Strauss and Corbin (1990, 1998), and a useful summary is available in Charmaz

(continued)

Table 7.B1 Continued

Article	References on axial coding	Quote(s)
		(1983). In the case of the current study a complete open coding was performed on the data. This was followed by an iterative process of axial and selective coding' (p. 188) 'In this sense, the coding schemes used in the analysis of the data develop throughout the coding process, from the initial open (or line by line) coding where many categories appear, to the axial coding where some categories are collapsed (or combined) into stronger, more refined categories and other categories are discarded. '[sic]' and finally onto selective coding where the density of each category is evaluated [...]' (pp. 197–198)
Espinosa *et al.* (2007)	No direct reference	'We then did axial coding of the data, which involves finding relationships among these themes, which we then used to produce a template with hierarchical codes' (p. 146)
Hackney *et al.* (2007)	No direct reference	'The subsequent analysis of the interview transcripts and documentary evidence closely followed the suggestions for axial and selective coding and the general suggestions given for the analysis of case study materials (Yin, 2003)' (p. 182)
Keil *et al.* (2007)	Strauss and Corbin (1998), Baskerville and Pries-Heje (2001)	'These responses were subjected to content analysis following the grounded theory approach described by Strauss and Corbin (1998), which involves three coding procedures: open coding, axial coding and selective coding' (p. 74) 'The second stage of the qualitative analysis involved axial coding which is a process of systematically relating categories in terms of their properties and dimensions. Our aim was to work towards developing a qualitative model consisting of concepts identified in the study and the causal chains between them (Baskerville and Pries-Heje, 2001)' (p. 75)
Larsen *et al.* (2007)	Corbin and Strauss (1990), Strauss (1987)	'Axial coding is the final step of the causal analysis mapping process (Strauss, 1987). By contrasting the consolidated causal map with the interview transcripts and the observation memos, the data were checked and revised. Finally, we cluster the wide range

(continued)

Table 7.B1 Continued

Article	References on axial coding	Quote(s)
		of variables potentially affecting project success by grouping them under a more abstract heading called category (Corbin and Strauss, 1990)' (p. 91)
Webb and Mallon (2007)	Strauss and Corbin (1990)	'Here, concepts are linked causally using the paradigm model to better reveal the story structure. Because we carry forward events and existents from the previous phase of analysis, this is primarily a deductive exercise (i.e., we are looking for preexisting codes in the data). Whereas axial coding usually requires some grouping of concepts prior to, or in addition to, applying the paradigm model, here they are simply pulled into the paradigm model directly without this intermediate step' (p. 376)
Xu and Ramesh (2007)	Strauss and Corbin (1990)	'After several iterations of open coding, axial coding was conducted in which the concepts were grouped into categories and subcategories and the relationships among them were identified' (p. 303)
Alvarez (2008)	Strauss and Corbin (1990)	*'The analysis advanced from open coding to axial coding (Strauss and Corbin, 1990)'* (p. 207)
Feller *et al.* (2008)	Strauss and Corbin (1990)	'The next step (*axial coding*) was the process of determining hypotheses about the relationships between a category and its subcategories – e.g., conditions, context, action/interaction strategies, and consequences' (p. 481)
Holmström Olsson *et al.* (2008)	Strauss and Corbin (1998)	'For the analysis we followed the *open coding* and *axial coding* techniques proposed by Strauss and Corbin (1998)' (p. 263) 'Axial coding is concerned with identifying the relationships between categories and validating these relationships in the data' (p. 263)
Smolander *et al.* (2008)	Strauss and Corbin (1990)	'The *third* phase, axial and selective coding, involved analysis of the categories and super-categories, including their values, with a view to building linkages among them' (p. 579)
Day *et al.* (2009)	Strauss and Corbin (1990)	'Axial coding was applied to match codes into the categories of the coding paradigm. Categories of axial coding are schematically summarized in Table 2 This part of the

(*continued*)

Table 7.B1 Continued

Article	References on axial coding	Quote(s)
		analysis required us to pay close attention to linking categories and subcategories while keeping the coding paradigm in mind' (p. 642)
Goo *et al.* (2009)	Strauss and Corbin (1990)	'Next, the axial coding technique (Strauss and Corbin, 1990) was employed to categorize the 11 SLA elements into 3 unique categories' (p. 129)
Goode and Gregor (2009)	Baskerville and Pries-Heje (1999)	'The next stage involved "axial coding" of the text, to discover differences and similarities among the categories (Baskerville and Pries-Heje, 1999)' (p. 7)
Mourmant *et al.* (2009)	No direct reference	Axial coding is mentioned in Figure B1 on page 520
Conboy (2010)	Strauss and Corbin (1998)	'The second phase of analysis used axial coding. Axial coding is defined by Strauss and Corbin (1998) as a set of procedures whereby data are put back together in new ways after open coding; whereas open coding fractures the data into categories, axial coding puts the data back together by making connections between the categories and sub-categories. As the data were coded, theoretical questions, propositions and code summaries arose' (p. 278)
Maldonado (2010)	Strauss and Corbin (1998)	'Axial coding defines causal relationships and the intervening conditions that mitigate those relationships' (p. 762)
O'Reilly and Finnegan (2010)	Strauss and Corbin (1990)	'The next step (axial coding) is the process of determining hypotheses about the relationships between a category and its subcategories, for example, conditions, context, action/interaction strategies and consequences' (p. 467)
Ramesh *et al.* (2010)	Strauss and Corbin (1990)	'After open coding, axial coding was conducted to achieve the theory-generation objective of this research. Data were analysed again to uncover relationships among categories and subcategories. This analysis resulted in the identification of concepts' (p. 455)
Remus and Wiener (2010)	Strauss and Corbin (1990)	'As our goal was not to create a whole new theory, we only used open and axial coding to identify the main categories and to make connections between categories, hereby identifying causal conditions, context, strategies and intervening conditions (Strauss and Corbin, 1990)' (p. 34)

(*continued*)

Table 7.B1   Continued

Article	References on axial coding	Quote(s)
Spears and Barki (2010)	No direct reference	'Finally, axial coding was used to identify relationships among existing code categories' (p. 507)
Strong and Volkoff (2010)	Strauss and Corbin (1998)	'We followed Strauss's recommendation of doing axial coding after open coding, but treated this technique as a method through which to discover relationships in the data, and not as an overly restrictive set of rules (Urquhart, 2007)' (p. 735)

Appendix C

Examples where it is possible that the S & C paradigm was applied, but there is not sufficient evidence

Work (2002), in a study of patterns of software quality management, writes about the use of axial coding: 'The second technique is axial coding which develops the categories further. The specific features of each category, such as the conditions which cause the category to occur, are validated against the data' (p. 64). Other paradigm items are not explicitly mentioned.

Maldonado (2010) writes: 'Axial coding defines causal relationships and the intervening conditions that mitigate those relationships' (p. 762). Again, no further paradigm items are mentioned.

Orlikowski (1993) says: 'This iterative examination [axial coding] yielded a set of broad categories and associated concepts that describe the salient conditions, events, experiences, and consequences associated with the adoption and use of CASE tools in SCC' (p. 314). With regard to this article, Urquhart *et al.* (2010) note: 'It is not clear whether the Strauss and Corbin (1990) coding paradigm [...] was used to assist the coding' (p. 374).

Other examples where one may speculate about the use of the paradigm include Goulielmos (2004) as well as Baskerville and Pries-Heje (2004).

Appendix D

Analytical dimensions

This appendix provides an overview of the analytical dimensions that were used in order to analyse those studies that applied the S & C coding paradigm.

Table 7.D1 Analytical dimensions

Analytical dimension	Description	Reference
1. Resulting theory/model	This dimension was chosen as we were particularly interested in whether the use of the paradigm impacts on the final product of research. For example, we investigated whether the resultant theories exhibit paradigm items as this may indicate conceptual description and forcing of data	—
2. Degree of conceptualization	With regard to the degree of conceptualization of grounded theory studies, Urquhart *et al.* (2010) distinguish three stages, namely, description, interpretation, and theory. While descriptions are the most basic conceptual products, resulting in categories and their properties, interpretation refers to the interpretation of categories and properties. The third stage, theory, refers to inferential and/or predictive statements, which may take the form of hypotheses. The criticism towards the S & C paradigm suggests that its application may be associated with low levels of conceptualization	Urquhart *et al.* (2010)
3. Theory scope	With regard to theory scope, Urquhart *et al.* (2010) distinguish between bounded context, substantive focus, and formal concepts. The first type refers to theories that comprises seed concepts and are bounded by their immediate context. Theories with a substantive focus have been described as being typical results of grounded theory studies. They are bound to a substantive area and are said to be of high-practical relevance. Formal concepts relate to the widest form of grounded theory as they usually apply to a set of several substantive areas. In particular against the background that Strauss and Corbin (1990) associate the use of grounded theory with the generation of non-theory, this dimension becomes relevant to the present study	Urquhart *et al.* (2010)
4. Theory type	With regard to theory type, Gregor (2006) distinguishes five types of theory in IS research, namely, theory for analysis and description, theory for explanation, theory for prediction, theory for explanation and prediction, and theory for prescription	Gregor (2006)
5. Conceptualization of the IT artefact	This dimension was chosen as the IT artefact is at the core of IS research. Orlikowski and Iacono (2001), for example, identify 14 different conceptualizations of IT in the IS literature, which are further clustered into 5 broader views, namely, the tool view, the ensemble view, the nominal view, the computational view, and the proxy view	Orlikowski and Iacono (2001)

Section III
Historical Approaches

8
The Use of History in IS Research: An Opportunity Missed?

Frank Land
London School of Economics, London, UK

Introduction

History is more or less bunk. It's tradition. We don't want tradition. We want to live in the present, and the only history that is worth a tinker's damn is the history that we make today. Henry Ford's edict on history has, in a sense, become a cliché derided by some as the ignorant spoutings of a self-opinionated, but highly successful entrepreneur, and praised by others for its forthright condemnation of the way historians described the past. It is perhaps ironic that Henry Ford has himself become a historical icon, and that 'Fordism' attached as a label to the kind of industrial organisation he put into place and espoused.

Further study of Ford's attitude has revealed that his view of history is rather more nuanced than the newspaper interview that yielded the quotation suggests. What offended Henry Ford was the concentration of historians on the affairs of state, on the doings of Kings and Presidents, rather than on commercial life and, his particular interest, the evolution of economic activity such as manufacturing.

The second quotation can be heard every day as another disaster unfolds. A search in Google on the phrase 'Lessons will be learned' yielded 46,200,000 finds. Like 'history is bunk', the phrase has become a cliché based on the assumption that the next time a complex system is rolled out the solutions that might have avoided the first disaster will be valid in the new situation.

Reprinted from 'The use of history in IS research: an opportunity missed?' by F. Land in *Journal of Information Technology*, 25, 2010, pp. 385–394. With kind permission from the Association for Information Technology Trust. All rights reserved.

Examples of failures, often in major projects, abound. These include Mitev's study of the French railway booking and reservation system SOCRATES (Mitev, 1996), Drummond's analysis of the failure of TAURUS, the London Stock Exchanges' ambitious IT project (Drummond, 1996), the recent Journal of Information Technology's special issue on the UK National Health Services National Programme for Information Technology (*Journal of Information Technology*, 2007) and the Denver Airport automated baggage handling case (De Neufville, 1994). And despite the analysis of past failings in academic journals, the incidence of failure shows little signs of diminishing.

Santayana's much-quoted aphorism 'Those who cannot remember the past are condemned to repeat it' first published in 1905 (republished Santayana, 2009) like the mantra 'we will learn the lessons', has some validity, but its underlying assumption that today's events are merely repetitions of the past will be questioned as will the assumption that we have the capacity and resources to actually learn from past experience.

In this paper, I will argue that the historiography of information systems (IS) is important for understanding IS and its evolution through time, and that understanding even the most transformative, revolutionary, innovations benefits from the study of the historical context. Henry Ford's viewpoint is too prevalent, and in my view damaging to IS research. A study and appreciation of history has a significant part to play in understanding the way information and communication technologies are transforming the world we live in. The argument will be supported by a number of examples.

The paper is set out as follows: Section 'Introduction' is followed by Section 'IS and History' – which notes the extent to which IS research is grounded in historical narrative and which suggests the various historical themes in which much of IS research is conducted. Section 'History, Historians and IS', reflects on aspects of historiography, distinguishing between the story of the past and the way historians interpret and manipulate that story. Section 'A digression on Lenses and Telescopes' defines Telescopes as a way for describing the many strands of IS research, which between them attempt to provide a comprehensive understanding of IS and what makes it a discipline in its own right. The final Section 'Learning and Understanding' is intended as a conclusion that reflects on some of the limits to our understanding and asks how the boundaries of the discipline are set and what aspects of IS are missing from our discourse. The appendix provides an example of the importance of understanding the context in which apparently new ideas are grounded and the pre-history from which the new ideas evolved.

IS and history

The part played by History in the study of IS is clear in the many research domains that are time-based and depend on the discovery of common patterns (Mason *et al.*, 1997a, b; Bannister, 2002). The empirical researcher from the positivistic perspective searches for patterns of activity and behaviour, which support or refute theory-based hypotheses. The interpretivist researcher infers patterns that can be used to build new theories, the grounded theory approach (Bryant and Charmaz, 2007), or patterns that support existing theoretical constructs. A good example of the latter is Drummond's use of escalation theory to explain the failure of the London Stock Exchange's TAURUS system (Drummond, 1996). Researchers coming from a critical theory perspective look for patterns of behaviour that support the critical view that explores, *inter alia*, power relationships and the way power has been used for the exploitation of those denied the power (Mitev and Howcroft, 2005).

The research domains include:

a. Research into Stages of Growth models that attempt to find some pattern in the development of IS at the enterprise level, the sector level or the universal level. The classic and most widely cited example is Nolan's paper in the Harvard Business Review in 1973 (Nolan, 1973). Nolan's model is based on an assumption that the path of development is primarily deterministic. Nolan elaborated his model on the basis of legitimate historical research involving the study of the computing budgets of a number of enterprises, and of their IS application portfolios. The consistency he appeared to find led him to hypothesize a regular pattern of development that would be universally applicable. Nevertheless, the original four stages of the model had to be modified to yield six stages.

The model has subsequently been subjected to critical reviews such as that of King and Kraemer (1984). They note that the principal tenets of the model have not been independently validated, and suggest the reason lies in problems in the formulation of the model's logical and empirical structure.

Despite, the criticism levelled at the Nolan Model, such models continue to proliferate. See, for example, the attempt to suggest a model of evolution for the adoption of knowledge management (KM) in the legal profession (Gottschalk, 2002). And the appeal of such models is clear. They appear to take the uncertainty out of the road ahead, and provide a guideline, from any position, on what steps to take next. Nevertheless, although they rely on the accumulation of historical data, the approach is strictly ahistorical in that it follows a very narrow thread that does not permit the exploration of variables outside that thread.

b. The study of innovation' diffusion in the context of IS is a major domain for IS research, which has yielded a large literature. Diffusion research sets out to discover the characteristics that determine the way an innovation – which can be an artefact, a process, or a system – becomes accepted, and used, and subsequently abandoned in favour of an alternative, perhaps newer artefact or process. In other words, it attempts to define the life cycle of inventions and innovations, usually in organisational settings. Once again, there is an underlying thrust to find deterministic models that enable us not only to understand the past, but also to model the future.

This is recognised by Marchetti, a researcher at the International Institute for Applied Systems Analysis (1980). Marchetti examines long-term innovation and diffusion life cycles for a wide range of human endeavours, finds an underlying consistency rooted in social behaviour, giving an appearance of uniformity to the life cycles. Nevertheless, he allows free will a role in the unfolding of actual events. The extent to which the uniformity found by Marchetti and others is an illusion, which disappears as the focus on actual events sharpens, is still not fully answered.

Much research in this domain is based, as is the work of Marchetti, on the collection of statistical data related to individual industrial sectors and demographic information. But other studies focus on the experience of individual organizations in the form of case studies, and attempt to derive generalizable explanations of the diffusion phenomenon from that experience. Swanson and Ramiller(1997) suggest an overtly historical approach with their notion of an 'organizing vision' rooted in the shared experiences of a community and lying behind the drive to adopt IS innovations.

Williams and Pollock (2009), as a result of their study of the implementation of ERP systems, point out the limitations of the typical case study approach in that it focuses narrowly on a particular episode within an organisational setting. To properly understand the complexity of what happens and to be able to make useful generalisations, it is necessary to take a much broader view involving not only the episode under review, but also the whole history of the artefacts and system being studied. They advocate what they call a 'biographical' study of, in their case, the ERP package being implemented. Their approach can be regarded as bringing a proper historical perspective to IS research. However, it has to be noted that, typically, each biography is unique; hence, they may help us to explain the past in relation to the artefact being studied, but their approach is limited in its ability to predict the future and to 'learn lessons'.

To extend our understanding, we may need to delve into the pre-history of the objects being studied. An example is the study of Decision Support pioneers by Daniel Power. Power asked a number of 'experts' questions about the origins of Decision Support Systems (DSS). The response from, for example, Frank Land (Appendix) suggests that the notions underlying modern DSS are rooted in age-old practices, and that an understanding of these practices can help in the design and implementation of IS systems such as DSS and Executive Information Systems (EIS).

Unfortunately, much current IS research neglects the prehistory and commences its analysis with the computer-based artefact or system, a tendency exacerbated by viewpoints that put prime focus in IS studies on the IT artefact exemplified by, for example, Benbesat and Zmud (2003).

The problems raised by the complexity of the situation in which events unfold might be explained by the following thought experiment:

Suppose we liken the introduction of an IS system (or change in system) to throwing a stone into a pond. We should be able to calculate the propagation of the ripples using laws derived from the study of Physics from some elementary knowledge about the stone and where it is being thrown. Now let us assume that, as in any real organisation, a number of events occur at more or less the same time. In our example, more than one stone differing in mass is thrown into the pond. Further, a passing truck sends a shower of stones into the pond. Now, the ripples from the various stones may combine or dissipate in an interference pattern. The path of the ripples becomes uncertain. The uncertainty is compounded if we bring in other factors such as a variable wind, and below the surface of the pond an unseen landscape with hillocks and valleys, which we might compare to tacit knowledge in the organisation.

The experiment reflects the complexity behind the introduction of new technology or systems. IS research is often grounded in an analysis based on something like the single stone event. A study of history would reveal the inherent uncertainty in attempting to predict outcomes and help to explain the lack of consistent results from IS empirical research.

A great deal of the research in this area is predicated on some kind of life cycle model, involving conception, birth, and finishing with the demise of what had been an innovation. Examples much quoted include the end of the thermionic valve as a component of computers and its replacement by semi-conductors, leading to a major restructuring of not only computer possibilities, but also the whole of the electronic manufacturing sector. But a less noted phenomenon is the rebirth of an old apparently discarded innovation under a new name, (Land, 1996). Perhaps the rebirth phenomenon is more common in human activity systems then in physical artefacts. Thus, the ideas propagated by the early LEO pioneers (Simmons, 1962) were reborn as Business Process Re-engineering (BPR) by Hammer (Hammer and Champy, 2001), only for it to be whispered that BPR is already dead.

c. The study of IS success and failure has become an important theme in IS research. The majority of the hundreds of studies are based on essentially historical research. Failure studies include: Lyytinen and Hirschheim (1987), Drummond (1996), Glass(1998). Success stories include reports on the applications and organizations, which appear to have built successful systems (Copeland *et al.*, 1995; Mumford, 2003; Land, 2006). Most of these studies attempt an analysis, which aims to explain the reasons that led to the outcome and to generalize from that into prescriptions. A number of papers have examined the research methods that are likely to be appropriate for such research (Dalcher and Drevin, 2003). Most researchers favour some kind of case study research, as, for example, Sauer (1993).

d. Management of change studies are again by their nature based on research that is grounded in a study of historical events. This is another area that has a long research tradition and has built up substantial literature. Pettigrew (1990) who has devoted much of his life as an academic to analysing why and how organisations change through time has set out a reasoned set of prescriptions for a researcher working in this field, which could be termed historiography, though he himself does not use that term. Pettigrew stresses, *inter alia*, the importance of understanding both the organisational context in which change takes place and the changing context in which the organisation itself exists. Management of change studies are usually longitudinal in nature, and the researcher is frequently present over at least part of the period of study as an observer of what takes place. Bannister (2002) notes the difference between longitudinal research and historical research.

e. Studies that set out the historical development of IS within the arena of business and organisational practice and studies of the evolution of IS as an academic discipline. The former are often in the form of historical narratives worshipping at the shrine of the pioneers, though some include analysis and attempt causal interpretations. Most of these studies concern the history of specific organisations; some concentrate on individual heroes. Examples of all of these include: Simmons (1962), Aris (2000), Land (2000), Baskerville (2003), Mason (2004), Porra *et al.* (2005). Research into the development of IS as an academic discipline was first published by Gary Dickson (1981). As Dickson's widely recognised historical treatment of the field, many studies of IS have tended to concentrate on the history of research perspectives and approaches either globally or in particular regions such as Australia or Europe (Khazanchi and Munkvold, 2000; Lyytinen and King, 2004 – a paper that has an excellent bibliography of relevant papers – Baskerville and Myers, 2002; Vessey *et al.*, 2002; Clarke, 2006), though the questioning of the continued relevance of the discipline by Carr (2003) has led to a number of papers examining and justifying IS as a legitimate academic discipline. Examples include: King and Lyytinen (2004), Piccoli (2004), Tapscott (2004). Moschella usefully defines four overlapping 'waves of power' as characterising the evolution of IS over the past decades (1997).

A major attempt to set out the development of the discipline by the selection and republishing of its seminal papers and thus recording its cumulative tradition, is the publication by Sage of the six volume 'Major Currents in Information Systems' (Willcocks and Lee, 2008). The historical development is split into *Information Systems Infrastructure* (Howcroft and Land (2008), *Information Systems Development* (Avison and Baskerville, 2008), *Design Science Theories and Research Practices* (Hevner, 2008), *Management and Information Systems* (Lacity, 2008), *Social and Organizational Information Systems Research* (Liebenau and Mitev, 2008), and *Information Systems, Globalization and Developing Countries* (Avgerou, 2008). Given a limit of 15/16 papers for each section, some important papers were not selected. Nevertheless, the six volumes provide an excellent review of the historical development of the discipline.

History, historians and IS

Historiography can be described as the study of historical methods, and the differences in the approaches to the study of history and what is presented as the historical narrative. Bannister provides an interesting review of the Historiography in Information Systems Research (2002). Bannister notes that what constitutes the historical narrative has changed with time. Namier (1971) taught that history was concerned with facts, as revealed by the study of, for example, exchequer rolls, while later historians concentrated more on interpretation (Collingwood, 1993).

It is important to distinguish between history and the historian – or the practice of history, historiography. History is the story of the past. That story is embodied in primary and secondary sources including archives such as repositories of, for example, exchequer rolls or clay tablets, memoirs and diaries, biographies, tracts and pamphlets, official reports and enquiries, plays, oral histories, artefacts including objects like Trajans column in Rome. Other secondary sources include accounts of history, written and verbal, and currently digitised, found in databases and data warehouses. Sometimes, it is far from clear whether the historical account is a primary or secondary source, and often it may have elements of both. What is clear is that no history is an unvarnished complete account of the past. Indeed, the study of history consists of making sense of the sources and attempting to fill in the numerous gaps in the historical record and excising parts that seem to the historian in question to be irrelevant or confusing, or sending the wrong (unwanted) message. The study of making sense – interpretation – of fragments is called hermeneutics. Each iteration of sense making – filling the gaps – yields more information, but also shows up anomalies in the interpretation. This requires a further attempt at sense making, involving the reinterpreting of earlier conclusions. A contemporary historian attempting to make sense of an earlier historian's interpretation of the past is engaged in the 'double hermeneutic' (Giddens, 1987), piling interpretation on interpretation and always at some remove from underlying history.

The work of all historians is instrumental – that is, it is done to serve some purpose. And that purpose is often hidden; indeed, it may be tacit in the sense that the historian is unaware that he or she is imparting a 'spin' on the facts revealed.

History is used to send all kind of messages. But the messages – the historical accounts – will be designed to persuade the recipient to think or act in a particular way. In normal discourse this is to be expected. Thus, it is not surprising that the French account of the 100-year war with England designed for French school children differs from that provided by English scholars for British school children. If there are lessons to be learned from the historical account they are different for French and British school children. Perhaps Henry Ford's stricture on history was based on his recognition that the problems lay, not with history, but with historians.[1]

We can see this at work in much IS research. Are the case studies of successful IS applications designed to reveal the truth, or is there a subsidiary aim to persuade readers of the centrality of IS in providing competitive advantage? Other good examples are the case studies reporting on events, and drawing on some theory to help explain the events. But looking deeper, what is sometimes at work is the exact opposite. The case study report is designed tacitly to illuminate the theory, and to enable the reader to make sense of the theory. One possible example is the study by Walsham and his Ph.D. student of an IS application in India (Walsham and Han, 1991; Walsham and Han, 1992). The study used elements of Gidden's Structuration Theory to help understand the unfolding events in the case. But to an extent the case was used to help in an understanding of Structuration Theory.

One of the success factors stressed by the literature is leadership quality at the level of the Chief Information Officer and general management. Indeed, leadership has, from intuitive insights and from numerous research studies, been seen to play an important role in ensuring success. As Armstrong and Sambamurthy show in their empirical study of IS managers and general management, certain leadership qualities and practices can be associated with organisational assimilation of IT systems (1999). Assimilation, which is implicitly associated with success, '... requires championship and executive leadership. Senior leadership becomes critical for such championship'. But the research tends to be biased towards the implicit association of assimilation with success, in that it does not investigate the cases, reported in anecdotal evidence, in which apparently strong leadership with the desirable qualities identified by the researchers has led an organization to disaster (Baskerville and Land, 2004).

Mohr made the distinction between 'variance'-based research – the model of research that searches for associations between variables by means of statistical analysis of typically survey-based data – and 'process'-based research, which attempts to trace the unfolding events including the antecedents that led to the current state (Mohr, 1982). The 'process' model is grounded in historical research. Applying the model to IS research, Shaw and Jarvenpaa note the predominance of the 'variance' model and lament the relative paucity of 'process'-based research (1997). However, their study finds that many IS research projects are of a hybrid nature, combining some 'process' – history-based – elements with the 'variance'-based research, though even the hybrid studies tend to be dominated by the 'variance' approach.

IS researchers in their quest for explanations tend to look for dominant patterns as typified by the leadership research noted above. They then use the explanations to advise practitioners on how to do IS.

However, in concentrating on the central part of the distribution, they tend to neglect the outliers; and as Taleb (2007) has shown, the realisation of the improbable can have far more profound impacts than the realisation of the expected. This suggests that IS research, regardless of whether it has a 'variance' or a 'process'-based orientation, needs to go beyond the 'mean' in investigating the IS phenomenon.

A digression on lenses and telescopes

The discussion of appropriate methods in IS research frequently uses the word 'lenses' as a metaphor for the chosen research perspective or approach. The implication of the metaphor is that different lenses can study the phenomenon at different magnifications, thus providing options for selecting the degree of granularity to be observed. Of course, different degrees of granularity reveal different aspects of the phenomenon studied. But the desired level of granularity to be observed is only one of the many research perspectives advocated for IS research.

Investigating the IS phenomenon[2] involves understanding a multiplicity of disciplines and a multiplicity of perspectives coming from a number of epistemological stances. Hence, the alternative metaphor of 'telescope' might be a better way of characterising the deployment of multiple IS research perspectives and approaches. Astronomers use different telescopes to provide different degrees of magnification, as do lenses. But many more differences in the phenomenon studied are revealed by the use of different types of telescopes – optical telescopes, radio telescopes, spectroscopic telescopes – which break the received light into the spectrum – X-ray telescopes, telescopes that view the object in the infra red, and so on. In the same way, IS research trains different epistemological telescopes onto the subject of study, the IS phenomenon, highlighting different aspects of the phenomenon and helping to answer different research questions. But between them, the different telescopes build up a comprehensive picture of the phenomenon under scrutiny.

What does the historical IS telescope reveal? At one level of magnification, it reveals the broad flow of IS evolution, leading at one extreme from the clay tablets of Babylon to the internet and Web2. What the flow shows is the remarkable continuity in human activity from the earliest days of civilization to our current state. At the same time, it indicates the major stepping stones amounting to breaks in the continuity of gradual evolution, highlighting the innovations that have resulted in changes and even transformations in the behaviour of human activity systems. It also reveals that the flow is cyclical with apparent repetitions of history, and that the direction is not always towards 'improvements'. It suggests that there has been a speeding up in the rate of change in the past 200 years and a further acceleration in the past decades, giving credence to the sociologist Zygmund Bauman's depiction of the state of today's society as 'liquid modernity' (Bauman, 2000). To paraphrase Bauman, the new condition is characterised by the flow of electronically mediated information. IT and IS play an important part in the speeding up and unfreezing of human activity systems. Nevertheless, through our telescopic view of change over the aeons, 'viscous modernity' might have been a better description.

A higher magnification with a narrower focus, typical of a case study, reveals more detail. If the telescope is used by a business school Management Information Systems researcher, the focus will characteristically be on IS in an enterprise setting, and issues such as competitiveness, strategy and economic evaluation (for example, Clemons and Row, 1991). If the perspective is that of a sociotechnical researcher, the focus will involve individual and organizational values and ethics (for example, Land *et al.*, 1983a,b), considerations that are less likely to be of concern to the business school researcher. A researcher coming from a perspective rooted in critical theory will focus on issues such as the impact of IS on the human condition, empowerment and exploitation, gender roles and organisational politics (for example, Ngwenyama, 1991). A researcher working in the IS-related topic of human–computer interaction is mainly concerned with the period the human user is working at the keyboard (or touch screen mobile), and the research may focus on tracing the user's eye movements during the time of interaction.

In a strange way, the IS telescope has a number of filters that inhibit the full examination of the phenomenon to be studied. Most theories providing explanations of IS phenomena have an underlying, and sometimes explicit, assumption that human behaviour, in the context of IS, is essentially rational (Avgerou and McGrath, 2007). Only rarely is the underlying rationality of the IS actor questioned, though, as Baskerville and Land noted, the apparently rational actions can have adverse outcomes (2004). One explicit exception is the notion of Drummond of an Icarus factor – a tendency for the IS strategist to have a level of ambition beyond the capability of the organisation to achieve (Drummond, 2008).

As in most human endeavours, in IS too, ignorance and incompetence, and the employment of copy-cat strategies play a significant role in determining outcomes. Yet none of these figure much as research questions or in explanatory models of even research topics such as the study of IS failures. Again in the real-world serendipity, the chance association of information may play a key role in the way events unfold. But few explanatory models or research questions address the role of serendipity in the history of the phenomenon being studied. Claudio Ciborra is one of the few IS scholars who captured the inherent uncertainty and the role played by serendipity and tinkering in his notion of *bricolage* (Ciborra, 1998). Would researchers schooled in historical research methods overcome the apparent taboos in what constitutes legitimate IS research and explanatory models?

In a world increasingly concerned about the growing incidence of cyber-crime and the use of Information and Communications Technology for anti-social purposes, or for use in warfare, there is a lack of history-based research of the 'biography' or 'ecology' underlying this trend in IS practice. Most research is focused on the way individuals, organisations and society can defend itself against attack. Yet without the understanding coming from studies exploring the history of, for example, cyber-crime, including its prehistory, the defensive prescriptions are almost bound to be one step behind the innovations stemming from the 'dark' elements in our society. Indeed, anecdotal evidence suggests that it takes about 9 months for a bank to learn how to plug the leaks following the latest cybercrime innovation. Criminology should, perhaps, be cited as one of the IS reference disciplines.

Learning and understanding

Does history have a role in throwing light on the many aspects of the IS phenomenon? History is of little use, as Henry Ford surmised, in comprehending all of the impacts of the here and now. For the IS scholar to predict how the latest advances in net and mobile technologies are going to impact society, the study of history may only be of a limited value. Nevertheless, could Henry Ford have developed his ideas about mass production without some understanding of the way manufacturing industry had developed in the late 18th and 19th century? Today's innovator builds on earlier works. Thus, Babbage got his ideas for the design of an automatic computer from visiting France and seeing the way a French mathematician, Gaspard de Prony, had organised the manual work of producing mathematical tables (Hyman, 1985).

KM is a relatively new field for IS study and discourse. It is based on the premise that ICT has transformed society to one based on knowledge – the 'knowledge society'. Knowledge driven and supported by Information Technology and embedded in IS will provide – taking the business school model of what matters – higher levels of efficiency and enhanced competitive advantage. Taking a more critical view of what matters, it is accepted that knowledge confers power on its owners – a truth proclaimed by Francis Bacon, in the 17th century. Acton, two centuries later, noted that power corrupts. A study of history underlines Acton's edict. Power legitimates what is understood to be knowledge in what Foucault describes as *regimes of truth* (Foucault, 1980, 1982; Avgerou and McGrath, 2007). The power of the Catholic Church with its God-granted 'knowledge' that the earth was the centre of the Universe, overruled the knowledge of Galileo derived from his observations with a telescope, and it was Galileo who was forced to recant (Land, 2009).

The study of KM provides another illustration of the failure of many IS (or in this case KM) researchers to use a more historical approach in their scholarship. A more historical approach would reveal that KM has an ancient lineage even if the term knowledge management was not used. The IS or KM practitioner has much to learn from, for example, Machiavelli and in modern as well as ancient times from the world of politics. But the business world equally has a long-standing record of KM (Land, 2009), though knowledge manipulation might be a more apposite name. It can be found, for example, in its more benign form in what today is termed customer relations management, and includes the KM processes of advertising and the public relations function. In its less benign form, it can be found in the business frauds typified by ENRON and the Ponzi schemes of Madoff. In some ways, KM can be seen at its most effective in the darker applications of its widely lauded processes.

Perhaps the 'productivity paradox' of earlier decades has now been replaced by the 'knowledge paradox'. Those who see Information Technology and IS as ushering in the age of universally shared knowledge, where knowledge is assumed to equate to the truth, might note the statistics of beliefs held by citizens worldwide. Believers in Intelligent Design and Creationism outnumber those who regard Evolution as providing an explanation of the diversity of species. The historian of the 22nd century, looking back at the credit crisis of 2007/2008 and its consequences, may wonder how in a 'knowledge society' replete with the highest technology such events could have caught the world unawares. The technology that the optimists regard as the gateway to the Knowledge Society has equally provided the means for the spreading of un-knowledge. The student of history would, perhaps, not be surprised by that trend.

History provides a richness in understanding which its neglect denies the IS researcher a vision of the whole story. And it is only with this understanding that we can learn lessons from past and current events. Searching through the record of IS research, we might be disappointed at the lack of explicit recognition of historiography as providing an important component for IS studies. Nevertheless, the topic is not entirely neglected. Indeed, as the citations in this paper indicate, there is a rich vein of research that uses some kind of historical method, and a small number including (Avgerou and McGrath, 2007) that would satisfy both the IS scholar and the critical historian. In order to grow that number and for the discipline to benefit from its insights, the relevance of history to the study of IS must be part of any IS curriculum and must be included in the training of our future researchers, today's cadre of Ph.D. students.

Notes

1. An interesting critique of historians and the value of using history as the basis for 'natural experiments' is provided by the essay *All the world's is a lab* (Diamond and Robinson, 2010).
2. The phrase 'IS Phenomenon' is used in this essay as an umbrella term denoting the whole range of topics concerned with IS which interest the IS scholar.

References

Aris, J. (2000). Inventing Systems Engineering, *IEEE Annals of the History of Computing* 22(3): 4–15.

Armstrong, C.P. and Sambamurthy, V. (1999). Information Technology Assimilation in Firms: The influence of senior leadership and IT infrastructures, *Information Systems Research* 10(4): 304–327.

Avgerou, C. (ed.) (2008). Information Systems, Gloalization and Developing Countries, in L.P. Willcocks and A.S. Lee, Series (eds.), Vol. VI, *Major Currents in Information Systems*, Los Angeles: Sage.

Avgerou, C. and McGrath, K. (2007). Power, Rationality, and the Art of Living through Socio-technical Change, *MIS Quarterly* 31(2): 1–21.

Avison, D. and Baskerville, R. (eds.) (2008). Information Systems Development, in L.P. Willcocks and A.S. Lee, Series (eds.), Vol. II, *Major Currents in Information Systems*, Los Angeles: Sage.

Bannister, F. (2002). The Dimension of Time: Historiography in information research, *Electronic Journal of Business Research Methods* 1(1): 1–10.

Baskerville, R. (2003). The LEO Principle: Perspectives on 50 years of business computing, *The Journal of Strategic Information Systems* 12(4): 255–263 Special LEO Conference Edition.

Baskerville, R. and Land, F.F. (2004). Socially Self-Destructive Systems, in C. Avgerou, C. Ciborra and F.F. Land (eds.) *The Social Study of Information and Communications Technology: Innovation, actors and contexts,* Oxford: Oxford University Press.

Baskerville, R. and Myers, M. (2002). Information Systems as a Reference Discipline, *MIS Quarterly* 26(1): 1–14.

Bauman, Z. (2000). *Liquid Modernity,* Cambridge: Polity Press.

Benbesat, I. and Zmud, R.W. (2003). The Identity Crisis within the is Discipline: Defining and communicating the discipline's core properties, *MIS Quarterly* 27(2): 183–194.

Bryant, A. and Charmaz, K. (eds.) (2007). *The Sage Handbook of Grounded Theory,* London: Sage Publications.

Carr, N.G. (2003). IT Doesn't Matter, *Harvard Business Review* 81(5): 41–49.

Ciborra, C.U. (1998). Crisis and Foundations: An inquiry into the nature and limits of models and methods in the information systems discipline, *Journal of Strategic Information Systems* 7(1): 5.

Clarke, R. (2006). Key Aspects of the History of the Information Systems Discipline in Australia, *Australian Journal of Information Systems* 14(1): 123–140.

Clemons, E.K. and Row, M. (1991). Sustaining IT Advantage: The role of structural differences, *MIS Quarterly* 15(3): 274–292 Special Issue.

Collingwood, R. (1993). *The Idea of History: With lectures,* Oxford: Oxford University Press.

Copeland, D.G., Mason, R.O. and McKenney, J.L. (1995). Sabre: The development of information-based competence and execution of information-based competition, *IEEE Annals of the History of Computing* 17(3): 30–57.

Dalcher, D. and Drevin, L. (2003). Learning from Information Systems Failures by Using Narrative and Ante-narrative Methods, in J. Bishop and D. Kourie (eds.) Proceedings of the 2005 Research Conference of the South African Institute of Computer Scientists and Information Technologists, SAICSIT, Published, Pretoria: South Africa, Vol. 47, pp. 137–142.

De Neufville, R. (1994). The Baggage System at Denver: Prospects and lessons, *Journal of Ait Transport Management* 1(4): 229–234.

Diamond, J. and Robinson, J.A. (2010). All the World's a Lab, *New Scientist* March 27: 28–31.

Dickson, G. (1981). Management Information Systems, Evolution and Status, in M. Yovits (ed.) *Advances in Computers,* New York: Academic Press.

Drummond, H. (1996). *Escalation in Decision Making: The tragedy of Taurus,* Oxford: Oxford University Press.

Drummond, H. (2008). The Icarus Paradox an Analysis of a Totally Destructive System, *Journal of Information Technology* 23(3): 176–184.

Foucault, M. (1980). *Power/Knowledge: Selected interviews and other writings 1972–1977,* New York: Prentice Hall.

Foucault, M. (1982). The Subject and Power, in M. Foucault, H. Dreyfus and P. Rabinow (eds.) *Beyond Structuralism and Hermeneutics,* Hemel Hempstead: Harvester Press, pp. 208–226.

Giddens, A. (1987). *Social Theory and Modern Sociology,* Cambridge: Polity Press.

Glass, R.L. (1998). *Software Runaways: Lessons learned from massive software project failures,* Upper Saddle River, New Jersey: Prentice Hall.

Gottschalk, P. (2002). Towards a Model of Growth Stages for Knowledge Management in Law Firms, *Informing Science* 5(2): 81–93.

Hammer, M. and Champy, J. (2001). *Reengineering the Corporation: A manifesto for business revolution*, New York: Harper Collins.

Hevner, A.R. (ed.) (2008). Design Science Theories and Research Practices, in L. P. Willcocks and A.S. Lee, Series (eds.), Vol. III, *Major Currents in Information Systems*, Los Angeles: Sage.

Howcroft, D. and Land, F. (eds.) (2008). Information Systems Infrastructure, in L.P. Willcocks and A.S. Lee, Series (eds.), Vol. I, *Major Currents in Information Systems*, Los Angeles: Sage.

Hyman, A. (1985). *Charles Babbage: Pioneer of the computer*, New Jersey: Princeton University Press.

Journal of Information Technology (JIT) (2007). Special Issue on NPfIT, **22**: 202–264.

Khazanchi, D. and Munkvold, B.E. (2000). Is Information Systems a Science? An Inquiry into the Nature of the Information Systems Discipline, *ACM SIGMIS Database* **31**(2): 24–42.

King, J.L. and Kraemer, K. (1984). Evolution and Organizational Information Systems: An assessment of Nolan's stage model, *Communications of the ACM* **27**(5): 466–475.

King, J.L. and Lyytinen, K. (2004). Reach and Grasp, *MIS Quarterly* **28**(4): 539–551.

Lacity, M.C. (ed.) (2008). The Management Information of Information Systems, in L.P. Willcocks and A.S. Lee, Series (eds.), Vol. IV, *Major Currents in Information Systems*, Los Angeles: Sage.

Land, F.F. (1996). The New Alchemist: Or how to transmute base organizations into corporations of gleaming gold, *Journal of Strategic Information Systems* **5**(1): 7–17.

Land, F.F. (2000). The First Business Computer: A case study in user-driven innovation, *IEEE Annals of the History of Computing* **22**(3): 16–26.

Land, F.F. (2006). LEO II and the Model T Ford, *Computer Journal* **49**(6): 650–656.

Land, F.F. (2009). Knowledge Management and the Management of Knowledge, in W.R. King (ed.) *Knowledge Management and Organizational Learning, Vol. 4, Annals of Information Systems*, New York: Springer, Chapter 2, pp. 15–25.

Land, F.F., Detjearuwat, N. and Smith, C. (1983a). Factors Affecting Social Control: The reasons and values – Part I, *Systems Objectives, Solutions* **3**(5): 155–164.

Land, F.F., Detjearuwat, N. and Smith, C. (1983b). Factors Affecting Social Control: The reasons and values – Part I, *Systems Objectives, Solutions* **3**(6): 207–224.

Liebenau, J. and Mitev, N.N. (eds.) (2008). Social and Organizational Information Systems Research, in L.P. Willcocks and A.S. Lee, Series (eds.), Vol. V, *Major Currents in Information Systems*, Los Angeles: Sage.

Lyytinen, K. and Hirschheim, R. (1987). Information Systems Failures: A survey and classification of the empirical literature, *Oxford Surveys in Information Technology* **4**: 257–309.

Lyytinen, K. and King, J.L. (2004). Nothing at the Center?: Academic legitimacy in the information systems field, *Journal of the Association for Information Systems* **5**(6): 220–246.

Marchetti, C. (1980). Society as Learning Systems: Discovery, invention and innovation cycles revisited, *Technological Forecasting and Social Change* **18**(4): 267–282.

Mason, R.O. (2004). The Legacy of LEO: Lessons learned from an English tea and cake company's pioneering efforts in information systems, *Journal of the*

Association for Information Systems 5(5), Article 7 [www document] http://aisel. aisnet.org/jais/vol5/iss5/7.

Mason, R.O., McKenney, J.L. and Copeland, D.G. (1997a). Developing a Historical Tradition in IS Research, *MIS Quarterly* 21(3): 257–278.

Mason, R.O., McKenney, J.L. and Copeland, D.G. (1997b). An Historical Research Method for MIS Research: Steps and assumptions, *MIS Quarterly* 21(3): 307–320.

Mitev, N.N. (1996). More than a Failure? The Computerized Reservation Systems at French Railways, *Information Technology & People* 9(4): 8–19.

Mitev, N.N. and Howcroft, D.A. (2005). The Role of History in IS research, in C.H.J. Gilson (ed.) Proceedings of Management Studies Conference (Cambridge, UK, 4–6th July 2005); Waikato Management School; New Zealand: South African Institute for Computer Scientists and Information Technologists.

Mohr, L. (1982). *Explaining Organizational Behaviour*, San Francisco: Jossey-Bass.

Moschella, D. (1997). *Waves of Power: Dynamics of global technology leadership 1964–2010*, New York: AMACOM.

Mumford, E. (2003). Designing an Expert System, in E. Mumford (ed.) *Redesigning Human Systems*, Herschey, Penn: IRM Press, Chapter 9, pp. 147–168.

Namier, J. (1971). *Lewis Namier: A biography*, New York: Oxford University Press.

Ngwenyama, O. (1991). The Critical Social Theory Approach to Information Systems: Problems and challenges, in H.E. Nissen, H. Klein and R. Hirschheim (eds.) *Information Systems Research*, Amsterdam: North Holland, pp. 267–294.

Nolan, R.L. (1973). Managing the Computer Resource: A stage hypothesis, *Harvard Business Review* 16(4): 399–405.

Pettigrew, A.M. (1990). Longitudinal Field Research on Change: Theory and practice, *Organization Science* 1(3): 267–292, Special Issue: Longitudinal Field Research.

Piccoli, G. (2004). Making IT Matter: A manager's guide to creating and sustaining competitive advantage with information systems, *CHR Reports* 4(9): 1–21.

Porra, J., Hirschheim, R. and Parks, M.S. (2005). The History of Texaco's Corporate Information Technology Function: A general systems theoretical interpretation, *MIS Quarterly* 29(4): 721–746.

Santayana, G. (2009). *The Life of Reason: Or the phases of human progress*, Vol. 1, Charleston, SC: Bibliobazaar.

Sauer, C. (1993). *Why Information Systems Fail: A case study approach*, Oxfordshire: Alfred Waller.

Shaw, T. and Jarvenpaa, S. (1997). Process Models of Information Systems Research, in A.S. Lee, J. Liebenau and J. DeGross (eds.) Information Systems and Qualitative Research, Proceedings of IFIP TC8.2 Conference Philadelphia, IFIP, Chapter 6, London: Chapman & Hall, Ltd. pp. 70–100.

Simmons, J.R.M. (1962). *LEO and the Managers*, London: MacDonald.

Swanson, E.B. and Ramiller, N.C. (1997). The Organizing Vision in Information Systems Innovation, *Organization Science* 8(6): 458–474.

Taleb, N.N. (2007). *The Black Swan: The impact of the highly improbable*, London: Random House.

Tapscott, D. (2004). The Engine that Drives Success, *CIO Magazine*, May.

Vessey, I., Ramesh, V. and Glass, R.L. (2002). Research in Information Systems: An empirical study of diversity in the discipline and its journals, *Journal of Management Information Systems* 19(2): 129–174.

Walsham, G. and Han, C.-K. (1991). Structuration Theory and Information Systems Research, *Journal of Applied Systems Analysis* 17: 77–85.

Walsham, G. and Han, C.K. (1992). Information Systems Strategy Formation and Implementation: The case of a central government agency, Research Paper No. 1992/18, Management Studies Group at the Department of Engineering, Cambridge University.

Willcocks, L.P. and Lee, A.S. series (eds.) (2008). *Major Currents in Information Systems*, Vol. 1–6. Los Angeles: Sage.

Williams, R. and Pollock, N. (2009). Beyond the ERP Implementation Study: A New Approach to the Study of Packaged Information Systems: The biography of artefacts framework, ICIS 2009 Proceedings, Paper 6 [www document] http://aisel.aisnet.org/icis2009/6.

Appendix

Frank Land responded by e-mail to six questions from Dan Power, DSSResources. com editor, about his past involvement with computerized decision support systems (DSS) and his current perspective on the issues that need to be addressed.

Q1: How did you get interested in computerized decision support?
Land's Response: Decision Support has an ancient history. Decision makers have always surrounded themselves with specialist staff to provide information as a crucial aid to decision making. In the army, for example, the decision support function was provided by the adjutant.

We can perhaps distinguish two kinds of DSS which we might term *Traditional* and *Modern*. Is there also a Post-Modern type?

Traditional DSS are the historic kind, though today still as important as ever – the decision makers being supported by a range of formal and often informal information and knowledge providers. These may be people, like the adjutant or accountant with formal support roles or informal like the business rival over a game of golf. Or they can be artefacts, formal, like an official report requested by the decision makers, or informal like a newspaper report seen by the decision maker at just the right moment. As is often the case serendipity plays an important role in reaching decisions.

Modern DSS are largely reliant on formal models whose expression and evaluation depends on computer technology. They rely to a considerable extent on mathematical modelling and simulation techniques. Many of the ideas stem from the decision sciences and operational research and were first developed in the run-up to the Second World War as part of the war effort.

My own involvement arose out of my first employment with J.Lyons & Co. in 1952.

J.Lyons & Co, were the largest and best organised company in the UK food trade – restaurants and hotels, food manufacturing including bakery products, confectionary, tea and coffee, and specialist caterers for events such as the annual Wimbledon Tennis Tournament, and the Royal Garden Parties, had established a Systems Research Office in the early 1930s.

In Lyons the management structure was, in a sense, based on decision support. Each functional unit – for example, the bread and cake bakery – had at its head a member of the Board. A liaison unit served that function providing detailed information on each days trading via a set of cost accounts. The head of each unit was directly responsible to the Board member. He/she were responsible for reporting variances and providing explanations of any variances discovered from the cost accounts to the manager in whose area of responsibility the variance occurred. In addition, the head of each unit was required to work out answers to questions from senior managers of the functional area served of a 'what if' nature. For example, what would be the impact of changing the production mix to increase the production of swiss rolls, or to replace raw material 'a' by raw material 'b'. In practice, they spent much of their time working on these problems and providing the required information for the decision makers. The kind of questions might be of a local operational nature or much more concerned with matters relating to company strategy.

The system had been designed and implemented by one of the true pioneers of Decision Support – JRM Simmons, a Director of J. Lyons, recruited by the company in the early 1920s directly from Cambridge University where he had graduated as the top mathematician of his year. It was John Simmons who had persuaded the Lyons Board to build their own digital computer, Lyons Electronic Office (LEO) to support the business in 1947. His book 'LEO and the Managers (Simmons, 1962) sets out his ideas and shows their development in the computer age.

Thus Lyons had, before the advent of computers, a well developed and effective decision support mechanism though Simmons recognised that computers would play a crucial role in making an effective system even more effective.

Another pioneer was David Caminer who had joined Lyons as a management trainee in the 1930s. On returning from war service David became manager of the Systems Research Office established by Simmons in 1932. David was made head of systems and programming when the decision to build the LEO computer was made. He played a crucial role in the design of most of the early computer applications for the Lyons business. It was perhaps natural for him to see the role of computers at Lyons as supporting the work of the liaison staff. Hence, nearly all early applications dating back to the early 1950s and subsequently incorporated decision support elements. There were numerous examples ranging from the system which helped the managers of the chain of Lyons tea shops in placing their daily orders on the factories and suppliers, to the Bakery Rounds application which printed an order form for each customer the bakery salesman called on, listing the items ordered in previous calls, as a reminder of that customers preferences.

I joined the Lyons computer team in 1953. After graduating from the London School of Economics (LSE) my first job in industry in 1952 was with Lyons working in one of the liaison units described above. As a result I absorbed the Lyons way of working and the way they had developed an organisation capable of supporting management in both its strategic and day-to-day operational decision making. When I became part of the Lyons computer team in 1953 these ideas were already deeply ingrained in my thinking.

Q2:   What do you consider your major contribution to helping support decision makers using computers? Why?
Land's Response: As part of the LEO team at Lyons I was responsible for the implementation of a number of computer based applications, at first exclusively for Lyons, and later, when LEO became a subsidiary manufacturing and selling

the LEO range of computers, for a number of industrial clients. The applications included a system for the ice cream business, which advised ice cream retailers how to fill their cabinets based on weather forecasts and the systems knowledge of each customer's ice cream sales history. This system was devised with the help of the Lyons Operational Research team and, looking at it in retrospect, was a step from Traditional DSS to Modern DSS. Another system I was responsible for implementing was the Tea Blending Programme, which supported the tea mangers in determining the best mix of blends to schedule each week based on tea prices and forecast demand. The system was in use, I believe for nearly 30 years.

Later (1967), I was recruited by the LSE to set up teaching and research in systems analysis. About 1970/71 the UK National Computing Centre set up a research project into evaluating the costs and benefits of computer-based information systems. Three of the researchers, Enid Mumford (Manchester Business School), John Hawgood (Durham University) and I (LSE) became interested in developing a tool which could be used by managers to choose between alternative views of what systems requirements really were and alternative methods of meeting the requirements. We developed a Decision Support System called BASYC based on the notions of multi-objective, multi-criteria decision making to be used for that purpose. An important insight gained from experiments with our system with savings banks was that the system enabled a group of decision makers to thoroughly explore the decision space and in doing so to surface often hidden assumptions. The process involved in using the DSS was as important as the numbers produced by the DSS (Land, 1975; Hawgood and Land, 1977).

I subsequently became interested in Executive Information Systems (EIS) and whilst at the London Business School developed an executive course in which EIS was demonstrated with course members role playing senior executives faced with choices on which direction to take.

Q3:   *What were your motivations for working in this area?*

Land's Response: Two archetypical positions had emerged with the growing power of computers and management science. The first, positivistic in its philosophy, has a strong belief in the power of science to model economic and business behaviour. Those who followed this line believed that decision making was best taken out of the hands of fallible human actors and computer armed with management models were the appropriate tools for this. In the 1950s, for example, Bob Deem, a management scientist working for BP, persuaded the company to let him develop a comprehensive computer system which would automate the scheduling of refinery production. Despite the ultimate failure of the system the underlying belief still has wide credence.

The second archetype has its origin in the social sciences. Amongst its tenets is the conviction that the behaviour of a system involving human actors is non-deterministic and emergent. Further, it is argued that the success of such systems requires the active engagement of its stake-holders. This would enable the Sociotechnical system to capture their knowledge, lead to further learning and provide motivation. Hence the role of the computer is to act as an assistant to, rather than as a replacement, of the human participant.

My interest was not in DSS *per se*, but in developing a repertoire of approaches and tools fitting in with my interest in a Sociotechnical view of Information

Systems. DSS and in particular GDSS provided a mechanism for utilising the Sociotechnical precepts.

Q4: Who were your important collaborators and what was their contribution?
Land's Response: Whilst at Lyons and LEO the main collaborators where the managers of the functional units – such as the managers of the tea factory and, of course, my seniors and in particular David Caminer.

My move from industry back to the LSE led to a much greater study of the systems literature. I was influences by Steven Alter's book on DSS which gave a name to some of the ideas I had carried tacitly from my days with LEO, and enabled me to articulate them more clearly.

But the greatest influence was my collaboration with Enid Mumford and John Hawgood. This led directly to our work with the savings bank. More importantly it helped me to find a rationale for the views I had adopted intuitively from my 16 years working with LEO.

My interest in evaluation, fired by the project noted above, was continued later working with David Target (London Business School and Imperial College, London)) and Barbara Farbey (LSE and University College, London). The partnership developed a real synergy resulting in a book and a number of papers based on our joint research with industrial partners.

Another important influence was (and is) Professor Lawrence Phillips Visiting Professor of Decision Science at the LSE (see http://www.lawrencephillips.net/). Larry is another pioneer in this area. He introduced the 'Pod' an environment for group decision making using a variety of aids to help arrive at difficult decisions in situations where radically different solutions are initially advocated. He has repeatedly demonstrated the power of his approach.

But it is impossible to list all the people with whom I collaborated or who contributed to my understanding and learning. Sometimes a conversation over coffee with a colleague was as influential as reading a paper or a book.

Q5: What are your major conclusions from your experiences with computerized decision support?
Land's Response: The best DSS are those which provide clear explanations of the rationale behind the alternatives offered up for consideration and permit the decision makers to explore the decision space and to bring to the surface underlying assumptions and hidden conflicts. But to make the process work it needs a facilitator with an understanding of group behaviour as well as of the way the DSS is constructed.

Without the assistance of a facilitator Managers sometimes find it difficult to follow the underlying logic of the DSS leading either to the dismissal of the DSS or to the blind acceptance of the recommendations without a full understanding of the implications of the choices made. However, at their best, when designed jointly with the decision makers, they can be highly successful.

A DSS which is simply parachuted into the decision situation has little chance of being adopted. Ideally the DSS is the outcome of collaboration between the decision makers and systems designers. The way the DSS is deployed is highly dependent on the working style of individual or group decision makers. The point is illustrated in the 1986 Ph.D. thesis of Richard Baskerville when my student at the LSE. The DSS was designed to support the activities of the Admiral of the US Navy in charge of its London Office. The very successful system designed to suit the officer in charge was sidelined when he was replaced by an officer with a very different working style (Baskerville and Land, 2004).

Q6:   What are the issues associated with decision support that we still need to address?
Land's Response: Note the importance of keeping the logic in line with changing conditions in a turbulent world. Too often decision makers, not fully understanding the underlying logic, rely on a model embedded in the DSS which has ceased to reflect the changed world. Designers, on the other hand, often do not ensure the mechanisms are provided for the rapid and easy updating of the models underlying the DSS.

The importance of the informal systems which run though most organisations. These often are more information rich than formal systems, which are restricted in the information they can gather. The importance of informal systems and their role in decision making is often neglected by systems designers.

However, developments in the use of the internet such as Web 2.0 and the ideas behind the open source movement are permitting the informal to infiltrate computer-based systems.

Perhaps most importantly we need to further improve our understanding of how decisions are made and the role played by non-instrumental issues such as 'office' politics, human relations and intelligence.

DSS References

Baskerville, R.L. and Land, F.F. (2004), Socially Self-Destructing Systems, in C. Avgerou, C. Ciborra and F.F. Land (eds.) *The Social Study of Information and Communications Technology: Innovation, actors and contexts*, Oxford: Oxford University Press, pp. 263–285.

Hawgood, J. and Land, F.F. (1977), The BASYC Approach to Planning, Evaluation and Designing Computer-based Systems, paper presented at Informationsforum: Die Wirtschaftlichkeit von Informations – und Kommunikations-systemen, Cologne, December.

Land, F.F. (1975), Evaluation of Systems Goals in Determining a Design Strategy for a Computer-based Information System, *Computer Journal* 19.

Simmons, J.M.M. (1962), *LEO and the Managers*, London: Macdonald.

9
Seizing the Opportunity: Towards a Historiography of Information Systems

Nathalie Mitev[1] and François-Xavier De Vaujany[2]
[1]*Department of Management, Information Systems and Innovation Group (ISIG), London School of Economics and Political Science, London, UK;*
[2]*Equipe de recherche Management & Organisation, DRM (UMR CNRS 7088), Université Paris-Dauphine, Paris, France*

Introduction

Since the late 1990s, a stream of research in IS has been promoting historical perspectives on organisational information systems (McKenney *et al.*, 1995, Mason, 1997a,b; Bannister, 2002; Porra *et al.*, 2005; Land, 2010). The adoption of historical sensitivity is likely to be helpful in a field that is often driven by the 'awesome potential' of advanced information and communication technologies (ICTs). We often lose sight of issues as we are blinded by the glare of technology (Bannister, 2002; Land, 2010). If we acquire a historical dimension we may avoid regurgitating ideas with little awareness of their historical context, and being victims of IT fads and fashions (Westrup, 2005) which often damage the potential competitive advantage of firms. A lack of historical consciousness means that concepts and themes are often repackaged several years on, with little thought given to their historical context and origin (Bannister, 2002).

In contrast, a historical approach to organisations and their technological capabilities is an opportunity to develop reflexivity and criticism. It is a way to combat the universalistic and 'presentist' tendencies of general so-called management theory, or 'Heathrow Organisation Theory' after Gibson Burrell (1997). The latter allows business researchers to escape without any real sensitivity to the issues raised by the humanities and social sciences, to view technology as neutral, technical progress as natural, and to view History[1] as hagiography (success stories, e.g., Peters and Waterman, success of IBM) rather than historiography.

From a managerial perspective, historical approaches can also help explore differently organisational assets through historical narratives about and by organisations (Brunninge, 2009) – for instance new elements for brand image, original corporate identities, memory, communication (Delahaye *et al.*, 2009), culture (Barney, 1986) or forgotten products or processes (e.g. quality management, see Karsten *et al.*, 2009). Corporate History has a relative malleability (Gioia *et al.*, 2002) and is a resource managers use for differentiation (Foster *et al.*, 2009).

Searching both for theoretical and methodological benefits, management and organisation studies have experienced a move towards History (see Goodman and Kruger, 1988; Kieser, 1989, 1994). According to Clark and Rowlinson (2004), the historic 'turn' represents a transformation of organisation studies in three senses, and this could apply equally well to IS research:

- turn against the view that organisation studies should constitute a branch of the *science* of society;
- turn towards history, conceptualising the past as process and context rather than as a *variable*;
- turn to historiographical debates and historical theories of *interpretation* which recognise the inherent ambiguity of the term History itself.

Indeed, the use of historical perspectives has been criticised, in the fields of organisation theory (Kieser, 1994; Clarke and Rowlinson, 2004; Üsdiken and Kieser, 2004), management (Goodman and Kruger, 1988; O'Brien *et al.*, 2004) and information systems (Bannister, 2002; Land, 2010) for its lack of achievement.

Clarke and Rowlinson (2004) provide a critical analysis of historical efforts in organisation studies. They argue that there have been minor rather than major applications of historical methods; for instance the discourse of contingency and strategic choice still seeks to identify universal characteristics, even if it is to allow for some variation between historical contexts. Research tries to include historical variability but still tends towards deterministic and universalist explanations. Some approaches like new institutionalism and organisational ecology have become more historical – with longitudinal studies of organisational fields and populations or use of large-scale historical data-bases. But their time frame is usually only a chronological time-line and presumes a linear account of history. Overall, organisation studies have only carried out limited historical research (*ibid*). The same question can be raised about IS research. According to Land (2010), one can wonder if History is not (still) a 'missed opportunity'. We argue here that there are ways of avoiding 'simple data dredging' (Goodman and Kruger, 1988) and we will make some suggestions to revisit and seize this historical opportunity.

This paper starts by examining IS historical research through a conceptual framework commonly used in management and organisation studies (Üsdiken and Kieser, 2004) in order to evaluate the use of History in IS research systematically. We explain this framework by relating it to the epistemological viewpoints of positivism, interpretivism and critical theory which are well-accepted in IS research and we briefly outline corresponding historiographical methods. We then use this historical conceptual framework to analyse a large data set of IS History papers and provide suggestions for further historical IS research.

Historiographical methods in organisation theory: a conceptual framework

Üsdiken and Kieser (2004)[2] have developed a typology which is summarised in Table 9.1. They classify different degrees of incorporation of historical approaches in organisational and management research and suggest that they fall into three categories:

- *supplementarist*, where historical 'context' is simply added and is only a complement to common positivist approaches still focusing on variables, although with a longer time span than usual. It 'adheres to the view of organisation theory as social scientistic[3] and merely adds History as another contextual variable, alongside other variables such as national cultures' (Booth and Rowlinson, 2004: 8);
- *integrationist*, or a full consideration of History with new or stronger links between organisation theory and history. The aim is 'to enrich organization theory by developing links with the humanities, including history, literary theory and philosophy, without completely abandoning a social scientific orientation' (*ibid*: 8); and
- *reorientationist* or post-positivist, which examines and repositions dominant discourses including our own (such as progress or efficiency), and produces a criticism and renewal of organisation theory itself, on the basis of history. This 'involves a thoroughgoing critique of existing theories of organization for their ahistorical orientation' (*ibid*: 8).

Table 9.1 A typology of historical perspectives in organisation studies (adapted from Üsdiken and Kieser, 2004)

Historical stances in organization studies	Principle	Example
Supplementarist historical perspective (i.e. peripheral use of history)	Longer time span than usual case studies. Limited use of historical concepts, theories or methods. Descriptive approaches. Consolidate existing theories. Positivist stance.	Structural contingency and strategic choice seek to identify salient universal contingencies even if it is to allow for variation between historical contexts. It tries to explain variability but tends towards determinism. See most research under the umbrella of the 'Heathrow theory' critique (Burrell, 1997).
Integrationist historical perspective (i.e. use of History to extend existing theoretical frameworks)	Integration of historical techniques and theories into organisational research. Extension of existing theories. Extending theories. Positivist or interpretivist stance.	Approaches like new institutionalism and organisational ecology have become more historical with longitudinal studies of organisational fields and populations, cross-sectional studies or use of large-scale historical databases. Their time frame is usually a simple time-line with a basic chronological account of history. See Kieser's (1989) work about monastic organisations which is a way to extend classic research about bureaucracy or protobureaucracy.
Reorientationist historical perspective (i.e. extensive use of historical data and historiography to deconstruct existing theoretical frameworks and to propose new ones)	Reorientation of organisational research (i.e. new organisation theories) on the basis of historiography. Challenging theories. Critical stance.	Reorientationist approaches are more present in the History of management, and of management ideas and thought. They help identify and analyse the following cliches: • History neglected and/or used to support a narrative about powerful new claims ('Heathrow Organisation Theory'); • History as science, designed for explanation of the past and prediction of the future (scientism). See Actor Network Theory based critical organisational historiographical analyses (Hartt *et al.*, 2009; Durepos and Mills, 2010).

Üsdiken and Kieser (2004) claim that supplementarist research seems to be more frequent in organisation theory than integrationist and reorientationist organisational research.

Examples of historical *supplementarist* approaches in management and organisation studies are how neo-institutional economics use historical analyses of corporate formations. Approaches like new institutionalism have become more 'historical': they study a small number of variables over longer historical periods, but usually are not rich contextual case studies of organisations on a long-term timescale. Their emphasis is on persistence and homogeneity, and they exhibit a fear of lapsing into narrative interpretations of historical events that stress their complexity, uniqueness and contingency.

Examples of *integrationist* work can be found in the business History perspective applied to the world of organisations. Business historians have progressed to realise the potential of their work to inform contemporary managerial decision-making. More *interpretivist* and inductive analyses of History in organisational studies (Kieser, 1989, 1994) have abandoned 'general models' that are conceptualised independently of the phenomena to be explained. They are longitudinal case studies which try to account for subtle temporal and institutional dimensions, use processual (as opposed to factor) approaches and focus on contextual differences, organisational change and culture.

Reorientationist approaches are present in the History of management, and of management ideas and thought. They move beyond the following false dichotomy: whether History is merely a literary or narrative form, designed for political and moral edification ('Heathrow Organisation Theory'); or a science, designed for explanation of the past and prediction of the future (scientist analytical schemas) in which the logic of efficiency has been superimposed onto the narratives of historians. The so-called 'efficiency principle' militates against both historical and ethical considerations. It presumes that History is efficient, and it subordinates History to conceptual modelling. But reorientationist research is rare in organisation studies (Üsdiken and Kieser, 2004).

These three perspectives make sense in the field of History itself, which has always drawn on multiple epistemological stances. For clarification purposes, we relate the supplementarist-integrationist-reorientationist typology to the three epistemological positions of positivism, interpretivism and critical research, well known in IS research (Hirschheim, 1985; Orlikowski and Baroudi, 1991; Walsham, 1993, 1995; Klein and Myers, 1999).

Etymologically, History is an inquiry (στορια [Historíai] means 'inquiry' in Greek). Historiography can refer either to the History of History, or to the investigation of historical methods (Furay and Salevouris, 2000). Our focus here is more on the latter, in relationship with epistemological stances.

Positivistic researchers have defined History as driven by the search for truth, that is to say, 'facts' (Seignobos, 1901; Carr, 1961). Carr wanted to 'show how it really was' (1961:3 quoted by Bannister, 2002). In classical historical research (Simiand, 1903) this often focuses on:

- chronologies which underscore the genealogy of present structures and habits and avoid the details specific to any particular period;
- centring History on the biography of individuals who embody a certain historical trend (like the common success and heroic stories in management);
- political ideas, that is giving priority to political History which underlines political ideology and trends, whose importance is often exaggerated;
- national interests (Le Goff, 2006) based on, or even legitimating, national frontiers. Continental or international world analyses are rarely carried out by classic historians.

A positivist historian will search for triangulation of traces and clues to get the 'real' picture of a context located in the past. Other researchers in historiography have challenged this view and proposed viewing History in a more *interpretivist* and *critical* way – see for instance Aron's (1938) invitation to work out a critical philosophy of History by drawing on Dilthey, Rickert, Simmel, and Max Weber. According to an *interpretivist* stance, Collingwood (1993) suggests defining History as 'the study of thought'; History is the 're-enactment in the historian's mind of the thought whose History he/she is studying'. Marrou (1954) invited historians to adopt a *critical* stance by concentrating on the fuzzy boundary between the study of the present and that of the past; she proposed that 'from a logical point of view, there is nothing specific in understanding related to the past. It involves the same process as the understanding of others in the present, in particular (as most of the time and in the best situation, the document taken into account is a "text") the comprehension of articulated language' (p. 83).

A *critical* historiographical perspective (Le Goff, 2006: 73) invites historians to 'build a new scientific chronology which dates phenomena according to the duration of their effectiveness in History instead of the starting-point of their production'. In other words, the emphasis is more on tracing the long-term effects and discourses associated with certain phenomena instead of the phenomena themselves. This leads to a stronger focus on institutions and social structures rather than isolated actions in organisations, and is a good way to answer Braudel's (1958) well-known call for a 'longue durée' (or long-term) perspective in history. There are few major social theories which are ahistorical or neglectful of this longue durée perspective. For instance institutionalism, evolutionism and structuration theory are all based on long-term historiographical logic and often, long-term observations.

To explain this further, let us look at one of the most fundamental questions debated in history: whether there is a 'typical' historical theorisation of social transformations within societies and organisations. An example in IS research could be the typical conceptualisation of IT providing a competitive advantage and transforming organisations which is (has been?) very dominant. This key question could be reversed. This would mean investigating its historiography, that is the long-term duration of this conceptualisation in its historical institutional and social context; for instance, the emergence of the notion of IT and competitive advantage in the context of deregulation and liberalisation in specific situations (e.g. US airlines which pioneered the use of IT for competitive advantage with SABRE in the 1980s), the relationship of IT to the shaping of free markets, and the social and economic effects on industry de/restructuring. It de-universalises these conceptualisations, provides a critical analysis of their effectiveness and leads to more sophisticated theorisations. Similarly, Sauer (2008: 65, 75) has argued that 'capitalism has motivated the exploitation of IT (...) for its potential rather than its actual value'; and more generally that historical 'backcasting' reveals 'series of mutual adjustments' rather than outputs of a linear model.

Although there is an apparent link between Üsdiken and Kieser's three categories and the respective epistemologies of *positivism, interpretivism*, and *critical* historical research above, there is an important difference. According to Orlikowski and Baroudi (1991: 5–6):

'Positivist studies are premised on the existence of *a priori* fixed relationships within phenomena which are typically investigated with structured instrumentation. Such studies serve primarily to test theory, in an attempt to increase predictive understanding of phenomena', whilst interpretive studies 'assume that people create and associate their own subjective and intersubjective meanings as they interact with the world around them' (*ibid*: 5). In contrast, 'critical studies aim to critique the *status quo*, through the exposure of what are believed to be deep-seated, structural contradictions within social systems, and thereby to transform these alienating and restrictive social conditions' (*ibid*: 5–6).

Whereas these three epistemologies are based on three distinctive views of knowledge and the social world, supplementarist, integrationist and reorientationist approaches form a continuum. This continuum is about the way in which the reference discipline (organisation studies or information systems in our case) is challenged by the historical approach. At the lowest end of the spectrum, supplementarism only adds History without affecting the premises of theory; for instance seeking correlations between variables (presumed to be stable) of organisational change over time. Integrationism goes a little further in identifying historical processes of, for instance, organisational change over time, although it still aims to improve theories; at the highest end, conceptualisations of organisational change theories themselves are questioned through the reorientationist historical perspective.

In addition, we believe that interpretivism (as described by Walsham, 1993) can be integrationist or even reorientationist; but that re-orientationism does not uniquely correspond to an interpretive perspective. Some reorientationist work can adopt an interpretivist, or even a positivist approach to critically de-construct organisation theory. On the other hand, we see a more direct correspondence between supplementarism (e.g. in its understanding of time and actors) and positivism, Integrationism can be positivist or interpretivist but not critical. Rather than just adopting different epistemological stances, historical approaches operate on a continuum:

- consolidating existing theories (*supplementarist*, positivist, never critical);
- extending theories (*integrationist*, positivist or interpretivist); or
- challenging theories (*re-orientationist*, positivist or interpretivist, and always critical).

An element of critical approaches, as already quoted above, is the exposure of deep-seated contradictions (Orlikowski and Baroudi, 1991). To achieve this, an important tenet of criticality is the centrality of discourse where the constitutive powers of language are emphasised and 'natural' or 'universal' objects are viewed as discursively and historically produced. This idea grew out of the 'linguistic turn' in French post-structuralist philosophy; it opposes the objectivists on the one hand, with their science aimed at predicting/controlling nature and people, and humanists on the other for privileging the individual's reported experience and a naïve version of human freedom (see Mitev and Howcroft, 2011). For instance, the Foucauldian version views discourses as systems of genealogical thought which are contingent upon, as well as informing, material practices (see Willcocks, 2004). Thus, tracing the historical emergence of 'strategy' discourses at a particular time can lead to identifying deep seated contradictions, including the sustaining and enhancement of the prerogatives of management, the generation of a sense of personal security for managers, the expression of a gendered masculinity, and the facilitation and legitimisation of the exercise of power (Alvesson and Deetz, 1996). A reorientationist perspective challenges theories (here strategy, see also Knights and Morgan, 1991, 1995) and is an often neglected element of critical approaches in management. Critical IS research in particular was initially guided by the emancipatory Frankfurt school and many have argued (e.g. Howcroft and Trauth, 2005) that the relative dominance of the Habermassian approach is unnecessarily limiting and have suggested that other approaches may be of benefit; we believe historical perspectives can contribute.

There have been tense debates about historiography as a method. Beyond the issue of the existence of specific historical methods (Veyne, 1971), History is a material which is handled, analysed and narrated by historians. Historians process materials left by past actions through access to recorded events. Those can be written or oral, based on monuments (archaeology is close to history), pictures, objects or documents. To select their primary material and develop an historical account, historians traditionally rely on the sets of criteria and associated questions outlined below (Langlois and Seignobos, 1897). Although positivist in their orientation, these criteria are still a deep part of historical rigour, whatever the epistemological position. They apply mainly to textual artefacts.

- *External* criteria: they deal with the physical features of materials under study (e.g. paper, ink or seals). To authenticate a document, skills in palaeography or epigraphy are often required. Historians of computing (e.g. Campbell-Kelly, 2010) include artefacts such as algorithms.
- *Internal* criteria: these are related to the internal coherence/consistency of a text, that is examining whether different parts of a text are coherent with one another.

- *Source* criteria: where does this material come from? This is often a way to evaluate the authenticity and accuracy of a testimony. In a corporate environment, a leaflet will not be valued in the same way as personal notes in a retired chairperson's diary. The temporal distance between events described and the period of their writing/ formalising in the document will also be taken into account.
- *Range/target* criteria, related to the receiver of a text. In what ways the artefact may have been received by people of that time? What could have been the expectations of the builder/sender of the artefact? How did she/he frame it to anticipate receivers' response?

Additionally, Garraghan (1946) has suggested the following six types of questions corresponding to some of these criteria. These questions show great potential for the study of IS and computer programmes in organisations.

- When was the document/artefact written (date)? – *External*
- Where was it produced (localisation)? – *External*
- By whom (authorship)? – *Source*
- From what pre-existing materials (analysis)? – *Source*
- In what original form (integrity)? – *Internal*
- With what evidential value (credibility)? – *Internal*

Beyond this critical examination of materials, historical methods focus on either the elaboration of a set of events (with the aim of constructing them 'objectively') or the understanding of perceptions/ representations (or interpretations) of actors involved in a specific spatio-temporal setting. For a *positivist* historian, facts will be isolated and then gathered according to their similarity or topicality. Each fact is linked to a cause or a set of causes which will be uncovered through a systematic study of materials. For a more *interpretivist* historian, imagination will play a stronger role. She/he will have to put himself/herself in the shoes of remote (in time and space) stakeholders of the society, organisation, tribe, etc. under study.

Eventually, whatever the epistemological stance (positivist, interpretivist or critical), comes the time of writing/narrating history. This stage of research has been thoroughly investigated recently with the 'linguistic turn'. According to Munslow (2001: 1), 'the recognition that History is a narrative about the past written in the here and now, rather than some distanced mirror of it, has been a significant issue within the profession for several years'. We believe that current debates in IS research about interpretivist and critical research could be renewed through an exploration of historiography, which can help address two key interdependent pitfalls[4]: anachronism and acontextuality (Booth and Rowlinson, 2004). Organisational scholars should give time serious consideration (see Orlikowski and Yates, 2002). Indeed, in many so-called historical studies, it is often assumed that 'any society, from the prehistoric to the present, faces the same organisational problems as our own'. Anachronism, presentism and universalism dominate. Universalism often 'emphasizes continuity over change' (Booth and Rowlinson, 2004: 6). Many organisational studies are not anchored enough in time, space and context. They present 'fictionalized organizations in a non-dated, extended present'. The historic turn problematises universalism and presentism:

> It raises the question of the extent to which organizations, and organizational research need to be historicized, that is, located in a specific historical context. For example, was the multinational enterprise born in ancient Greece? Or is it a form of organization that is specific to a globalized, capitalist economy? In which case, were the forms of foreign direct investment during the first age of globalization comparable to those of the late 20th century? And in terms of the present, how generalizable across time and space are the findings of an ethnographer from a fictionalized and supposedly typical organization? (Booth and Rowlinson, 2004: 6)

There have been similar calls by Kieser (1989, 1994) for more interpretivist and inductive analyses of History in organisational studies and for abandoning 'general models' that are conceptualised independently of the phenomena to be explained.

Can the same difficulties be noticed in IS research? Has IS research been mainly supplementarist, integrationist or re-orientationist? How historical has been positivist, interpretivist and critical IS research? How can we revisit the opportunity offered by historiography (see Land, 2010)? These will be the issues which will be addressed next. We first examine existing historical IS research critically, using Üsdiken and Kieser's (2004) classification to rank different degrees of incorporation of historical approaches into IS research. We then illustrate what the potential could be for historical analyses of IS.

From historical perspectives in organisation theory to historical perspectives in is research

In order to examine how historical approaches have been applied to IS research, we first present a thematic analysis of all papers on History and IS found through a systematic search of the ABI bibliographic database. We classify them using Üsdiken and Kieser's (2004) typology already presented in the introduction above. Using a further search of Google Scholar™ and pre-existing literature reviews, we then propose a qualitative analysis of a few papers typical of each of Üsdiken and Kieser's categories in order to discuss the main trends identified.

We provide an overview of IS papers with a historical perspective. In order to do this we concentrated on refereed journal articles since they are the type of publication that are regarded as being of highest quality, as compared to international conference papers or books.[5] Our concern is with papers deemed to be of a standard sufficiently high for international journal publication and thereby legitimized as worthy of interest to an international community. In addition, we focused specifically on journals that were located within the IS discipline and only considered papers which were located unequivocally within this literature. The journals chosen had information systems as their primary focus as opposed to management science, computer science, or information science. We selected journals whose principal readership is intended for those involved in the IS field.

The aim of this literature review is to provide an illustration of the quantity and nature of the types of papers that have been published in IS journals. We do not claim that the survey is exhaustive; nor do we assume that a more comprehensive survey (e.g. including conference proceedings or using other databases) would deliver significantly different results. The analysis involved the identification of all research papers in ABI that might broadly be defined as a historical perspective on information systems. Using a further search on Google Scholar™ (http://scholar.google.com/),[6] we double checked our primary analysis in order to confirm general tendencies and identify complementary references, used in our discussion. Therefore, in our survey of relevant literature our intention is to focus on material that is published in outlets specifically targeted as IS. Our research goal is to learn how a historical perspective has been incorporated into the IS literature.

We constructed a data set by retrieving all academic papers with the words 'information systems' and 'history' (in citation and abstract) from ABI. Our search focused on full text academic papers. This resulted in 384 papers from 1972 to 2009. Among the 384 papers, we found a lot of irrelevant papers, that is papers using the word History from a technical perspective (e.g. 'historical customer data') or only incidentally. We identified only 64 papers which were historical in their content. We

Table 9.2 Relative distribution of IS historical papers

	Number of historical papers per category	Percentage of historical papers per category	Number of papers in IS journals	Percentage in IS journals
Supplementarist	34	53.1	19	59.38
Integrationist	29	45.31	11	37.5
Reorientationist	1	1.56	1	3
Total	64	100	31	100

Table 9.3 Distribution of IS historical papers per decade

Decades	1970s	1980s	1990s	2000s
Supplementarist	1	3	1	29
Integrationist	0	5	5	19
Reorientationist	0	0	1	0

then used the three dimensions mentioned earlier (supplementarist, integrationist, reorientationist) to code each paper (see Appendices 1 and 2 for raw data and additional analysis). The results are presented in a succinct form in Tables 9.2 and 9.3. An extract of the full list of papers identified on ABI along with their analytical coding can be found in Appendix C.

The main findings are:

- the very small number of historical papers (only 64 from 1972 to 2009, see also Appendix C);
- a limited use of History for challenging theories (only 1.6% of reorientationist papers);
- the sharp increase of supplementarist papers consolidating existing theories (in particular in the 2000s, see also Figure 9.1);
- the fact that there is a moderate number of IS journals (see Table 9.1). Many interesting papers we found were published in journals in information science, history, computer science or economics.

Beyond this, historical IS papers follow a pattern: almost entirely absent reorientationist papers, a steady increase of integrationist publications and a dramatic increase of supplementarist articles (see Figure 9.1).

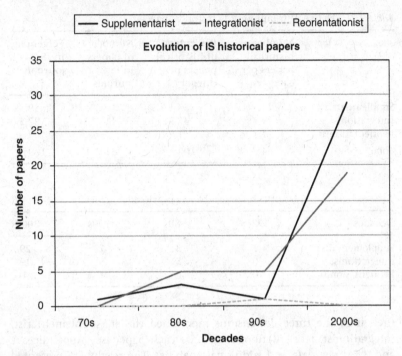

Figure 9.1 Evolution of supplementarist, integrationist and reorientationist publications in IS historical research (per decade)

History is therefore entering IS research through supplementarism (i.e. longer time span of data collection and a focus on processes rather than variables or factors). From the mid-1990s, it seems nonetheless that an increasing number of (integrationist) papers borrowed theories, concepts or methods from history. But this does not result in specific IS historical perspectives. Perhaps this is due to the fact that IS phenomena are relatively recent so historical 'data' are only slowly accumulating and IS scholars need historical distance to be able to distinguish long-term historical trends.

Our additional analysis based on Google Scholar™ produces the same results as our ABI analysis (see Appendix D). From the 1970s to the early 2000s, we identified 190 papers. The bulk was published in the 1990s, with an increase in the late 1990s. In addition, most articles were not published in IS journals and could be classified as supplementarist or integrationist (although we did not carry out such a systematic analysis as the one we did with ABI).

Discussion

From long-term research to historiography

Analysing these historical papers shows that: most are a description of events broadly covering a couple of decades of IS, within a single organisation (see Land, 2000; Maier *et al.*, 2002; Chen and Hirschheim, 2004; D'Arcy *et al.*, 2008); some focused on using a few historical concepts or techniques applied to a broader time scale (Robey and Newman, 1996; McKenney *et al.*, 1997a,b; Yates, 1997, 1999); researchers often relied on second-hand data; their theorisation was not strongly linked to History; they developed concepts which could have been developed on the basis of non-historical data; and they did not include long-term analyses or broader institutional contexts. This is also confirmed by a more general analysis of historical papers, by means of Google Scholar™ (see Appendix D), complemented by Bannister (2002)[7] and previous literature reviews by de Vaujany (2006) and Mitev and Howcroft (2005).

Clearly, historical research on organisational information systems has been relatively rare (Bannister, 2002). The Porra *et al.* (2005) History of the Texaco corporate information technology functions, Yates' work (1999, 2005) on the structuring of early computer use in the life insurance industry, Winter and Taylor's (2001) analysis of the role of IT in proto-industrial and post-industrial organisations, or the Harvard MIS History project (McKenney *et al.*, 1995) are among the rare, often cited references of historical works by IS scholars. Outside IS research, some historians of computing have also been interested in organisational computer systems. For instance, Wells (2000) studied artefacts and outdated computers in Wall Street and Heide (2004) analysed record management systems in France between 1935 and 1944.

If some of this research has adopted a descriptive stance shedding light on the evolution of various forms of IS, there are few writings in IS that have worked out a historiography of IS. Among the rare historiographical conceptualisations within the field, Mason *et al.* (1997a,b) and Yates (1997, 1999) are worth examining further.

Mason *et al* first suggest that there are three main roles, which can be endorsed by historical figures: the leader (identifying phases of crisis), the 'maestro' (mastering key business or technological domains) and the 'supertech' (who will develop relevant innovations to overcome the crisis). Second, they propose two key concepts; in their notion of cascade, these researchers insist on the importance of discontinuities in the flow of events, which is very close to the well-known notion of punctuated equilibrium and strategic alignment (see Majchrzak *et al.*, 2000).

Following a crisis, IS would gradually converge to a balanced configuration of technology and human assets. This conceptualisation of historical change proposes a three-part method consisting in the identification of key roles and variables, the specification of units of analysis, and the gathering of evidence.

Other IS historical studies have drawn on interpretive frameworks. For instance, Yates based her work on Giddens' structuration theory (Yates, 1997, 1999). Her method is less based on crisis identification and more on everyday continuous enactment of structure.

To better understand the supplementarist, integrationist and reorientationist approaches to IS History and their implications, we examined a sample of papers in more depth (see Table 9.4).

Supplementarist research tends to have a descriptive understanding of historical research to consolidate existing IS theories. For instance, Simon *et al.* (2009, see also Table 9.4) juxtaposed the History of a leading US multinational company and its offshore vendors with the literature on offshore outsourcing to refine attributes of best practices/maturity for a model for mature IT governance. By contrast, Mason *et al.* (1997a, b) can be classified as *integrationist*; they use historical evidence to build and extend the theory that IT has become 'the most influential force leading to restructuring of business and political economy as a whole'. Their aim is to 'reveal how IT forces have changed businesses, organisations, and industries' and they draw on the Schumpeterian creative/destructive approach to economic cycles. Their research base is 'exemplary' IT-based business histories to 'demonstrate' the effects of investments in IT on companies, industries and societies, exemplified by the Harvard MIS History Project. It consists of accounts of success stories at Bank of America (McKenney *et al.*, 1997), American Airlines, FedEx, Bank One, Wal-Mart, Frito-Lay and American Hospital Supply.

Studies for explaining IS in organisations can present both historical accounts and multivariate analysis, using a supplementarist approach, but can also expand into integrationist approaches to enrich IS theories. Accordingly, they recognise that present organisational forms and socio-technical arrangements have been shaped by past events (e.g. economic cycles) and their course of development has been influenced by the broader historical context. It implies turning to: processes of organisational and institutional change over time; development of organisational forms and variations across societal settings; path dependencies and continuities in organisational ideas and practices over time; historically specific material, social and cultural settings and their relations with organisations and technologies – these settings can include education,

Table 9.4 Classification and examples of historical perspectives in IS research

Historical stances	IS historical research
Supplementarist	See Appendix C. Most ABI articles we found include longer time spans but use an ahistorical stance. History is only a variable. Creating Better Governance of Offshore Services (Simon *et al.*, 2009)
Integrationist	From ABI: The History of Texaco's corporate information technology function (Porra *et al.*, 2005). The historical perspective is used to extend the general systems theory as applied to IS. Use History to reflect on IS and large organisations (Yates, 1999). IT and organisational transformation (Elbanna, 2002). Cross-History of IT and organisational change in the British Census from 1801 to 1911 (Campbell-Kelly and Aspray, 1996). From Google Scholar: The History of SAP proposed by Pollock and Williams (2008).
Reorientationist	From ABI: A Historical Method for MIS Research: Steps and Assumptions (Mason *et al.*, 1997a), Developing a Historical Tradition in MIS Research (Mason *et al.*, 1997b). The role of IT in the transformation of work. A comparison between proto and post industrial organisations. Reconceptualisation of the role of IT in organisations (Winter and Taylor, 1996). From Google Scholar: Drawing on structuration theory, Yates (1999) shows the 'conservative influence of existing patterns' (in the insurance industry of the 1950s) which is often underestimated in non-historical research about IT. It sheds light on new and innovative uses of computer technology in insurance from a longue durée perspective.

national institutions, economic and political history, the role of the State, religion, etc.

Supplementarist and integrationist stances dominate our ABI findings, and reorientationist research is rare. Reorientationist perspectives could challenge existing theories, generate new research questions as well as look at old questions in new ways (Üsdiken and Kieser, 2004). By anchoring research findings more clearly to their social origins can push thinking about alternative explanations for phenomena, help identify more and less stable concepts, and expand research horizons. The reorientationist historical approach can help frame theory and research within their time-related boundaries, and provide perspective on the present through the past. Reorientationism helps confront current and popular organisational and managerial ideas with practices in the past likely to reveal continuities and similarities. Studying the fate of earlier approaches and their features enables critical assessments of ideas that are currently promulgated. Universalist ahistorical stances are challenged and debates around what is made of History and how it is done are favoured.

For instance, revisiting the well-known stock of pioneer IT success stories would help understand how these discourses constituted our world at certain times and in certain spaces, and what their deep seated contradictions were. It would expose universalist Chandlerian heroic accounts of how particular technical solutions were seen as yielding superior results, and the effects of 'ideal types' of IT innovation such as cascade and crisis. Examining these mechanisms in the past would help understand the History of our intellectual constructs and their own historicity and help challenge the construction of current theories. As avenues for further historiographical research in IS, some of the ways in which History can help to extend or reshape IS theoretical underpinnings are explored further below.

Suggestions for further research

From the *integrationist* perspective, we believe a longue-durée historiographical outlook can help grasping the specificity of the institutional context of IS design, use or implementation in contemporary organisations. An example of a long-cycle approach is Martins' (2009) study of first-tier managers' roles from the industrial revolution to the 21st century which concludes that 'if key factors are not considered from an in-depth historical perspective (...) the people management role will remain a major organisational dilemma'. Neo-institutional frameworks (DiMaggio and Powell, 1983; Scott, 2001), structuration theory (Giddens, 1984), evolutionary economics (Nelson and Winter, 1982) or social critical realism (Archer, 1995), to name but a few, can help modelling the dynamic of society, organisational fields or populations of organisations. Such theories can help understanding socio-technical path-dependencies (Van Driel and Dolfsma, 2009). Notions such as increasing returns, lock-in or self-reinforcement are promising ways to extend organisational perspectives (Page, 2006). Models used in IS such as absorptive capability, critical success factors of IT project management or strategic alignment models of IS could be extended by the inclusion of these broader institutional factors and their history. Such is also the case of rising socio-material approaches (see Orlikowski, 2007). The integration of long-term perspectives could be a way to make sense of materiality and the evolution of its social meaning through time.

From a *reorientationist* perspective, historiography could also be a way to deconstruct IS frameworks and their relationship to managerial decision-making. Indeed, organisational History (and of information systems) could be conceptualised as a managerial asset; historians have shown that corporate History has a relative malleability (Gioia *et al.*, 2002). It is a resource managers can use for differentiation (Foster *et al.*, 2009). Firstly, because narratives about IT itself can become a differentiating myth, like the famous SABRE case-study (Hopper, 1990; Copeland, 1991). There has been debate (Adam, 1990; Monteiro and Macdonald, 1996; Mitev, 2004) about whether SABRE really helped to gain a competitive advantage *per se*, when there were other major influences such as airline deregulation. But what it clear is that this software has become a differentiating myth for American Airlines. Long-term History of financial, human and technical resources can help conceptualise further how the combination of resources over the History of an organisation evolves (see Penrose, 1959) and is intertwined with IT (Porra *et al.*, 2006).

Historiography can also be a way to narrate IS differently and challenge existing theories, through more reflexive approaches. Examples in management studies which could inspire IS researchers are: Cooke's (1999) historiography of the concept of change management; Zan's (1994, 2004) History of accounting histories; and the historical institutional analysis by Caswill and Wensley (2007) on how relevance and rigour have been constituted in management research in the UK. A critical example about the History of IS is Haigh's (2001) historical exploration of the role and vested interests of various professional bodies in 'inventing' information systems. Rayward (1996) uses Braudel's notions of 'longue', 'moyenne' and 'courte durée' to provide a new perspective on the History of information science; and the notions of synchrony and diachrony[8] to suggest other approaches to its historical study, in particular its interdisciplinarity over time.

The work of historians such as Le Goff (2006) could be an inspiration to write our scientific articles, books, case narratives differently, maybe in a more innovative and a more critical way. Grey and Sinclair (2006) suggest critical forms of writing to address aesthetic, moral and political concerns and ask questions on what our ways of writing accomplish in political terms. Using historical fiction is another example of writing which opens up the possibility of new critical insights (Czarniawska, 1999); and so is the use of History for critically examining management education (Down, 2001; Zald, 2002). Finally, and more reflectively, Hatchuel and Glise (2003) propose a redefinition of management research based on a historical analysis which could also be carried out in IS research.

Beyond suggesting these broad avenues for further research, we now illustrate what these avenues could look like. We concentrate in particular on two re-orientationist examples since our main finding is that there is very little evidence of reorientationist IS research, so it may be more difficult to carry out. We expand two IS topics which we think lend themselves to a critical reorientationist analysis: outsourcing/ centralisation with a positivist reorientationist approach; and action research/empowerment with an interpretivist reorientationist approach.

The History of the 'putting out' systems (Kieser, 1994) could be compared to current outsourcing and issues of de/centralisation. Putting out was a complex network of contracts of manufacture, usually analysed through labour process analysis (workers' control of product and process, division of labour, factory systems, technical superiority, matching of technology with skills, family lives) during the industrial revolution in Western societies, especially the UK. Historical material shows that putting out was a consequence – rather than the cause – of a division of work that was already in existence across rural communities in the North West of England in the textile industry. The centralisation of production was triggered by the need to fill the capacity of large-scale machinery, but putting out systems were far more effective than the centralised factory. Factory owners were forced to compromise as they were unable to find a technology for decentralised production. One could see parallels with the contracting out of workers through increasingly mobile ICTs, which takes place within countries and globally across borders, as opposed to just within regions. It may be possible to contrast and compare across cases, to highlight features particular to each historical context in order to gain some unexpected insights into current practices. While we are not suggesting that History repeats itself, informed historical analyses could serve to reflect on current thinking and critique existing theories of IT-enabled work design, for instance the consequences of offshoring on communities both in Southern and Northern parts of the world (see Howcroft and Richardson, 2010).

The historiography of influential ideas and thinkers on action research and change management could bring insights into the topic of participatory design and empowerment through ICTs. Cooke (1999) looked at the work of Kurt Lewin (1946), who is noted for the development of action research in organisational studies. Action research methods are concerned with changing the social system through engagement on the part of the researcher with the intention of making a contribution to social problems. However, action research was originally developed to deal with 'minority' problems, group dynamics and race relations, in a context of inter-ethnic conflict (US black apartheid). And participatory anthropology had been used by the British Empire and its liberal colonial administration's principle of 'indirect rule'. This principle was the stimulus for the development of action research, throwing an ambiguous light on the origins and aims of these methods, providing an interesting lens through which query current participatory or community-based technologies.

Similarly, Cooke (1999) also examined how the change management discourse has rewritten its own History and how its very construction has been a political process,[9] which has excluded a certain understanding of radical change, and 'shaped an understanding of change as technocratic and ideologically neutral'. Change management deals with the 'correct' understanding of the need for change and of who the subjects of change are. Cooke (1999) argues that Edgar Schein (1961) incorporated 'radical' ideas into the dominant management orthodoxy of the time and that his change management techniques draw on representations of an oriental 'other', in the context of a US military opposing liberation struggles in Asian countries. Participatory 'liberation' management does not question the right of those controlling the process. Social political and ideological circumstances in which it is applied are assumed to be uncontested and objectively given. Change management is therefore analysed as arising from drives to make 'subjects', whose voices are never represented, manageable. The current and growing use of ubiquitous managerial technologies to empower IT users and employees could be examined with these histories in mind.

Concluding remarks: an historical opportunity

Our literature survey and classification of IS historical journal papers over the last 38 years show that IS historical research has mainly been supplementarist (confirming existing theories) rather than integrationist (extending theories) or reorientationist (questioning theories), although the two latter have potential for a critical understanding of IS-related organisational changes. In the last section, we have made proposals to inspire integrationist and reorientationist historical IS researchers. Reviewing examples in related disciplines such as business history, management and organisational history and the social history of technology may provide further inspiration and broaden the scope of IS History research in the future.

There are still debates within the discipline of History, in particular about the focus on discourses and the use of historical narratives. Linear narratives tend to attribute a causal relation between events which is misleading. And historians have a problem with the indifference to the origin and context of historical texts. But the focus on metaphors, material/cultural practices and historically based analyses of discourses about technologies can help reject scientific and historical notions of 'progress' (e.g. technological progress), avoid inferences of causality and universal truths, and bring some distance on present organisations and technologies by making them unfamiliar. As Rowlinson and Carter (2002: 400) state:

> History is about lies, not truth. It is a struggle for domination acted out in a play of wills (...) in order to demonstrate the historical specificity of (...) organisations that have generally been overlooked in the discourse of organisation studies, historical research is required (...) and that necessitates the provision of concrete histories of organisations, practices and institutions.

We can add here concrete histories of their information systems and technologies in order to enrich, extend and question existing theories about their rationales, uses and effects. Whether IS researchers will be interested in carrying out this type of research in order to refute Ford's provocative statement 'History is bunk' (Land, 2010) remains to be seen.

Notes

1. To improve understanding we use the traditional distinction between 'history' (the past) and History (historical science).
2. For broader discussions about historical approaches in management and organisation studies, see a new journal set up in 2006: *Management & Organization History* (http://moh.sagepub.com/). This unique journal corresponds to a community of organisational historians which departs from the business history community, through its focus on 'the study of management, organizations and organizing'. It is related to a regular track at the European Group in Organizations Studies (EGOS) conference about 'historical perspectives in organizations studies' (see http://www.egos2012.net/2011/06/sub-theme-08-swg-historical-perspectives-in-organization-studies/).
3. Scientism refers to a belief in the universal applicability of the systematic methods and approach of science, especially the view that empirical science constitutes the most authoritative worldview or most valuable part of human learning, to the exclusion of other viewpoints.
4. Booth and Rowlinson use the metaphors of the 'Flintstone method' and the 'Simpsons method' to describe these two situations.
5. Books are clearly a better example of historical research and there are a few in IS. However, the pressures on researchers to publish in journals have grown

enormously and there are hardly any rewards in publishing research monographs, particularly in business schools. This is another debate.
6. Based on the same search terms as for ABI, see Appendix C.
7. Beyond the references mentioned in this paper, see also Bannister's website for an inventory of IS historical literature: http://is2.lse.ac.uk/leo/historio.htm.
8. Synchronic analysis views phenomena only at one point in time, usually the present; a diachronic analysis regards a phenomenon in terms of developments through time.
9. This is a good example of what we meant earlier by historiography as the History of History.

References

Adam, R. (1990). A License to Steal? The Growth and Development of Airline Information Systems, *Journal of Information Science* 16(2): 77–91.

Alvesson, M. and Deetz, S. (1996). Critical Theory and Postmodernism Approaches to Organizational Studies, in S.R. Clegg, C. Hardy and W.R. Nord (eds.) *Handbook of Organization Studies*, Thousand Oaks: Sage Publications, pp. 191–217 [Reprinted in Grey, C. and Willmott, H. (2005). Critical Management Studies: A Reader, Oxford: Oxford University Press (Oxford Management Readers), pp. 60–106].

Archer, M. (1995). *Realist Social Theory: The morphogenetic approach*, Cambridge: Cambridge University Press.

Aron, R. (1938). *Introduction à la philosophie de l'histoire. Essai sur les limites de l'objectivité historique*, Paris: Gallimard.

Bannister, F. (2002). The Dimension of Time: Historiography in information systems research, *Electronic Journal of Business Research Methods* 1(1): 1–10.

Barney, J.B. (1986). Organizational Culture: Can it be a source of sustained competitive advantage? *Academy of Management Review* 11(3): 656–665.

Booth, C. and Rowlinson, M. (2004). Management and Organizational History: Prospects, *Management & Organizational History* 1(1): 5–30.

Braudel, F. (1958). La longue durée, *Annales* 4(Oct-Nov): 725–753.

Brunninge, O. (2009). Using History in Organizations: How managers make purposeful reference to history in strategy processes, *Journal of Organizational Change Management* 22(1): 8–26.

Burrell, G. (1997). *Pandemonium: Towards a retro-organization theory*, London: Sage.

Campbell-Kelly, M. (2010). Historical Reflections: Victorian data processing, *Communications of the ACM* 53(10): 19–21.

Campbell-Kelly, M. and Aspray, W. (1996). *Computer: A history of the information machine*, New York: Basic Books.

Carr, E. (1961). *What is History?* London: Macmillan Press.

Caswill, C. and Wensley, R. (2007). Doors and Boundaries: A recent history of the relationship between research and practice in UK organizational and management research, *Business History* 49(3): 293–320.

Chen, W. and Hirschheim, R. (2004). A Paradigmatic and Methodological Examination of Information Systems Research from 1991 to 2001, *Information Systems Journal* 14(3): 197–207.

Clark, P. and Rowlinson, M. (2004). The Treatment of History in Organisation Studies. Towards an 'Historic Turn'? *Business History* 46(3): 331–352.

Collingwood, R. (1993). *The Idea of History: With lectures 1926–1928*, Oxford: Oxford University Press.

Cooke, B. (1999). Writing the Left out of Management Theory: The historiography of the management of change, *Organization* 6(1): 81–105.

Copeland, D.G. (1991). So You Want to Build the Next Sabre System? *Business Quarterly* 56(Winter): 56–60.

Czarniawska, B. (1999). *Writing Management: Organization theory as a literary genre*, Oxford: Oxford University Press.

D'Arcy, C., Holman, J., John Bass, A., Rosman, D.L. and Smith, M.B. (2008). A Decade of Data Linkage in Western Australia: Strategic design, applications and benefits of the WA data linkage system, *Australian Health Review* 32(4): 766–778.

Delahaye, A., Booth, C., Clark, P., Procter, S. and Rowlinson, M. (2009). The Genre of Corporate History, *Journal of Organizational Change Management* 22(1): 27–48.

de Vaujany, F.X. (2006). Conceptualizing IS Archetypes Through History: The case of the Roman Curia, in International Conference on Information Systems (ICIS) (Milwaukee, Wisconsin, December 2006). Wisconsin: Association for Information Systems, University of Milwaukee.

DiMaggio, P.J. and Powell, W. (1983). The Iron Cage Revisited: Institutional isomorphism and collective rationality in organizational fields, *American Sociological Review* 48(2): 147–160.

Down, S. (2001). The Use of History in Business and Management Learning, and Some Implications for Management Learning, *Management Learning* 32(3): 393–410.

Durepos, G. and Mills, A.J. (2010). Actor-network Theory: ANTi-history and critical organizational historiography, in Academy of Management Annual Meeting (Montreal, 6–10 August 2010).

Elbanna, A.R. (2002). Information Technology and Organisational Transformation: History, rhetoric and practice, *Information Technology & People* 15(2): 175–179.

Foster, W.M., Suddaby, R. and Wiebe, E.M. (2009). Organizational History and Tradition: Can it be the source of a sustained competitive advantage? In 25th European Group on Organisation Studies (EGOS) Colloquium (Barcelona, Spain, July 2009), Sub-theme 43: Historical perspectives in organization studies. Barcelona, Spain: ESADE Business School.

Furay, C. and Salevouris, M.J. (2000). *The Methods and Skills of History: A practical guide*, 2nd edn, New York: Harlan Davidson.

Garraghan, J.G. (1946). *A Guide to Historical Method*, New York: Fordham University Press.

Giddens, A. (1984). *The Constitution of Society. Outline of the Theory of Structuration*, Cambridge: Polity.

Gioia, D.A., Corley, K.G. and Fabbri, T. (2002). Revising the Past (While Thinking in the Future Perfect Tense), *Journal of Organizational Change Management* 15(6): 622.

Goodman, R.S. and Kruger, E.V. (1988). Data Dredging or Legitimate Research Method? Historiography and Its Potential for Management Research, *The Academy of Management Review* 13(2): 315–325.

Grey, C. and Sinclair, A. (2006). Writing Differently, *Organization* 13(3): 443–453.

Haigh, T. (2001). Inventing Information Systems: The systems men and the computer, 1950–1968, *Business History Review* 75(1): 15–61.

Hartt, C.M., Durepos, G. and Mills, A.J. (2009). Performing the Past: Anti-history, gendered spaces and feminist practice, in 26th European Group on Organisation Studies (EGOS) Colloquium (Lisbon, June 2010). Lisbon, Portugal: Universidade Nove de Lisboa.

Hatchuel, H. and Glise, H. (2003). Rebuilding Management: A historical perspective, in N. Adler, A.B. Shani and A. Styhre (eds.) *Collaborative Research in Organisations: Foundations for learning, change and theoretical development*, Thousand Oaks, USA: Sage Publications.

Heide, L. (2004). Monitoring People: Dynamics and hazards of record management in France, 1935-1944, *Technology and Culture* 45(1): 80-101.

Hirschheim, R.A. (1985). Information Systems Epistemology: An historical perspective, in E. Mumford, R. Hirschheim and G. Fitzgerald (eds.) *Research Methods in Information Systems*, North-Holland: Amsterdam, pp. 13-38.

Hopper, M.D. (1990). Rattling Sabre: News ways to compete on information, *Harvard Business Review* 68(3): 118-125.

Howcroft, D. and Richardson, H. (eds.) (2010). *Work and Life in the Global Economy: A gendered analysis of service work*, Basingstoke: Palgrave Macmillan, p. 284.

Howcroft, D. and Trauth, E.M. (2005). Choosing Critical IS Research, in D. Howcroft and E.M. Trauth (eds.) *Handbook of Critical Information Systems Research*, Cheltenham: Edward Elgar, pp. 1-16.

Karsten, L., Keulen, S., Kroeze, R. and Peters, R. (2009). Leadership Style and Entrepreneurial Change: The centurion operation at Philips Electronics, *Journal of Organizational Change Management* 22(1): 73-91.

Kieser, A. (1989). Organizational, Institutional and Societal Evolution: Medieval craft guilds and the genesis of formal organizations, *Administrative Science Quarterly* 34(4): 540-564.

Kieser, A. (1994). Why Organization Theory Needs Historical Analyses – and How This Should be Performed, *Organization Science* 5(4): 608-620.

Klein, H.K. and Myers, M.D. (1999). A Set of Principles for Conducting and Evaluating Interpretive Field Studies in Information Systems, *MIS Quarterly* 23(1): 67-88.

Knights, D. and Morgan, G. (1991). Corporate Strategy, Organizations and Subjectivity: A critique, *Organization Studies* 12(9): 251-273.

Knights, D. and Morgan, G. (1995). Strategy Under the Microscope, *Journal of Management Studies* 33(2): 191-214.

Land, F. (2000). The First Business Computer: A case study in user-driven innovation, *IEEE Annals of the History of Computing* 22(3): 16-26.

Land, F. (2010). The Use of History in IS Research: An opportunity missed? *Journal of Information Technology* 25(4): 385-394.

Langlois, C.V. and Seignobos, C. (1897). *Introduction aux études historiques*, Paris: Editions Kime, (Collection Sens de l'Histoire), 1992.

Le Goff, J. (2006). (eds.) *La nouvelle histoire*, Paris: Complexe Editions.

Lewin, K. (1946). Action Research and Minority Problems, *Journal of Social Issues* 2(4): 34-46.

Maier, J.L., Greer, T. and Clark, J.F. (2002). The Management Information Systems (MIS) Job Market Late 1970s-Late 1990s, *The Journal of Computer Information Systems* 42(4): 44-50.

Majchrzak, A., Rice, R.A., Malhotra, A., King, N. and Ba, S. (2000). Technology Adaptation: The case of a computer-supported inter-organizational team, *MIS Quarterly* 24(4): 569-600.

Martins, L.-P. (2009). The Nature of the Changing Role of First-tier Managers: A long-cycle approach, *Journal of Organizational Change Management* 22(1): 92-123.

Marrou, H.I. (1954). *De la connaissance historique*, Paris: Editions du Seuil.

Mason, R., McKenney, J.L. and Copeland, D. (1997a). An Historical Method for MIS Research: Steps and assumptions, *MIS Quarterly* 21(3): 307–320.

Mason, R.O., McKenney, J.L. and Copeland, D.G. (1997b). Developing an Historical Tradition in MIS Research, *MIS Quarterly* 21(3): 257–278.

McKenney, J., Copeland, D. and Mason, R. (1995). *Waves of Change: Business evolution through information technology*, Boston: Harvard Business School Press.

McKenney, J.L., Mason, R.O. and Copeland, D.G. (1997). Bank of America: The crest and trough of technological leadership, *MIS Quarterly* 21(3): 321–353.

Mitev, N.N. (2004). Trains, Planes and Computers: From high-speed trains to computerised reservation systems, *Journal of Transport History* 25(2): 101–123.

Mitev, N.N. and Howcroft, D.A. (2005). The Role of History in IS Research, in *Critical Management Studies* (CMS) Conference (Cambridge, UK, 4–6 July 2005). Cambridge, UK: Judge Institute of Management Studies, Cambridge University.

Mitev, N. and Howcroft, D. (2011). Poststructuralism, Science and Technology Studies and Actor Network Theory: What can they bring to IS research? In B. Galliers and W. Currie (eds.) *Oxford Handbook of Management Information Systems*, Oxford: Oxford University Press.

Monteiro, L. and Macdonald, S. (1996). From Efficiency to Flexibility: The strategic use of information in the airline industry, *Journal of Strategic Information Systems* 5(3): 169–188.

Munslow, A. (2001). What History is, *History in Focus*, Issue 2 (What is History?) University of London. [WWW document] http://www.history.ac.uk/ihr/Focus/Whatishistory/munslow6.html.

Nelson, R. and Winter, S. (1982). *An Evolutionary Theory of Economic Change*, Harvard: Harvard University Press.

O'Brien, J., Remenyi, D. and Keaney, A. (2004). Historiography – A neglected research method in business and management studies, *Electronic Journal of Business Research Methods* 2(2): 135–144.

Orlikowski, W.J. (2007). Sociomaterial Practices: Exploring technology at work, *Organization Studies* 28(9): 1435–1448.

Orlikowski, W.J. and Baroudi, J.J. (1991). Studying Information Technology in Organizations: Research approaches and assumptions, *Information Systems Research* 2(1): 1–28.

Orlikowski, W.J. and Yates, J. (2002). It's About Time: Temporal structuring in organizations, *Organization Science* 13(6): 684–700.

Page, S. (2006). Path Dependence, *Quarterly Journal of Political Science* 1: 87–115.

Penrose, E.T. (1959). *The Theory of the Growth of the Firm*, New York: Wiley.

Pollock, N. and Williams, R. (2008). *Software and Organisations: The biography of the enterprise-wide system or how SAP conquered the world*, London: Routledge.

Porra, J., Hirschheim, R. and Parks, M.S. (2005). The History of Texaco's Corporate Information Technology Function: A general systems theoretical interpretation, *MIS Quarterly* 29(4): 721–746.

Porra, J., Hirschheim, R. and Parks, M.S. (2006). Forty Years of the Corporate Information Technology Function at Texaco Inc. – A history, *Information and Organization* 16(1): 82–107.

Rayward, W.B. (1996). The History and Historiography of Information Science: Some reflections, *Information Processing and Management* 32(1): 3–17.

Robey, D. and Newman, M. (1996). Sequential Patterns in Information Systems Development: An application of a social process model, *ACM Transactions on Information Systems* 14(1): 30–63.

Rowlinson, M. and Carter, C. (2002). Foucault and History in Organization Studies, *Organization* 9(4): 527–547.

Sauer, C. (2008). The Technology of the Possible – IT, innovation, capitalism and globalisation, in S. Dopson, M.J. Earl and P. Snow (eds.) *Mapping the Management Journey: Practice, theory and context*, Oxford: Oxford University Press, pp. 63–79.

Schein, E.H. (1961). *Coercive Persuasion: A socio-psychological analysis of the 'brainwashing' of American civilian prisoners by the Chinese Communists*, New York: W. W. Norton.

Scott, W.R. (2001). *Institutions and Organizations*, Thousand Oaks, CA: Sage.

Seignobos, C. (1901). *La méthode historique appliquée aux sciences sociales*, Paris: F. Alcan.

Simiand, F. (1903). Notes Critiques, *Sciences sociales* 4–6. Also published in Simiand, F. (1987). Méthode historique et sciences socials, Paris: Éditions des archives contemporaines, pp. 177–178.

Simon, J.C., Poston, R.S. and Kettinger, B. (2009). Creating Better Governance of Offshore Services, *Information Systems Management* 26(2): 110.

Üsdiken, B. and Kieser, A. (2004). Introduction: History in organization studies, *Business History* 46(3): 321–330.

Van Driel, H. and Dolfsma, W. (2009). Path Dependence, Initial Conditions and Routines in Organizations: The Toyota production system reexamined, *Journal of Organizational Change Management* 22(1): 49–72.

Veyne, P. (1971). *Comment on écrit l'histoire. Essai d'épistémologie*, Paris: Seuil.

Walsham, G. (1993). *Interpreting Information Systems in Organizations*, Chichester: Wiley.

Walsham, G. (1995). Interpretive Case Studies in IS Research: Nature and method, *European Journal of Information Systems* 4(2): 74–81.

Wells, W. (2000). Certificates and Computers: The remaking of Wall Street 1967–1971, *The Business History Review* 74(2): 193–235.

Westrup, C. (2005). Management Fashions and Information Systems, in D. Howcroft and E.M. Trauth (eds.) *Handbook of Critical Information Systems Research: Theory and application*, London: Edward Elgar.

Willcocks, L.P. (2004). Foucault, Power/Knowledge and Information Systems, in L. Willcocks and J. Mingers (eds.) *Social Theory and Philosophy for Information Systems*, New York: John Wiley, Information Systems Series, pp. 238–296.

Winter, S. and Taylor, L. (1996). The Role of IT in the Transformation of Work: A comparison of post-industrial, industrial and proto-industrial organizations, *Information Systems Research* 7: 5–21.

Winter, S. and Taylor, L. (2001). The Role of Information Technology in the Transformation of Work: A comparison of post-industrial, industrial and proto-industrial organization, in J. Yates and J. Van Maanen (eds.) *Information Technology and Organizational Transformation: History, rhetoric and practice*, London: Sage, pp. 7–34.

Yates, J. (1997). Using Giddens' Structuration Theory to Inform Business History, *Business and Economic History* 26(1): 159–183.

Yates, J. (1999). The Structuring of Early Computer Use in Life Insurance, *Journal of Design History* **12**(1): 5–24.

Yates, J. (2005). *Structuring the Information Age: Life insurance and information technology in the 20th century*, Baltimore, MD: Johns Hopkins University Press.

Zald, M. (2002). Spinning Disciplines: Critical management studies in the context of the transformation of management education, *Organization* **9**(3): 365–385.

Zan, L. (1994). Toward a History of Accounting Histories, *European Accounting Review* **3**(2): 255–307.

Zan, L. (2004). Accounting and Management Discourse in Protoindustrial Settings: The Venice Arsenal in the turn of the XVI century, *Accounting and Business Research* **32**(2): 145–175.

Appendix A

Results of ABI thematic coding per year and per decade
Request: 'information systems' + 'history'

Target: citation and abstract. Focused on academic (i.e. peer-reviewed) journals and those with full text version (which allowed a real exploration of abstracts and if necessary to confirm classification, the full text).

Period: 1972–2009.

Results: 384 papers, among which 64 with a non-anecdotal use of the notion of history, and 31 published in IS journals.

NB: we chose to target citation and abstract to increase the likelihood to get real History-oriented papers, and not incidental uses of the notion of history. We defined a journal as an IS journal if present in the IS world ranking.
(see: http://ais.affiniscape.com/displaycommon.cfm?an=1&subarticlenbr=432)

Evolution per year (See Figure 9.A1; Table 9.A1)

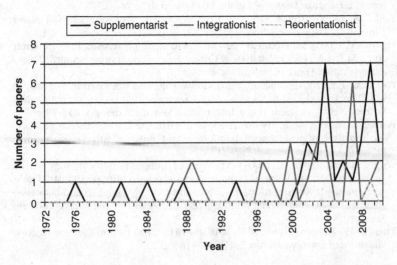

Figure 9.A1   Evolution of IS historical papers per year

Table 9.A1 Evolution per decade

	1970s	1980s	1990s	2000s
Supplementarist	1	3	1	29
Integrationist	0	5	5	19
Reorientationist	0	0	1	0

Appendix B

Distribution of historical stance (supplementarist, integrationist or reorientationist) in IS papers published in academic journals overall and in IS journals in particular (See Figure 9.B1).

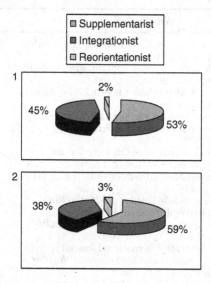

Figure 9.B1 (1) Distribution of supplementarist, integrationist and reorientationist papers and (2) Distribution of supplementarist, integrationist and reorientationist papers in IS journals

Appendix C

Coding of a selection of historical papers (from ABI)
Classification scheme applied for our coding: NR, S, I or R

NR: Not Relevant, rejected. Only incidental use of historical approaches. The word 'history' is used in the paper, but only incidentally.

S: Supplementarist. A historical perspective is claimed. But it is only a case narrative or the use of long-term data without any specific conceptualisation.

Historical material is not used to produce a specific theorisation. Nor do authors use historical concepts or methods.

I: Integrationist. Historical material is used to produce a specific theorisation. Alternatively, authors use historical concepts or methods. This is done so as to extend current theories.

R: Re-orientationist. Historical material is used to produce a specific theorisation. Alternatively, authors use historical concepts or methods. This is not done to extend current theories. It is done to develop specific theorisations about historical perspectives on IS (See Table 9.C1).

Table 9.C1　Extract of the thematic coding (full list of 54 pages is available upon request)

Articles	CODING
1. The Influence of Weather Conditions on the Relative Incident Rate of Fishing Vessels Yue Wu, Ronald P Pelot, Casey Hilliard. *Risk Analysis*. Oxford: Jul 2009. Vol. 29, Iss. 7; p. 985	NR
2. Inventory Control with Product Returns: The impact of imperfect information Marisa P de Brito, Erwin A van der Laan. *European Journal of Operational Research*. Amsterdam: Apr 1, 2009. Vol. 194, Iss. 1; p. 85	S
3. Creating Better Governance of Offshore Services Judith C Simon, Robin S Poston, Bill Kettinger. *Information Systems Management*. Boston: Spring 2009. Vol. 26, Iss. 2; p. 110	S
4. Improving Access to Safe Drinking Water in Rural, Remote and Least-Wealthy Small Islands: Non-traditional methods in Chuuk State, Federated States of Micronesia William James Smith Jr. International *Journal of Environmental Technology and Management*. Wolverton Mill: 2009. Vol. 10, Iss. 2; p. 167	NR
5. Modeling Propensity to Move After Job Change Using Event History Analysis and Temporal GIS Marie-Hélène Vandersmissen, Anne-Marie Séguin, Marius Thériault, Christophe Claramunt. *Journal of Geographical Systems*. Heidelberg: Mar 2009. Vol. 11, Iss. 1; p. 37 (29 pages)	I
6. String Alignment for Automated Document Versioning Wei Lee Woon, Kuok-Shoong Daniel Wong. *Knowledge and Information Systems*. London: Mar 2009. Vol. 18, Iss. 3; p. 293 (17 pages)	S
7. Neolithic Informatics: The nature of information Paul Beynon-Davies. *International Journal of Information Management*. Kidlington: Feb 2009. Vol. 29, Iss. 1; p. 3.	I

(*continued*)

Table 9.C1   Continued

Articles	CODING
8. A Framework for Information Systems Metaresearch: The quest for identity Viju Raghupathi, Linda Weiser Friedman. *Communications of the Association for Information Systems.* Atlanta: 2009. Vol. 24, Iss. 1; p. 50.	NR
9. Explaining Information Systems Change: A punctuated socio-technical change model Kalle Lyytinen, Mike Newman. *European Journal of Information Systems.* Basingstoke: Dec 2008. Vol. 17, Iss. 6; p. 589 (25 pages).	I
10. Credit Information System Act Anonymous. *International Financial Law Review.* London: Dec 2008/Jan 2009.	NR
11. Supporting Spatial Semantics with SPARQL Dave Kolas. *Transactions in GIS.* Oxford: Dec 2008. Vol. 12, Iss. s1; p. 5.	NR
12. Changes in the Importance of Topics in Auditing Education: 2000–2005 Jack Armitage. *Managerial Auditing Journal.* Bradford: 2008. Vol. 23, Iss. 9; p. 935. (...)	NR

Appendix D

Google scholar search results
For the query: history + 'information systems', only in the title
Period: 1972–2009
Number of results: 190 (See Figure 9.D1)

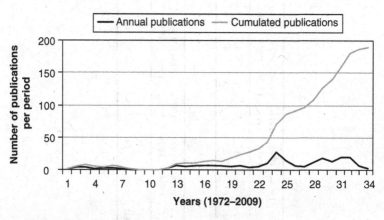

Figure 9.D1   Evolution of IS historical publication (for Google Scholar)

Year	1974–1975	1975–1976	1976–1977	1978–1979	1979–1980	1980–1981	1981–1982	1982–1983	1983–1984	1984–1985	1985–1986	1986–1987	1987–1988	1988–1989	1989–1990	1990–1991	1991–1992	1992–1993
Year	1	4	4	1	3	3	1	0	0	0	0	3	6	5	6	7	7	6
Total	1	5	8	5	4	6	4	1	0	0	0	3	9	11	11	13	14	13

Year	1993–1994	1994–1995	1995–1996	1996–1997	1997–1998	1998–1999	1999–2000	2000–2001	2001–2002	2002–2003	2003–2004	2004–2005	2005–2006	2006–2007	2007–2008	2008–2009
Year	5	6	4	5	10	28	15	6	5	12	18	13	20	20	7	3
Total	18	24	28	33	43	71	86	92	97	109	127	140	160	180	187	190

10
History and IS – Broadening Our View and Understanding: Actor–Network Theory as a Methodology

William (Bill) Bonner
Faculty of Business Administration, University of Regina, Regina,
Saskatchewan, Canada

Introduction

The call for a historic turn in IS studies is mirrored in business studies generally and is the explicit recognition of the predominance of present-ism and universalism in research. It is an implicit but unstated assumption that the present is the product of an extended, unproblematic and universally shared past (Booth and Rowlinson, 2006). 'Presentism results in research being reported as if it occurred in a decontextualized extended present' (Booth and Rowlinson, 2006: 6). This critical assumption centers the present as if it were a stable entity stripped of its messiness and uncertainty leading to the observation that, 'Most of our mainstream journals [organizational studies, in this case] are written as if they apply to some disembodied abstract realm' (Zald, 1996: 256).

The past, if it is addressed at all, is summed up in a paragraph of an article or Chapter 2 of a text (Jacques, 2006), which draws cursory connections between the past and present, providing a helicopter summary of the past (Clark and Rowlinson, 2004). From this high vantage point, selected elements of the past are used to validate current positions and understandings, while ignoring anything from the past that would contradict that position. This unproblematic rendition of the past justifies an exclusive focus on the present as a self-contained and the logical

Reprinted from 'History and IS – Broadening our view and understanding: Actor–Network Theory as a methodology,' by W. Bonner in *Journal of Information Technology*, 28, 2013, pp. 111–123. With kind permission from the Association for Information Technology Trust. All rights reserved.

outcome of the past (Zald, 1996). 'This common genre of anachronistic writing trivializes history because, since everything has always been the same anyway, what can the past offer except exotic examples to illustrate today's mundane issues' (Jacques, 2006: 41).

The call to history in IS research is a call for context to test and to challenge existing theories and methods (Ciborra, 1998), to test our framing of the problems we identify (Preston, 1991) and to challenge potential complacency in the field (Boland and O'Leary, 1991). First, the call to history is a call to recognize contingent presents, the unique circumstances of a setting or settings in which a new artifact comes to be shaped, interpreted and enacted or rejected (Swanson, 2002). Promoters of change involving technology encounter unique settings in which other technologies, their advocates and the word views already exist and are understood (Bannister, 2002; Chae and Poole, 2005).

Second, the call to history is a call to avoid the consequences of inserting divides in time, through a focus on an artifact. An example would be the modern computer, creating a post-computer world and an irrelevant void before it (Land, 2010). Issues, practices and ideas, which may be magnified by computer technology, often have a prior life and history that shape their manifestation in the present (Scranton and Horowitx, 1997).

If our theories and explanations fail to account for context and are restricted to presentist abstracts of the 'world out there' that others may not see and experience, this raises serious challenges about the work that we do, the value of that work to others, and is cause for reflection on our impact as educators (Land, 1996). The call for a historic turn is a call to question and challenge ourselves.

If the challenge is accepted the question becomes, how does one do history? Pointing out problems with presentism does not offer a solution or a way forward. This paper proposes and demonstrates the application of Actor– Network Theory (ANT) as a means of conducting historical research that reduces the likelihood of presentism. ANT enables this by viewing the present as an outcome, something that requires explanation. To understand this outcome, we must go back to moments in time when it could have been otherwise, when the outcome (the present) was merely one option among many. From these moments we must discover, trace and recreate past actions, however diverse, that combined to produce the present.

The next section articulates the central tenants of ANT as they relate to historical inquiry, and then demonstrates the use of ANT in a case study. This is followed by a discussion of insights gained in terms of this specific case, followed by concluding comments.

Actor–Network Theory

ANT is not a theory so much as it is a philosophical view that, if embraced, leads to a simple but overriding principle, 'follow the agents themselves' (Latour, 1999a: 128).

> Actors know what they do and we have to learn from them not only what they do, but how and why they do it. It is *us*, the social scientists, who lack knowledge of what they do, and not *they* who are missing the explanation of why they are unwittingly manipulated by forces exterior to themselves and known to the social scientist's powerful gaze and methods. (Latour, 1999b: 19; emphasis in original)

This statement reflects ANT's basic ontological assumption. The 'world out there' and the pieces of it that we wish to understand is the product of diverse past actions and association that come together, over time, to produce the present. Coming to know reality, epistemology, requires identifying and following those actually involved in its creation. Find them, follow them and trace the prior work, actions and associations that combined to configure and produce the present. Thus the essential focus of ANT is on the 'How?' question.[1]

> ANT does not tell anyone the shape that is to be drawn – circles, cubes or lines – but only *how* to go about systematically recording the world-building abilities of the sites to be documented and registered. (Latour, 1999b: 21, emphasis added)

The term actor–network needs to be examined to explain the idea of 'world-building.' Actor refers to anyone or anything that enables or causes others to act (Latour, 1992). An actor can be human, non-human or a combination of both. The human aspect is fairly straightforward while the non-human aspect is problematic for some, although it should not be in our field. Imagine taking your conference presentation material, stored on a memory stick, into a conference room that only has an overhead projector or has a computer projector but the bulb does not work. You the presenter and your presentation are defined and define each other in conjunction with technology (non-humans). Humans and non-humans define each other in action. They are actor–networks.

The term network is more problematic for our field because it has pre-existing connotations. We tend to think of wired or wireless networks that have fixed properties such as telephone lines, transmission towers and switching stations: elements of fixed infrastructure (Latour, 1999b). Network in the sense used in ANT are more like associations with varying degrees of stability. Networks are connected local actor–networks nodes (Callon, 1991). This transition from micro to macro (associated micros) requires local actor–networks to willingly align (converge) around something, such as an idea, a goal, a technology potential, a public hearing, a profession, or some other intermediary. To enlist others, or for other actor–networks to willingly align around it, an intermediary must permit translation, negotiation, drift around its interpretation and substance so that different local actor–network interests can be accommodated and combined (Latour, 1999c). What eventually emerges from this constant negotiation of and with the intermediary may have little bearing with how it was originally conceived. Subsequent events and actions determine its shape and trajectory. In itself this is a challenge to presentist tendencies, the inability to assume a straight line between what an advocate proposed and what eventually emerged. Additional ANT features that resist presentism are discussed shortly.

The linking of local actor–networks in action and apparent alignment around this flexible intermediary may be fleeting, say for the installation of a new piece of technology, or more durable if it results in the creation of a profession, for instance accountants. Network building may never get off the ground for failing to enlist the willingness of others to act on the intermediary's behalf,[2] or network building may be so successful that the outcomes become irreversible (at least for the foreseeable future) that the outcome becomes punctualized, that it becomes a taken for granted, a black box (Callon, 1991). These black boxes, say for instance communication standards, become built into subsequent infrastructure and deeply embedded in many actor–networks (Hanseth and Monteiro, 1997). Once created, these black boxes inscribe behavior and become obligatory passage points (Callon, 1986; Latour, 1992). If you wish to communicate using electronic data interchange, there are very specific standards to follow. If you wish to drive your automobile on public streets, there are standards around which side of the road you should drive on. This is where the hyphen between actor and network is critical; it does not hold actors and networks apart, rather it stresses the inter-relationship between the terms as defining each other in action.

With this understanding of the ways in which reality and the present come to be, ANT then asks us to work backwards and 'follow the agents' to uncover and reveal the 'world building abilities' of the actor–networks involved that produced and may still be producing the present. ANT suggests that we 'follow the agents [actor–networks] themselves.' How do we identify the actor–networks we should follow and how do we avoid presentism and universalism? This leads to the final two elements of ANT that are critical for this discussion of ANT's potential for historical inquiry in IS: controversies and the insertion of divides.

Controversies represent moments in time where a degree of symmetry and equivalence exists between competing ideas. These ideas are subjected to 'trials of strength,' a competition between the ideas and their supporting actor– networks. Black boxes or 'taken for granteds' represent asymmetry; they emerge from the settlement of past controversies (Latour, 1988). Thus ANT seeks to understand the closure of controversies, how black boxes, taken for granted or obligatory points of passage, emerged from controversies through rediscovering, understanding and explaining 'the work that generates inequivalence and asymmetry' (Latour, 1988: 169). Controversies are vehicles for discovery because in controversies actor–networks for competing positions are most visible and can be seen. These are the actor–networks to follow, the actor–networks that have something to teach us about the present. 'The aim [of empirical ANT work] is to open up these black boxes, these simplifications that we take for granted all too often and expose the way that translations occur and associations are generated' (Doolin and Lowe, 2002: 73). Questioning the taken for granted and focusing on prior controversies helps us avoid presentism by tracing events forward from an uncertain past rather than searching for evidence of the present in the past. The actual paths taken from the past to the present can meander; paths drawn from the present to the past tend to be unnaturally straight.

Finally, the issue of inserted divides concerns severing connections and decontextualizing the present. Technology and humans are not divisible in action but are defined in action together. Dividing them and treating them separately severs the threads that connect. Similarly, separating the micro and macro obscures the movements that turn local action involving local actor–networks into networks of actor–networks. This makes the micro and macro difficult to understand (Callon, 1991). Inserting divides in time has the potential to sever past threads that still exist and shape the present. For instance if we divide time based on the modern computer, we create pre and post computer time. In the process we may sever continuing threads, such as questions of ethics and propriety generally, or historical employee–employer relationships that transcend the divide. Inserting divides decontextualizes the content of the setting being investigated, reducing the 'world out there' to a 'disembodied abstract realm.' Abstracts of reality facilitate universalist tendencies as the context that makes each setting unique is removed. Inserting divides in time, such as pre- and post-modern computer time also facilitates presentist tendencies to treat the past as irrelevant or easily explained away.

ANT has been used in a number of empirical IS studies highlighting the contingent nature of the present and the rich context in which sites of negotiation involving technology are embedded. In addition to the ones already mentioned, IS studies using ANT have also shown how outcomes are negotiations and trials of strength involving an Enterprise Resource Planning system at a university (Scott and Wagner, 2003: 308), and resource management systems in heathcare facilities (Bloomfield *et al.*, 1992: 212).

What this study adds to ANT's contribution to IS is a demonstration of its application as an historical methodology in IS studies. What follows is an ANT informed case study that emerged from the resolution of a privacy controversy through an appeal to two black boxes. As foundations for the decision made, these black boxes appeared to possess substance (they were employed as arguments) but on the surface it was unclear how one managed to trump the other. The focus of this paper, within the limits of journal space, is on the practical application of ANT as an historical methodology and why it matters.

ANT as a methodology for historical research – A practical application

A controversy is closed through an appeal to black boxes

A privacy audit was conducted by the Offices of the Auditor General of Alberta and the Information and Privacy Commissioner of Alberta on the department responsible for the Motor Vehicle Registry (the MVR). At issue was the use of personal information collected from Albertans when, as required by law, Albertans registered their motor vehicles. The privacy audit was requested by the government on the basis that:

> The disclosure of this information [personal information in data banks], and in particular the selling of it, has been raised a number of times with the Minister, with myself [Deputy Minister] and other department officials. As a result, ensuring adequate privacy practices are adopted – especially as they relate to the FOIP [Freedom of Information and Protection of Privacy] Act – is important to us. (Office of the Information and Privacy Commissioner and the Auditor General of Alberta, 1998: 3)

The personal information maintained in MVR databases includes names, addresses, telephone numbers, birth dates, heights, weights, and hair and eye colors (Office of the Information and Privacy Commissioner and the Auditor General of Alberta, 1998). The privacy audit revealed the sale or release of MVR data to a host of organizations including 'public bodies, municipalities, federal government bodies, hospitals, post secondary institutions, parking companies and private sector businesses' as well as 'law firms, private investigators, collection agencies, small businesses, private parking companies, etc.' (Office of the Information and Privacy Commissioner and the Auditor General of Alberta, 1998: 22).

The audit findings drew attention to the issue of lack of legislative authority for selling or releasing MVR data and the fact that the MVR had been granted an outright exemption from Alberta privacy legislation, passed a few years earlier. These audit issues (controversies) remained unresolved for a year until a government committee, charged with reviewing privacy legislation, recommended that no changes be made to existing activities.

> Considering the historical purposes and practices of public registries and the review process currently under way by Alberta Registries [responsible for the MVR], the Committee recommended that Registries should continue to be excluded from the scope of the Act under section 4(1) (h) [The Freedom of Information and Protection of Privacy Act]. (Select Special Freedom of Information and Protection of Privacy Act Review Committee, 1999: 32)

Thus the Committee's closure of the controversy weighed historical purposes and practices ('The review process under way by Alberta Registries' was at a standstill. Alberta Registries was waiting for the recommendation of the Committee) against a standard for privacy protection (FOIP) and decided in favor of historical purposes and practices. This relationship and result is depicted in Figure 10.1. On the one hand, there is the black box of historical purposes. No information was provided as to what those practices were and why they were justified. On the other side of the balancing act is the black box of privacy's representative. Thus, Figure 10.1 identifies the trails to follow, the trails necessary to follow to discover the contents of the 'historical purposes and practices' and the FOIP black boxes.

FOIP as privacy's representative

The Deputy Minister established FOIP as privacy's representative in calling for the audit, 'As a result, ensuring adequate privacy practices are

Committee Recommendation: Closure of controversy

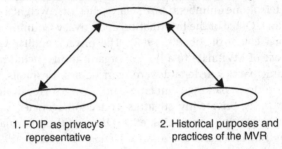

1. FOIP as privacy's
representative

2. Historical purposes and
practices of the MVR

Figure 10.1   Trails to follow: opening the black boxes used to close the controversy

adopted – especially as they relate to the FOIP Act – is important to us' (Office of the Information and Privacy Commissioner and the Auditor General of Alberta, 1998: 3). We could accept that FOIP represents privacy, granting it the substance that the Deputy Minister claimed for it, but FOIP was defeated through an appeal to 'historical purposes and practices' by the FOIP review committee. Yet this counterweight set against FOIP had no identifiable substance, making FOIP a puzzle rather than something self-explanatory.

To understand FOIP as it appeared in the privacy audit we must first understand the development of FOIP and how freedom of information is somehow tied to the idea of privacy protection. Freedom of information refers to the public right of access to information possessed by governments. Governments, generally, would like to limit or control access to potentially embarrassing information while opposition parties and the media thrive on such information. Thus, the shaping of the access to information side of FOIP-type legislation is highly contentious. The protection of privacy part, in this context, arises from the challenge posed by the question, 'How do we protect personal citizen information contained in government documents if we are going to release government documents?' This tight tying of privacy to the context of access to information is reflected in the fact that over the 6 days of debate in the Alberta legislation (March 31, April 18, May 15, 19, 30 and 31, 1994), privacy as a distinct right and issue (separate from questions of access to information) was only mentioned twice (Alberta Hansard, 1994a, b). This mirrors what happened federally, 12 years earlier. Federally, the committee responsible for the legislation left deliberation of the entire privacy portion of the legislation to a lengthy session in the afternoon of the last meeting (Standing Committee on Justice and Legal Affairs, 1981).

This background provides the context for the development of FOIP, but does not speak to the contents of the privacy protection elements of FOIP that were set up against 'historical purposes and practices.' The contents were specifically referred to, in the privacy audit, as 'Generally accepted principles known as "fair information practices"' incorporated into FOIP (Office of the Information and Privacy Commissioner and the Auditor General of Alberta, 1998: 22). Alberta Privacy Commissioner annual reports in 1998 and 1999 also reference fair information principles (FIP) as the foundation of the privacy aspects of FOIP, and the 1999 report cites the Organization for Economic Co-operation and Development OECD specifically as the source of FIP (Office of the Information and Privacy Commissioner of Alberta, 1998, 1999). Others make the same reference to FIP as the foundation of privacy legislation in Canada (Gillis, 1987), Europe (Mayer-Schonberger, 1997), the United States (Laudon, 1996) and Australia, New Zealand and Hong Kong (Slane, 2000). FIP clearly has status as privacy's representative, but they did not formally exist before 1973 (Secretary's Advisory Committee on Automated Personal Data Systems, 1973) with OECD principles not emerging until 1980 (Organisation for Economic Co-Operation and Development, 1980). To understand FIP in the privacy audit context, we need to understand FIP and in tracing the origins of FIP we find controversy.

The controversy involved tensions between government and large organization actor–networks perceiving benefits in the data-processing potential of the modern computer and public concerns about that very same potential: the potential to build dossiers on citizens. The emergence of FIP themselves is directly traceable to these tensions around the computer, but public concerns about organizational practices were not new, as reflected in the popularity of books such as *Nineteen Eighty-Four* (Orwell, 1936), *The Naked Society* (Packard, 1964), and *The Privacy Invaders* (Brenton, 1964).

In Europe, the concern for potential computer user actor– networks was that public pressure might lead individual countries to pass unique pieces of legislation that would restrict the flow of digital data across Europe (Organisation for Economic Co-Operation and Development, 1980). These actor–networks had the resources and desire to align around the intermediary of interest, the computer and data, and work toward ensuring the flow of data against a substantial but undefined and unorganized opposition. Gradually, the issue at stake came to be increasingly defined and translated into an issue involving personal data, the thing that computers process. This is reflected in the title of an OECD publication at the time, *Digital Information and the Privacy Problem* (Niblett, 1971). This is where asymmetry developed, where the 'problem' was defined and translated with solutions developed for the translated problem. FIP emerged from this process as general principles about organizational handling of personal data and, on the surface, appeared to give individuals a degree of control over personal data possessed by organizations.

FIP started from the assumption that individuals should know what organizations have data about them (the assumption being that the large-scale centralized computers of the day would be the norm in the future). Individuals should then be able to approach these organizations and see what personal data they have and challenge the possession, and the accuracy, of that data. Organizations would be responsible for responding to individuals for these purposes, securing personal data possessed, seeking consent before collecting data, limiting secondary use of that data, and limiting the collection of personal data. The OECD version of FIP required that member countries restrict the flow of personal data to other countries that do not have substantially similar legislation.

This is where FIP came into FOIP legislation. Canada, as an OECD member with this obligation, also had to solve its access to information problem (freedom of information) and protect personal data that might be in that information. FIP, handy and required through OECD membership, fit the bill and was incorporated into FOIP legislation. This happened federally and was copied provincially.

Thus, privacy's representative in the enactment of balance in the privacy audit controversy, FIP, is the product of earlier controversies. In substance, FIP deals with a narrow concept of privacy's potential, digitized, personal data. FIP came to be employed in Canada to address a thorny side issue raised in the controversy surrounding access to government information. FIP lost in the Committee's enactment of balance against historical purposes and practices after the privacy audit, but it lost earlier, when FOIP legislation was passed in 1994. The Committee's recommendation was that '[The MVR] should continue to be excluded from the Act [FOIP] under section 4(1) (h).' Under that section, uses made of MVR records were exempted from FOIP. The question this audit raised was should that decision be reversed, and the answer was negative for its impact on historical purposes and practices.

Tracing events and opening the black box of FOIP reveals the presence of another black box: FIP, privacy's apparently universal representative. Yet FIP does not have universal, fixed properties that diffuse, unchanged from setting to setting. FIP are, at their core, principles that, once met, permit the collection, use and dissemination of personal data. They are on the one hand data protection principles, while on the other they are data movement principles. This contradiction is built right into the documents creating FIP. 'These Guidelines [FIP] should be regarded as the minimum standards which are capable of being supplemented by additional measures for the protection of privacy and individual liberties' (Organisation for Economic Co-Operation and Development, 1980: 10). In the same document but 12 pages later, OECD member countries are advised to 'Avoid undue interference with the flows of personal data between Member countries' (Organisation for Economic Co-Operation and Development, 1980: 22). FIP are flexible intermediaries with room for interpretation and translation built into them. The OECD source document for FIP ensures that the minimum standards are not exceeded. In effect, the minimum standards become the maximum.

The 1998 committee, in the most recent enactment of balancing privacy against other interests, recommended that FIP not be applied to the MVR now, due to historical purposes and practices. Tracing of the development of FOIP has provided a sense of the substance of FOIP and while this review reveals that it represents a fairly weak conception of privacy's potential, but it does possess some substance. This begs the question, what is the substance of historical purposes and practices?

Historical purposes and practices of the MVR

Where does one begin? The review committee appealed to historical purposes and practices, and therefore the committee was the logical starting point. Fortunately, the meetings of the committee were recorded, transcribed and published, producing 700 pages of text. Unfortunately, there was almost no discussion on the history or current practices of the MVR. The committee was struck to review the entire FOIP Act, and the few times the MVR issue came up, it was mixed up with the Land Titles Registry, one of a number of registries gathered under the umbrella of Alberta Registries. The following example exemplifies the confusion that appeared a number of times (Alberta Legislature, 1998a, b, c).

> I think it's important also to recognize that when the information that registries gather was originally established, part of the reason was not just for the protection of the person who got the license or the permit or whatever it was but also to provide that information for the benefit of others. [He then used an example of someone purchasing a property and accessing the Land Titles registry to see who

owned adjacent property and any use limitations that might exist on the property].

The Chair then continued,

> I think it is the same thing if you are buying a car. It's important to know, to be able to find out – and I'm talking about a used car – who owned the vehicle before you. So it was not put there strictly to protect an individual or create some privacy. I think the intent was to make certain information available, and as long as that information is reasonably necessary to afford that purpose, it would be wrong to make changes now. (Alberta Legislature, 1998a: 37)

The confusion stems from the fact that the Land Registry is defined as a public registry for the purposes mentioned as well as a way for citizens to assure themselves that property tax assessments are transparent and fairly applied across properties. No evidence was gathered or offered that the MVR was established as a public registry. Quite the opposite in fact, the privacy audit revealed that there was no provision in MVR legislation permitting the sale of MVR data (Office of the Information and Privacy Commissioner and the Auditor General of Alberta, 1998: 22). This confusion continued throughout the committee's meeting and in one of the final meetings culminated in a statement that closely mirrored the final recommendation.

> Recognizing that much information collected by various registries is for the purpose of protecting the interests of other people than the applicant, that historical practices of providing that information be upheld to the extent that it is necessary for those purposes and that registry services remain outside of the FOIP Act. (Alberta Legislature, 1998c: 10)

Perhaps the MVR issue was just too small a component of the overall FOIP review to spend a lot of time on it. Perhaps the Chair and committee members could not wrap their minds around registry differences. Perhaps the Chair and the committee had marching orders from the government to make sure that this was the committee's conclusion. We do not know, but historical purposes and practices as an argument carried the day, and its actual substance is not evident from the work of the review committee. The substance has to be found elsewhere.

In-person interviews were conducted with people who currently worked with the MVR, people who conducted the audit and members

Table 10.1   Identifying and following the agents

History of MVB	1994 FOIP Act	1972 Invasion of privacy study
Step 1: Initial trails, actor–networks to follow		
Information Sources:	Information Sources:	Information Sources:
Documents, interviews	Limited documents, interviews	Documents, interviews, audio tapes
Step 2: Go back farther, the Archives:		
Thread A: Anything on:		*Thread B: Anything on:*
Wiggins: What is it, where did it come from?		R. L. Polk Canada (Polk)
Addressograph/Graphotype machines: Why were they set up to produce a seventh 'wiggins' form?		

of the FOIP review committee. From these interviews, a number of potential trails were identified and shown in Step 1 of Table 10.1. First, a long-time employee of the Motor Vehicle Branch (MVB), where motor vehicle registration actually took place, had started writing a history of the MVB in the year prior to his retirement in 1985. That might be useful. Second, the MVR was exempted from FOIP legislation in 1994. That required explanation. Third, mention was made of a 1972 Invasion of Privacy study by the Alberta government. That might be interesting.

The first trail involved an incomplete and unpublished manuscript on the history of the MVB. This manuscript, only partially organized and completed, was acquired from the department and its author was identified. The manuscript covered the period from the earlier 1940s through the late 1950s (Hogg, 1985). The author was later discovered and interviewed, and it turned out that he was part of a network of retired MVB employees. Three more individuals were interviewed from this cohort. They shared their general recollections on people, procedures and techniques, as well as organizational changes to the MVB over time. The history and interviews mentioned the 'wiggins' form, a duplicate form made of the vehicle registration that was batched and mailed to a firm in Winnipeg, Manitoba.

> The 'wiggins' portion [copy of the vehicle registration form] was detached and forwarded to a statistical gathering service in Winnipeg who made tables and charts indicating how many vehicles were registered in each province, the size of the vehicles by wheelbase, license fee costs and revenue collected, number of different vehicles by make, year and model number. The firm was eventually purchased by R. L. Polk and Company Ltd. who at this time operated basically in the United States. (Hogg, 1985: 32)

Registration forms were produced on Addressograph and Graphotype machines from the early 1940s onwards. When these retirees started working in the MVB in the early 1940s, the Graphotype and Addressograph machines generated copies of the registration form, including the 'wiggins' form. These retirees had the impression that these machines had 'always' been there.

The second trail involved identifying and interviewing individuals involved in passing and writing the FOIP Act in 1994, as well as accessing transcripts of debate in the Alberta Legislature. There was no formal committee charged with creating FOIP, and therefore no formal records of deliberation were created or kept. Interviews revealed that writers of the Alberta legislation (government staff not politicians) gathered similar legislation from other provinces and cut and paste sections to create the Alberta legislation. All such legislation had exempted the MVRs of their respective provinces. It was made clear to the actual writers of the Alberta legislation that this was desired in Alberta. The wording of legislation from other provinces was altered slightly to reflect conditions in Alberta. One individual interviewed related how they had watched the debate in the Legislature hoping no one would say anything, and no one did. This reflects the fact that the focus of the debate in the Legislature was on the access to information side of the legislation, as already discussed. As to why exempting the MVR was desired, the most cited reason offered in interviews was that in 1993 the MVR had been rolled into something called Alberta Registries (Registries), which housed all Alberta registries including Vital Statistics, Corporate Registry, Land Titles and the Personal Property Registry. Through Registries, the delivery of registry services was privatized. Since the access to information portion of FOIP applied to public and not private companies, Registries therefore had to be excluded from that side of the legislation somehow and it was easier to grant an outright exemption.

The last trail identified in the initial interviews was the 1971 Invasion of Privacy Study produced by a committee of the Alberta Legislature (Simpson *et al.*, 1970). This was located in the library of the Alberta Legislature. Elected officials who were on the committee and in the Alberta Legislature were identified, located and interviewed. Neither the study or interviews mentioned the MVR, but the motion put forward in the Legislature that led to the study did.

Whereas there are now no laws protecting the right of privacy of Alberta citizens [...] Now therefore be it resolved that this Legislative Assembly request the Alberta Government to set up a Special Committee on the

Invasion of Privacy to examine and review all matters related to the invasion of privacy in Alberta and, in particular [points 1, 2 and 3 and 4] 'The desirability of continuing the sale by the Alberta Government of the names and addresses of over 800,000 Alberta motorists to an organization selling the names and addresses to "junk mail" companies.' (Clerk of the Legislature of the Province of Alberta, 1970)

This motion was amended in the Legislature to drop the specific references (points 1 through 4). A review of the audio tapes of the debate in the legislature[3] revealed that the company referred to in point 4 above was R.L. Polk Canada (Polk). The question that emerged from this trail was who or what is Polk, and how was it getting the names and addresses of all Alberta motorists?

Table 10.1, Step 1, depicts the three trails initially followed. The trail on the exemption of the MVR from the 1994 FOIP Act was completed outside of the archives. The other two trails required going into the archives. Step 2 (Table 10.1), *Thread A*, focused on the 'wiggins' form as it represented a leak of personal information outside of the government. What was the 'wiggins' form used for and how did it come to be that the processes around the Addressograph and Graphotype technologies generated it? The second trail, *Thread B*, focused on anything related to Polk, another outsider who was getting MVR data.

Into the archives

Chronologically, it is convenient to present the findings discovered by following the agents Wiggins and Polk in that order but the actual research was much less linear; the actor–networks paths overlapped.

Following Thread A (Table 10.1) meant focusing on the MVB to find anything on 'wiggins.' Unfortunately, there was no file in the archives called 'wiggins.' Therefore the search had to focus on motor vehicles, motor vehicle registration and the departments responsible for motor vehicles. Further research indentified the branches of the government responsible for motor vehicles over time: the Provincial Secretary (1905–1955), the Ministry of Highways (1955–1975) and the Solicitor General (1975 onwards). All records had to be searched for any information that they might possess on the MVB. This search through these records for anything at all on motor vehicles involved hundreds and hundreds of hours. The first Provincial Secretary left 42 meters of records, the second left 12 meters while the third, fourth and fifth left no records at all. The same was true for Ministers of Highways. Some left a lot of records and some very few and the MVB was a relatively minor activity within the Ministry. The Solicitor General's department raised the same sort of issues as the Ministry of Highways, but was compounded by relative recentness of records deposited in the archives records, with some being sealed for 25 years from the date of deposit. There were also scattered listings in the archives related to motor vehicles in some fashion and they were pursued as well.

Through this searching, some details related to motor vehicle registration emerged. From the beginning of Alberta as a separate province in Canada in 1905, motor vehicles had to be registered every year. From 1905 to 1910, a list of registered motor vehicles was tabled in the Alberta Legislature until it grew too large (41 vehicles in 1905, 423 in 1910). Then there is gap where the next mention of a list is the absence of such a list. A town constable in Innesfree, Alberta wrote a letter to the Provincial Secretary in 1918.

If the department has a list of the motor licenses issued with owners' names and addresses, in a booklet form, I would be pleased if you would send me a copy. Some of the drivers in this district are very careless in regard to the rules of the road, as described in the Motor Vehicle Act. (Defoe, 1918)

The response offered was:

The Deputy Provincial Secretary advises that no such list is published. In any particular case if you will write the Deputy Provincial Secretary giving him the number of the car he will be able to give you the address of the owner. (Forbes, 1918)

Thus, in 1918 there appears to be no list, but at some point this changes. Try as I might I could find nothing in the Alberta archives on Wiggins. A call to the provincial archives in Manitoba revealed nothing in their files, although a suggestion was offered to contact the Companies Office in Winnipeg. That would only be helpful if I had a company name. I reviewed the Winnipeg telephone directories in the 1940s and found two firms with the name Wiggins in them. Presented with the two names, the MVB retirees immediately identified Wigglis Systems Limited (Wiggins) as the recipient of the 'wiggins' form. This opened up two new trails to follow. What services did it sell and what happened to this company?

A review of Henderson Directory business advertisements revealed that Wiggins started as a printing company in 1913. In the 1920 advertisement, Wiggins services included 'multigraph letters, mailing work, addressing.' The 1930 advertisement services include 'Good mailing lists, human interest copy, attractive printing, multigraphing, neat addressing and careful mailing work will profitably sell any kind of merchandise.' The 1940 and 1950 advertisements expand the offerings to include 'All Advertising Service within One Organization. Newspaper. Magazine. Radio. Direct Mail. Market surveys, copy and plan, multigraphing, mimeographing, mailing lists, addressing and mailing.'

In the 1960 directory, the company is not listed. Contact with the Companies Offices in Winnipeg revealed that the company went bankrupt in 1958 and the principal reason for this was the 'loss of volume due to the automotive trades taking their direct mailing contract from him to an agency operating in Eastern Canada' (Canadian Credit Men's Trust Association Limited, 1958).

Discussing the 'agency operating in Eastern Canada' will be deferred for the moment as it leads into Thread B. There is and still remains a gap in the story. Nothing in the Alberta Archives was discovered that mentioned Wiggins at all, but ongoing curiosity has led to the subsequent discovery of actual Wiggins Mailing Lists in British Columbia (1922) and Saskatchewan (1951) archives. The BC Mailing list is a motor vehicle count (Wiggins Systems Limited Mailing List, 1922). In addition, cash reconciliations prepared for the Provincial Secretary of Saskatchewan in 1925 and 1926, on the MVB of Saskatchewan within the Provincial Secretary's Department, reveal that Wiggins was buying copies of registrations, for one cent apiece (Provincial Secretary of Saskatchewan, 1926).

With these pieces of information, we can see that Wiggins bought copies of all registration slips (90,419 slips in 1926, according to the cash reconciliations) and used this information for marketing purposes in Western Canada. Despite extensive searches, nothing has been discovered as to how this practice of releasing registration slips to Wiggins came about or why, but it is far more than the committee that appealed to historical purposes and practices appears to have known.

This leads to Thread B of Step 2 (Table 10.1), what is Polk's involvement with MVR data? The history of the MVB branch, discussed earlier, mentioned that Polk bought Wiggins but that is not quite right. Wiggins was not purchased. Wiggins declared bankruptcy in 1958 'due to the automotive trades taking their direct mail contract from him to an agency operating in Eastern Canada.' Fortunately, Polk did appear as an indexed item in the main reference cards of the Alberta Archives. This index pointed directly to a controversy in 1972 centered on Polk

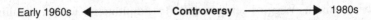

Early 1960s ◄————————— **Controversy** —————————► 1980s

Figure 10.2 The 1972 controversy shed light on events before and after it

and its access to MVR data. This access point shed light on Polk at that controversial moment. It also shed some light on events before and after the controversy and this is depicted in Figure 10.2.

In late 1971, a new government was elected and one of the first actions of the new Minister of Highways, responsible for the MVR, was to cut off Polk's access to MVR data in 1972. Being cut off appears to have caught Polk by surprise. This ties into a comment made in a phone interview with a retired individual who was a senior official at Polk, at around this time. It was Polk's practice to monitor any significant personnel change at the provincial level (a Minister, Deputy Minister or Registrar) and schedule visits with the new individual to keep the actor–network aligned and the practice going. The change in government (the former party had governed Alberta for 30 consecutive years) and the Minister's actions took place before Polk had a chance to visit.

The controversy and Polk's attempts to re-establish access to MVR data forced Polk to respond to the Minister's demands for information and reveal practices that had evolved around its access to MVR data. In 1971, 1,916,057 mailings were made from the MVR file to Albertans (Heil, 1972a). Polk, over time, had become the center of a network of actor–networks that had aligned around MVR data, as depicted in Figure 10.3. Polk argued that direct mail advertising was a relatively small part of its operation but that it was good for the economy as a whole. Polk also stressed the value of the information to assist auto and auto-part manufacturing industries establish demand (Heil, 1972b). In addition, Polk processed MVR data for the War Amputees, who did not have their own computer. Six months later, largely due to pressure to accommodate the War Amputees, contracts were signed with Polk to continue to get computer tapes of all motor vehicle registrations, including names and addresses. The new contract placed strict conditions that the personal data could be used for statistical purposes only and not for direct contact with individuals (Copithorne, 1973, #2057).

What changed between Thread A (the Wiggins story) and Thread B (this initial encounter with Polk, 14 years after Wiggins declares bankruptcy) is that MVR data was now on digital tape. The modern computer had become part of actor–networks around MVR data. This is important not as a divide in time, but as a point where multiple possible futures exist. The enlistment of the modern computer in the MVR registration process

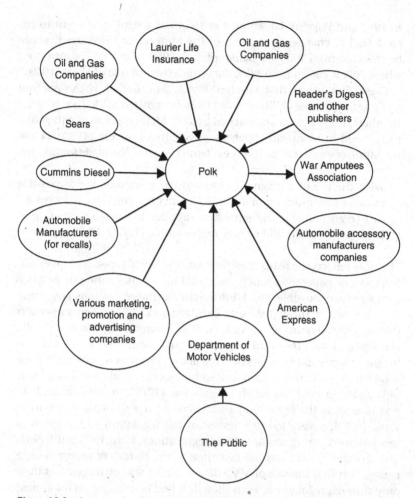

Figure 10.3 Actor–networks aligned around MVR data, exposed in controversy. All connections between Polk and its clients are one way, from the client to Polk, with the exception of the War Amputees Association. For the War Amputees, Polk sorted and provided the full listing of registered motor vehicle owners. In all other cases, Polk accepted client mailing criteria (people living in certain areas, car-type owners, numbers of people in household pulled from city directories, etc.) and the letters and envelopes the client wanted sent to prospects. Polk culled its data (bases or tables), selected prospects and put prospect names on the supplied letters and envelopes and did the actual mailing. Other than the War Amputees Association, Polk clients did not get access to the lists

in 1962 and Wiggins' bankruptcy in 1958 was a significant event to create a trail of changes in the files of the Ministry of Highways that can be followed from Wiggins' bankruptcy in 1958 to the 1972 controversy where Polk is cut off from MVR data (the left-hand side of Figure 10.2).

These files reveal that Gordon Taylor, Minister of Highways, was intrigued by the possibility enabled by now digitized MVR data, to sell it to others. He had been approached by O.E. McIntyre (a marketing company based in Montreal) about the possibility of buying MVR data and the Minister was in favor. This is explained in a note he made for his files.

> With the use of a magnetic tape and the computer, it was possible to make the information available to anyone. The price is 1 cent for each registration if the purchaser supplies the magnetic tape plus $900 for the microfilm of new registrations. (Taylor, 1968)

The note reflects the realization that data on digital tapes, no longer tied to pieces of paper, was much more mobile. To make the sale of MVR data to others possible, the Minister altered the regulations governing MVR legislation, through Alberta Regulation 453/67, changing a section that set out the terms of sale of bulk MRV information. The word 'Polk' was replaced with the word 'person' and specific reference was made to magnetic tapes and the costs detailed above. Previous regulatory change shows that the entire section altered by Alberta Regulation 453/67 was only added in 1962, via Alberta Regulation 417/62. In this change, Polk was named as the buyer and costs were related to paper registration slips. This discovery led to a review of the legislation and supporting regulations covering motor vehicle registrations, from 1905 until 1962. The change in 1962 was the first time in the history of motor vehicle registration that the sale of MVR data was ever acknowledged and then only through regulations, even though it had been going on for almost 40 years. This lack of legislative authority and weakness of regulations as a source of legitimacy is acknowledged in a 1968 internal memo between the Deputy Minister and Minister of Highways.

> I have your memo of June 3rd dealing with the marginally noted [Polk] and would agree that our authority for selling registration data to the marginally noted [Polk] is very vague.

> Mr. Syska [solicitor, Ministry of Highways] suggests and I agree that specific amendment [to the legislation] should be introduced at the next Session to give us clear cut authority for our actions. (McManus, 1968)

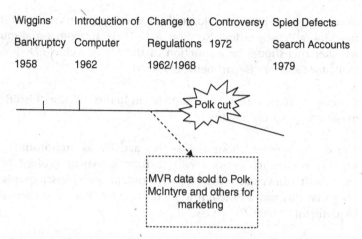

Figure 10.4 Trajectories

Thus it would appear that Wiggins' bankruptcy in 1958 required a change to the processes involving the recipient of the 'wiggins' form, still being produced by the Addressograph and Graphotype machines. This raised questions about a practice that had been going on so long it was almost invisible. Questions regarding legislative authority emerged at the same time paper slips were replaced by magnetic tapes. The Minister of Highways was ideologically in favor of expanding the sale of MVR data to others as indicated by changes he made to the regulations and the note he wrote in his files, referred to earlier.

Given these activities, the continued and expanded sale of MVR data seemed the likely future, depicted in the dotted line of Figure 10.4, but that trajectory of events was changed abruptly by a new Minister of Highways in 1972. He had a different view and this view reflected a growing public concern about privacy as was discussed earlier. If the story ended here with the controversy and its apparent resolution, one would expect that the sale of MVR data would be a non-issue into the future, but the privacy audit of 1997 revealed that not to be the case. While Polk was less and less a factor through the 1970s, the lack of legislative authority continued to be a problem. A 1979 project started by the Solicitor General's department, but never finished, 'spied defects' that stem in part from the unresolved question of legislative authority in the early 1960s.

Officials of the department have spied defects in the practice of imparting information to whomever requests it merely upon payment of the fee proscribed by section 6 (h) of the regulations issued under the Motor Vehicle Administration Act. There is room for dispute whether this should be a function of the Motor Vehicle Division. (Solicitor General's Department, 1979a: 4)

The study offered a striking comment in terms of the 'historical purposes and practices' argument.

The cardinal point about the MVD's activity as an information supplier is that its service seems to have grown or evolved into its present dimensions with little record of any conscious planning that this was a function to be undertaken. (Solicitor General's Department, 1979b: 9)

While these 'defects' were spied, they were being noted because of rising concern about the unchecked growth of search accounts enabled by the advent of databases. Over 1000 search accounts had been created in less than a decade. These accounts were set up by and with the MVB to enable outsiders to search MVR records. A branch within the government, making use of modern computers, had replaced Polk and a new collection of actor–networks had emerged around MVR. This is depicted in the far right part of Figure 10.4. The practice of releasing MVR continued, but in a different form: it was not linear but a change in trajectory. The largest search account holders included bank branches, finance companies, collection agencies, insurance companies, car dealerships, investigation companies, department stores, and others whose names do not indicate their type of business. The reason for examining account holders specifically was that, 'It is this kind of recipient that most troubles those officials in the MVD who are sensitive to the security issues suggested by the wide disclosure of personal data' (Solicitor General's Department, 1979b: 5). This project provides a good description of the issues but the project appears to have been abandoned (Leblanc, 1982).

Issues around the sale of MVR data appear to have continued into the 1980s. The discovered concerns raised in the 1980s range from potential liability if people became aware that others were reaching them through access to the MVR (Armstrong, 1982), concern that female motorists might be placed at risk through being traced through the license plate on their car, and generally attempting to find the 'balance between the rights of an individual to privacy and the legitimate requirements of some other persons to obtain information' (Harle, 1982).

From here the trail fizzles. The radiance of the bright spotlight shed on actor–networks in the 1972 controversy only reaches so far. Absent new controversy, the practice slides back into the background in the 1980s until it emerges again in controversy in the 1997 privacy audit, where many of the same issues of the past reappear. Specifically, legislative authority for selling access to MVR and control over search accounts.

The issue of how the resolution of the privacy audit controversy in 1998 was resolved, between privacy's representative (FIP) and the counterweight employed in the act of balance (historical purposes and practices), is no less strange than it was, but it is more understandable. It is strange in the sense that actual historical purposes and practices were unknown by the committee members. This investigation revealed that it was largely unknown and little discussed over many decades by those actually involved in releasing the information. A common question that arose, when it was acknowledged and discussed, was whether this was something the government should even do and under what authority. Thus, the resolution remains strange because the substance of the actual history, and the uncertainty through time about the practice itself, was used to justify no change and continuation of those same practices.

At the same time, the particular resolution of the privacy audit is understandable in the sense that the historical purposes and practice argument presented was never tested. It was not subjected to trials of strength. Even without substantiation FIP, privacy's representative, did not triumph but FIP may not possess the substance they are granted as privacy's representative. This raises numerous interesting questions about the current debate on privacy generally, but they are specifically discussed in detail elsewhere (cf. (Bonner and Chiasson, 2005; Bonner, *et al.*, 2009). The focus of the remainder of this paper is a discussion of two unexpected questions that emerged from this study and what these say about the present, followed by concluding comments on ANT as an appropriate historical methodology.

Unexpected questions

Two critical questions emerged from this study that has changed the way I personally look at organizations, perhaps forever. What is an organization? And who can speak for it? These questions have also made me wonder if the present, in the context of organizational practices around data, is really any different now than it was in the past. If it is not, inserting a divide in the present that severs off the past from the present is going to lead to a very mysterious understanding of the issues in the present. I will speak to these in turn.

I will develop the basis for the two questions by focusing on the public, at the bottom of Figure 10.3. The public was largely unaware of the web of actor–networks that surrounded the data they provided.[4] A vehicle owner was and is required by law to register their motor vehicles. In doing so, the public provided the MVB data about their vehicle and themselves. This department, a department within the Ministry of Highways, itself one of many Ministries within the Alberta government each with its own departments, sold this information to Polk on magnetic tapes (at this time, paper copies 10 years earlier and for the previous 40 years). Polk in turn provided services around this information to other actor–networks that had aligned around this data. In the chain of knowledge about these activities, the public was unaware that the 'government' sold what it forced them to provide. However, strictly speaking most of the people in that same 'government' were also unaware that a department within one of its Ministries was and still is selling MRV data. Even within the specific department selling the data and the Ministry it was located in, there was limited awareness of the sale of the information to Polk and no awareness of the extent of the subsequent dispersal and uses made of that data by Polk. With this view of an organization as a loose connection of varied actor–networks, the second question emerges from this study, 'Who can speak for an organization?'

In the case studied here, who would have spoken for the Alberta government on its handling of citizen data? What would this spokesperson actually know? In being briefed on the subject, would those doing the briefing be aware of what was going on in a small department of one of the many Ministries? Would they know enough to have probed deep enough? If they did become aware of Polk, would they have probed any deeper than those who were aware of Polk ever did, before the controversy erupted? Would the people the spokesperson relied upon even be aware of the web of actor–networks that had formed around government-collected personal information?

Emerging from the above is the question, 'is the present any different?' I am going to invoke an image to help visualize the question. To appreciate the position of the public in Figure 10.3, picture that person standing on the side of a country road that borders a cornfield, late in the growing season. Corn plants are 8–9 feet tall, thick with corn stalks, leaves and ears of corn. It is a field of impressive green. Looking into the field from the road level the density of the plants is such that details within the cornfield itself are limited after 10 feet or so; the foliage is too thick to discern details. Imagine the size of the cornfield to be proportionate to that of an individual relative to the size of an organization, say the cornfield occupies a section of land (1 square mile).

In this scenario, the individual public member is on the road at the edge of the cornfield and the person she is dealing with, taking her registration data (and money), is seated at a desk cut into the first row of corn. The required data is collected, recorded and sent off by the person at the desk back into the cornfield somewhere. The deal is completed from the woman's point of view; she complied with the law, paid the required amount and walks away with the required paperwork and/ or license plate. The deal may be finished from her perspective, but unknown to her new deals are made around that deal, within the cornfield, by people and departments of the government she has not directly engaged, with Polk and then between Polk and others.

Continuing with the imagery, take Figure 10.3 and make it proportionate to the size of the cornfield. Then overlay this enlarged Figure 10.3 onto the cornfield, from above the cornfield, and burn it into the cornfield so that the circles are now small, cleared pockets on the ground within the cornfield, and the lines connecting the circles are narrow pathways that join the pockets on the ground. The idea of expanding Figure 10.3 is to create enough space between the pockets so that each pocket (node in a network) may or may not be aware of the other nodes of the network of which they are a part. Other departments of the government (nodes in the cornfield connected to the desk taking her registration data, not depicted in Figure 10.3) did not know of Polk's presence in the cornfield, but they were connected to Polk through creating and enforcing legislation that required her to provide personal information. *Reader's Digest* knew of Polk but may or may not have known of its link through Polk to Sears or Oil and Gas companies. The woman who registered her vehicle knew of her link to the MVB as the face of the government requiring her to register her vehicle, but she was unaware that she was part of an extended actor–network involving license plates, magnetic tapes, registration slips,[5] marketing programs, databases, auto makers and sales generation.

The essential question raised here is, What is different today about actual within-organization and interorganizational practices involving personal information and what is the same? I do not pretend to have an answer that transcends this specific case but the question raises serious challenges to interpreting studies that ignore the question entirely.

ANT and the call to history

Is ANT *the* answer to the call to history? No, of course not, but it has potential, largely unrealized at the moment, because its philosophical underpinnings challenge presentist tendencies. ANT keeps its eyes on and continually develops context, making 'taken-for-granteds' and inserted divides, things that require explanations rather than being explanations in themselves.

But what did the modern computer really change? It was implicated in change but it did not result in a complete break from the past, as depicted in Figure 10.4. The enlistment of the modern computer in the registration of motor vehicles almost resulted in an increase in the number of firms purchasing MVR data for marketing purposes, but that potential trajectory did not solidify. The Polk actor– networks around MVR data gradually dissolved while another emerged around search accounts. The practice of selling MVR though did not start with the modern computer; it was only altered by its adoption. ANT keeps the continuities visible avoiding the presentist tendency to assume away the past. ANT, like historical research, seeks to keep the context in the present. Perhaps it is better stated the other way around. The value of ANT, like historical research, lies in not truncating that which gives the presence substance and meaning, but in working with a present that those living in it would recognize.

ANT is offered here, in an opening of a discussion on historiography in IS research, as *a* tool, albeit a powerful tool, for conducting histori- cal IS research. ANT has been used in IS research but it can be pushed much farther into the past. Is the story told in this paper *the* story of the past? I cannot make that claim. It is an understanding based initially on curiosity about an outcome, that shaped the framing of the questions to be investigated, and my efforts and understanding in discovering and following trails, followed by decisions about ordering the material to tell the story forward in time.

I believe privacy is an important idea but I would be hard-pressed to define it. This belief framed the questions but is not what drove the research. I wanted to understand this specific enactment of balance without any idea as to how it came about. ANT is a powerful tool for this. 'Actors know what they do and we have to learn from them not only what they do, but how and why they do it' (Latour, 1999b: 19). Focusing on the actors who created the present helps researchers avoid inserting divides or taken-for-granteds that the actors themselves do not acknowledge.

Delving into the past was fascinating in discovering what was, what could have been and what seems to have continued into the present. I interviewed the first computer programmer in the Alberta government. From whom did he learn programming? Moments like that made it apparent those times were different. Since 1905 it has been the law in Alberta that motor vehicles be registered. Drivers' licenses though were not introduced until 1927. That awareness helped explain the frustration a Constable experienced trying to keep a blind man from driving a registered vehicle on public roads, in 1917. I did not find everything I would like to have found as there were gaps in the available material. I could not find out exactly how long Addressograph and Graphotype machines came to be embedded in the paper-based processing of motor vehicle registrations, nor how they came to generate an extra copy of the registration slip for Polk. I also would like to have met, but was unable to find, any of the 'hundreds of homeworkers'[6] who processed paper-based registrations. Through this process, however, I became aware of the continuity of personal data use for marketing that has been done and done effectively long before the computer entered the picture.

Our field is relatively recent, but issues that emerge around the artifact of our interest may or may not be. The risk of presentism is that we limit our view and focus too narrowly on the present. The more limited that view is, the easier it is to see differences and read change into them. If we broaden our focus and investigate those differences, we are more likely to see those differences as continuities and this produces a very different understanding of the present.

Acknowledgements

I acknowledge the support of the Social Sciences and Humanities Research Council (Canada).

Notes

1. In reading this section, a reviewer was reminded of a technique employed by research historians known as prosopography. A branch of this technique seeks to explain political outcomes by tracing webs of interplay between small groups that create unity and political force (Stone, 1971). It is not clear what role, if any, non-humans play in this technique.
2. Holmstrom and Stalder (2001) show how a cash card technology in Sweden failed for exactly this reason.
3. Alberta did not have a transcribed record of debate in the Legislature (a Hansard) until 1972. In anticipation of the Hansard debates were recorded on magnetic tape a few years earlier and fortunately included the above.

These recordings are available, but the speakers are identified by role and not name.

4. There were occasional letters from the public in the archives and the occasional newspaper editorial commentary but they were very few, had no details to work with, and were easily dismissed. The issue would briefly appear and then disappear. Like a shooting star in the night sky, if you blinked you missed it.

5. At this time, Polk was purchasing MVR data from all provinces and some had not computerized the registration process. Polk was still receiving paper copies of registration slips from some provinces, including Ontario, well into the 1970s.

6. This was the terminology used by a retired senior Polk official describing how lists were created before the computer. This is a pre-computer version of distributed data processing and Wiggins must have employed this technique as well.

References

Alberta Hansard (1994a). Alberta Hansard, May 5, 1994. Edmonton, Legislature of Alberta.

Alberta Hansard (1994b). Alberta Hansard, May 30, 1994. Edmonton, Legislature of Alberta.

Alberta Legislature (1998a). Freedom of Information and Protection of Privacy Act Review Committee, 17 November. Edmonton, Government of Alberta.

Alberta Legislature (1998b). Freedom of Information and Protection of Privacy Act Review Committee, 23 November. Edmonton, Government of Alberta.

Alberta Legislature (1998c). Freedom of Information and Protection of Privacy Act Review Committee, October 20, 1998. Edmonton, Government of Alberta.

Armstrong, R. (1982). Letter written to G.L. Harle, Solicitor General of Alberta, written by SOS columnist at the *Edmonton Journal*, 10 May. Provincial Archives of Alberta, Accession number: 93.191, File/item number: 11.

Bannister, F. (2002). The Dimension of Time: Historiography in information systems research, *Electronic Journal of Business Research Methods* 1(1): 1–10.

Bloomfield, B.P., Coombs, R., Cooper, D.J. and Rera, D. (1992). Machines and Manoeuvres: Responsibility accounting and the construction of hospital information systems, *Accounting, Management and Information Technologies* 2(4): 197–219.

Boland, R.J. and O'Leary, T. (1991). Technologies of Inscribing and Organizing, *Accounting, Management and Information Technologies* 1(1): 1–7.

Bonner, W.T. and Chiasson, M. (2005). If Fair Information Principles are the Answer, What was the Question? *An Actor Network Theory Investigation of the Modern Constitution of Privacy, Information & Organization* 15(4): 267–293.

Bonner, W.T., Chiasson, M. and Gopal, A. (2009). Restoring Balance: How history tilts the scales against privacy, *An Actor-Network Theory Investigation, Information & Organization* 19(2): 84–102.

Booth, C. and Rowlinson, M. (2006). Management and Organizational History: Prospects, *Management & Organizational History* 1(1): 5–30.

Brenton, M. (1964). *The Privacy Invaders*, Toronto: Longmans Canada Limited.

Callon, M. (1986). Some Elements of a Sociology of Translation: Domestication of the scallops and the fishermen of St. Brieuc Ba, in J. Law (ed.) *Power, Action and Belief: A new sociology of knowledge*, London: Routledge & Kegan Paul, pp. 196–233.

Callon, M. (1991). Techno-Economic Networks and Irreversibility, in J. Law (ed.) *A Sociology of Monsters: Essays on power, technology and domination*, London: Routledge, pp. 132–155.

Canadian Credit Men's Trust Association Limited (1958). Contained in files of Wiggins Systems Limited, maintained by the Companies Office, Winnipeg, Manitoba.

Chae, B. and Poole, M.S. (2005). The Surface of Emergence in Systems Development: Agency, institutions and large-scale information systems, *European Journal of Information Systems* 14(1): 19–36.

Ciborra, C.U. (1998). Crisis and Foundations: An inquiry into the nature and limits of models in the information systems discipline, *Journal of Strategic Information Systems* 7(1): 5–16.

Clark, P. and Rowlinson, M. (2004). The Treatment of History in Organisation Studies: Towards an 'historic turn'? *Business History* 46(3): 331–352.

Clerk of the Legislature of the Province of Alberta (1970). Third Session of the 16th Legislative Assembly of the Province of Alberta, Mr. Hyndman's motion in the Legislature, 25 February. Provincial Archives of Alberta audio tape reference, P.A.A. DUPE 70.397/44, from 3:30 p.m. to 5:30 p.m., Edmonton, Alberta.

Copithorne, C. (1973). Letter from the Minister of Highways (Clarence Copithorne) to Mr. Heil (V.P. Polk Canada), voicing surprise and strong objection to Heil's suggestion that MVR data be used for a marketing survey for Ford Canada Limited. Provincial Archives of Alberta, Accession number: 76.346, File/item number: 50100, Box 32.

Defoe, G. (1918). Letter from Constable G. Defoe, Innesfree, Alberta, to the Provincial Secretary, requesting a list of persons given licenses for motor cars in Alberta. Provincial Archives of Alberta, Accession number: 75.126, Box 48, Motor Vehicle Act – General File 1917–1921.

Doolin, B. and Lowe, A. (2002). To Reveal is to Critique: Actor-network theory and critical information systems research, *Journal of Information Technology* 17(2): 69–78.

Forbes, W. (1918). Letter from Wilfred Forbes, Acting Deputy Attorney General, to Constable G. Defoe, Innesfree, Alberta, regarding list of persons given licenses for motor cars. Provincial Archives of Alberta, Accession number: 75.126, Box 48, Motor Vehicle Act – General File 1917–1921.

Gillis, P. (1987). The Privacy Act: A legislative history and overview, *Canadian Human Rights Yearbook* 4(1987): 119–147.

Hanseth, O. and Monteiro, E. (1997). Inscribing Behaviour in Information Infrastructure Standards, *Accounting, Management and Information Technologies* 7(4): 183–211.

Harle, G.L. (1982). Memo from G.L. Harle, Solicitor General, to R.J. LeBlanc, Deputy Solicitor General. Provincial Archives of Alberta, Accession number: 93.191, File/item number: 11. 3 June.

Heil, J.P. (1972a). Letter from VP of R.L. Polk (Canada) Ltd, listing every mailing made into Alberta in 1971. Provincial Archives of Alberta, Accession number: 76.346, File/item number: 50100, Box 32. 9 May.

Heil, J.P. (1972b). Letter from VP of R. L. Polk (Canada) Ltd, talking generally about what Polk does, including assisting in motor vehicle recall notices. Provincial Archives of Alberta, Accession number: 76.346, File/item number: 50100, Box 32. 18 April.

Hogg, B. (1985). History of the Motor Vehicle Division, (unpublished). Alberta Registries, Government of Alberta, Edmonton, Alberta.

Holmstrom, J. and Stalder, F. (2001). Drifting Technologies and Multi-Purpose Networks: The case of the Swedish cashcard, *Information & Organization* 11(3): 187–206.

Jacques, R.T. (2006). History, Histography and Organization Studies: The challenge and the potential, *Management & Organizational History* 1(1): 31–49.

Land, F. (1996). The New Alchemist: Or how to transmute base organizations into corporations of gleaming gold, *Journal of Strategic Information Systems* 5(1): 7–17.

Land, F. (2010). The Use of History in IS Research: An opportunity missed? *Journal of Information Technology Case and Application Research* 25(4): 385–392.

Latour, B. (1988). *The Pasteurization of France*, Cambridge, MA: Harvard University Press.

Latour, B. (1992). Where are the Missing Masses? The Sociology of a Few Mundane Artifacts, in W.E. Bijker and J. Law (eds.) *Shaping Technology/ Building Society: Studies in sociotechnical change*, Cambridge, MA: MIT Press.

Latour, B. (1999a). For David Bloor and Beyond: A reply to David Bloor's 'anti-Latour', *Studies in the History and Philosophy of Science* 30(1): 113–129.

Latour, B. (1999b). On Recalling ANT, in J. Law and J. Hassard (eds.) *Actor Network Theory and After*, Oxford: Blackwell Publishers, pp. 14–25.

Latour, B. (1999c). *Pandora's Hope: Essays on the reality of science studies*, Cambridge, MA: Harvard University Press.

Laudon, K.C. (1996). Markets and Privacy, *Communications of the ACM* 39(9): 92–104.

LeBlanc, R.J. (1982). Memo from R.J. Leblanc, Deputy Solicitor General, to G.L. Harle, Solicitor General. Provincial Archives of Alberta, Accession number: 93.191, File/item number: 10. 13 August.

McManus, L.H. (1968). Re: R.L. Polk – Registration Data, Memo from L.H. McManus, Deputy Minister, Department of Highways, to Gordon Taylor, Minister of Highways. Provincial Archives of Alberta, Accession number: 76.346, File/item number: 50100, Box 32. 10 July.

Mayer-Schonberger, V. (1997). Generational Development of Data Protection in Europe, in P.E. Agre and M. Rotenberg (eds.) *Technology and Privacy: The new landscape*, Cambridge, MA: The MIT Press, pp. 219–241.

Niblett, G.B.F. (1971). *Digital Information and the Privacy Problem*, Paris: Organisation for Economic Co-operation and Development.

Office of the Information and Privacy Commissioner of Alberta (1998). 1997–98 Annual Report, Edmonton.

Office of the Information and Privacy Commissioner of Alberta (1999). 1998–99 Annual Report, Edmonton.

Office of the Information and Privacy Commissioner and the Auditor General of Alberta (1998). Alberta Registries: Report to the Minister of Municipal Affairs, 15 April, Edmonton, Alberta.

Organisation for Economic Co-operation and Development (1980). *Guidelines on the Protection of Privacy and Transborder Flows of Personal Data*, Paris: Organisation for Economic Co-operation and Development.

Orwell, G. (1936). *Nineteen Eighty-Four*, London: Secker & Warburg, Originally published: London: V. Gollancz.

Packard, V.O. (1964). *The Naked Society*, New York: David McKay.

Preston, A.M. (1991). The 'Problem' in and of Management Information Systems, *Accounting, Management and Information Technologies* 1(1): 43–69.

Provincial Secretary of Saskatchewan (1926). Motor License Branch, Reconciliation of Receipts with Treasury Deposits for the Year Ending 30 April, Saskatchewan Archives. Accession number S-P Se.2i.

Scott, S.V. and Wagner, E.L. (2003). Networks, Negotiations and New Times: The implementation of enterprise resource planning into an academic administration, *Journal of Information Technology* 17(2): 285–313.

Scranton, P. and Horowitx, R. (1997). The Future of Business History: An introduction, *Business and Economic History* 26(1): 1–4.

Secretary's Advisory Committee on Automated Personal Data Systems (1973). *Records, Computers, and the Rights of Citizens*, U.S: Department of Health, Education & Welfare.

Select Special Freedom of Information and Protection of Privacy Act Review Committee (1999). Final Report, Edmonton: Legislative Assembly of Alberta.

Simpson, R., Ludwig, A., Miller, D., Werry, L.F., Switzer, W. and Copithorne, C. (1970). A Report to the Alberta Legislature of the Special Select Committee on Invasion of Privacy, Edmonton: Alberta Legislature.

Slane, B.H. (2000). Killing the Goose? Information Privacy Issues on the Web, Auckland, Office of the Privacy Commissioner, Notes for address by the Privacy Commissioner. Bruce Slane address to the Untangling Web Law Conferencze. [WWW document] http://privacy.org.nz//11172191.pdf (last accessed 8 March 2013).

Solicitor General's Department (1979a). Legal Research Project, Edmonton: Government of Alberta. Provincial Archives of Alberta, Accession number: 93.191, Item/File number: 23 May 1979 report.

Solicitor General's Department (1979b). Legal Research Project, Edmonton: Government of Alberta. Provincial Archives of Alberta, Accession number: 93.191, Item/File number: 23 June 1979 report.

Stone, L. (1971). Prosopography, *Daedalus* 100(1): 46–79.

Standing Committee on Justice and Legal Affairs (1981). Deliberation of Bill C-43, Freedom of Information and Protection of Privacy Act, Federal Government of Canada, Archives of Canada reference, RB 14 ACC 199091/119, Box 105, Wallet 23-1.

Swanson, E.B. (2002). Talking the IS Innovation Walk, in Proceedings of the IFIP WG8.2 Working Conference on Global and Organizational Discourse about Information Technology (Barcelona, Spain), 15–31.

Taylor, G.E. (1968). Note for File. Re: R.L. Polk. Provincial Archives of Alberta, Accession number: 76.346, File/item number: 50100, Box 32. 18 April.

Wiggins Systems Limited (1922). Wiggins Systems Limited Mailing List, Automobile Counts for 1922, British Columbia, British Columbia Archives, Call number GR 665, Volume 47.

Wiggins Systems Limited (1951). Wiggins Systems Limited Mailing List, Numerical List for the City of Regina (passenger), Saskatchewan Archives, R E1502, Mailing lists for owners, 23 January.

Zald, M.N. (1996). More Fragmentation? Unfinished Business in Linking the Social Sciences and the Humanities, *Administrative Science Quarterly* **41**(2): 251–261.

Printed in the United States
By Bookmasters